PART III
1861–1882

LIST OF ILLUSTRATIONS

ACKNOWLEDGEMENTS

Figures 1, 2, 23, 24, 25, 35, 38, 51, 52, 53, and 61 are from the *Radio Times Hulton Picture Library*. Figures 49 and 50 are reproduced by permission of the proprietors of *Punch* and 7, 8, 9, 10, 15, 16, 41, 42, 43, 44, 45, 46, 47, 48, 54, 55, 56, 57, 58 and 59 by permission of the proprietor of the *Illustrated London News*. Figure 39 by permission of the Director of the *Museo del Risorgimento*, Milan, and the rest by permission of the Secretary General of the *Istituto per la Storia del Risorgimento Italiano*, Rome.

PLANS

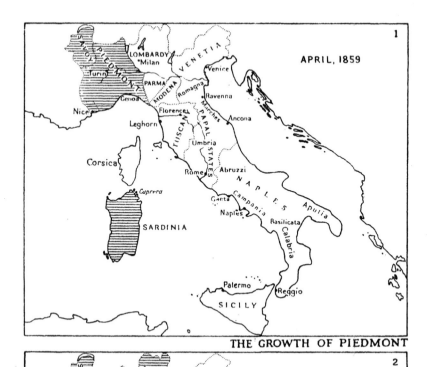

APRIL, 1859

THE GROWTH OF PIEDMONT

AUGUST, 1859

MAY, 1860

3

INTO THE KINGDOM OF ITALY

NOVEMBER, 1860

4

FOREWORD

The British historian A. J. P. Taylor once wrote that Giuseppe Garibaldi was 'the only wholly admirable figure in modern history'. Admirable figures do not necessarily make the choicest biographical subjects, but Garibaldi – freedom fighter, master of guerrilla warfare, founding father of modern Italy – would seem a rare gift. Arguably the greatest figure of the nineteenth century, he mesmerized his contemporaries. 'What of Garibaldi!' enthused the Russian novelist Ivan Turgenev. 'One cannot believe it – one's heart stops beating'. For an awestruck Henry Adams, who saw him in London in 1864, the Italian hero 'covered too much space for simple measurement'. Garibaldi, he claimed, was 'beyond any process yet reached by the education of Henry Adams'.

Christopher Hibbert took the measure of Garibaldi in this masterful biography. The book is a superb match of biographer and subject: the life of one of history's most charismatic figures narrated by the man who for the past fifty years has been one of our most accessible and entertaining historians. Born in 1924, Hibbert studied history at Oxford University before serving as an officer in the British Army during World War II. He saw action as platoon commander in Sicily – the stage, coincidentally, for some of Garibaldi's greatest heroics – and was wounded twice. For his courage on the battlefield he received the Military Cross, an award granted 'in recognition of exemplary gallantry'. He learned Italian while convalescing from his wounds, then completed his studies at Oxford after leaving the Army in 1945. For the next decade he worked in the property business, and only in the late 1950s, when he reached his mid-thirties, did he embark on what has become a truly exceptional career as a biographer and historian.

Garibaldi was Hibbert's tenth book. It followed works on, among other things, the Gordon Riots, the Battle of Quebec, and the Crimean War. These histories specialized in setting controversial, eccentric, and sometimes tragic figures, such as Lord George Gordon and Lord Raglan, against the backdrop of tumultuous historical events. Scrupulously researching a wide variety of sources, he infused them

with intimate and telling details, thereby setting the model for the
'personal histories' – with their focus on character and relationships –
that he would later write of more well known figures such as Nelson,
Wellington, and Queen Victoria.

Garibaldi was a figure tailor-made for Hibbert, whose histories are
animated by individual personalities. As he writes in his preface,
Garibaldi 'is about people and events rather than ideas and conditions'.
Ideas and conditions are undoubtedly vital for the shaping – and for
the studying – of history. But somehow arguments about the economic
causes of the Risorgimento are less likely to captivate the public
imagination than the vision of the bearded, poncho-wearing Garibaldi
astride his white horse at the head of a band of Red Shirts chanting
'Rome or Death!' And it is into this world that Hibbert delivers us.

Hibbert's command of his sources and his grasp of history's broad
sweep are strong enough that 'professional' historians – that is, those
whose salaries are paid by universities – can find little to quibble
about in his evocations of complex personalities at the expense of
reams of economic data or footnotes about social conditions. Hibbert
may wear his learning lightly – but his learning is immense and
hard-won. As the late British politician Roy Jenkins (himself a fine
biographer) wrote in the *New York Times Book Review*, in Hibbert's
work we find 'no inaccuracies to offend the historian, no solecisms
to irritate the fastidious and no *longeurs* to weary the general reader'.
As Hibbert himself once told an interviewer: 'You've got to make
the reader want to know what's going to happen next'.

It is this rare combination of historical exactitude and narrative
skill that we find in *Garibaldi*. Here we witness Garibaldi's irresistible
rise from his humble origins as a cabin-boy on a merchant ship to his
worldwide reputation achieved after military glory in South America
and Italy. Along the way we are witness to his rivalries with other
heroes of the Risorgimento such Mazzini and Cavour, his love affairs,
and his somewhat unlikely interludes raising goats on the rugged
island of Caprera. We are also treated to a remarkable portrait of
Garibaldi's beloved first wife, Anita, pregnant with their first child,
tramping through the Brazilian jungle and then, after the boy's birth,
toting him through bamboo swamps in a sling around her neck. Such
details are related in the effortlessly urbane style that is Hibbert's

trademark (an American reviewer for *Time* expressed admiration for the 'cool British way' in which Hibbert was able to convey the confusing and sometimes farcical shenanigans of Italian political life).

A century ago Giovanni Giolitti, the Prime Minister of Italy, claimed it would not be proper to let 'beautiful legends be discredited by historical criticism'. Hibbert does not shy away from criticism of Garibaldi: his vanity, his susceptibility to flattery, his sometimes unwise political maneuverings, and even his 'distressingly bad' novel (hastily penned to keep the wolf from the door). But he keeps the 'beautiful legend' more or less intact. The story of Garibaldi's life is truly a remarkable one, and in these pages Christopher Hibbert brings the legend to life.

– Ross King

PREFACE

A hundred years ago Garibaldi was, perhaps, the best-known name in the world. There were streets and squares named after him in a hundred different towns from Naples to Montevideo; statuettes of him, busts, medallions, china figurines were almost as common in Manchester as in Milan, in Boston as in Bologna; postcards garishly depicting his messianic features were sold in their millions; you could drink a Garibaldi wine, wear a Garibaldi blouse, see a Garibaldi musical, eat a Garibaldi biscuit.

When the legendary figure came to New York in 1850 he was, as the *New York Tribune* declared, already 'world-famed'. And in London in 1864 *The Times* reported that such a welcome as he received had never before been known; everyone flocked to him from the Prince of Wales to the Archbishop of Canterbury; workingmen cheered him till they were hoarse; ladies fainted at the sight of him.

But when reviewing Arthur James Whyte's *The Evolution of Modern Italy* some years ago in *Belfagor*, Piero Treves felt constrained to express the hope that the Garibaldian legend had not been forgotten outside Italy. For it seemed to him that Dr. Whyte had paid scant tribute to the General's achievements and had denied him the historical recognition which foreign liberal historians had traditionally accorded him.

Reference was made in this review, with a kind of nostalgic admiration, to the work of G. M. Trevelyan, who dedicated the first volume of his splendid trilogy to 'the immortal memory of Giuseppe Garibaldi'. And certainly this trilogy will always remain an inspiration both as a work of scholarship and of art. No book could pretend to take its place. But Professor Trevelyan's 'chanson de geste about the paladin Garibold', as Bernard Berenson called it, was written over half a century ago, and recent research has rendered parts of it out of date and cast doubts on some of its conclusions.

The portrait that I have painted is necessarily less flattering than Trevelyan's, for it has been painted in the darker light that the disillusioning effects of recent history and changing attitudes of

xvii

mind have cast upon it. As one of the women who loved Garibaldi wrote at the end of her memoirs of him, 'in history Garibaldi will always remain resplendent as the sun; yet even the sun has its spots'. But although I have not found it possible to interpret the Garibaldian legend in the same way as Professor Trevelyan (or, indeed, as some of the General's more recent Italian biographers) I have tried in this book to indicate that his contribution to the making of Italy can still be regarded by a modern non-Italian as essential and unique.

The subtitle of the book suggests the limits of its scope: it is only indirectly concerned with social and economic problems, with arguments about the extent to which the revolution was, in Giovanni Gentile's phrase, 'an authentic nationalist movement'; and it is scarcely concerned at all with what Luigi Salvatorelli has called the 'spiritual process' of the Risorgimento. It is about people and events rather than ideas and conditions. It highlights those men whom Piero Gobetti condemned in his *Risorgimento senza eroi* as being unequal to their tasks; and throws into the background 'those various groups of uncommitted liberals' whose 'anonymous collective action', Gaetano Salvemini believed, was the 'principal factor in the Risorgimento'.

Over the space of twenty years I have visited nearly all the places mentioned in this book, beginning in 1945 by the waters of the Lake of Commachio, where Garibaldi's first wife died, and ending last year on the island of Caprera where he died himself. On the final stages of this intermittent journey I have received most generous help from the directors and staffs of the various Risorgimento libraries and museums which are to be found all over Italy; and in particular I want to thank those of the Museo Civico del I^0 e II^0 Risorgimento, Bolgna; the Museo del Risorgimento e Raccolte Storiche, Milan; the Società Toscana per la Storia del Risorgimento Italiano, Florence; the Istituto Mazziniano, Genoa; the Museo Nazionale del Risorgimento Italiano, Turin; the Istituto per la Storia del Risorgimento Italiano, and the Biblioteca di Storia Moderna e Contemporanea, Rome.

Italian scholars have been delving so long in these and other fields, however, that it would be absurdly pretentious to suggest that I have unearthed anything of importance that is new, particularly as 'the eagerness of the Italians to publish everything, however trivial, on the revolution', so Bolton King suggested in 1899, 'reaches almost to a literary mania'.

For guiding me through this vast accumulation of published material I am extremely grateful to Professor Vittorio Gabrieli and his colleagues at the University of Turin, to Professor Rosario Romeo of the Istituto di Storia Moderna, Rome, and to Mr. Denis Mack Smith of All Souls College, Oxford. For their help in a variety of ways I want also to thank Miss Jane Carroll, Miss Geraldine Ranson, Mrs. Joan St. George Saunders, Mrs. Louise Hollingworth, the Countess of Sutherland, Signorina Elisa Costa and her staff in the Library of the Istituto Italiano di Cultura in Belgrave Square, Professor Leonardo Patanè of the Rassegna Scolastica Siciliani di Cultura e Informazioni, Catania, Sicily, Professor Roberto Weiss, Mr. Hamish Francis, and my wife and sons.

For permission to reproduce copyright material I am grateful to the authors, editors, agents and publishers of the following books: *Le memorie nella redazione definitiva* (*ed. naz. degli scritti di Giuseppe Garibaldi*, Cappelli, Bologna, 1932); *Some Revolutions and other Diplomatic Experiences of the late Rt. Hon. Sir Henry G. Elliot, G.C.B. Edited by his Daughter* (John Murray, Ltd., London, 1922); G.M. Trevelyan, *Garibaldi's Defence of the Roman Republic* (Longmans, Green, 1907); *Queen Victoria's Letters* (John Murray, Ltd., 1907-1932); *The Correspondence of Arthur Hugh Clough* (Ed. Frederick L. Mulhauser, O.U.P., 1957); *La liberazione del Mezzogiorno* (*Carteggi di Camillo Cavour*, Zanichelli; Bologna, 1961); *Scritti editi ed inediti di Giuseppe Mazzini* (*ed. naz. degli scritti di GiuseppeMazzini*, Imola, 1906-1943); Giuseppe Tomasi di Lampedusa, *Il Gattopardo* (Feltrinelli, Milan, 1958, and William Collins Sons & Co. Ltd., 1961); *Scritte e discorsi politici e militari* (*ed. naz. degli scritti di Giuseppe Garibaldi*, Cappelli, Bologna, 1934).

For helping me when I was working in Rome I owe a particular debt of gratitude to Professor Emilia Morelli of the Istituto per la Storia del Risorgimento Italiano. And I am most grateful to Signora Alda de Caprariis for her great kindness in having put her wide knowledge of Garibaldi and his period at my disposal, and in having read the manuscript.

C. H.

PART I
1807-1859

1

'APOSTLES OF A NEW RELIGION'

Between Corsica and Sardinia, south of the lighthouses that guide the ships steaming at night past the rocks in the Strait of Bonifacio, lies the little island of Caprera. Here in the winter of 1872, sitting by the fire in the untidy bedroom of his bare, uncomfortable house, Giuseppe Garibaldi rewrote the autobiography that he had begun over twenty years before. He was sixty-five. His life's work was over and he could look back upon it as one of the most compelling of the forces that had made Italy one nation. It was the memories of his adventures as a seaman, however, and, even more than these, the recollections of his youth in South America that stirred him most deeply.

'Bending with stiffened limbs over the fire,' he wrote, 'I recall with emotion those scenes of the past, when life seemed to smile on me. I myself am old and worn now. But where are those splendid horses? Where are the bulls, the antelopes and the ostriches which made those lovely hills so beautiful and so much alive?'

He remembered, 'as though he had seen them yesterday', the wild stallions of the pampas, their unshod hoofs white as ivory, their glossy backs shining in the sun, their tangled manes streaming behind them in the wind; and the great black bulls running towards him across the short grass of the plains of Uruguay, and then suddenly stopping short 'to stare in amazement at a two-legged creature they had never seen before'; and the ostriches half-running, half-flying as they sped away from their pursuers until they were brought crashing to the ground with the cords and balls of the bolas entangled round their legs. And he remembered, most vividly of all, the marches and the battles, the hardships suffered for the freedom enjoyed, the exhilaration of leading a few brave men who admired, obeyed and trusted him, of throwing himself into a career which had 'an immense attraction' for him, 'even more than that of the sea'.[1]

*　　*　　*

He had been born to the sea, only a few yards from the Mediterranean water's edge. His father, Domenico, was a sailor and the son
of a sailor, owner of a merchant ship that plied an uncertain trade in
wine and oil along the Ligurian coast, and Giuseppe himself had gone
to sea as a cabin-boy apprentice when he was sixteen and a half. It
was a late age to begin work for a boy from a poor home, but his
parents – and, in particular, his kind and thrifty mother, whose
'tenderness' for him, the son afterwards decided, 'was perhaps
excessive' – had been determined that he should have a good
education and did all they could to persuade him not to follow in his
father's and grandfather's footsteps.

In later life he liked to present himself as a simple man of the
people, most of whose knowledge had been self-acquired from the
lonely study of books;[2] but his education as a child had not been
neglected, and at a dinner-party in London at the house of Sir
Anthony Panizzi in 1864 he told Gladstone that he 'was at school in
Genoa'.[3] Perhaps he had not wanted to admit this to an Italian
because the school was a religious seminary and he had lived his
whole life as an enemy of the priesthood, that 'emanation from hell',
that 'black brood, pestilent scum of humanity', 'the enemy of the
whole human race', the 'very scourge of God'. Certainly both his
father and his pious mother would have liked him to become a
priest and they employed as his first tutor an old Augustinian monk.[4]

They could ill afford to do so. They had three other children –
their first child had died before her second birthday and their sixth
before her third – and Domenico's trade was never a profitable one.
They did not own a house, and when Giuseppe was born on
4 July 1807 they were living with an old relative in a cramped alley
by the harbour wall at Nice.

Nice had been taken from the Kingdom of Piedmont by Napoleon
ten years before, and so Giuseppe was born a French citizen and
remained one until 1815 when the town was returned to the House
of Savoy. The inhabitants of Nice were partly French and partly
Italian, but both Domenico and his wife, Rosa Raimondi, were
wholly Italian, though the name Garibaldi and Giuseppe's fair
colouring betokened a more northern origin. Domenico had come
west from Chiavari near Rapallo, Rosa from Loano north of Alassio.
They were good, kind people, honest and devout; and Giuseppe's

childhood was a happy one. He loved swimming in the sea and fishing and trawling for oysters and clambering up the rigging of the boats in the harbour, and playing draughts or reading in the shade of the olive trees. Sometimes he would climb up into the mountains with a borrowed gun and a game-bag, and once, so he said later, when he was coming home, he helped a woman who had fallen into a deep ditch used for steeping hemp. 'Though small for my age and encumbered with my game-bag', he recalled, 'I jumped in after her, and succeeded in pulling her out. In after years', he added in one of those many unconsciously self-dramatising passages in his *Memorie* that strike so disarmingly immodest a note in the modern ear, 'I have never shrunk from helping any fellow creature in danger, even at the risk of my own life'.[5]

He admitted, too, that he was a gentle, indeed an emotionally soft-hearted boy, capable of crying bitterly for hours when he accidentally broke the leg of a pet cricket. But he was adventurous, impatient and restless as well as compassionate, and he did not take kindly to his lessons. The language spoken in his home was the Ligurian dialect and his second language was French, but Italian did not come easily to him – in later life, his accent, grammar and spelling all betrayed his frontier origins – and although he acquired a little Latin, showed some aptitude for mathematics and geometry, and developed an interest in history and geography, it was to the sea that he felt irresistibly drawn. And after he and some friends had tried to steal a boat and sail away in her, his parents felt compelled to give way.[6]

In 1824 he was allowed to sign on in the *Costanza* and he sailed to Odessa under the Russian flag. It was a deeply moving experience for the impressionable boy. The wide decks of the *Costanza*, her stout sides and lofty rigging, the broad-breasted figurehead of the woman on her prow, the songs that the sailors sang, remained fixed in his memory for ever; and for ever afterwards he remained grateful to her captain, Angelo Pesante, who gave him his first lessons in the art of seamanship. Deeply as this first voyage affected him, however, the experience was not as disturbing and inspiring as a journey he made with his father in the following year to the coast of the Papal States and then on up the Tiber in a small boat drawn by oxen, with a cargo of wine for Rome.

'The Rome that I beheld with the eyes of my youthful imagination', he wrote, 'was the Rome of the future – the Rome that I never despaired of even when I was shipwrecked, dying, banished to the farthest depths of the American forests – the dominant thought and inspiration of my whole life.'[7]

It was quite true that it became so later, an obsession from which he could never escape. But for the moment he was far from feeling this overwhelming sense that Rome was the symbol of United Italy; for he had not yet come into contact with people who talked of such things – certainly his conservative parents did not, certainly the priests did not, nor the easy-going crews of the *Costanza* and of his father's boat *La Santa Reparata*. Soon, though, he was to sail with other crews from different parts of Italy – to the Middle East and Gibraltar, to the Canary Islands and Constantinople, to Marseilles and Tunis and Rio de Janeiro – and he was to learn from them, and from the Italian exiles he met in foreign ports, that the movement which was seething beneath the surface of life in the Italian peninsula was one to which he could and must dedicate his life.

He had already, on a voyage to Constantinople in 1833, when he was mate of the brig *La Clorinda*, come into contact with the Saint-Simonians, 'persecuted apostles', as he called them, of 'a new religion'.[8] A group of these self-appointed apostles of the gospel of the Comte de Saint-Simon, author of the *Nouveau Christianisme*, had sailed with him to the Bosphorus and had immediately caught his imagination. They wore long red gowns and loose white tunics, with belts, gloves and boots of black leather, and black scarves round their necks over which their hair and beards flowed uncombed and uncut. Their flamboyant appearance – their leader, Emile Barrault, assured him – their extravagant ritual and dramatically emotive songs served an essential purpose: to stir men's souls to enthusiasm for their cause. It was a lesson that Garibaldi never forgot. Nor did he ever forget the lessons of their faith – that, in the words of Saint-Simon, 'the whole of society ought to strive towards the improvement of the conditions, both moral and physical, of the poorest class'; that the State should be organised into a social hierarchy dominated by a leader, ascetic, simple and selfless; that women should be emancipated and gain entire equality with men; and that the body should be given its due honour as a creation of God and as a source of sexual pleasure by what was termed the 'Rehabilitation of the Flesh'. These beliefs, propounded to him by Emile Barrault, made so profound an impression on the young Garibaldi that he remained influenced by them for the rest of his life.

He did not yet look like a prophet himself. He had not grown the beard and the long hair that were later to encourage men to see in him a new Messiah. He was not, in fact, of remarkable appearance. Rather bow-legged and stocky – less than 5 ft. 7 in. – with broad shoulders and hips and a narrow waist, he had a round face, a fresh complexion and fair, reddish hair. His small brown eyes deeply set and rather close together were divided by a long, aquiline nose, with a very high bridge, so that it seemed on occasions that he had a slight squint.* He had well-defined eyebrows and long, fine lashes, and a friendly, charming smile. If not, at this time the strikingly handsome, even beautiful face that his more recklessly enthusiastic biographers have described, it was a pleasant face, open and kind. Only when he was angry and the eyes took on a darker hue and the features set, hard, relentless and stubborn, giving warning of a different man, less reasonable and far more emphatic, did it lose its air of placid frankness.

He was not often angry, though; nor had he yet developed that capacity for implacable resentment to which the disappointments, rebuffs and setbacks of the future gave rise. In his twenties he was, it appears, a contented, sometimes even hearty sailor who loved singing the songs of the sea and the regular exercise of a strong and healthy body. This body he was always to tend and wash with a meticulous care, paying to his hair and his nails an attention that seemed to some of his companions strangely feminine in a man so irresistibly drawn to danger and adventure, with so profound an admiration for physical stamina, such contempt of cowardice. He spoke slowly and calmly, without the gestures which were later to be so marked a feature of his public oratory; and he moved with a firm deliberation, rolling slightly as sailors are said to do. In times of danger, when fighting pirates and in shipwrecks, he seems always

---

* His eyes are often described as having been blue; and certainly in his later life many of his contemporaries wrote of them as such. To Maxime Du Camp they appeared '*d'un bleu barbeau*'. But his family and official documents agreed in calling them brown.

to have been brave and always self-reliant. He was easily flattered, easily impressed. He had no sense of humour. His mind was not dull, however, and his outlook never conventional. He saw, in what seemed to most of his contemporaries the outlandish views of the Saint-Simonians, both a satisfying philosophy of life and a valid programme for action. His conversations with them on board the *Clorinda* opened up a whole new world for him. It was as if, so he put it himself, a strange light had broken in on his mind.

*   *   *

Soon after this experience another light was to break in on his mind – a light that revealed a specific cause for which to fight as well as a belief worth fighting for. It happened, as he confessed, quite suddenly and unexpectedly: one day at sea or ashore (he did not remember which) he had overheard an argument. A young man had been talking about a secret organisation which he had joined, an organisation known as *La Giovine Italia* – Young Italy – when one of his companions commented derisively, 'What do you mean, Italy? What *is* Italy?' The young patriot turned round and said passionately, 'I mean the new Italy . . . United Italy. The Italy of all the Italians.' Listening to these words Garibaldi felt 'as Columbus must have done when he first caught sight of land'.[9] He went over and shook his fellow countrymen enthusiastically by the hand.

*   *   *

Italy had need of the enthusiasm of such men as these. For, after all, what did Italy mean in the early 1830s? Outside the Peninsula most people thought it was – as Metternich was soon to say it was – '*ein geographischer Begriff*', a mere geographical expression. And inside the Peninsula, too, there was not, nor never had been, a widespread feeling that it ought to be made into something more dynamic.*

---

* Earlier and more romantic interpretations of the history of the Risorgimento suggested that such men as Dante and Petrarch were the precursors of the national movement, and even if they so much as mentioned the word Italy were granted a place in the Risorgimento pantheon. This interpretation no longer commands support and although recent research has revealed much nationalist sentiment during the period of the Napoleonic occupation, this sentiment was usually limited, as Gaetano Salvemini has observed, to 'vague projects and Arcadian laments'.

Napoleon, proud of his Italian descent, fascinated by the Roman Empire and conscious of the need for a barrier against Austria, had encouraged a nationalist spirit. He had swept away the eleven states of the Peninsula and, except for some small enclaves which he gave to his family or officials, he had divided Italy into three. The Kingdom of Piedmont and Savoy (which included Sardinia), the Grand Duchy of Tuscany, the Duchy of Parma, the republic of Genoa, the Dalmatian provinces of the Republic of Venice and the Papal States west of the Apennines were incorporated into France. Lombardy, the Romagna and the Marches, the Duchy of Modena and continental Venice were formed into the 'Kingdom of Italy' under the rule of the Empress Josephine's son Eugène de Beauharnais. While the south of Italy (excluding Sicily which remained under Bourbon rule) was transferred to Napoleon's brother Joseph, as King of Naples, and, after Joseph's promotion to the throne of Spain, to General Joachim Murat, the husband of Napoleon's sister Caroline.

But after Napoleon's fall, the Congress of Vienna set about the task of breaking up Italy again into its former small components and handing the pieces back, wherever possible, to their old rulers. The watchword of the Congress was 'legitimacy' – a doctrine invented by Talleyrand to express the advantages of the Bourbon restoration in France. And in the pursuit of legitimacy in Italy, the Bourbons were restored to the Kingdom of Naples (to which Sicily was united), the Pope was returned to his temporal power in the central states, and in the north the House of Savoy recovered the crown of Piedmont and Sardinia whose territories were extended to include Savoy and Nice as well as the former Republic of Genoa.

The Italian policy of the Congress of Vienna was guided not only by the doctrine of legitimacy, however, but also by Metternich's determination that Italy should be kept divided so that Austria could maintain her hold over Lombardy and Venetia. Metternich, an extremely good-looking man with carefully powdered hair and a capacity for talking at great length and in a harsh, nasal voice in a variety of languages, was much disliked by his contemporaries. But 'although in the day-to-day conduct of affairs he displayed an opportunism which bounded upon levity, the main principles which guided his political course were', as Sir Harold Nicolson has said, 'unvarying and rigid'. He was dedicated to stability. And in 'international affairs the balance of power was an almost cosmic principle. Without internal and external equilibrium there could be no repose; and repose was essential to the normal happiness of man.'[10]

Despite some rebuffs, Metternich had his way at Vienna. He did not get all that he wanted, but he won for Austria a commanding power in Italy. Lombardy and Venetia were ceded to her; Tuscany was accorded to an Austrian arch-duke; and Parma to the Empress Marie Louise, daughter of the Austrian Emperor, Francis II. Austria, in fact, was restored to the dominant position she had enjoyed in the Italian Peninsula at the end of the eighteenth century. And not only in those territories which she dominated, but in all those other parts of Italy to which the restored rulers returned, the clouds of reaction and repression gathered and darkened. Police spies, clerical privileges and press censorship became once more an accepted part of life from Milan to Naples. Italy retreated from progress.

In the Kingdom of Naples and Sicily – the Two Sicilies of diplomatic language – a proclamation promising a constitution was suppressed. In the Papal States all officials who had served the French were dismissed from their posts; the French codes of law were destroyed; street-lighting, public drainage and vaccination were abolished; education was limited while taxes were increased; power was concentrated in the hands of the Cardinal Secretary of State and the ecclesiastics appointed to direct the various departments of the Government. In Piedmont, Victor Emmanuel I forbade recognition of any change made in the Government since 1770.

From time to time the people revolted against their new masters. In the Neapolitan territories, General Pepe led an army of rebels on the capital; in Piedmont agitators and mutinous troops demanded a constitution and secured the abdication of Victor Emmanuel; and in the Papal States, after some reforms effected by Cardinal Consalvi, Pius VII's Secretary of State, had been nullified by Pius's successor, Leo XII, conspirators set up a provisional government. All these rebellions, however, were crushed by Austrian troops.

But although the demands of the rebels were for independence, constitutions and reforms, it is a too simple interpretation to suggest that the revolts were prompted by any deep feeling for national unity. In Naples, for example, General Pepe's military supporters had been angered by the embezzlement of army pay by corrupt civil servants, his aristocratic supporters had been roused by their new King's failure to annul the changes in land ownership brought about by French reforms, and all his supporters had been dismayed by the failure of the Bourbon Government to deal with the depredations of growing bands of brigands. In the Papal States the main cause of complaint was the failure of the Papacy to restore municipal liberties, and its refusal to allow laymen to play any part in government.

Despite the attempts made by some historians – particularly fascist historians* – to make it appear so, there was, in fact, no question of the uprisings being inspired by any sudden upsurge of patriotism. 'Censorship was only partly to blame. The forces working against nationalism were very great indeed. Italians of north and south were virtually unknown to each other; even members of the aristocracy spoke mutually unintelligible dialects';[11] and in so many districts the calls for freedom and better government arose purely from economic pressures and social discontents.

Also, the reaction was less violent and cruel than some political exiles suggested and less widely resented than many liberal and anti-Catholic writers have pretended. The rulers who were returned to Italy by the Congress of Vienna were wholly unsympathetic to the spirit of revolutionary France, but they were not all blind to the welfare of the people. Duke Francis IV of Modena was, perhaps, characteristic of them. Gentle, patient and polite, he had a real interest in his subjects and in their moral welfare. He took pains to ensure that they did not suffer either in body or in soul. He demanded in return obedience and subordination. 'He held it a prince's sacred duty, at whatever cost to himself and subjects, to save society from

---

* In 1932 the *Società Nazionale de la Storia del Risorgimento* and its review *Rassegna Storica del Risorgimento* were drawn into the circle of fascist propaganda under General C. M. De Vecchi (one of the *Quadrumviri* of the 'March on Rome' in 1922) who became president of the one and editor of the other. The statutory definition of the Risorgimento was 'the creation of Italian unity and the presupposition of the Fascist Revolution' – Kent Roberts Greenfield, 'The Historiography of the Risorgimento since 1920' in *The Journal of Modern History* (1935, vii, 65). It is this sort of interpretation which Luigi Salvatorelli condemns in his *Pensiero e azione del Risorgimento* (Einaudi, Turin, 1960), 13–16.

Liberalism and its disintegrating influence. "The Liberals," he said,
"are sinners. Pray for their repentance, but punish the unre-
pentant." '12

It was inevitable, of course, that this sort of belief should bring
him, and rulers like him, into conflict with all that was most
progressive in Italian life and, in particular – since there were no
constitutional channels through which opposition and protest could
be expressed – with the secret organisations which were working for
liberty.

By far the most influential of these secret societies was that of the
Carbonari who took their name, symbolically, from *carbone* (coal)
which, black and lifeless, burns brightly when it is kindled. The
Carbonari had evolved in Southern Italy, virtually as an offshoot of
Italian freemasonry, and spread northwards as a liberal organisation
which contemplated, at some unspecified future date and by vaguely
suggested means, the attainment of freedom from foreign domination and the ultimate unity of the Italian states. But although it had
many thousands of members, it was never a cohesive organisation
working for definite aims.

One of its members, however, was determined that such a society,
less vague and more positively national in outlook, should and could
be formed. Its aim, this young member insisted, must be to inspire
the people of Italy to achieve – through widespread revolt – independence, liberty and unity in a republic.

Giuseppe Mazzini had been born in June 1805 in Genoa. His
father was a doctor who had become professor of anatomy at the
University, his mother, a convinced Jansenist, was a gentle, beautiful,
affectionate woman devoted to her husband and son and to her three
daughters. It was a happy home, but Giuseppe had not been a
contented child. Restless, impatient, moody, slow to make friends
and quick to take offence, he seemed already burdened with the
ambitions, the sorrows and the disappointments that were later to
dominate his life. When he was nearly sixteen the suppression of the
insurrection against Victor Emmanuel I filled Genoa with political
criminals and Carbonari hoping to escape to Spain; and his imagination was haunted by the sight of them. He took to wearing black
which he always afterwards wore; he read all he could of their exploits
and defeat; he brooded over the writings of Ugo Foscolo; and his

mother feared that, like the hero of Foscolo's *Letter di Jacopo Ortis*, he too might kill himself.

He recovered his balance, but he could not get the Carbonari out of his mind. He thought of becoming a doctor like his father, but he fainted while watching his first operation and turned to law. He had little enthusiasm for this either, and though he did well enough in his examinations he was a difficult, troublesome and argumentative student. He was by now a remarkable personality as well – forceful, determined and fiercely eloquent, with a beautiful voice and striking features. His eyes were dark and flashing, the only eyes that one man who knew him had ever seen that 'looked like flames', his skin was smooth and olive, its pallor emphasised by his long, thick black hair, his forehead was high and domed. He walked quickly with a feline grace, holding his head forward. When he was well and happy he could be generous, charming, lively, even gay; but when he was tired or dispirited he was irritable, exacting and didactic. He permitted himself few pleasures and his only luxuries were expensive writing paper and scent. He smoked cigars with his friends and sang to his guitar, and in later life it seems that his friend Giuditta Sidoli bore him a child;[13] but he was always a puritan in spirit.

He joined the Carbonari, the inspiration of his boyhood, soon after he had taken his degree; but the *opera buffa* ceremony of the ritualistic initiation, in which he was required to swear allegiance to unknown leaders on a bared dagger, the vagueness of the oath insisting on obedience without defining any aims, the ultimate obscurity of their intentions as well as their means, all struck him as absurd. Also he could not accept their reliance on middle-aged and often aristo-cratic leaders who were, apparently, out of sympathy with republican sentiments and without any real faith in Italian unity. And for Mazzini unity was not only possible but vitally necessary, more necessary even than the republic itself.

'He insisted upon it with single-minded obstinacy', Gaetano Salvemini has written, 'and dedicated his whole life, from his early, ardent youth to his grief-striken old age, to realising it. He preached it incessantly, in the face of ridicule, disappointment and defeat; and communicated his own faith to others simply by virtue of being all the more unshaken in his convictions.'[14]

'Mine is a matter of deep conviction', he would say with characteristic dogmatism. 'It is impossible for me to modify or alter it.'[15] And this very refusal to compromise, this blind dedication to an ideal that allowed him to disregard the hard facts in the way of its realisation, this intolerance of views other than his own, formed his unique and essential contribution to the birth of his country. In his writings his arguments are often illogical, and even contradictory, his omissions and gaps numerous, his historical foundations uncertain, his social theories unformed, his religious teachings quite without influence; but it was, nevertheless, 'Mazzini and Mazzini alone, who imposed upon the Italian liberal-nationalist groups the one dominating idea to which through all the vicissitudes of the making of Italy, everything else was to become subordinated'.[16]

Provided Italy became one nation, he was even prepared to accept a monarchy. 'I am republican in my aims for every country and above all for Italy,' he told his friend Sismondi. 'But I would adapt myself to a monarchy if, for instance (as is far from probable) a King of Piedmont or of Naples would for this price give us the nucleus of an army and a supply of arms.'[17] But the monarchy, to be acceptable, would have to abandon itself to the national cause. And so would the social reformers.

Mazzini urged the necessity of social reform, but at the same time he insisted that national unity was an essential preliminary, an indispensable basis, and that all classes must unite in achieving it. This insistence by an accepted revolutionary that social reform should wait upon national unity, for a long time 'served as a barrier against the spread of communist ideas' and is one of the main reasons, of course, why Mazzini appears as so distasteful and shabbily ineffective a figure to communist writers and in Marxist interpretations of nineteenth-century history. In E. J. Hobsbawm's brilliant and stimulating *The Age of Revolution* Mazzini is presented as a 'woolly and ineffective self-dramatiser' whose mere presence in the 'Youth' movements of the day 'would have been enough to ensure their total ineffectiveness'.[18]

To contemporary Europeans he appeared, of course, quite differently. The influence of the organisation *La Giovine Italia*, which he himself founded as a vigorous society dedicated to the cause of revolt and to 'insurrection by means of guerrilla bands', soon spread far beyond the boundaries of Italy. It caused Metternich to call Mazzini the 'most dangerous man in Europe'.[19] It led, as Mr. Hobsbawm says, to the 'disintegration of the European revolutionary movement into national segments',[20] but it led also to the ultimate acceptance by thousands of young Italians, mostly from the middle classes, that they must no longer look upon their country as '*ein geographischer Begriff*' but that, in the words of the oath of *La Giovine Italia*, they must work 'wholly and for ever to constitute Italy one, free and independent'. From that, Mazzini taught, great things would follow.

For he offered more than a revolutionary nationalist programme. He offered a national religion, 'a creed and an apostolate'.

The guiding principle of Young Italy – '*Dio e popolo*' ('God and the People') – expressed the religious foundation of the national cause. Mazzini had grown up in a Europe pervaded by an atmosphere of romanticism and idealism, reacting strongly against Voltaire's anti-clericalism and Diderot's materialism; but while the conservative forces had been drawn towards the absolute monarchs and the Catholic Church, he had declared war on the Catholic Church 'not in the name of philosophic rationalism but in that of a new mysticism which claims to be more in conformity with the humaner spirit of the Gospels'.[21]

We are no followers of the eighteenth century and Voltaire [he declared]. They denied and destroyed. Where they destroyed, we seek to find. Where they denied, we affirm. Humanity is, now as ever, deeply, inevitably religious, and because it is religious, it makes war upon the Papacy. . . . The Papacy is only a form . . . and Catholicism is only a sect, an erroneous application, the materialism of Christianity. But remember that Christianity is a revelation and a statement of principles. . . . The martyrdom and word of Christ are not in opposition to our principles.[22]

       ★   ★   ★

These were views that Garibaldi, honouring Christ, 'the man of the people', but hating the Papacy with all the special virulence of the nineteenth-century Italian liberal conscience and with all the force of a peculiarly impressionable mind, felt immediately drawn to share. By the end of 1833 he had joined Young Italy.

He had also joined the Royal Piedmontese Navy. The second step, according to his own account, was prompted by the first. For the leaders of 'Young Italy' had instructed him to leave the Merchant Service 'to make converts for the revolution' in the Navy, and to help seize whatever ship in which he might be serving when the revolution broke out.[23]

The revolution, however, never did break out. For although Young Italy was highly successful as a society for the dissemination of propaganda, its leaders were incapable of organising active resistance, even had the people as a whole been willing to follow them. An uprising planned to take place in Genoa at the beginning of 1834 was, like all the other and more ambitious attempts at insurrection, a complete disaster; and Garibaldi (whose far from clandestine efforts to suborn not only the sailors on his ship but also various soldiers he met in harbour cafés had soon been noticed by the authorities) was condemned to death. The verdict, however, was given in the absence of the accused and by the time he read of it he had managed to escape to Marseilles. He did not attempt to disguise his pride at seeing his name in a newspaper for the first time, but he knew that it would now be many months and perhaps many years before he could return to his 'own dear, ill-used country'.

In December 1835, after spending eighteen months under an assumed name and doing what work he could find, he stepped ashore in Rio de Janeiro to begin a new life and to acquire new skills and new ideas, new loyalties and beliefs that were to alter that 'dear, ill-used' country for ever.

2

'AN EAGLE HOVERING IN THE UPPER HEIGHTS'

'A man who defends his own country or attacks another's is no more than a soldier. . . . But he, who adopts some other country as his own and makes offer of his sword and his blood, is more than a soldier. He is a hero.'[1]

Emile Barrault's words, spoken three years before aboard *La Clorinda*, were at once a comfort and an inspiration. At first Garibaldi, in partnership with another of those numerous Italian exiles who had crossed the Atlantic, had earned his living as a trader in brandy, sugar and flour, sailing in a small ship along the eastern coasts of Brazil. But it was a sadly dispiriting life for an adventurous young man who had enjoyed the exhilaration of conspiracy and the hope of revolution; and a disappointingly unprofitable one for a man so trusting and guileless without any of the sharp business sense of so many of those other Italians who shared his exile. He longed to escape from its monotony.

'*Per Dio*, I am tired of this dreary life of a trading sailor, so useless to our country,' he wrote impatiently to Giambattista Cuneo, a fellow member of Young Italy. 'I am impatient to resort to extremes. Write to P['Pippo' Mazzini], tell him to give us a prescription, and we will get it made up. We were destined for greater things.'[2]

But he could not wait for a prescription from Mazzini. He looked round with a kind of desperation for a people struggling against tyranny to whom he could offer his blood and his sword.

He found one early the following year in the south of Brazil where a revolutionary leader had declared an independent republic. Garibaldi offered his services. They were accepted; and he left immediately for the fighting.

He was granted letters of marque by the rebel government of Rio Grande do Sul, and though he knew that his own personal problems were now solved and his frustrations dispersed at last, he

entered upon his new life as a buccaneer with some feelings of misgiving as to whether this was the sort of prescription that Mazzini
and Young Italy would have supplied. He asked Cuneo, who had
gone to start a newspaper for the Italian colony in Montevideo, to
see that this 'new path' on which he was setting out, was presented
'in its true light'.[3]

Soon all misgivings that he was not perhaps serving the true cause
of liberty were dispelled, however. Once at sea in his little ship, the
Mazzini, 'a feeling of happiness and pride' came over him. When he
went ashore one day and climbed a high hill and looked down at the
water so far below him, he 'uttered a cry such as the eagle gives when
she is hovering in the upper heights'. He felt as though all the ocean
were his empire and he was setting out to take possession of it.[4] He
was going to fight – and he would be fighting in the cause of liberty.

For twelve years, first at sea and then on land, he fought his way
along this new path that the republic of Rio Grande do Sul, and
afterwards the republics of Santa Caterina and Uruguay, had opened
up for him. Shipwrecked, ambushed, shot through the neck,
captured, imprisoned, strung up by his wrists for attempting to
escape and refusing to say who had helped him, marching exhausted
for days on end through the jungle with nothing to eat but the roots
of plants, and riding at night over the cold sierras, through suffering,
violence and the unquestioned belief that he was 'helping the cause
of nations', he grew to love the wild and trackless immensities of the
continent where he was serving so invaluable an apprenticeship.
Throughout his later life he looked back with pride and a kind of
sad longing to those days, talking of his achievements with a
satisfaction that he could not find in later triumphs, remembering
their details with a sharp and revealing clarity, comparing the men
he led, the 'brave sons of Columbus', with some of his own 'unwarlike and effeminate countrymen . . . incapable of keeping the field a
month without three meals a day'.[5]

There were days, of course, that he could wish to forget, and men
whose behaviour disgusted him; for despite the rough and violent
life he led, his was never a rough nor cruel nature. Once he was given
the task of sacking a village and afterwards he confessed that he had
never passed a day of such remorse. His men, a motley ragbag of
Italian exiles, European adventurers, released Negro slaves and South

Americans, behaved like 'unchained wild beasts', pillaging, murder-
ing, raping, wild with drink and lust for blood and women. He was
forced to cut down several of the worst offenders himself before he
could restore order and get the others back aboard his ship where,
looking down the hatchway, he saw them gambling round the
corpse of a German sergeant which he had ordered them to bury.
'Their brutal faces, seen by the light of tallow candles stuck in
bottles placed on the breast of the corpse, seemed those of demons
playing at dice for souls.'[6]

These memories, though, were not obtrusive. It was the space and
the freedom that he remembered and talked about most often; the
beautiful forests of pine and bamboo by the banks of the *arroyos*, the
tall, reed-like grass in the valleys, the immense herds of cattle, the
peons on the skyline, the swirl of the lassoo and the sound of hundreds
of galloping hooves, the rides at sunset to a new camp at the head of
a few devoted men, with the woman he loved beside him.

The woman was Anna Ribeiro da Silva, a short, masculine woman
of mixed Portuguese and Indian descent, with big breasts, small
features and glistening long black hair, which in the opinion of a
surgeon who met her later in Rome was 'her only ornament'. In
Garibaldi's eyes, though, she was beautiful. She was also strong and
brave and passionate. 'She looked upon battles', he wrote admiringly,
'as a pleasure, and the hardships of camp life as a pleasant pastime.'[7]

He saw her for the first time, so he said, through a telescope from
the quarter-deck of his ship. He was feeling lonely and disheartened.
He had recently lost his previous ship which had been wrecked in a
storm, and the seven Italians in the crew, including Edoardo Mutru, a
boyhood friend who had been condemned to death with him in
1834, had all been drowned. 'I needed a human heart to love me,'
he confessed. 'I felt that unless I found one immediately life would
become intolerable.'[8]

It was not only sympathy he wanted, of course. He was a passionate man with an impulsive and urgent sexual appetite. He was
capable of writing and thinking of women in terms of romantic
respect – 'the most perfect of God's creations', 'wonderful things',
'creatures of higher perfection than men' – but he expressed himself
just as characteristically when he admitted to a friend that he had no
time for a woman who was attracted by him but would not give

herself to him. 'When a woman takes my fancy, I say, *Est ce que tu m'aimes? Je t'aime! Tu ne m'aimes pas? Tant pis pour toi!*'[9]

Here now, at Laguna, was a woman he was determined to attract and to have. He gave orders for a boat to take him ashore. He walked up the hill where he had seen her; he looked for her, but could not find her. Instead he found a man he had met on his first arrival in the port. This man invited him to his house for a cup of coffee. He went with him, entered his house and there, facing him, was the woman he had seen from his ship. He stared at her:

> We both remained enraptured and silent, gazing at one another like two people who meet not for the first time, and seek in each other's faces something which makes it easier to recall the forgotten past. At last I greeted her by saying, '*Tu devi esser mia*' – 'You should be mine.' I could speak but little Portuguese, and uttered the bold words in Italian. Yet my insolence was magnetic. I had formed a tie, pronounced a decree, which death alone could annul. I had come upon a forbidden treasure, but yet a treasure of great price.
>
> If guilt there was, it was mine, alone. And there was guilt. Two hearts were joined in an infinite love; but an innocent existence was shattered. ... I sinned greatly, but I sinned alone.[10]

When Alexandre Dumas was editing the *Mémoires de Garibaldi* which were published in Brussels in 1860, he handed Garibaldi the page of the manuscript on which this passage occurred, and asked for further enlightenment. What did it mean exactly? ' "Read this, my dear friend, it does not seem clear." Garibaldi did read it; and then, after a moment's pause, said with a sigh:

' "It must remain as it is." '[11]

Garibaldi did not care, evidently, to reveal the whole truth to Dumas or, indeed, to anyone else; and it used generally to be supposed that the sin of which he spoke was that of taking her from her peaceful home to a life of danger, and that he did not marry her at once because he could not obtain the consent of her father who had betrothed her to a man much older and richer than himself. These suppositions, however, were far less dramatic than what may now be accepted as the truth: he did not marry her at once because she was already married.[12]

This does not seem, however, to have disturbed the happiness of

Garibaldi

Mazzini

their life together. The Saint-Simonians had taught him that there was nothing necessarily indissoluble in marriage and that the gratification of the sexual appetite could be purifying and inspiring. Instinctively he felt that this was so; and Anita was for him the ideal companion, sensual and loving, tender yet violent. Within a few weeks of his leaving Laguna, she was fighting alongside his men, cursing those who gave way to their fear, driving them back into the fight. And at the end of the day she would go to her lover and they would lie down together under the stars.

Even when she was pregnant she went on fighting, marching through jungles where the decayed stalks and leaves of the bamboos lay so thick in the undergrowth that they swallowed up and buried those who stepped amongst them, riding through the *maciega* with the strength and grace of an Amazon, helping to kill and to cook the great carcasses of beef on which the guerrillas existed.

On 16 September 1840 their first child was born. They called him Menotti, after the executed leader of the insurrection of 1831, and twelve days later she had to ride away with him to escape the regular troops. They nearly starved in the jungle where the rain fell down upon them in torrents for weeks on end, and at night wet and cold she pressed her baby between her breasts. She was terrified of losing him, Garibaldi said, 'and indeed it was a miracle that we saved him. In the steepest part of the tracks and when crossing the torrential rivers, I carried him, slung from my neck in a handkerchief.'[13]

With his child's life in danger, the cause for which he had been fighting virtually lost, and, in any event, doubting by now that it was a cause worthy of victory, Garibaldi decided at last to make for Montevideo and a quieter life. For a time he settled down to domesticity, earning his living in a variety of more commonplace ways, from commercial traveller in pasta and textiles to teacher of history and mathematics. And on 26 March 1842 he married Anita, when they heard that her husband might be dead.

But he could not settle down happily for long, and when the independence of the Republic of Uruguay was threatened by the Argentinian dictator, Juan Manuel Rosas, Garibaldi persuaded himself that a fresh opportunity had come to 'serve the cause of nations'. By April 1843 he had formed the Italian Legion from amongst the ever increasing number of Italians in Montevideo, some of them genuine political exiles, others those waifs and strays of fortune who drifted from port to port along the South American coastline. The Italian Legion served to create in Europe the first Garibaldian legend. Its initial engagement, fought two months after its formation, was a disaster ending in an embarrassing retreat which made Garibaldi feel he was 'ready to die of shame and grief'.[14] But he was not dismayed for long. He never once in his life gave himself up to despair, he wrote proudly years later, and he did not do so now. Helped by his old and experienced friend, Francesco Anzani, readily acknowledged by Garibaldi as a far more capable organiser than himself, he worked hard to train the Legion to become a more skilful and dedicated fighting force, and to instil into those who fought in it the belief that they were not merely fighting for the independence of Uruguay but for the future of their own country, too. He succeeded. Soon they were fighting well in a series of skirmishes which, though tactically irrelevant, provided them with experience and confidence, and which, though not always worthy of report, provided Mazzini with the material he needed to propagate 'the heroism of those Italians who had taken up arms in the name of liberty and of their great leader Giuseppe Garibaldi'. By the time a real victory had been won, and won against superior numbers of regular troops, Mazzini's *L'Apostolato Repubblicano* and other papers had made the name of the Italian Legion and its inspired leader well known all over Europe.

Their flag was black, indicating the sorrow of mourning Italy, and in its centre was a volcano, symbolising the power of the hidden fires that burned within her. Their uniform was a long, loose, red shirt. There was no symbolism in this, however. The Legion had to be clothed cheaply and there lay in a warehouse in Montevideo a large stock of red, smock-like shirts that had been intended for export to the Argentine where they were used by men employed in the slaughter-houses. They camouflaged the blood of the cattle; they would camouflage the blood of the men. At the same time they would make conspicuous those who attempted to skulk away from the battlefield, as the less dedicated members of the Legion had on occasions shown themselves prone to do.[15]

Once he had equipped himself with a red shirt, Garibaldi was rarely seen without one. Its prosaic origins were forgotten and it became, like the flag of the Legion, a symbol of all that he stood for and all that he fought for.

★   ★   ★

For five years the Italian Legion helped to defend Montevideo; and Garibaldi, its leader, began to enjoy his first intoxicating taste of power and popularity. 'Italians and Uruguayans,' he said, – and was proud to say it – 'both loved me; and I might, without fearing any man, have set myself up as dictator.'[16]

But he chose to live in strict austerity, refusing the money and land that the Government offered him, more proud of his worn-out clothes, as such men are, than concerned by the poverty of his family, as moved by the hardships of others as by those of his dependants. He was ready to give a stranger what little money he had in his pocket as to bring it home to a wife who, so the stories went, badgered and nagged him, angry that he kept them all so poor, jealous of his many women admirers, so much better looking than herself. There were four children now – Menotti, Rosita born in November 1843, Teresa born in February 1845, and Ricciotti born in February 1847, and named after the patriot who had been shot with the Bandiera brothers following the failure of the 1844 revolt in the Kingdom of Naples.

Rosita, a most precociously intelligent child, seems to have been his favourite. She was, he thought, 'the most beautiful, the sweetest of little girls', and her death at the age of four distressed him profoundly.

He could not bear the thought that her little body should be buried and her bones for ever remain in South America; and he longed, more than ever now, to go home.

For many months he had been disillusioned by the political under-currents of life in Montevideo – a disillusionment that was to leave him with a life-long distrust of politicians – and angered by what he took to be the selfish attitude of the European merchants and diplomats in the town. In Italy he hoped that he might find a different, a cleaner atmosphere. Certainly it seemed from recent events that he was needed there. He sent Anita and the children back to Nice; and in April 1848, three months before his forty-first birthday, he followed them, taking Rosita's coffin with him.[17]

3

'A MAN OF DESTINY'

'There is storm in the air,' Pope Gregory XVI had said to a friend shortly before his death. 'Revolutions will soon break out.'[1] An obscurantist of the most reactionary kind he had gone so far as to prohibit the building of railways in the Papal States, fearing that they might 'work harm to religion' and lead to the arrival in Rome of deputations of malcontents from the restless provinces beyond the Apennines. He set his face blank against reform and in Cardinal Lambruschini he had an adviser, though far more personally attractive than himself, no less uncompromising. When the Pope died in the summer of 1846 there remained in the Papal States only the pretence of good government.[2]

Most of the cardinals came to the Conclave to elect a new Pope knowing, or at least uneasily aware, that some concessions to liberal if not to national sentiments could no longer be delayed. None of them doubted that the possession of a strip of territory across the middle of Italy was essential to the independence and dignity of the Holy See. Indeed, this was accepted by more or less the whole Roman Catholic Church. 'God has entrusted the State,' Cardinal Lambruschini's predecessor as Secretary of State, Cardinal Bernetti, had written, 'to his Vicar on earth for the freer exercise of the Pontifical primacy all over the world.' It was a view which found wide acceptance throughout Catholic Europe. But it was clear to the cardinals as they gathered together for the Conclave in June 1846 that there would have to be changes in the manner in which this God-given State was administered.

There were sixty-two members of the Sacred College, thirty of whom lived in Rome, seventeen in the papal provinces, eight in other parts of Italy and seven outside Italy. Europe had settled on no particular candidate, but in Italy the popular choice had fallen on the aged liberal Cardinal Gizzi, and on Cardinal Micara who was also believed to be strongly in favour of reform. When Micara's carriage arrived at the Quirinal, however, and the people rushed up to it, greeting him as the new Pope, he stood up and cried out in his strong, deep voice, 'Be careful! With me you will get the gallows as well as bread.' To Lambruschini, he is said to have whispered later, 'if the Devil gets his finger in the voting, it will certainly be one of us'.[3]

The first vote was taken on the morning of 15 June. Of the fifty-two cardinals present many abstained, unwilling to commit themselves until a strong candidate emerged. But fifteen of the voting slips which were completed bore Lambruschini's name. Thirteen, however, bore the name of the kindly, polite, good-looking and, until then, little-known Cardinal Mastai Ferretti, the fifty-four-year-old Bishop of Imola.

During the course of the day Mastai's candidature slowly began to gather more support; and in the evening he polled seventeen votes, four more than his rival Lambruschini. The following morning Mastai's lead increased so encouragingly that by the time of their midday meal, several cardinals had decided to spend their siesta going round from cell to cell to enlist more votes for a man of whom 'they knew much that was good, but nothing bad'. Cardinal Mastai himself remained alone and in prayer.

After the afternoon vote had been taken it was clear that this canvassing had had its effect. Cardinal Mastai, who had been chosen as one of the three scrutineers of the voting slips, and whose duty it was to read out the names, showed so much nervousness as he did so that the others thought he might faint. His hands were trembling and it was remembered with apprehension that he had suffered from epilepsy as a boy. He had already counted his name eighteen times when he asked if someone else would take over the duty of teller from him. But as this would have made the vote invalid he was advised to wait for a few minutes until he felt well enough to carry on.

He agreed to do so and during the interval jokes at his expense were made by the more lively of the cardinals. Bernetti, one of these, leant over to his neighbour and whispered in his ear, 'Well, after the policemen come the ladies.'

At length Mastai recovered his strength and the counting began again; but, according to one account, the excitement once more proved too much for him and when he saw that he had received six more votes he collapsed in his chair. Another report has it that on his election (with thirty-six votes of the fifty cast) he knelt down with folded hands begging the cardinals to choose someone else, and then giving himself up to prayer. 'Oh, God!' he said, and his voice was shaking, 'I am Thy unworthy servant.'[4]

The white smoke came up through the chimney and the crowd learned that the Marshal of the Conclave had told the waiting diplomats that the papal clothes had been sent for and shoes of a very small size were required. The word went round that the little Cardinal Gizzi must certainly have been chosen. Excited messengers rushed to Gizzi's house, where his servants observed the traditional custom of breaking up all the belongings of their master which he would not need in the Vatican.

On the appearance of the Bishop of Imola who was presented to the people pressing round the Quirinal as their new Pope, Pius IX, it was not only the members of Cardinal Gizzi's household who were dismayed. Pio Nono was greeted with cold suspicion. Many of those in the crowd had not even heard of him before. But then he 'faced the crowd outside the Quirinal and three times gave, with his strong and melodious voice, the apostolic benediction, his arms raised slowly to the sky to outline, with the full papal gesture, the sign of the cross'.[5] And gradually the tense atmosphere relaxed. By the time he was driven away to the Vatican in his glass carriage the mood of the people had entirely changed. His calm, handsome face, and gentle gestures impressed all who saw him. '*Ah!*' the women said, '*Ah! che bello!*'[6]

He was soon recognised as much more than *bello*. He showed himself to be a man of sensitivity and generosity, pious and simple yet with a charming self-deprecating humour. He showed himself above all to be what Metternich condemned as a contradiction in terms, a reforming Pope. Immediately he made economies in the papal household, dismissed his predecessor's Swiss Guard, formed a Council to watch over all branches of the administration and to investigate proposals for modernisation and change. He promised to support scientific congresses, appointed a commission on railways and on the civil and penal codes, granted an amnesty for political offences, planned gas lighting in the streets, the formation of an Agricultural Institute, and the introduction of laymen into the government. He appointed Cardinal Gizzi his Secretary of State. Metternich was horrified. 'We were prepared for everything but a liberal Pope,' he said, appalled at what was happening, 'and now that we have one, who can tell what may happen?' It was 'the greatest misfortune of the age'. 'A new era' was approaching.[7]

Metternich was right. A new era *was* approaching. But Pio Nono was not a man who could or would wish to remain its inspiration. Despite his proclaimed disapproval of Pope Gregory's rule and his recognition that the Papacy must ally itself with liberal Europe, he had no real sympathy with the motives behind the liberal movement; and despite his fine figure and commanding voice he did not have the strength of character to fulfil the hopes and control the enthusiasm of the applauding thousands who followed him through the streets shouting their '*evviva!*' and waving the scarves and handkerchiefs they had made in his colours. He enjoyed the acclaim, his enemies said, but he was nervous of its consequences, of the implications of the repeated cry, '*Viva Pio Nono, solo! solo!*' and of the sour faces of the old régime.

He was drawn towards the idea, propounded by Vincenzo Gioberti in his *Del Primato morale e civile degli Italiani*, that the Papacy was the divinely appointed agency for Italy's regeneration, and that there should be a confederation of Italian states under the Pope's presidency. He had a genuine feeling for Italy; and, although deeply alarmed, he was at the same time flattered to receive a letter from Mazzini, addressed to the 'most powerful man' in Europe and calling upon him to fulfil the mission entrusted to him by God and unify Italy.[8] He was said also to have been pleased by a letter from Garibaldi, forwarded by the Papal Nunzio in Rio de Janeiro, offering the Italian Legion 'to further the work of redemption of Pius IX'.[9] But at heart he did not believe that representative government could be reconciled with papal authority, nor did he believe himself capable, even if he had been willing, to lead a national movement to its fulfilment. They wanted to make a Napoleon out of him, he complained, when he was really nothing but a priest.

As the months passed and the demands of the liberals increased, he shrank back from the consequences of his early example. He saw that he was being held up for popular acclaim not so much as a reforming Pope but as one who had sided with 'the revolution against tradition'.[10] His cautious and sensible reforms were dismissed as unworthy of the times; he was caricatured no longer as a saint, but as a tortoise; he was still subjected to popular acclamations of embarrassing extravagance, but the leader of the Roman democratic party, Angelo Brunetti, a strong, fat, good-natured and ill-educated wine dealer, nicknamed Ciceruacchio, began to speak to the people in the teeming slums of the Trastevere, less of Pio Nono's shining qualities than of the corruption of his advisers.

Men were gradually persuaded to feel that Mazzini might be right in dismissing Pio Nono as merely well disposed, after all, 'without any of those Italian intentions which others have been determined to see in his first acts'. Whatever were the intentions behind those first acts, however, they had awakened desires and hopes that were surging beyond his control.

In Tuscany, where unrest had long been growing, events in the Papal States strengthened the liberal party and its leader Baron Ricasoli, and led to the Grand Duke's granting a Council of State like the one which had been instituted in Rome. In Lombardy and Venetia new spirit was given to the movement for freedom from Austrian rule. And in Piedmont, the new King, Charles Albert, devout, self-tormenting, diffident and indecisive, was given fresh encouragement to live his romantic dream. Cesare Balbo's *Delle speranze d'Italia* had already suggested that although it was absurd to consider the possibility of a single Italian state such as Mazzini's self-styled 'party of action' proposed, it behoved the King of Piedmont to play the leading part in the formation of a federation of allied states. This moderate view was later endorsed by Massimo d'Azeglio's *Degli ultimi casi di Romagna* which suggested that the papal government was too backward ever to play the important role in Italian affairs which Gioberti had envisaged, but that the Papal States should become a part of federated Italy once representative institutions had been introduced. Of course, an Italian federation presupposed a challenge to Austria and this the King of Piedmont now showed himself willing to give. 'If God permits a war for the freedom of Italy,' he wrote to the Pope, waiting for a sign, for the guidance he so desperately sought, 'I will place myself at the head of the army.'

At the beginning of the following year revolutions broke out all over Italy, from Sicily and Naples to Florence and Milan, while the fall of the Orleans Monarchy in France and the declaration of the Second Republic loosened a general European revolt against the post-Napoleonic restorations. Metternich was forced to fly from Vienna; and in Austrian-dominated Lombardy, Marshal Radetzky was compelled to evacuate Milan after the famous 'Five Days' of furious fighting in which 300 Milanese were killed. In Venice, the old republic was restored and a provisional government proclaimed under the guidance of Daniele Manin – a brilliant lawyer of Jewish descent. In Parma and Modena, the Austrian garrisons withdrew, leaving the people free to join the volunteer armies.

Charles Albert, the 'Re Tentenna' – the 'Wobbly King' – decided to act at last. Since the Piedmontese revolt of 1821, in which he believed the liberals had betrayed him, he had felt inclined to regard nationalism as a dangerous movement designed to weaken monarchy; and in 1833 he had repressed a Mazzinian conspiracy with stern severity, urging the judges to act with relentless implacability. But now that revolt in Milan had led to the declaration of war on Austria by Tuscany and to the danger that Lombardy might become a republic, he felt the time had come to march against the common enemy. The new era which Metternich had prophesied seemed about to unfold.

★   ★   ★

Garibaldi was at sea when he heard the news. The *Speranza*, in which he and about sixty men of the Italian Legion had sailed from Montevideo, had put in at a little Spanish port to pick up fresh supplies, and the captain had rushed back on board to shout to the crew and passengers that 'Palermo, Milan, Venice and a hundred sister cities, had brought about the momentous revolution. The Piedmontese army was pursuing the scattered remnants of the Austrians, and all Italy, replying as one man to the call of arms, was sending her contingents of brave men to the holy war'.[11]

There was a sudden uproar in the ship. Men dashed upon deck shouting and laughing, hugging one another, 'crying for very joy'. They had sailed the Atlantic in ignorance of the events that had been the talk of Europe for days. Expecting that when they arrived in Italy they might have to put ashore on a hostile coast, they had sung each night a patriotic song standing in a circle on the deck, and to Francesco Anzani it had seemed rather a lament than a hymn of hope. But now there was no further cause for apprehension: they would land at Nice in triumph to take part in the war of liberation which it seemed would soon be won.

Italy, however, was far farther from liberation than Garibaldi and his friends imagined. The Austrian army had certainly been driven from Milan, but although the Empire was falling into ruins behind it, it was still holding out in the fortresses of Verona, Mantua, Peschiera and Legnago south of the Brenner Pass. And elsewhere in Italy, in the Kingdom of the Two Sicilies, in Tuscany and in the Papal States, although concessions had been made in the face of popular demands, neither King Ferdinand, nor the Grand Duke Leopold, nor Pio Nono were prepared to give way to the movement for national unity. And even in Piedmont there was as little agreement as to how it should be achieved and under what form of government as there was co-operation between those who were attempting to create the necessary conditions for its realization by defeating the Austrians in the field.

When Garibaldi arrived at King Charles Albert's headquarters to offer his services, he was welcomed far less warmly than he had expected and was sent back to Turin to see the Minister of War, who told him coldly that he ought to go to Venice where Daniele Manin had contrived an Austrian withdrawal from the city and proclaimed a radical republic. That seemed a more suitable place for this self-important rebel who had once been condemned to death for treason and sedition, this farouche *corsaro* and his band of adventurers. Besides, the Royal Piedmontese Army would prove itself quite capable of fighting its own battles. 'You ought to go to Venice,' the Minister said to him, so Garibaldi told Giacomo Medici, one of the young officers who had come with him from South America. 'They will give you some small ship and you can ply your trade as a buccaneer. That's your place – there's no place for you here.'[12]

Angry and embittered by this rejection of his services and disillusioned by what he took to be the King's subsequent cowardice, Garibaldi never forgave Charles Albert. 'I will not open the grave of that dead man to pronounce on his conduct,' he wrote years later. 'I leave it to history to judge him,* and will only say that, called by his position, by circumstances and by the voice of the majority of Italians, to the leadership in the war of redemption, he did not respond to the trust reposed in him, and not only showed himself incapable of making use of the enormous resources at his disposal, but proved the principal cause of our ruin.'[13]

The verdict was unjust, but then Garibaldi's character did not allow him always to be just to those who thwarted or slighted him. His certainty of his mission and his uncompromising assumptions made it impossible for him to see that those who did not agree with him might have valid reasons for doing so, that they did not necessarily act out of cowardice, ambition or personal animosity. Because of this he was, of course, an easy man to quarrel with. Medici, who found him in so bitter a mood at Turin, had quarrelled with him recently himself; and Mazzini was soon to quarrel with him, too.

Garibaldi was also, though, an easy man to forgive, not only because of the essentially responsive warmth of his nature, not only because while he was often an irritating man he was never a self-seeking one, but also because his romantic feeling for Italy was both passionate and inspiring. Francesco Anzani whose health, worn down by twenty-seven years of exile and war, had not been able to stand up to the Atlantic crossing, had understood all this. 'Don't be too hard on Garibaldi,' he had said to Medici shortly before he died, 'I myself have quarrelled with him more than once; but being convinced of his mission I have always been the first to make it up. He is a man of destiny. A great part of the future of Italy depends on him. It would be a grave error to abandon him.'[14]

There were men on Charles Albert's staff who recognised this, too. 'It was a great mistake not to use him,' General La Marmora decided. 'I do not believe he is a Republican in principle. . . . When there is another war, he is a man to employ. Garibaldi is no common man.'[15]

For the moment, however, he was refused all employment in

* The historical verdict has, perhaps, been best summed up by the Marquis Arconati: 'He was not a very talented man, but his belief that he might be one was his great misfortune.' See Adolfo Omodeo, *Difesa del Risorgimento* (Einaudi, Turin, 1951), 222.

Piedmont, and he crossed into Lombardy with Medici, to offer his services to the revolutionary committee in Milan. But although he was greeted with more enthusiasm than he had been able to arouse in Turin, and was permitted to enrol volunteers, when he raised the matter of weapons he was told that he must supply his own, and as for uniforms he must make do with what he could find in the Austrian barracks. And so the volunteers marched from Milan for Bergamo wearing blouses made from the white linen jackets of the Austrian infantry, looking 'like a regiment of cooks'.¹⁶

Whether or not they could fight better than their appearance suggested was, however, never put to the test; for soon after their arrival in Bergamo they learned that Charles Albert had surrendered. Many of the volunteers immediately decided to go home; but to prevent the dispersal of the rest, Garibaldi, protesting that the capitulation had 'nothing to do' with him, made a vehement speech in which he advocated the spirited prosecution of the war by guerrilla bands.¹⁷

But his listeners were more impressed by his passion than his arguments and by the time of roll-call next day less than 500 volunteers remained with him. He was determined, however, not to give in, and when, mainly through the efforts of Medici, 250 more men had been collected, he decided, with this pitiably small force, to take the field against the victorious Austrian armies.

He scored a few minor successes against far superior numbers, mainly in stubbornly defensive actions; and he succeeded 'in producing a feeling of insecurity,' his enemies conceded, 'by making rapid appearances and disappearances at various points in the district'.¹⁸ But it was a hopeless struggle from the beginning; and Garibaldi, suffering from a fever as well as from acutely painful attacks of the arthritis that his years in South America had given him, was in no condition to continue it.

The fighting in and around the mountain villages south of the frontier had, however, served a vital purpose: it had enhanced Garibaldi's prestige as a guerrilla leader of remarkable talents, and provided a basis for the propaganda of the future. It had also made him a popular hero, a hero not afraid to act outside the law, a man of courage and ability, of determination and passion, a simple man given to grandiloquent and apocalyptic announcements, but a man of shining sincerity in a murky and selfish world.

He was determined to live up to the part. The only question to be decided was where next to fight, how best to arouse the Italians to an awareness of their destiny.

He considered going to join Manin in Venice; he considered going to attack King Ferdinand, who had revoked the constitution he had granted in Naples; and he went so far as to set sail on a sudden whim for Palermo with about seventy companions – most of them officers who had served in the Italian Legion in Montevideo – with the intention of liberating Sicily. But on his way he put in at Leghorn and was greeted with such wild enthusiasm that he made it known that he would not be opposed to 'offering his services to the Tuscan Government'. The Tuscan Government, however, had other ideas. Their position was politically precarious and they were naturally reluctant to open the way either to democrats or reactionaries by embarking on the war against the Kingdom of the Two Sicilies that Garibaldi was now pressing upon them. When, therefore, a telegram arrived in Florence from Garibaldi – couched in terms which were soon to be recognised as characteristic: 'Garibaldi wants to know if you are putting him in command of Tuscan forces to fight against Bourbons. Answer yes or no,' – the Government decided not to answer the question at all.[19]

They were anxious enough, however, that he should leave Tuscany with his followers. 'They are like a plague of locusts,' one of the ministers, Guerrazzi, said. 'We must do all we can to get them away quickly.'[20] And they were delighted when news came that Garibaldi had decided to go to Venice after all. They readily granted him permission to recruit men in Tuscany and showed themselves willing to grant him all the help he needed provided he got quickly over the border. They were even more concerned that he should leave without delay when he arrived in Florence on his way from Leghorn and made an inflammatory speech to a cheering crowd in which he declared that the 'Tuscan Government should not only be pushed: it should be forced and whipped along. . . . Italy can choose one of two ways with her rulers. She can drag them along with her or she can overthrow them.'[21]

However much these sentiments appeared to be to the taste of his audience, though, few men felt inclined to be forced and whipped along to the war in the ranks of the Italian Legion which, by the time it reached Tuscany's northern frontier, numbered scarcely more than a hundred men.

They presented a pitiable sight as they climbed up the Apennines in the snow, looking now 'more like a caravan of bedouins than a body of men ready to fight for their country'.

'It was cruel to see those gallant young fellows in that bitter weather up in the mountains, clad for the most part in linen, some in rags, and without food in their native country,' Garibaldi thought, 'when all the thieves and scoundrels of the world have enough and to spare.'[22] It was even more cruel when, having crossed the frontier, they were halted in the freezing mountain passes.

For to reach Venice from Tuscany they had to cross the Romagna, one of the Papal States, and the Government in Rome had decided that they should not do so. In Bologna, twenty miles from the Tuscan frontier and the centre of the late democratic rising that had found such impassioned advocates in the Barbanites, Alessandro Gavazzi and Ugo Bassi, the movement for reform had been forced to a standstill. And the Pope's advisers in Rome, like the Government in Tuscany, were anxious to avoid a recurrence of the sort of trouble that the presence of Garibaldi and his legionaries in the city might be expected to arouse.

Eventually permission came from Rome for the Legion to cross the Romagna to Marina di Ravenna, provided they relinquished their arms until they reached the Adriatic coast and provided no one entered Bologna itself, except Garibaldi.

The last concession had had to be made for the citizens of Bologna had demanded it with such intimidating insistence that the military governor had felt compelled to give way. Garibaldi had entered the city in triumph, had been conducted to the Hotel Brun in a torch-light procession and had been given the opportunity of talking with Ugo Bassi and with Angelo Masina, a rich young democrat who raised a squadron of lancers to accompany the Legion to Marina di Ravenna.

On 10 November Garibaldi himself arrived in Ravenna. But to the annoyance of the Papal authorities he did not embark for Venice immediately. He was reluctant to do so, for Manin's republic seemed already doomed, and it was so far from the centre of the stage. Surely, somewhere else in Italy something would soon happen, in some city a people too long suppressed would break out in violent protest, someone would act to break through the clouds of apathy that were everywhere descending to darken the brief hopes of that now ending year of revolutions.

On 15 November 1848 on the steps of the Palazzo della Cancelleria in Rome, such an event as Garibaldi had waited for took place.

Events in the north had been welcomed in Rome and the Papal States with wild excitement; and had led to many of the Pope's subjects marching to Lombardy to join in the war of liberation against the Austrians. But Pio Nono refused to countenance the war which one of his earlier pronouncements – 'O Lord God, bless Italy' – had hopefully been taken to encourage; and on 29 April he had delivered an Allocution, separating himself once and for all from the nationalists, from those who wanted war and, indeed, from the Risorgimento itself: 'We assert clearly and openly that war with Austria is far from our thoughts, since we, however unworthy, are the Vicar of Him who is the author of peace and the lover of concord.'*[23]

The storm of resentment which this bravely unequivocal announcement provoked led to the temporary appointment of the liberal Count Terenzio Mamiani della Rovere as head of the ministry which the Pope had been forced to accept under the terms of a constitution granted the previous March. In the middle of September, however, the ministry was placed in the hands of the conservative anti-democrat Count Pellegrino Rossi.

Rossi, a pale, tired-looking scholar, was a man of strong character and high attainments. A Tuscan by birth he had been exiled for supporting Murat's attempts to revive the Napoleonic Kingdom of Italy. He had gone to Paris where his lectures at the University had so impressed Guizot that he had been asked to represent France at

---

* He had tried to separate himself from politics altogether. Marco Minghetti, one of his Ministers, recorded that when he and his colleagues called to see him on urgent business they would as likely as not find him 'unavailable', closeted with the Grand Penitentiary discussing 'some monk in America' – Marco Minghetti, *Ricordi* (Turin, 1889), i, 349.

Rome and to negotiate for the suppression of the French Jesuits. He had a Protestant wife; his books were on the Index; he was thoroughly disliked by the hierarchy. But the Pope liked and trusted him, for Rossi saw in the Papacy 'the one great thing that was left to Italy'; and he was determined to preserve its temporal power, not by making concessions to the democrats but by wise economic reform and enlightened administration. Late as his appointment came, he might well have succeeded in his work, he might even have earned the respect of the people, had he been a less proud, aloof and provocatively contemptuous man. For 'of all the Italian patriots living in foreign lands there was perhaps none whose career so genuinely proved him to be one of the distinguished men of Europe, as Pellegrino Rossi. . . . He stood for the existing Constitution, the Statuto; he believed in using the Papal States as a haven or refuge within which to develop Italian nationality on a federal basis; and above all he intended to restore law and order.'[24] But he took no trouble to hide his disdain of his opponents, both among the reactionaries and more particularly among the democratic extremists; he did not hesitate to make enemies by a cold and cruel sarcasm, while rejecting any suggestion that the animosity he provoked might cost him his life with a dismissive, 'they would not dare'.

But they did dare. On 15 November as he dismounted from his carriage in the piazza before the Palazza della Cancelleria to attend the new session of the Council of Deputies, he noticed that the crowd was in a hostile and even dangerous mood, and that at the entrance to the palace were several evil-looking men in the uniform of the *Reduci*, the volunteers who had returned from the Lombard campaign after Charles Albert's surrender. They shouted insults at Rossi as he approached, a tall, thin figure in a dark blue overcoat; but he ignored them and came on, very pale but entirely controlled. *'Abbasso Rossi! Abbasso Rossi! Morte a Rossi!'* The shouts grew louder as he walked towards the broad stone steps of the Palace, his features marked by an expression of scorn and distaste, or, as some said, a slight contemptuous smile. On the steps a man struck him; and then another, believed to be Luigi Brunetti, a son of the democratic leader Ciceruacchio, lunged at him and stabbed him through the neck with a hunting knife. As the blood spurted from Rossi's

Cardinal Antonelli

Pius IX

Pellegrino Rossi

Ugo Bassi

Garibaldian staff officers outside their headquarters at the San Silvestri convent, Rome

A group of Garibaldini

A Garibaldian Lancer carrying a message through the streets

Garibaldi and Aguyar

Giacomo Medici

Nino Bixio

Luciano Manara

Candido Augusto Vecchi

severed caratid artery, Brunetti's companions lifted their daggers so that the assassin should not be identified and then they covered him with a cloak.[25]

The news of Rossi's death was received by the deputies in silence; but next morning the town was in uproar. Armed gangs roamed through the streets singing songs in praise of the assassin, and a mob, including soldiers, policemen and several well-known citizens, demonstrated outside the Quirinal demanding positive pledges of a democratic programme.

At first the Pope refused to yield; but after the mob had attacked his Palace, tried to set fire to the door and fired several shots through the windows, killing his Latin secretary, he gave way to the radicals. Protesting that he did so only because he was forced, he accepted a cabinet which included Pietro Sterbini and another member of Young Italy, Giuseppe Galletti.

A few days later, in the guise of an ordinary priest and wearing large spectacles, he left Rome in a carriage belonging to the Bavarian envoy. On the advice of the artful, sensual, able and avaricious Cardinal Antonelli, whose charm of manner and evasive humour concealed a compelling ambition, the Pope made south for Gaeta in the Kingdom of Naples and from there wrote to King Ferdinand that he had left his capital and sought refuge outside the Papal States 'in order not to compromise his dignity, or by his silence appear to approve of the excesses that had taken place and might take place in Rome'.[26]

In Gaeta the Pope, still accompanied by Cardinal Antonelli, demanded the submission of the rebels. He appointed a Regency, which the Roman leaders ignored, and when it was announced in Rome that a Constituent Assembly would be elected on the basis of universal suffrage, he virulently denounced this 'monstrous act of unconcealed treason and open rebellion', this proposal so wicked that it would arouse 'holy indignation'. Wholeheartedly believing that he must on no account separate his spiritual from his temporal sovereignty, he threatened anyone who voted with the 'Greater Excommunication'.

He protested in vain. Had he offered terms to the rebels, he would no doubt have been welcomed back by the people, for his personal popularity had not yet been dispelled, and he was, after all, the Vicar

of Christ. But the enthusiasm in Rome could not now be checked
by the uncompromising stand that he was persuaded to adopt.

*   *   *

When news of the assassination of Rossi reached Ravenna, Garibaldi's thoughts were immediately turned to Rome. No longer need
he take his men to fight in Venice. Now he could take them to the
centre of the stage.

A self-confessed disciple of Cesare Beccaria and therefore 'opposed
to capital punishment', he was compelled, he said later, 'to condemn
the dagger of Brutus'. At the same time he could not but share the
feeling of excitement which the deed of the 'young Roman who had
recovered the steel of Brutus' had aroused throughout the Papal
States.[27] The clever American-born Marchioness Ossoli, then living
in Rome, told her mother that she thought that she could 'never have
heard of a violent death with satisfaction', but that this one had
affected her 'as one of terrible justice'.[28] To Garibaldi, born amongst
a people whose views on political murder might be expected to be
somewhat more elastic than those of the former school-teacher from
Boston, the dagger seemed not only justified, but a timely and
terrible warning to all advocates of compromise with foreign
powers 'that the people they suborned by falsehood and treachery'
would not submit to slavery.

Freed from the pressure formerly put upon them to leave the
Romagna, Garibaldi's Legion left Ravenna and moved south
towards Cesena. Recruiting began to improve and, including
Masina's lancers who had now joined the Legion as its small but
dashing complement of cavalry, it soon increased its numbers
to about 550.

These men wandered slowly south through the Apennines
towards Rome, while Garibaldi and Masina went on ahead of them
to obtain some definite guarantee of employment from the provisional government. They did not succeed in doing so. They were
welcomed with enthusiasm when they appeared in the streets of
Rome; but with wary caution by the government who envisaged
the same sort of problems that were being reported from the
provinces.

It was not that the Legion was continuously disorderly, for

discipline, when their leader was there, was strict. It was well known, indeed, that despite his professed respect for Beccaria, Garibaldi had no hesitation in ordering a soldier found looting or raping to be pilloried or shot, and he would do so, as one of his officers later remarked, 'without taking the cigar out of his mouth'.[29] But it was well known, too, that he had no money, and that his demands for wages and provisions for his men were made to the communes through which he took them with the sort of determination that did not envisage a refusal.

It was grudgingly admitted that many of the men were perfectly respectable despite their rather wild appearance. A number of them, in fact, were students; many others were intelligent young men from the professional and artisan classes of the towns of the Romagna, Lombardy and Venetia; very few were peasants (for the peasants as Garibaldi had already discovered were for the most part left unmoved by appeals to patriotism, feeling more for their Church than for their country, an abstraction which they could not fully comprehend). Nearly all of the officers, also, came from the North; twenty-two were Italians who had been with Garibaldi in Montevideo; two were South Americans. But there were also in the Legion a large number of professional criminals as well as restless adventurers whose extravagant endorsement of their comrades' political or religious views was often a cloak for acts of outright, if frequently exaggerated, brigandage.

The government in Rome, therefore, listened to Garibaldi's requests and offers of assistance with misgiving. They granted him the rank of Lieutenant-Colonel in the Roman Army and the authority to maintain a force of 500 men. But, despite the urgings of Pietro Sterbini, they refused to hold themselves responsible for supplying it.

Garibaldi returned to Umbria discontented and disillusioned, suffering from that strong sense of injustice and persecution which his treatment at Charles Albert's headquarters had recently aroused and which was later in life to be fanned, by those who called themselves his friends, into states of intermittent paranoia. He had, however, secured himself a candidature for the new Constituent Assembly and with the help of the votes of his Legion, which was marched *in toto* to the polls (although none of its members was, in fact, entitled to a vote), he was elected. On 5 February, unable to walk because his arthritis was so bad that day, he was carried into the Assembly by one of his officers. He sat down on the back row '*in costume guerrigliero*' and immediately every eye turned round to him. 'Why are we losing time in vain formalities?' he demanded of the startled deputies. 'The delay of even a minute is a crime. Long live the Republic.' The audience in the galleries applauded, but 'a buzz rose among the other deputies' who also wanted their say; and it was not until four days later, at nine o'clock at night, after thirteen hours of passionate oratory, that the Republic was born.[30]

It was a lonely child, disliked by its neighbours and, indeed, by the whole of Catholic Europe which considered the Pope to have been grossly ill-used. Republicans from all over Italy flocked towards it; but its life was already despaired of. Already the Pope had appealed to France, Spain, Austria and Naples to smother it. King Ferdinand, determined not to be left behind in the race to restore the Pope to his dominions, moved his army up to the frontier.

Austria, for the moment at least, had other problems. For King Charles Albert, brooding in Turin on the fate of Milan, which he had abandoned the previous August, was prompted by his Parliament and the force of his conscience to renounce the armistice. On 20 March he marched once more across the Ticino into Lombardy. It was a brave gesture, bravely supported by a heroic army. But neither he nor his generals had the military skill of Marshal Radetzky who, by overwhelming him at Novara, forced him into abdication and to an early death in Portugal that same summer.

The defeat of Charles Albert at Novara, the sad end of a man who had earned forgiveness for the past by risking both his life and his crown for Italy, brought the death of the Roman Republic closer than ever.

But as the Austrians moved south from Novara towards the Romagna, it prepared itself to fight for its existence by creating a Triumvirate to dictate its policy in the coming emergency. The Triumvirs chosen were Count Aurelio Saffi, the leader of the liberals from the Romagna, 'all mildness and philosophy', Carlo Armellini, a quiet Roman lawyer, and Giuseppe Mazzini.

*   *   *

Mazzini had appeared briefly in Italy in August the previous year. He had rushed from his exile in London as soon as he heard the news of Charles Albert's decision to support the revolt in Milan. 'Notwithstanding all my aversion to Charles Albert as the executioner of my best friends, and the contempt I feel for his weak and cowardly nature,' he had said, 'notwithstanding all the democratic yearnings of my own heart—yet, could I believe him possessed even of sufficient true ambition to enable him to unite Italy for his own advantage – I could cry, Amen!'[31]

But soon after Mazzini had returned to Italy, the resistance to the Austrians had begun to collapse, and there was nothing left for him to do but join Garibaldi's Legion then at Bergamo. He appeared amongst them with a rifle (the gift of Mrs. Ashurst, an English friend) slung over his shoulder; and he asked to join the vanguard which was about to leave by forced marches to Monza.

'A general acclamation saluted the great Italian,' wrote Medici, the vanguard's commander, 'and the Legion unanimously confided its banner which bore the device "God and the People" to his charge. . . . The march was very fatiguing. Rain fell in torrents. We were drenched to the skin. Although accustomed to a life of study and little fit for the violent exercise of forced marches, his constancy and serenity never forsook him for an instant.'[32]

But it was a hopeless cause and Mazzini had neither the physical stamina nor the temperament to support a form of guerrilla warfare which he could not control. He withdrew once more into exile.

The flight of the Pope to Gaeta, however, had given him fresh hope; and, elected to the Constituent Assembly in his absence, he had set out once more for his homeland, encouraged by a message of three words sent to him by the young poet, Goffredo Mameli: '*Roma, Repubblica, Venite!*'[33]

'Rome was the dream of my young years,' he wrote, 'the religion of my soul. I entered the city one evening, early in March, with a deep sense of awe, almost of worship. . . . I had journeyed towards the sacred city with a heart sick unto death from the defeat of Lombardy, the new deceptions I had met with in Tuscany, and the dismemberment of our republican party over the whole of Italy. Yet, nevertheless, as I passed through the Porta del Popolo, I felt an electric thrill run through me – a spring of new life.'[34]

He was inspired by the wild hope that the liberation of Italy would be accomplished in a pure, spreading fire set off by a spark in Rome. 'We must act like men who have the enemy at their gates,' he told the Assembly, 'and at the same time like men who are working for Eternity.'

There are not five Italies, or four Italies or three Italies. There is only one Italy. God, who, in creating her, smiled upon her land, has awarded her the two most sublime frontiers in Europe, symbols of eternal strength and eternal motion – the Alps and the sea. . . . Rome shall be the holy Ark of your redemption, the temple of your nation. . . . Rome, by the design of Providence, and as the People have divined, is the *Eternal City* to which is entrusted the mission of disseminating the word that will unite the world. . . . Just as to the *Rome of the Caesars*, which through action united a great part of Europe, there succeeded the *Rome of the Popes*, which united Europe and America in the realm of the spirit, so the *Rome of the People* will succeed them both, to unite Europe, America and every part of the terrestrial globe in a faith that will make thought and action one. . . . The destiny of Rome and Italy is that of the world.[35]

With such grand and prophetic pronouncements Mazzini inspired the Romans with something of his own feverish, almost hysterical, enthusiasm. Immediately after his arrival he had become the leader of the Assembly, and was soon the undisputed dictator of the Republic, pushing it forward under his banner – 'God and the People'.

He made enemies, of course, for he would brook no argument, nor any rival, seeing truth as a reflection of his own ideas, opposition as treachery. 'Mazzini thinks he is Pope and infallible,' Giovanni Ruffini had already written of him; and Luigi Carlo Farini was soon to say, 'He is pontiff, prince, apostle, priest. When the clericals have gone he will be thoroughly at home in Rome. . . . He has the nature of a priest more than of a statesman. He wants to tether the world to his own immutable idea.'[36]

But the Republic, if it were to have any relevance at all, had need of such a man. Certainly its short life could have served little purpose without him. And how short its life would be, how little time there was to make it serve its purpose in the fight for Italy, was clear to

Mazzini from the beginning. Soon after his arrival he had called on the Marchioness Ossoli, looking, she thought, 'more divine than ever after all his new strange sufferings'. But he had been doubtful about the future. The foes, he told her, were 'too many, too strong, too subtle'.[37]

The most immediate of these foes was France where Louis Napoleon – whose election the year before to the French Assembly had been likened by a newspaper to the sudden and unexpected appearance of a demon in a pantomime – had recently been proclaimed its President. Louis Napoleon, nephew of the Emperor, had been preferred to his rivals not only because his name seemed to promise law and order, but also because the bourgeoisie were hungry for a more dynamic policy and, perhaps, a second Empire.

Ready to indulge the people in these ambitions, and needing the support of the clericals to achieve them, the new President listened to the Pope's appeal with interest, and after Novara he was ready to act. Pio Nono's choice of the Kingdom of Naples for his temporary exile had been interpreted as a diplomatic defeat for France, but so long as King Ferdinand remained inactive on the Roman frontier there was still time to recover prestige. There was another reason, too, for Louis Napoleon's anxiety to act in Italy: Austria could not be allowed to extend her influence there. She had been prevented from making extravagant claims on Piedmont after Novara; she must now be checked also at Rome.* And so, although Louis Napoleon had a personal sympathy with the aspirations of the Italian nationalists – and had, in fact, risked his life as a young Carbonaro fighting against the misgovernment of the Papal States – he saw that, if his own ambitions were to be fulfilled, he must 'liberate' Rome from the 'foreigners who had come from all parts of Italy' to force their socialist views on an intimidated populace. There was also no doubt that opinion in France was strongly sympathetic towards the Pope, so roughly expelled from Rome, and encouraged action to restore him. And so on 25 April 1849 a French army under General Oudinot landed at Civitavecchia.

---

* 'It was not for the sake of the Roman people, or the Pope, or Catholicism that we went to Rome,' Thiers wrote; 'it was for the sake of France . . . to maintain our right to have one half of Italy if Austria seized the other.' Quoted by J. M. Thompson, *Louis Napoleon and the Second Empire* (Basil Blackwell, 1954), 198.

The following day a French staff officer, Colonel Leblanc, arrived in Rome. Until then there had been doubt, intensified by General Oudinot's equivocal statements, as to the exact purpose of the French intervention. There was even hope that they had come merely to save Rome from the Austrians. But Colonel Leblanc removed all these fanciful illusions. He told Mazzini that the French had come to restore the Pope.

'And if the people do not want the Pope restored,' Mazzini replied, 'what then?'

'He will be restored,' the Colonel said, 'just the same.'[38]

Mazzini took this categoric answer to the Assembly and asked for a decision as to whether the gates of Rome should be opened to the French, or the papal troops and the people called upon to defend them. 'After a short tumult and brief delay' the Triumvirs were charged with the safety of the Republic and commanded 'to oppose force by force'.[39]

A few days before, Garibaldi had written to Mazzini reminding him that the Legion, now numbering over a thousand men stationed at Rieti, were still his 'friends in the faith'.

Now, at last, they were wanted.

4

THE SIEGE OF ROME

On the afternoon of 27 April 1849, Garibaldi's Legionaries entered Rome. And as they pushed their way through the crowds down the Corso towards the Piazza Colonna the people looked at them with astonishment. They looked more like brigands than soldiers. Their bearded faces, shaded by the brims of high-crowned, black-plumed hats, were covered with dust; their hair was long and unkempt; some carried lances, others muskets and all of them wore in their black belts a heavy dagger. The officers and orderlies of the staff wore red blouses instead of the dark-blue tunics of most of the men, but otherwise there seemed little distinction between them.

There was, though, no mistaking the broad-shouldered figure on the white horse. Despite the freckled skin burnt red by the sun and the flamboyant black felt hat with its high plume of ostrich feathers, Garibaldi looked, as the people had been told he would look, like a new Messiah. The fair beard, the loose, brown hair worn down to the shoulders, the long, high-bridged nose, the broad smooth brow, and the deep-set eyes in the calm, sad face, marked him out from the others as a man alone and apart.

'I shall never forget that day when I first saw him on his beautiful white horse,' said a young artist who left his studio to become one of his soldiers. 'He reminded us of nothing so much as of our Saviour's head in the galleries – everyone said the same. I could not resist him. I went after him; thousands did likewise. He only had to show himself. We all worshipped him. We could not help it.'[1]

It was not only Italian artists who were thus affected. During the next few days Englishmen, Belgians, Swiss, Dutchmen (and even one Frenchman) whose habit it had been to meet at an artists' cafe in the afternoons, enlisted either in the Italian Legion or in the Civic Guard, or else joined the Students' Corps which was composed for the most part of men from the University. Schoolboys joined as well as artists and students, and hundreds of older men who felt in the air, as Mazzini had felt, 'the pulsations of the immense eternal life of Rome, the immortality stirring beneath those ruins of two epochs, two worlds'.[2]

Already the battalions of the National Guard had shown on parade before the Palace of the Assembly that they were eager to fight for the Republic. Their officers had doubted it at first, but when Mazzini had spoken to them himself, 'the universal shout of *"Guerra!"* that arose from the ranks drowned in an instant the timid doubts of their leaders'.[3]

The papal troops in Rome also promised their support, and though many of them were prepared to fight against the Pope's friends not so much because they felt the Pope had stood in the way of liberation and unity as because their own neglect at the expense of the Swiss regiments had embittered them, there were others who shared the enthusiasm of the leading Garibaldini. There were, however, no more than 2,500 of these regular troops under arms, and scarcely more than 1,000 men in the National Guard. And were these enough, Mazzini's critics wondered, even when reinforced by Garibaldi's irregulars and the citizen volunteers, to make even a token resistance?

Certainly his detractors outside the walls of Rome believed that resistance was futile. When *The Times* leader-writer spoke of the 'degenerate remnant of the Roman people' preparing to fight in the mistaken belief that they were heroes,[4] he was expressing sentiments common to European opinion. Palmerston, unaware how uncompromising the Pope's attitude had become, advised Mazzini to accept a return to papal rule in exchange for the establishment of liberal institutions.[5]

For Mazzini, of course, such a solution was unthinkable. Rome was to him now, more than ever, 'the natural centre of Italian unity', and the eyes of the world must be directed towards her. The Republic would fall if no help came from the other provinces of Italy, but by its fall the Italian people would regain their 'Religion of Rome' and from the ashes of its defeat would rise a new spirit, fierce and purified.

However fanciful and extravagant such beliefs might appear to statesmen in the North, they provided in Rome both an inspiration and a stimulus. And Mazzini himself lived up to them. Occupying a small room in the Quirinal, he made himself accessible to everyone who wished to see him, workmen and officials alike. Walking the streets, 'with the same smile and warm handshake for all'; working endlessly by day and dining at night in a cheap restaurant, or eating a supper of bread and raisins in his room; spending almost the whole of his Triumvir's modest salary of £32 a month on others; relaxing only in the evenings when, left by himself at last, he sang to his guitar, he gave an example of serenity and self-abnegation to which it was difficult not to respond.[6]

And the people did respond. At first, of course, there was much scepticism. An English resident told a visitor that he was quite sure the present government would soon be put down, that the Roman soldiers would run away at the first shot and that the people wanted the French to help them get rid of the Republic. It was only Garibaldi and his men who supported the Republic, and they 'were a parcel of brigands'. A week later, however, it had to be grudgingly admitted that 'enthusiasm was gaining ground'.[7]

For it was not only a matter of resisting a foreign invasion; there was much in the achievements of the Republic that was truly impressive, much to indicate that given time and a less haphazard approach to economic problems it might live up to its declared programme of 'no war of classes, no hostility to existing wealth, no wanton or unjust violation of the rights of property; but a constant endeavour to ameliorate the material condition of the classes least favoured by fortune'.[8]

Legal, financial and municipal reforms had been put into effect; a charity commission had been appointed; the universities had been made free; money had been spent on the encouragement of art; the offices of the Inquisition had been turned into flats; a scheme had been prepared to partition ecclesiastical estates into small-holdings to be let at nominal rents.

But although Church property was to be nationalised and the Church itself subordinated to the State, the Republic rigidly opposed all persecution of priests, even those who preached against its policies; for it was vital both for the internal stability of the Republic and for the appeasement of Catholic opinion abroad that the Government should be seen not as an enemy of Catholicism but as a champion of liberty, order and Christian ideals, that Mazzini's Republic was essentially, in fact, the religious organization which he had always conceived it to be.

And, as it happened, except in country districts where Antonelli's agents encouraged the peasants' native conservatism and superstition, there was little open opposition by the clergy; and although Mazzini never won them over to his ideas as he had ingenuously hoped to do, many of them quietly ignored the Pope's excommunication of the Assembly's electors. It was impossible, indeed, for the priests, as it was for laymen, not to admit that the Republic's maxim, 'stiffness in particles, toleration to individuals', was not empty propaganda. Press censorship was lifted, and the views of papal writers circulated freely.[9]

Naturally, a policy of such permissiveness, after so long a period of authoritarian control, led to outbreaks of crime and violence, particularly in the provinces, where the opportunity for revenge and the prosecution of personal vendettas were found to be irresistible. In the Romagna and the Marches there were numerous outrages; and at Ancona twenty-eight *Sanfedisti*, murderous anti-liberals who acted in the name of the Holy Faith, were assassinated. While in Rome itself the report that a hole in the dungeons of the Inquisition had been found stuffed with skeletons and human hair led to an outburst of violence; and later, after the siege had begun, several priests, some but not all of whom had fired at soldiers, and three peasants, who were mistaken for spies, were all murdered.

But the crimes were isolated and sporadic; and only for a short period in May when Collimaco Zambianchi – a rough, savagely anti-clerical terrorist from Forlì, who had been placed in command of a volunteer regiment of customs house officers from the provinces – instigated a number of violent crimes in the Trastevere quarter, did the outrages seem beyond the control of the government and the citizen guard. *The Times* correspondent, who was not in Rome at the time, gave credence to the most highly coloured reports that came out of the capital, creating the impression that a reign of terror had been proclaimed and that priests 'who had the courage to appear in public' had been 'butchered in open day and their flesh, cut up in morsels, thrown in to the Tiber'.[10]

In fact, no one who lived in the city during those days could doubt that the reports that filled not only *The Times* but much of the Press of the world outside, had been wilfully exaggerated; nor could they doubt that what outbreaks of violence occurred were due less to the

policy or indifference of the government than to the provocation of
its enemies, and to the personal, non-political crimes of those who
professed to be its most ardent supporters.[11]

'Priests walk about in great comfort,' Arthur Clough assured his
friends who might have supposed from the reports in *The Times*
that Rome had become, as the Pope said it had become, 'a den of
wild beasts, crammed full of men of all nations, who, being apostates
or heretics, or teachers of Communism or Socialism and animated by
the most terrible hatred against Catholic truth, strive to teach and
disseminate pestiferous errors of every description . . . appropriate
the property of priests' persons, infringe the personal liberty of the
well-disposed and expose their lives to the daggers of cut-throats'.[12]

'Assure yourself there is nothing to deserve the name of "terror",'
Clough went on calmly. 'The worst thing I have witnessed has been
a paper in manuscript put up in two places in the Corso, pointing out
seven or eight men for popular resentment. This has been done by
night; before the next evening a proclamation was posted in all the
streets, from (I am sure) Mazzini's pen, severely and scornfully
castigating such proceedings.'[13]

On occasions Mazzini personally intervened; and once when a
mob dragged the confessional boxes from a church for use as barricades he prevailed upon the ringleaders to take them back.[14]

*   *   *

After the arrival of the Garibaldini the preparations for the defence
of Rome took on a more intense as well as a more practical note. For
political reasons the Triumvirs – and this term was understood to
mean Mazzini since he it was who ruled them – felt that they could
not appoint Garibaldi commander-in-chief. It seemed to them
essential, in view of the papal allegations that Rome had been taken
over by foreigners, that a Roman should be given the supreme
command. It was important, too, that the regular troops should be
given no grounds for complaint that they had been placed under the
orders of a guerrilla: 'they might as well have proposed an Indian
chief to command the Roman army'.[15] It was Garibaldi, nevertheless, whom the population regarded as their natural leader.[16]

When he appeared in the streets, where barricades were being
thrown up in sudden outbursts of energy, or on the outskirts of the

city, where the existing fortifications were being strengthened by all sorts of the city's inhabitants, the people rested on their spades to look at him, and 'hardly had the General, with his melodious penetrating voice, spoken a few words, when an uproarious cheering broke out'.[17] And when he trotted away, followed by the huge, fierce-looking Negro, Andrea Aguyar, a man of 'gigantic form and Herculean strength' who had followed him from South America and was now his orderly, the cheering grew louder than ever. Aguyar was always with him dressed in clothes no less striking than those of his master – 'a dark cloak like a cope over his red tunic, a beret on his head, his trousers blue with green stripes, and in his hand a long lance decorated near the point with a red streamer'.[18] Whenever these two appeared in the streets, hundreds of people hurried towards them – workmen in smocks, clerks in top hats, ladies in silk dresses, youths and boys, 'even mothers who held the children up to show them the man whose name was on everyone's lips'.[19]

There was no mistaking the enthusiasm in Rome now as ramparts were raised and loopholes made in the walls, as the covered way from the Vatican to the Castle of Sant' Angelo was destroyed, the fine trees in the Villa Borghese torn down to make barricades, and the 'villas, haunts of sacred beauty, that seemed the possession of the world for ever' were sacrificed to the pressing military needs of the moment.[20]

In every *rione* deputies were appointed to take command of the citizens when the bells of the Capitol and Montecitorio summoned them to arms; platforms were erected in the squares for the use of the most forceful orators in the Assembly; pensions were promised to the families of those who might lose their lives in the defence of Rome; priests and nuns were asked to pray for victory; and Princess Belgioioso, joined by nearly six thousand volunteer nurses, organised hospitals for those who might be wounded in striving to achieve it.[21]

There were those, of course, who were still sceptical of the effect of this enthusiasm. Mrs. William Wetmore Story, who was then staying in Rome with her husband, the writer and sculptor, went one day to watch the barricade-making at Porta San Giovanni where they 'voted the workmen too lazy to live';[22] another day they went to Porta Cavaleggeri and Porta Angelica 'to see the barricades, or rather earth mounds, ramparts, stockades, which the Romans are building in the event of the French. They had been working at these some thirty hours', her husband recorded in his diary, 'and in some places had done three feet. Bunker Hill ramparts were thicker. Here nothing is right earnest. The labourers were leaning picturesquely on their spades, doing nothing, and everything was going on as leisurely as if the enemy were in France instead of a 'few hours' march of the city.'

The following day Story went out early with a friend 'to Piazza Santa Apostoli to see the Guardia Civica meet and be harangued. Sterbini asked them if at the cost of their blood they were ready to defend the city; to which they screamed '*Si!*' and held up their hats on their bayonets, making the Piazza ring with huzzas. But the enthusiasm did not seem of the right stuff – it was rather a *festa* demonstration.'[23]

Emilio Dandolo who entered Rome with a regiment of *bersaglieri* from Lombardy the next day, 29 April, formed the same impression. He thought that the applause that greeted his men from the windows and coffee-houses on every side indicated only too clearly that they had arrived in time to be present at the last scene of some absurd comedy. 'There was the same superabundance of standards, of cockades, of badges of party that had characterised the last few months of Milan's liberty,' he wrote, 'the same clanking of swords along the public streets, and those various and varied uniforms of officers, not one matching with the other, but all seeming more suitable for the embellishment of the stage than for military service; those epaulettes thrown, as it were by chance, on the shoulders of men whose very faces seemed to declare their unfitness to wear them. . . . All this array of warriors in glittering helmets with double-barrelled guns and with belts full of daggers, reconciled us but little to the scanty numbers of real, well-drilled soldiers.'[24]

Dandolo's *bersaglieri*, for their part, were at first considered unlikely to add much either to the life or lustre of the Republic. They looked well enough, it was admitted, in their dramatic broad-brimmed hats crowned with plumes of dark green feathers, but some of the men were former bandits, others had deserted from the Austrian army, many more were callow youths, while most of their officers were rich young men from noble families, inexperienced and intractable. They were the 'Aristocratic Corps', convinced monarchists, few of whom 'felt any sympathy for the government which had Mazzini at the head', and many of whom persisted in retaining on their sword belts the Cross of Savoy 'in order to convince everyone', as Dandolo said, 'that if we were foremost in peril under the walls of Rome, we were so only from the ardent desire of defending an Italian city from a foreign invasion'.

They had, in fact, come to Rome largely because they had nowhere else to go. Their brigade, about 600 strong, had been formed by Luciano Manara, a young Milanese aristocrat, from Lombard exiles who had fled to Piedmont after the recapture of Milan by the Austrians. They had sworn loyalty to their new King, Victor Emmanuel II, Charles Albert's son and successor, but he was not yet in a strong enough position to make use of them or even to allow them to remain in his country. And as they could not go back to Lombardy, they had wandered south, answering with relief on their landing at Anzio a request for help from General Giuseppe Avezzana, the Roman Republic's Minister of War. They were not prepared, however, to accept General Avezzana's political beliefs. When he reviewed them after their entry into the city and made a speech which he rather tactlessly ended with the words '*Viva la Repubblica!*' the soldiers remained silent and motionless.

'Present arms! *Viva l'Italia!*' shouted Manara quickly, noticing the Minister's embarrassment.[25]

But although the *bersaglieri* disliked the idea of a republic and distrusted the capacity of its supporters to defend it, and although they themselves were viewed at first with widespread misgiving, opinions on both sides were soon to change. That night when drums beat in the town 'all of a sudden the whole city was in movement to resist the approach of the French'.

'In all the streets in the neighbourhood of Porta Angelica and Porta Cavalleggeri were bivouacked small but admirable regiments of the line,' Dandolo wrote, 'two magnificent battalions of carabineers, with four or five parks of field artillery. Two regiments of cavalry were stationed in Piazza Navona; numerous bodies of volunteers kept watch on the walls; and the whole of the National Guard were all in perfect order at their respective quarters. . . . We passed the night in the square of St. Peter's enchanted with the

View of the Janiculum from the roof tops of Rome

French troops attempting to enter Rome through the Porta Cavalleggeri on 30 April 1849

A French Battery firing on the Janiculum defences

French troops advancing their siege works

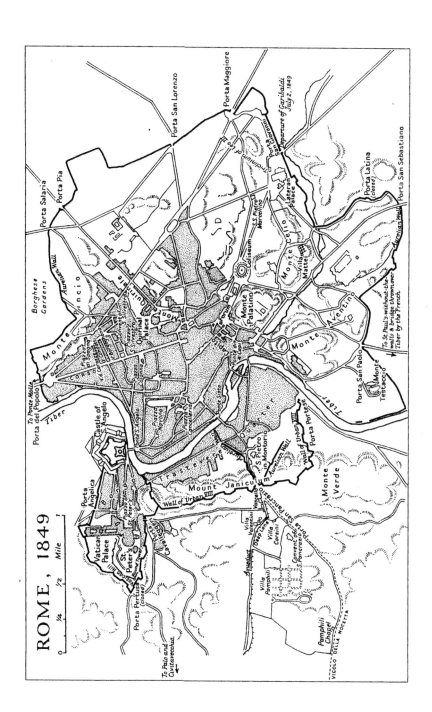

ROME, 1849

0   ¼   ½   Mile

To Ponte Molle
Porta del Popolo

Porta Salaria
Porta Pia

Borghese
Gardens

Aurelian Wall

Monte Pincio

Porta San Lorenzo

Porta Maggiore

Superature of Garibaldi
July 2, 1849

Porta San Giovanni
Porta Ferdinando

Porta San Lorenzo

Porta San Sebastiano

Porta Latina
(closed)

Lateran
Palace

S.S. Pietro
Marcellino

Coliseum

Monte Celio

Villa
Mattei

Monte Aventino

Monte Esquilino

Monte
Palatino

Forum

Quirinal
Palace

Monte Quirinale

Monte Viminale

Monte Verde

Tiber

Porta San Paolo

Monte
Testaccio

To St. Paul's without the
walls & bridge thrown over
Tiber by the French

Tiber

Castle of
Angelo

Ponte S. Angelo

Piazza
Navona

Trastevere

S. Pietro
in Montorio

Wall of Urban VIII

Porta Portese

Aurelian Wall

Mount Janiculum

Wall of Urban VIII

Monte
Verde

Porta
Angelica

Vatican
Palace

St. Peter's

Porta
Cavalleggieri

Porta Pertusa
(closed)

To Palo and
Civitavecchia

Villa
Valentini

Villa
Desplora

Villa
Corsini

Convent of
S. Pancrazio

Porta San Pancrazio

Aqueduct

Villa
Pamphili

Pamphili
Chapel

VICOLO DELLA NOCETTA

spectacle, and with finding ourselves in the midst of soldiers, and of a confident and resolute population.'[26]

The troops were concentrated round St. Peter's and the Vatican Palace for it was here and against the high ground of the Janiculum Hill south of Porta Cavalleggeri that the French, marching down from Civitavecchia and Palo, were expected to launch their attack. This part of Rome, on the western bank of the Tiber, was protected by a line of walls stretching from the Castle of Sant' Angelo in the north and then round the Vatican Hill to Porta Portese in the south. The fortifications, most of which had been either built or extended by Urban VIII after the development of gunpowder had revolutionised the art of siege warfare, were much more capable of resisting bombardment and much more capable of being used offensively by artillerymen than the ancient walls that encircled greater Rome to the east. But they had a serious disadvantage; the ground beyond them was as high as the defences, and in one place it was even higher. Here the mouths of the besiegers' cannon could look down upon the besieged.

It was this dangerous part of the front, where the gardens of two villas – the Villa Corsini and the Villa Pamphili – overlooked the fortifications by the Porta San Pancrazio, which Avezzana gave Garibaldi to protect. In reserve Avezzana posted about 1,800 troops of the Papal Army under Colonel Bartolomeo Galletti together with some companies of the National Guard; and along the whole line of the Vatican Hill he placed two battalions of the National Guard and two battalions of papal troops, a force of about 2,000 men, under Colonel Masi.[27]

Garibaldi's command included about 300 civilian volunteers, mostly students and artists, and rather less than 1,000 other volunteers from the Papal States as well as his own Italian Legion, about 2,500 men in all. It was immediately clear to him that these men must fight outside the walls of the city on the high ground where the villas stood. So there, in the Villa Corsini, he established his headquarters.

In the valley below him the sun shone on the vineyards; and beyond them, out of sight to the north, the French marched confidently down the road from Palo.

★   ★   ★

They marched in the hot morning sun of 30 April through a countryside deserted. On the walls of empty houses were posters in heavy type which carried, in sardonic simplicity, the bare text of the fifth article of the newly adopted French constitution:

France respects foreign nationalities. Her might will never be employed against the liberty of any people.[28]

There seemed to be no cause for alarm, and the officers apparently felt none. Assured by sympathisers that the gates of Rome would be opened as soon as the advance-guard came into sight, or at least when the first shot was fired, they marched towards the city in their beautiful uniforms and white gloves, without siege guns or scaling ladders, their scouts only a short way in front of the dense columns. 'We shall not meet as enemies either the citizens or the soldiers of Rome,' General Oudinot had assured them. 'Both consider us as liberators.' And then he added a private opinion for the benefit of those who doubted him: 'Italians never fight.'[29] It was a view which his officers clearly shared.*

Sometime before eleven o'clock the advance-guard caught sight of an old round tower, part of the fortifications that Leo IV had built on the summit of the Vatican hill as a defence against the Saracens. Oudinot's plan was to enter Rome either by the gate beneath this tower, the Porta Pertusa (which, although walled up many years before was still shown on some recently printed French maps), or by the Porta Angelica, between the Vatican Palace and the Castle of Sant' Angelo. But when the leading troops came to within a hundred yards of the Porta Pertusa, two cannon on the walls above their heads opened up on them.

One French officer, still convinced that no opposition would be met, confidently assured his companions that this must be the usual signal for midday.[30] When the first shots were followed by several more, however, the officers in command of the advance-guard, surprised rather than dismayed by this evidence that the Romans were prepared, after all, to offer a token resistance, gave orders for

* The French had been encouraged in this view by the attitude shown towards their landing by the people at Civitavecchia. According to *The Times* correspondent, who witnessed the disembarkation, all classes of people looked on with 'stupid amazement', gaping, wondering and saying nothing. 'Not one word of approbation or disapprobation was heard.' – *The Times*, 8 May 1849.

their own artillery to be unlimbered and for the fire to be returned. A mile away to the south, on the terrace on the Villa Corsini, Garibaldi's staff stood looking down on the movements of the French troops clearly visible in the now fiercely burning sun. They saw a company of infantry in white coats and heavy shakos rush at the Vatican walls, make an attempt to climb them and then fall back under heavy fire behind the cover of the mounds and dykes that cut across the valley beneath the Vatican hill; they saw a column of troops move off and march north round the curve of the hill where, out of sight, they also came under heavy fire from the National Guard in the hanging gardens above; and they saw another and larger column come down into the vineyards on the other side of the round tower and head towards the Porta Cavalleggeri. The men in this column, too, were met by a spirited fire from the cannon and muskets on the battlements which dominated the approaches to the gate and, like the troops on the other side of the Vatican Palace, they could make no headway. After half an hour it had become clear to the French commanders that they could not hope to storm the walls without further preparations and a more coherent plan. Their troops had already shown they were capable of fighting with great courage and resource, but the defence of Rome was obviously not in the irresolute hands that would have allowed such virtues immediately to triumph.

Garibaldi saw his opportunity. The French had not been repulsed, but for the moment they had been halted. If he attacked them now, while they were reorganising, he might drive them away from the walls, back towards Palo. So sending about three hundred of his students down from the gardens of the Villa Pamphili as an advance-guard, he gave orders for his own legionaries to follow them.

At the bottom of the steep slope beyond the Pamphili gardens, however, there was a deep walled lane, the Via Aurelia Antica, that ran from the Porta San Pancrazio to the Palo road; and here beneath the arches of the Pauline Aqueduct the untrained students came suddenly face to face with eight companies of the 20me de Ligne. The excited young men immediately opened fire and some of them rushed forward brandishing their bayonets and shouting patriotic slogans. At first the French infantry fell back, astounded by so violent and unexpected an onslaught; but they soon recovered and within a few minutes were driving the students back up the slope and then across the Pamphili gardens towards the Villa Corsini. Units of Garibaldi's legion came up to their assistance, but they too were forced back by the regular troops, and Garibaldi was constrained to send for help from the reserves in the city. When eight hundred of these reserves arrived, it was time for Garibaldi to act in the way that he loved to act. Rallying the legionaries who had already been engaged in the fight, and surrounded by those who had not yet fought and by Colonel Galletti's papal troops, he rode out with majestic calm to lead the counter-charge, shouting 'Come on, boys, put the French to flight like a mass of carrion! Onward with the bayonet, *bersaglieri!*'[31]

Encouraged by these cries and by the sight of the *'Duce'* sitting astride his horse, with the poncho falling from his shoulders, excited by the sort of hysteria that violence and the sight of blood and death can arouse, the Italians rushed forward towards the stream that divided the grounds of the Villa Corsini from those of the Villa Pamphili. They threw themselves at the French, shouting and cheering, stabbing at the bodies in the heavy uniforms, splashing with blood the flowers and the stone statues and the lead figures beside the pools where the fountains played, running past the huts and outhouses where other volunteers, by-passed in the French attack, were still holding out. They poured across the gardens, already covered with a pall of smoke and down the slope towards the sunken lane. For a time the French, outnumbered in this part of the field, held their ground here; but not for long. The repeated rushes of the volunteers, whom a French officer described as being 'as wild as dervishes, clawing at us even with their hands', forced them back beyond the aqueduct into the vineyards and then across the Palo road and into the deserted country over which they had so confidently advanced only six hours before. They left behind them 365 prisoners and about 500 killed and wounded.[32]

It was a wonderfully inspiriting victory, a victory which Garibaldi later generously attributed to the planning and organisation of General Avezzana.[33] That night the uncurtained windows of the city were ablaze with light, the streets and piazzas full of proud and happy people, the cafés and restaurants crowded to the doors. 'The Romans are all elated and surprised at themselves,' William Story wrote in his diary. And Arthur Clough who from the Pincian Hill

had seen the smoke and heard 'the occasional big cannon and the
sharp succession of skirmishers' volleys bang, bang, bang – away
beyond St. Peter's', told Thomas Arnold that the Roman Republic
had shown 'under Mazzini's inspiration a wonderful energy'.[34]
'The Italians fought like lions,' the Marchioness Ossoli confirmed.
'It is a truly heroic spirit that animates them. They make a stand here
for honour and their rights, with little ground for hope that they
can resist, now that they are betrayed by France.'[35]
Yet it was still Mazzini's hope that, despite this betrayal, France
could even now become the Republic's friend; and he, for his part,
was determined to do all that he could to make the *rapprochement*
possible. The French prisoners were treated with an almost elaborate
courtesy, given cigars and wine and food, and shown the sights of
Rome before being returned to their companions beyond the city
walls.* The French wounded were nursed with the same care as the
Republic's defenders and they, too, were returned to their regiments when they were well enough to leave the hospital. And, for
the same reason, no advantage was taken of the Republic's initial
repulse of the French army.

To Garibaldi this failure to follow up the victory of 30 April was
a disastrous mistake. And Mazzini's refusal to permit a pursuit, on
the grounds that 'the Republic was not at war with France, merely in
a state of defence',[36] became a 'burning question' between them, and
the cause of a new series of quarrels that forever embittered their
relationship.†[37]

Garibaldi never outgrew his disappointment at this first check
upon the designs prompted by his uncomplicated mind, nor ever

---

* 50,000 cigars, together with proclamations stigmatising the French Government as one '*de traîtes et de lâches renegats*' were sent to the French camp outside
the walls. Émile Bourgeois et E. Clermont, *Rome et Napoleon III, 1849–1870*
(Paris, 1907), 137.

† This relationship had already been embittered by Garibaldi's ready offer of
his services to Charles Albert on his return from South America. Mazzini's
letters of that time are full of his 'disappointment' and 'disillusionment' with
Garibaldi. 'I am very upset,' he told his mother, 'that Garibaldi allows himself to
be persuaded to come as a Colonel or even as a General into the regular army.
He will no longer be the Garibaldi that Italy used to love and admire.' – Giacomo
Emilio Curàtulo, *Il dissidio fra Garibaldi e Mazzini* (Milan, 1928), 66.

forgave Mazzini for what he took to be his military incapacity. Years later he was caustically to write, 'If Mazzini had been willing to understand that I might possibly know something about war as well as he . . . how differently would things have turned out. . . . If he had had as much practical capacity and fertility of imagination in planning movements and enterprises and if he had possessed – what he always claimed to have – a genius for directing warlike affairs if, moreover, he had been willing to listen to some of his friends, who, from their antecedents might be expected to know something, he would have made fewer mistakes.'[38] He had always had 'an urge to be a general, but he did not know the first thing about it'.[39]

Mazzini's belief that so long as there was still a strong and influential republican feeling in France he might yet succeed in a policy of conciliation, was based on two misconceptions: a misunderstanding of the political atmosphere in Paris, and a miscalculation of Louis Napoleon's likely reactions to Oudinot's repulse. In fact, as soon as he heard of it, the French President took the repulse as a defeat which could not be tolerated. 'Our military honour is in peril,' he told Oudinot. 'I will not allow it to be compromised. You can be certain of being reinforced.'[40]

Garibaldi reacted in a similar way. To him, Mazzini's failure to use his exhilarated forces either to drive its enemies back into the sea or to attack the Austrians, was a betrayal of all that the Republic stood for.* Garibaldi really believed that the Republic could survive if Mazzini acted decisively. And the day after the victory over the French, although he was in pain from a stomach wound which he had asked the surgeons to keep secret, he was urging the Triumvirs to grant him an independent and overriding command which would allow him to advance on the enemy north of the capital.[41]

He was refused permission to act in this way, but on 4 May he was allowed to leave Rome to meet a danger that threatened

---

* According to *The Times* correspondent who was with the French troops, Garibaldi would have stood little chance against them in the open field. They were not in the least disheartened by their setback on 30 April. They 'are in admirable order and in the highest spirits,' he wrote on 2 May. 'I never saw such smart active fellows. . . . I have seen many troops in motion, but I have never met any which equal those now before me in smartness and expedition.' *The Times*, 12 May 1849.

the Republic on the other side of the Tiber – a threat from the Neapolitan army of King Ferdinand of the Two Sicilies.

The troops which Garibaldi took with him were almost all volunteers, the same men who had driven the French out of the Pamphili gardens on 30 April, together with some troops of Angelo Masina's Bolognese cavalry and Manara's *bersaglieri*, about 2,300 men in all.[42] Luciano Manara, the young Milanese aristocrat who prided himself on his 'disciplined, proud, silent, gentlemanly regiment', placed his men under Garibaldi's command with reluctance. The flamboyant guerrilla leader was 'a devil, a panther', he thought, and his followers 'a troop of brigands'.[43]

One of Manara's officers described how wild the Garibaldini seemed to the *bersaglieri* when, on the day after their departure from Rome, they encamped with them in the grounds of Hadrian's villa near Tivoli.

'Garibaldi and his staff were dressed in scarlet blouses,' he wrote, 'with hats of every possible form, without distinctions of any kind, or any pretension to military ornament. They rode on American saddles and seemed to pride themselves on their contempt for all the observances more strictly enjoined on regular troops.'[44]

The immediate impression they gave was one of indefatigable movement. They galloped about amongst the ruins and the camp fires, followed by their South American orderlies, now forming in little groups, now dispersing, shouting to each other, swinging their lassos above their heads. Suddenly they would leap to the ground, pull the saddles from their horses' backs, unroll them and form them quickly into a kind of tent.

The officers all looked after their own horses, groomed them, and gave them their water. Indeed, the *bersaglieri* soon realised how little difference there was between officers and men, how a brave man might be suddenly commissioned in the field without regard to his age or length of service in the Legion, how an officer might as suddenly find himself reduced to the ranks and carrying a musket, yet how many more officers there were than amongst regular troops – even Garibaldi's cook was a lieutenant.

If they failed in procuring provisions from the neighbouring villages, three or four colonels and majors threw themselves on the bare backs of their horses, and, armed with long lassoos, set off at full speed through the *Campagna* in search of sheep or oxen. When they had collected a sufficient quantity they returned, driving their ill-gotten flocks before them; a certain portion was divided among each company, and then all indiscriminately, officers and men, fell to, killing, cutting up, and roasting at enormous fires, quarters of oxen, besides kids and young pigs, to say nothing of booty of a smaller sort, such as poultry, geese, etc.[45]

Rough, disorderly and consciously theatrical as they seemed, however, the Garibaldini soon earned the respect, at first grudging, but afterwards unreserved, of most of the *bersaglieri*. No one could deny their bravery in action, nor could it be said that despite the occasional lawlessness of their conduct they were a generally undisciplined force. Luigi Carlo Farini complained that they acted 'without discipline and without orders', that their only merits were 'boldness and good luck'.[46] He has, however, found few serious supporters. As Giuseppe Guerzoni said, 'some biassed historians may have alleged that the whole Legion was a gang of delinquents, and jail-birds and that their leader protected or tolerated them, but no honest writer will repeat this'.[47]

Garibaldi's rules were few but they were known and they were respected. Looting church property was, within limits, tolerated, but violence was not; and while a man might go into a convent and come out with a pocketful of candles, he could not go into a house and come out with a bottle of wine.

Within a few days, by the force of his personality, as well as by his commanding and dramatic appearance, Garibaldi had succeeded in imposing himself as unquestioned leader on all the heterogeneous units under his command. A few hours after leaving Rome some young men from the Students' Corps entered a house in search of drink. Garibaldi rode up to them on his white horse, his long fair hair falling to the white poncho on his back.

'What! You have only just left Rome, and already you must call for wine! I lived five years on flesh and water.'

The reprimand was met, not with silence and downcast looks but by immediate shouts of '*Evviva! Evviva!* Garibaldi!'

'Silence!' he commanded. 'This is no time for cheers. When we have defeated the enemy, then we will cheer.'[48]

He rode away and they watched him silently; and during the rest of that campaign he would often ride up to them to show that they were forgiven, to talk to them, to encourage them; not to laugh with them, for he rarely laughed, but sometimes to smile, a sad and gentle smile – and it seemed like a benediction. There was nothing of 'the devil, the panther' in him then; and Manara who had described him thus, became his chief of staff a month later and grew to love as well as to admire him.

It was his 'patriarchal simplicity', his calm presence of mind and courage in the heat of combat that appealed to men like Manara. They knew he was not a great general; they were soon, indeed, to learn that he was not yet even a good one when fighting a pitched battle; but as a guerrilla leader he was at once inspired and inspiring. And it was as a guerrilla that he was conducting this operation.

Conscious that he must at all events avoid a headlong clash between his small force and the far more numerous troops of the Neapolitan army stationed on the Alban Hills, he had made a night march towards Tivoli and then turned south to the little hill-town of Palestrina to harry the enemy's right flank.

From Palestrina detachments of his force made so many successful raids on the Neapolitan outposts that the Bourbon general, Ferdinando Lanza, received orders to march from Albano and deliver an attack on Palestrina with the intention of driving the guerrillas back into Rome.

At noon on 9 May while standing with his staff on the walls of the Castel San Pietro on the high ground to the north of Palestrina, Garibaldi watched Lanza's 5,000 troops approach from Valmontone in two long, straggling columns. He did not wait for them to attack, but sent his men hurtling down the slopes and through the cobbled streets of the town to throw the Neapolitans out of it. Within three hours the short but fierce engagement was over; and King Ferdinand's troops were in full retreat.

That night Palestrina was as gay as Rome had been on the night of 30 April. Every window was illuminated and from the deserted monastery crowds of *bersaglieri* could be seen

emerging from the different cells; one fellow wearing a large Dominican hat; another with a long white tunic over his uniform; while a third stalked along draped in a cope. All of them made their appearance at the calling of the roll with thick, lighted wax tapers in their hands; and the monastery that night, at least, was splendidly illuminated. Even the correspondence of the poor brothers was not respected and the soldiers brought out not a few letters and some diaries which would have brought many a blush to the cheeks of the monastery's chaste founders.[49]

The next night was spent less cheerfully. Mazzini, afraid now that Oudinot was about to return to the attack, ordered Garibaldi's immediate recall to Rome. And so in the early morning of 11 May, tired out and parched with thirst, the guerrillas filed back into the city.

Four days later, however, it seemed that their painful and exhausting march had been unnecessary. For Ferdinand de Lesseps arrived from Paris on a diplomatic mission which gave hope of a negotiated peace. De Lesseps, then an energetic consul-general whose imagination was already fired by the thought of one day building a canal across the isthmus of Suez, seems to have had no idea that he was being used by the French government merely to gain time. But this was the real purpose of his presence in Rome.

For Louis Napoleon and his ministers were determined to avenge their defeat before it became known in Paris that Oudinot's despatch describing the 'affair of 30 April' as 'one of the most brilliant in which French troops have taken part since our great wars' was, to say the least, misleading. The President's whole personal future, as well as the future of the Catholic party in France, had been endangered by this military setback. It was essential, then, to deceive both the French electorate and the Roman Triumvirate until reinforcements for the expeditionary force, together with France's greatest military engineer, General Vaillant, arrived in Italy, to turn the fortunes of an initially inglorious campaign.

After a fortnight's negotiation de Lesseps, whose emotional nature was deeply impressed by Mazzini and the spirit of his Republic, was able to come to an understanding with the Triumvirs whereby it was agreed that the French forces would remain outside the city walls and protect Rome from the Austrians who were now approaching from the north, and from the Neapolitans who still threatened the Republic in the south. Since the future of the Republic was not mentioned, nor yet the possibility of a papal restoration, and since the terms were entirely favourable to the Romans, de Lesseps thought it advisable to add a proviso to the effect that the treaty required ratification by the Paris Government who were, of course, in no way inclined to confirm it.

While these negotiations were continuing Garibaldi once more left Rome to attack the Neapolitans. This time, instead of the 2,300 men with whom he had left for Palestrina, he was accompanied by almost 11,000.[50] He himself, however, was not their leader as the Triumvirs had thought it as well to give the command to Colonel Pietro Roselli, a professional officer and a Roman, and to appoint Carlo Pisacane, a Neapolitan duke who had also received a formal military education, as Roselli's chief of staff.

Roselli was told that Garibaldi had been offered the command and had refused it; but with a liberal-conservative majority in the Assembly and an army composed mainly of regular troops or volunteers from the Papal States, the Triumvirate can scarcely have hoped that he would accept it. Roselli was, politically, a far wiser choice. He had been born in Rome, was a regular soldier of 'much knowledge and singular modesty',[51] and, while not an inspiring or energetic officer, was universally respected. He had no strong republican feelings – although his acceptance of the command and his promotion to general led men for the rest of his life to think that he had – but he did have a profound respect for Mazzini, 'a man of pure heart, courageous spirit, sound morals and incorruptible honesty, a man of his word – in fact, the best Italian of our time'.[52]

But although politically sound, Roselli's appointment was militarily dangerous. It is far more difficult for a good regular soldier, accustomed to disciplined obedience, to command volunteer and irregular troops than it is for a good guerrilla leader to command regulars. And the arrangement led to the army moving south with what Professor Trevelyan graphically described as the 'uncomfortable and jerky motion of a man with an excitable dog in leash; Garibaldi dashed about in front, locating and engaging the enemy, and then was forced to wait till Roselli came sulkily lumbering up with the bulk of the troops. On an expedition like this, such a general was about as fit to be put in command of Garibaldi as

Parker was to be put in command of Nelson; indeed, the case was much worse, for though himself a modest man, Roselli was surrounded by a staff of regular officers who urged him to assert himself, regarding the guerrilla with a professional jealousy which none of the captains of Copenhagen felt against the victor of the Nile'.[53] At Roselli's headquarters Garibaldi was dismissed as '*il corsaro*'.[54]

It was not only professional jealousy, however, for Roselli had drawn up a detailed plan of attack which Garibaldi's lively activities were rendering unworkable. Although nominally in command of the central division of the army, Garibaldi spent much of his time with the advance-guard. Always preferring to do his own reconnaissance he had, during the previous short campaign which had ended at Palestrina, often disguised himself as a peasant to get a close view of the enemy's position and 'passed whole hours, seated on some commanding elevation, examining the environs with the aid of a telescope'.[55] He continued to carry out his own reconnaissance now; and in the early morning of 19 May he was galloping along the Velletri road from Valmontone when he discovered that the Neapolitans, discouraged by the French from interfering in the campaign, were retreating from the Alban Hills, no longer, in any case, a tenable position since their flank and rear were threatened by a force larger than their own, a force which King Ferdinand believed, in fact, consisted of almost the entire strength of the Republican army.

Determined that they should not escape, Garibaldi, on his own responsibility, gave orders to the advance-guard to engage the enemy and at the same time sent back a message to Roselli asking him to hasten the arrival of his own central division. Having given these tactically correct but insubordinate instructions, Garibaldi watched Masina's Bolognese lancers charge headlong down the road and then come galloping back again, their course having been blocked by a much larger body of Neapolitan cavalry. Masina himself was not there that day and his men were retreating in disorder. Convinced that such demoralising behaviour could not be tolerated, Garibaldi, with Aguyar beside him, drew up his horse in the path of the retreating lancers. They came galloping back towards him. The banks on either side of the road were too steep for there to be any possibility of their avoiding him; but he did not move. He sat in his saddle, indignant and furious, looking down upon the retreating cavalry. They rode into him, unable to control their frightened horses, knocked him to the ground, trampled over him, and left him so bruised and entangled with his saddle and stirrups that he could not get to his feet.

The Neapolitan cavalry came charging towards him and, had not a group of boys from his Legion (some of whom were only fourteen) come dashing up to him to carry him to safety, he would certainly have been captured.

The Neapolitans' charge had taken them into the very centre of the advance-guard's position where they were caught as if in an ambush. Under fire from both flanks they had no alternative but to rein up and turn back, leaving thirty prisoners behind them.

By the time General Roselli and the main body of his army arrived, the advance-guard had resumed the offensive and were moving bravely down into Velletri, driving the increasingly alarmed Neapolitan troops before them. But the cautious commander-in-chief, concerned to find how deeply Garibaldi had committed him, refused to continue the attack and insisted that no further advance should be made into the Neapolitan position until their own positions had been consolidated. So that night the Republican's troops were halted at Velletri and Garibaldi went to sleep in a bed that had been occupied the night before by King Ferdinand himself. Having dropped his only shirt in the bath, he was wearing the habit of an Augustinian monk which the doctor who treated him for his bruises had found in a nearby monastery.[56]

Next morning Garibaldi continued to insist that the enemy were already demoralised and a full-scale attack would drive them in disorder across the Neapolitan frontier.*[57] But his advice was ignored. And now that the Austrians were advancing fast across the

---

* It may even have been true, for the sharp engagement at Velletri following his victory at Palestrina had undoubtedly unnerved the Bourbon troops. Niccola Nisco believed that had Garibaldi been supported by the whole Republican army he might well have succeeded, so demoralised had the Neapolitans become – *Storia del Reame di Napoli dal 1824 al 1860* (Naples, 1908), iii, 272. Certainly as Roselli's biographer, Professor Emilia Morelli has observed, they never forgot this day which led to Mazzini agreeing that Garibaldi was 'the terror of the Neapolitan soldiers. In 1860 that episode of eleven years before was not entirely forgotten.' – Emilia Morelli, *Tre profili (Quaderni del Risorgimento, ix)* (Edizioni dell'Ateneo, Rome, 1955), 118.

Romagna and the Marches towards Ancona (determined, in the words of their commander, Count Wimpffen, 'to restore the Papal government overthrown by a perverse faction'[58]) Mazzini felt compelled to recall the bulk of the army to Rome. Garibaldi was, however, allowed to take his Legion and the *bersaglieri* down towards the Neapolitan kingdom.

And as they advanced beside the waters of the Liris River, through Frosinone to the frontier that divided the Papal States from Naples, they were excitedly welcomed by the villagers on their route who greeted them as their liberators from the Neapolitan invaders.[59] When they approached the frontier town of Arce, however, the fear of the Garibaldians – 'ogres let loose by the devil to devour children and burn down houses' as King Ferdinand's propagandists had described them – led the inhabitants to desert the town and take refuge in the hills.

'We found the houses shut up and deserted, and not a human being in the whole place,' wrote Emilio Dandolo. But although the volunteers were 'indignant at this want of confidence', thanks to the influence of Garibaldi and Ugo Bassi, the fiery, eloquent and passionately dedicated Bolognese priest whom Mazzini had appointed chaplain to the Legion, 'no pillaging took place, and in that deserted village not a single door was forced. We sat down on the ground in the square; and, when the terrified inhabitants observed from the surrounding heights this admirable spirit of order and restraint they hurried down to welcome us, threw open their houses and shops, and in a few minutes the whole village had resumed its accustomed activity'.[60]

Garibaldi felt sure that this enthusiasm would be repeated all over the kingdom – that to attack the Neapolitan army would be to defeat it, and that to defeat it would be to bring about the realisation of his dreams.* 'A battle won under Capua will give Italy into our

---

* He had always advocated and continued to advocate taking the battle for Rome outside its walls, rather than enclosing it within them. He had an exaggerated view of the willingness of the people in the Papal States to rise and support him and, indeed, of the readiness of the Italy of 1849 for the sort of uprising that alone could make such action successful. From a military point of view his plan was more inspired than that of the High Command which was dictated by Mazzini's obsessional feeling for Rome itself, not only as the capital of the Republic but as the 'angel of the Italian nation'.

hands,' he told his officers in Arce's main piazza. 'Here the destinies of Italy can be decided.'[61]

His hopes of so sudden and dramatic an end to the struggle were soon to be dispelled, however. For at Arce Garibaldi received orders to return immediately to Rome where the threat from the Austrians in the north was growing ever more alarming.

He chose to return through the Abruzzi in the hope that he might encounter some Austrians on the way. And in that event, as he told Masina in a ferocious order, the Legionaries were to get it into their heads that the *tedeschi* were the most terrible of their enemies. 'Let them think of a charge with cold steel and of sticking a sharp bayonet into the flank of a cannibal. . . . Give an order of the day making the following prayer compulsory: "Oh God! Grant me the grace that I may put all the steel of my bayonet inside a *tedesco*, and not deign to pull the trigger but keep my shot to kill a second *tedesco* at not more than ten paces." '[62]

The Austrians he himself could never forgive for setting fire to whole villages in Lombardy. For this and other 'atrocious practices usual with them',[63] his men must never forgive them either.*

*   *   *

The real danger, as Garibaldi discovered, soon after his arrival back in Rome at the end of the month, was not, however, from the Austrians, but from the French. For Oudinot's reinforcements had arrived, and many more with additional guns and siege equipment were on the way. Replying to a letter from General Roselli which suggested that one day the armies of the French and Roman republics would be fighting side by side and went on to ask for an armistice *sine die* 'and a fortnight's notice of any intention to resume hostilities' so that the Romans could concentrate on the Austrians, Oudinot had written:

* Many of the *bersaglieri*, at least, found it difficult to do so; for the Austrians, according to one of their officers, had behaved in Milan with the 'most refined barbarity', mutilating their prisoners, burning them, and burying hostages alive in quicklime. Emilio Dandolo, who reported that a Croat soldier had walked through the streets with a baby impaled on his bayonet, was 'horror struck' by what he found in the Castello after the Austrian troops had evacuated the city – 'bodies disgustingly mutilated and a boy nailed to a doorway' – Emilio Dandolo, *op. cit.*, 36–37.

General – My Government's orders are positive; they require me to enter Rome as soon as possible. I have told the Roman authorities that I have abrogated the verbal armistice which, at the instance of M. de Lesseps, I agreed to grant for the time being. I have warned your outposts that either army has the right to reopen hostilities. Solely, to give time to any of our French residents to leave Rome . . . I am deferring the attack upon the place until Monday morning.[64]

When he saw this alarming and unexpected letter, Mazzini immediately wrote to Garibaldi for his advice. Garibaldi was in bed in his lodgings in Via delle Carozze near Piazza di Spagna, suffering from an attack of rheumatism aggravated by the rough treatment he had received from the horses' hooves at Velletri and by the still festering wound he had received in the Pamphili gardens the month before. Nevertheless he gave Mazzini a spirited, typical and highly ambitious reply:

Mazzini – You ask me to choose what I want. I tell you that I can exist for the good of the Republic only in one of two ways – a dictator with unlimited powers or a simple soldier. Choose! Always yours, Garibaldi.[65]

So simple a solution to the problem, while it might have military advantages, did not of course recommend itself to Mazzini and the other Triumvirs who saw in it far more widespread political repercussions than Garibaldi himself could envisage. They wrote to him again, not mentioning the proposed dictatorship, and repeated their request for his military opinion. He told them simply that General Avezzana should replace Roselli as commander-in-chief; and that was as much as they could get out of him. They decided to ask him to return to the command of the most vulnerable sector of the defences where his men had so distinguished themselves on 30 April. But he replied that he could not do so, giving his reasons in a series of notes all dated 2 June:

I regret to inform you that I am unable to accept the honourable appointment conferred upon me, as I am at present ill. I submit my resignation from the command of the 1st Division and would be pleased if you would give orders directly to it.

I reiterate my resignation from the position to which I have been appointed, and I am an ordinary soldier of the Italian Legion. Give my orders direct to the corps which formerly obeyed me.

I am truly indisposed. However, if necessary, I shall be at the walls of Rome as a soldier of the Italian Legion, if they want me.[66]

And so he remained in bed in the Via delle Carozze, intending to stay there until the time of Oudinot's truce had expired.

Oudinot had promised in his letter to defer his attack 'upon the place' until Monday morning, 4 June. Although it was afterwards realised how ambiguous this description was, it was accepted in Rome at the time that 'the place' meant not only the city itself but all its outposts, including the Corsini and Pamphili villas which were essential to its defence. But Oudinot intended – or could at least later claim that he intended – to refer only to the city, and his promise not to attack 'the place' before Monday did not preclude his attacking its outposts on Sunday.

This was, in fact, precisely what he and General Vaillant were preparing to do. They had rejected the idea of breaching the walls on the other side of Rome, for although the fortifications were far weaker there, to enter the city on that side would surely have the effect of driving the defenders to the barricades they had prepared, and then days of street fighting, in which the treasures of Rome would be in danger, would no doubt ensue. To enter Rome from the west, however, would give the French immediate possession of the ground that dominated the city.

But before regular siege could be laid to Rome by the usual methods of digging parallels and advancing batteries in the style perfected by Vaillant's military engineers, the villas that would dominate these works must be captured. And in the early hours of Sunday morning they were. The 400 volunteers in the gardens (assured by Roselli the previous day that no attack need be expected until Monday)[67] were fast asleep in their bivouacs when the French poured up the slopes, drove in the isolated pickets, swept across the Pamphili gardens and, having brought up artillery to soften the growing resistance in the Corsini gardens, stormed their way not only into the house that Garibaldi had chosen as his headquarters five weeks before, but entered also the Vascello Villa at the foot of the slope.

5

THE FRENCH ATTACK

At three o'clock in the morning of 3 June, Garibaldi's chief of staff, Francesco Daverio, burst into the General's room in Via delle Carozze. Garibaldi dressed and buckled on his sword-belt to the sound of cannon 'thundering the alarm' from beyond the Janiculum. Then, accompanied by Daverio and Masina, he rode out across the Tiber. All over the city now the bells were ringing in the campanili, people cheering in the piazzas, drums beating, officers and orderlies galloping and running up and down the streets as the Garibaldini rushed out of their quarters in San Silvestro and their officers out of the villas where they had been comfortably billeted.

Pushing his way through the noisy confusion of shouting soldiers and excited cab-drivers offering their help with the transport of the wounded, Garibaldi arrived at Porta Cavalleggeri only to discover that any troops who took part in a sortie from that gate would surely be wiped out by the French now firmly entrenched in the villas to the north. He decided immediately that those villas must be retaken at all costs, and he rode down to Porta San Pancrazio to direct his counter-attack from there.

Porta San Pancrazio was at that time approached from the low-lying Trastevere quarter of Rome by means of a steep lane shaded by trees and the crumbling walls of palace gardens; and it was up this lane, already crowded with wounded men stumbling back or being pushed in wheelbarrows from the villas on the heights outside the gate, that Garibaldi rode to study the ground over which he was now to fight. He rode through the gateway at about half past five in the morning.

Rather more than a quarter of a mile in front of him was the Villa Corsini, tall, ornate and isolated on the crest of its hill, the two lower of its four storeys hidden by a stone wall and an outside double staircase that led up to a balcony beneath its second-floor windows. On either side of the villa, in line with its front, ran a low wall, on the top of which was a line of big pots each containing an orange tree, and behind this wall French sharpshooters crouched, covering with their fire the whole of the slope between the villa and the Porta San Pancrazio.

In front of the villa was another wall which ran along the garden boundaries on each side of the entrance gates and then met the wall of the Pamphili gardens at the back. To take the Villa Corsini by means of a frontal attack, then, the assaulting troops would have to pour out of the narrow Porta San Pancrazio in the papal walls, run across the open ground towards the boundary walls of the villa, close up again to pass through the garden gateway, run up the drive between the high box hedges that flanked it, and then up the narrow steps of the villa itself. And all the way they would be under heavy fire from the well-protected French. Even if they succeeded in breaking through the bottleneck at the villa gate in sufficient numbers to capture the house, the French could re-form in the grounds of the Villa Pamphili and then move in to the counter-attack on a wide front supported by artillery.

Since the frontal attack was an almost suicidal venture, an out-flanking movement seemed an obvious alternative. But on the one side the villa was protected not only by its high boundary wall but by the deep lane where Garibaldi's volunteers had stumbled into the French infantry on 30 April, and on the other side by the continua-tion of this same wall and by the trees that lined the Vicolo della Nocetta. Garibaldi determined, therefore, that his men must attempt to storm the Villa Corsini from the front. Covering fire would be given by the battery on the papal walls at Casa Merluzzo, to the left of the Porta San Pancrazio, and by small-arms fire from the Vascello Villa at the foot of the Corsini hill, which Colonel Galletti had managed to recapture before the arrival of the Garibaldini.

For the whole of that morning frontal assaults were launched, repulsed and repeated. The villa had been taken: it must be retaken. Garibaldi's objective was as single-minded as his method of achieving it. Time after time, with a wild and pathetic bravery, the young volunteers responded to Garibaldi's shouts of 'Courage! Courage, my boys!' with cries of 'Long live the Roman Republic! Long live Garibaldi!' and then rushed up that exposed slope, between the vineyards and fields on the left and the Vascello Villa on the right, to die beneath the sweltering sun. Inside the San Pancrazio gateway behind the city walls, crowds cheered them as they went out and received the few wounded that managed to crawl back; while a band, endlessly and at full blast, played the *Marseillaise*, hoping that its stirring notes would fill the French republican army with shame.

Sitting on his white horse outside the gateway, Garibaldi directed the desperate attacks, throwing one assault party after another across the open ground and through the narrow entrance of the villa gate beyond it. More often than not, the gate was never reached, and the volunteers, too few and too haphazardly supported, were broken up by the French troops firing at them from behind the cover of the stone walls and the orange trees. Sometimes, though, a party of Italians would survive the dangers of the approach to the gate, pass through it and rush up the drive between the box hedges towards the villa steps. And once or twice they reached the steps and, dashing up on to the balcony, bayonet in hand, ran into the entrance hall and toppled the defenders out of the windows, using the corpses of the dead as cover for firing at the supporting French troops in the Pamphili gardens farther back. But the heroism was always in vain. Never was a temporary success supported in time to prevent the surviving volunteers being driven out of the villa by a French counter-attack.

Hundreds of men died in these repeated attempts to take and keep the villa. Garibaldi later admitted that he had never seen anything in his life to equal the butchery of that day. Francesco Daverio, his chief of staff, was killed during the morning, and Angelo Masina and Nino Bixio, two others of his most trusted officers, were both wounded. He himself escaped death only by what his followers took to be a miracle, for his poncho and the huge hat he was wearing were torn in many places by musket balls and scraps of flying metal.

By the time the *bersaglieri* arrived at about eight o'clock the situation seemed catastrophic. Medici was still holding out in the Vascello Villa which he had taken over from Colonel Galletti; but his men, under constant fire from the upper windows of the Villa Valentini behind them, as well as from the Villa Corsini, were now threatened by a large force of French troops which had advanced towards them under cover of the garden wall. While farther south, groups of tirailleurs had pushed forward in the cornfields to open fire at close range on the Casa Merluzzo battery which covered the approaches to the San Pancrazio gate.

As soon as the *bersaglieri* came up, Garibaldi sent one company to occupy the Casa Giacometti opposite the Vascello Villa on the other side of the Corsini garden, and two other companies forward into yet another frontal assault at the tall, forbidding villa. Unsupported by any previous bombardment or prolonged musket fire, Manara led his men into the attack.

It was a horrifying sight. About 400 men took part in the assault, poured through the bottleneck of the Corsini garden gate, and ran up the hill towards the villa steps in the ever burning sun. But the concentrated fire that met them was too much: men fell to the ground on every side, and before the steps were reached the *bersaglieri* were forced to halt. But they did not turn back. As if they had come to a wall behind which they could now rest and re-form, they knelt down to open fire at the villa windows and at the heads behind the walls. For a few moments Manara stood behind his kneeling men, watching them fire and watching them die; and then accepting at last the impossibility of success he gave orders for the bugler to sound the retreat.

As they ran back towards the walls of Rome, one of their officers, the Swiss Gustav von Hoffstetter, saw so many of them fall to the ground that he imagined at first that they had 'stumbled in their haste over the roots of the vines. But their motionless bodies soon showed [him] the truth. Those hurrying past would try to drag away fallen comrades; but the man who stretched out his hand to help would bring it suddenly back to clutch at his own death-wound. Others, who had already reached the shelter of the house or the garden gate, would dash to help some comrade who was still alive; but then, a shudder, a spasmodic movement of the limbs— and they lie beside their friend.'[1]

Emilio Dandolo, who had been left with his men as a reserve inside the San Pancrazio gate, watched his fellow *bersaglieri*, most of them wounded, limp back past him. He was told that his brother was believed to be very seriously wounded, and he paced up and down 'compulsively gnawing the barrel of a pistol' in his struggle to keep back his tears.

At this moment of unspeakable suffering [he wrote later], Garibaldi came in our direction, and I heard him say. 'I shall require twenty resolute men and an officer for a difficult undertaking.' I rushed forward desirous at least to liberate myself from a state of inaction, and to suffocate in the excitement of danger the anguish which threatened to turn my brain. 'Go,' said Garibaldi to me, 'with twenty of your bravest men, and take Villa Corsini at the point of the bayonet.'

Involuntarily I remained transfixed with astonishment – with twenty men to hurry forward to attack a position which two of our companies and the whole of Garibaldi's Legion, after unheard of exertions, had failed in carrying! I thought that perhaps he gave me these orders because, as there had been a few minutes' pause in the report of the enemy's musketry, he wanted to discover if anything fresh had occurred. The idea glanced through my mind afterwards, but at the time I did not answer a word, merely pointing to those who were to accompany me. 'Spare your ammunition. To the bayonet at once,' said Garibaldi.

'Do not fear General,' I replied. 'They have perhaps killed my brother and I shall do my best.'

Seeing Dandolo in such an agitated state, a friend of his joined him and said that he would go into the attack with him. They ran away together to the Vascello Villa to which their Colonel, Manara, had retreated with the remnants of the regiment that were still fit to fight, since they 'did not know what on earth was to be done with only twenty men'. But they could not find the Colonel who had crossed over to the Casa Giacometti, and they felt obliged to go on without support. They dashed through the garden gate 'and up the long deserted avenue which led straight up to the villa'. Several of their small force were shot before they had covered the length of the drive and by the time they reached the villa steps, only twelve men were left. 'I looked round me,' Dandolo said. 'We were there alone. A shower of bullets fell fearfully round us from the half-closed windows. What could twelve men do against a place occupied by several hundreds of the enemy?' They stood 'intrepid, silent, ready for any effort'. But how could he ask them to die when success was impossible?

He gave the order to retreat, and as he ran back across the villa grounds six more of them were shot, and both he and his friend were wounded in the thigh.

His severe wound, however, did not stop him spending the rest of the afternoon looking for his brother. He asked several men in his regiment if they knew what had become of him; but they dared not tell him, for they knew that he was dead. At length he found his way to the Casa Giacometti.

'Do not look for your brother any more,' Colonel Manara said to him. 'It's too late now. I will be a brother to you.' Already exhausted by loss of blood, Dandolo fell fainting into his Colonel's arms. Manara picked him up and carried him away.[2]

By now the firing had died down and the smoke and dust began to drift away under the blue and cloudless sky. After hours of bombardment from the battery at Casa Merluzzo, the Villa Corsini, occasionally bursting into flames, had begun to collapse into ruins, and from the walls of Rome men could see the floors give way and the French defenders clinging on to the ends of the shattered beams.

Garibaldi determined to make yet another assault. Sending forward the wounded Angelo Masina with his Bolognese lancers to lead the attack, he followed it up himself with the remnants of infantry that remained to him.

Now it seemed that the Italians would succeed at last. Masina and Colonel Galletti, who had bravely decided to accompany him, managed to gallop through the garden gate, and to lead the lancers across the villa grounds and up the steps; while the infantry, following closely after them, helped to push the French out of the ruined villa and off the hill on which it stood. Watching this success from the walls of Rome, the rest of Garibaldi's force, together with many civilian spectators, were overcome with excitement; and, rushing out of the San Pancrazio gate, they poured up the slope of the hill.

Garibaldi and his officers managed to arrange the excited and disorderly volunteers in some sort of defensive position in the Corsini gardens before the French counter-attack was mounted. When the attack came, however, the force of professional and well-directed troops was irresistible. The Italians were once more thrown out of the grounds of the villa, already littered with their dead. Garibaldi,

Galletti and Manara survived; but Masina did not return and for the rest of the month his body lay on the slopes beneath the villa steps, putrefying in the heat.[3]

* * *

Unknown numbers of dead lay around Masina's body; and it was supposed by many of his officers that Garibaldi was largely to blame for their sacrifice. He 'had shown himself', Dandolo wrote after the bitterness caused by his brother's death had somewhat faded in his mind, 'to be as incapable of being a general of a division as he proved himself to be an able and efficient leader in the skirmishes and marches against the Neapolitans. Without any well-considered and matured plans he sent first one company and then another against the enemy as was suggested to him by the danger of the moment, without either measuring the forces, or calculating the resistance we were to meet with; in short he was utterly incapable of directing the manœuvres of masses of men.'[4] Carlo Pisacane agreed with him. 'Garibaldi did not know how to reply to the operations of the enemy or how to direct his attack,' he wrote. 'His men were sent up in small, confused parties, ten or twenty at a time, merely to charge with the bayonet.'[5] And the bayonet charge, though effective enough against the Neapolitans, was not a method of attack likely to be effective against the more stable French – particularly when unsupported by artillery fire which Garibaldi had had little experience in directing.

There is much that can be said in his defence: the force under his command – less than half as numerous as the French opposed to him – were never within his control all at the same time, for the *bersaglieri* arrived only when the Garibaldini were almost exhausted, and the papal troops, which he threw into the attack as a last desperate gamble when the assault led by Masina's lancers had failed, arrived after the *bersaglieri* had been defeated. Also, it must be admitted that a flank attack (which the circumstances seem theoretically to have demanded), would, perhaps, have failed owing to the strength of the Pamphili position and its numerous defenders; and that Roselli's failure (during Garibaldi's illness after his return from Velletri) to entrench the Corsini position made it all the more difficult for the Italians to hold the villa once they had taken it. But the conclusion is nevertheless inevitable – that Garibaldi fought this critical battle without any of the skill with which he had previously been credited.

It says much, though, for the power of his remarkable personality that in Rome when the sun had set that night few voices were raised against him. The counter-attacks had failed, but without him they would not even have been made; and now, while his officers lay down exhausted or sat drinking in the Caffè Babuino, 'Garibaldi's white cloak could still be seen in the darkness as he rode round the field giving orders to drive back any new French attack that might be launched.'⁶ All, or nearly all, of the responsibility for the terrible slaughter of the day was laid at the door of Roselli who had declined to weaken his defences elsewhere by sending men to Garibaldi's support and, less controversially, at the door of the Republic's enemies – 'Cardinal Oudinot and his master, the Pope'.

'These blackguard French are attacking us again,' Arthur Hugh Clough had written in a letter to Thomas Arnold at ten o'clock that morning. 'May the Lord scatter and confound them. For a fortnight or more they have been negotiating and talking, and inducing the government to send off men against the Austrians at Ancona, and now here they are with their cannon.'⁷

It was a universal complaint. Several French prisoners were killed as soon as they surrendered, and many more were hissed and threatened on their way into the city. The Marchioness Ossoli found that the Italian wounded in the hospitals were 'in a transport of indignation'. 'You will have heard how all went,' she wrote home, 'how Lesseps, after appearing here fifteen days as plenipotentiary, signed a treaty not dishonourable to Rome; then Oudinot refused to ratify it, saying *"the plenipotentiary had surpassed his powers"*. Lesseps runs back to Paris and Oudinot attacks – an affair alike infamous for the French from the beginning to end.'⁸

And William Story, who a few days before had left Rome for Florence, which he found 'full of Austrians . . . jingling through the streets', heard the 'melancholy news of the battle' and was dismayed. 'What will be the end?' he wrote in his diary. 'Fatal, I fear, for Rome. Yet how bravely and resolutely she has acted; how glorious her position compared with that of the French!'⁹

But it was not only anger with the French that took men's minds from disappointment at Garibaldi's failure. For what Italians craved for in that summer of 1849 was, as Professor Trevelyan rightly said, 'not tactics but heroism'. And the heroism which Garibaldi had inspired in the defenders of the Republic, 'culminating on this day of sacrifice, made Rome splendid as the capital of the Italy to be. . . . So the sacrifice made on the third of June, and in the month that followed, of so many of the best lives that Italy could give, had great political, because it had great spiritual significance. . . . Because men remembered and told with pride and anguish the story of the uncalculating devotion of those young lives in this hopeless struggle, there grew up as the years went by, an unconquerable purpose in the whole nation to have their capital; there rose that cry of the heart – *Roma o Morte!* – so magical even in years of discord and derision, that soon or late the Catholic world was bound to yield to it, as to a will stronger and more lasting even than its own'.*[10]

Mazzini, of course, was already aware of this truth. That morning his proclamation to the Republic had been full of bitterness:

> Romans – To the crime of assailing a friendly Republic with Republican troops, General Oudinot has added the infamy of treachery. He has violated his written promise, now in our hands, that he would not begin the attack before Monday. Romans, arise! To the walls, to the gates, to the barricades! Let us show that not even treachery can vanquish Rome. . . . Let right triumph and eternal infamy weigh upon the ally of Austria.

In the evening, however, his message to the people of Rome had a different and prophetic note:

> Romans – You have sustained the honour of Rome, the honour of

---

* It is a view which has since been endorsed by most historians of the Risorgimento, both Italian and foreign. Garibaldi's defence of Rome was 'a glorious legend which would go further towards the creation of the new nationality than any other influence during the Risorgimento. It proved that there were thousands of Italians who felt it better to throw their lives to the winds than to see their cause fail without honour. And such an example went straight to the heart of the people. More than any other episode in the story it inspired the romantic tradition which has been the strength and the making of modern Italy' – G. F-H. and J. Berkeley, *Italy in the Making. January 1848 to November 1848* (Cambridge University Press, 1940), 398.

Italy. . . . May God bless you, guardians of the honour of your fore-
fathers, as we, proud of having rightly judged the elements of greatness
within you, bless you in the name of Italy.

Romans! This day is a day of heroes, a page of history. Yesterday we
said to you, be great; today we say to you, you are great. Continue so.
Be constant.

Of the Roman people one may ask miracles. And we say with perfect
trust in the people, in the National Guard, and in the youth of every
class, that Rome is inviolable. Watch over her walls this night;
within those walls is the future of the nation. . . . The angel of your land
is the angel of the Italian nation. Long live the Republic![11]

6

THE FALL OF ROME

Although the outcome of the siege was decided by nightfall on 3 June, the Romans held out until the end of the month. Throughout these weeks the volunteers and papal troops on the Janiculum and in their outposts in the Vascello Villa and Casa Giacometti replied as best they could to the French batteries now established on the commanding heights of the Corsini hill. General Vaillant conducted his siege operations with skill and deliberation, pushing his trenches nearer and nearer to the city and to the two crumbling but still bravely defended villas on either side of the entrance to the Villa Corsini.

Inspired by their leaders the Italian defenders continued to resist the advance with what appeared to the French to be tireless energy. Loading, firing, sponging down and reloading the guns in the batteries, rushing out with the bayonet to repel the enemy's attacks on exposed parts of their line, working under fire with pick and spade to repair emplacements and dig new defences, they seemed to be wholly unaware of the inevitability of their ultimate defeat. To some observers inside Rome, however, the energy was more intermittent and less conspicuous now. Many of the defenders seemed to have grown tired of their apparently unprofitable resistance. The guards on the walls were with difficulty persuaded to go on improving the fortifications as well as to keep watch; while so few civilians volunteered to help with their digging that on at least one occasion they had to be driven up by the bayonet; and the gunners instead of concentrating on the demolition of chosen targets fired their shots haphazardly at random.

Garibaldi and his staff now occupied the Villa Savorelli, a tall and once beautiful house standing high above Via di Porta San Pancrazio just inside the gate. And the General himself, calm and dignified as always under fire, directed the defensive operations on this part of the front as though the possibility of defeat had never occurred to him. Every day he would ride about along the line of walls, his long hair shining in the sun, his white poncho thrown back to reveal the red of his shirt, the Negro Aguyar trotting faithfully after him.

The red shirt was now no longer the uniform only of his staff, for after his return from Palestrina he had given orders for several hundreds to be made so that all the Garibaldini could wear this unmistakable and flamboyant emblem of the Italian Legion. The shirts – they were really more like smocks or full-sleeved surplices, for they had long skirts that came down half-way to the knee – were not yet ready, but many men had been able to get hold of one and they were worn with a pride that was often taken for bluster.

Garibaldi's vanity was of a different sort. He saw, of course, in the extravagant uniform in which he clothed his men, a striking symbol of their shared dedication as well as a means of flattering the suscep-tibilities and gratifying the needs of youth. And he himself wore his eccentric clothing – his 'fancy dress' as an Englishman was later to call it – and let his well-washed hair grow so long on his shoulders, and dressed up his huge Negro attendant in colours so vividly contrasting with his own, not only because he liked to indulge a taste for theatrical gestures but also because these kinds of gesture served a practical purpose.

No one could fail to recognise him; no one could overlook him; no one was likely to forget him. His panache was the beginning of his influence.*

There was no mistaking, of course, the pleasure he took in his dramatic appearance and in the fascination and excitement it evoked, just as there was no mistaking the pleasure he took in drawing attention to the well-known simplicity of his life. The night after the engagement with the Neapolitan rearguard at Velletri, the night his

---

* One of the most admired and influential of the South American warrior-presidents for whom Garibaldi had fought was Benito Gonçalves, a romantic leader of humble origins and gracious manners. Gonçalves was a fine horseman who wore strikingly picturesque clothes and was enthusiastically followed by his men. The resemblance between him and the Garibaldi of later years, as Denis Mack Smith has observed, was 'probably not altogether accidental'. Garibaldi himself described Gonçalves as 'an extraordinary man on whom nature had bestowed her most precious gifts'. The bravest, most generous and honest of leaders, he was *'il tipo guerriero brillante e magnanimo'* – *Le Memorie di Garibaldi nella redazione definitiva* (Bologna, Cappelli, 1932), 54.

shirt fell into his bath, he had laughed so loudly that his servant in the next room called out: 'What is it, General?'

'My shirt's dropped in the bath,' he replied cheerfully, 'and it's the only daughter of a widowed mother.'[1]

Nor was there any mistaking the pleasure he took in inspiring men, and especially young men and boys, to follow him, and to die, if necessary, for Italy's sake. The pleasure, indeed, was part of the inspiration – a sort of reactive enthusiasm. One of these young men, enraptured by his glance, remembered for the rest of his life the day at dawn, when sleeping on the ramparts, he had 'opened his eyes, dreamily half aware that a horse was stepping tenderly across his body. . . . He had a vision of the rider's face looking down at him out of masses of curling golden hair. It was imprinted on his brain as one of the noblest things in art or nature which he had ever seen'.[2]

Those who saw Garibaldi at his headquarters in the Villa Savorelli, or when he went on his rounds to encourage the defenders, were affected in the same way. His benign and reassuring calm, the adoration of his loyal staff (led now, since Daverio's death, by Manara, who was so obviously devoted to the man he had recently dismissed as 'a devil, a panther'), his complete disregard of danger (which was not the bravado of a man who demands admiration as he challenges death, but the consistent courage of a man who is afraid of neither life nor death) – all these grounds for the belief that the nobility of his features was matched by the nobility of his character were unforgettably impressive.

Every morning at dawn he would go up to the watch-tower on the roof of the villa where he 'was immediately greeted by the French sharpshooters who gave him their particular attention all day long', one of his staff recorded. 'But Garibaldi, after throwing a glance at the enemy used to light his cigar, which was never extinguished till evening.'[3]

He seemed, in fact, almost to enjoy being under fire, even to be amused by his extraordinary escape from serious injury. 'The mania on the part of the French for riddling my poor headquarters with bullets, shells and cannon balls sometimes led to amusing scenes,' he wrote in the *Mémoirs* which Alexandre Dumas so jauntily edited from his manuscripts.

'On 6th or 7th June, Vecchi [a rich lawyer who had left his villa near Genoa to join the Legion] came to see us at dinner-time,' he remembered, and was asked to stay for a meal. Vecchi gladly accepted: a hot dinner was a rare treat, for only occasionally did the tin boxes from a restaurant on the other side of the Tiber arrive at the Villa Savorelli, since as often as not the kitchen workers who were sent with them turned back when they arrived at Via di Porta San Pancrazio and heard the mortar bombs exploding and saw the wounded bodies in the streets. Once, indeed, Garibaldi had nothing at all for forty-eight hours except a cup of coffee and two or three glasses of beer. But on this occasion there was more than enough for Garibaldi and his guests, and they went out to eat in the garden. Shells and shot were pounding the walls of the villa and the earth shook beneath them; and at one point during the meal a shell screamed towards them and the dinner party flew away to safety in all directions. Vecchi himself jumped up and was about to leap away, too, when he felt Garibaldi's strong hand grip him by the wrist. He sat down again. The shell burst on the other side of the villa.

A few days later, Vecchi was at the villa again and was obviously tempted by the risotto on Garibaldi's table. The General asked him to sit down and join him; but Manara said earnestly, 'don't do anything of the sort, Vecchi. For three consecutive days officers who have accepted the General's invitations to dinner have been killed before they have had time to digest it.'

It was quite true, but Vecchi who told them that as a boy he had been warned by a gypsy that he would die in Rome, thought that now was probably as good a time as any and merely added, 'Help me to some of that risotto, General!'

'For God's sake, General,' protested Manara with the utmost seriousness, 'for God's sake, don't send Vecchi anywhere today.'

After the meal Vecchi, who had been on duty for two nights running, asked if he could lie down for a time. While he was asleep Garibaldi went up to the watch tower and saw the French placing gabions in the trench which they had opened up opposite one of the bastions. Wanting someone to take a party of snipers to pick them off, he felt reluctant to disturb Vecchi, but there was no one else to be found so he pulled at his legs and woke him.

Sometime later Garibaldi was appalled by the news that Vecchi was missing. Within an hour, however, he caught sight of him. The young lawyer had been taking cover behind a sandbag which had been ripped open by a musket ball; sand had poured out over him, and the collapse of the bag had resulted in ten or twelve other bags toppling over on to Vecchi's head and temporarily burying him. The ball that had caused the 'amusing' incident ricocheted off a stone and flew into the back of a young soldier who soon afterwards died on a stretcher on the way to hospital. An officer who had been accompanying the stretcher burst into tears and threw himself on the dead body and covered it with kisses. The officer's name was Ponzio, the young soldier was Colomba, his wife.

'It reminded me of Anita who was also so calm under fire', commented Garibaldi. 'I had left her at Rieti, without regard to her own desires in the matter. She was pregnant and for the sake of the child to which she would give birth, I persuaded her to separate from me.'[4]

In fact, Anita had decided to disobey her husband and come to Rome. She had left Rieti and gone back to her mother-in-law and children in Nice; but when the news of Oudinot's attack on 3 June reached her she felt that, although she was ill as well as pregnant, she must leave her children with their grandmother and return to her husband. Not knowing of her decision Garibaldi wrote to her on 21 June:

> My dear Anita – I know you have been ill, and perhaps still are; but I wish I could see your handwriting and my mother's, and then I should not feel so uneasy.
>
> Cardinal Oudinot's Gallic-friars content themselves with cannonading us, and we are too much accustomed to it to care. Here the women and children run after the balls and shells and struggle for their possession.
>
> We are fighting on the Janiculum and these people are worthy of their past greatness. Here they live, die and suffer amputation, all to the cry of '*Viva la Repubblica!*' One hour of our life in Rome is worth a century of ordinary existence.
>
> Last night, thirty of our men, surprised in a house outside the wall by 150 of the Gallic-friars, used the bayonet, killed a captain and three soldiers, made four prisoners and wounded several others. . . . We had one sergeant killed and a soldier wounded. . . .

Get well. Kiss Mamma and the babies for me. Menotti has sent me a letter for which I am grateful. Love me much. Your Garibaldi.[5]

The news of the incident which Garibaldi mentioned in his letter – the decisive repulse of a large French raiding party from the Casa Giacometti by thirty-five papal troops of the Unione Regiment – had come to him as a welcome relief after several days of disappointment. For the tiring, nerve-wracking work upon which his volunteers were now engaged was not the sort of fighting in which ill-trained and inexperienced troops can ever hope to excel. And there was no doubt that the French, laboriously plodding as they sometimes appeared in their slowly approaching siege-works, were gradually proving themselves superior as soldiers, particularly in night-fighting, to the tired defenders whose nerves often seemed on the point of breaking. Indeed, on one occasion at least, Garibaldi felt constrained to tell his own Legion that they were unworthy of their name. The gunners in the bastions, prevented at last by Hoffstetter from sending over a few scattering shots in the hope of hitting something rather than concentrating on a single target, now replied to the French fire with impressive accuracy; the tough and wily Medici with his gallant force still held out amidst the tumbled ruins of the Vascello Villa; the Unione Regiment could not yet be forced out of the stone rubble that had once been Casa Giacometti. But too many good officers and men had now been killed and wounded; the spirit was being drained by exhaustion out of many of those who remained; and, in any case, the Vascello and Giacometti outposts became of less and less importance as the French, supported by fire from their batteries on Monte Verde as well as on the Corsini hill, were concentrating now not on Porta San Pancrazio but on the central bastion and Casa Barberini farther north.

It was Garibaldi's persistent complaint that the Roman military command, directed by Roselli and supported by Mazzini, were withholding from him troops which should have been available for the defence of the constantly bombarded and repeatedly attacked lines on the Janiculum. The complaint was understandable, of course, but Roselli insisted that although the main threat to Rome seemed, indeed, to be from the west, Garibaldi must remember that there were large numbers of French troops both in the south around

St. Paul's Without-the-Walls and in the north by Ponte Molle, which they had captured on 3 June; while to the east squadrons of light cavalry roamed through the Campagna cutting communications with the rest of the Republic and intercepting food convoys. So long as other parts of the Roman defences were thus threatened, and occasionally bombarded, Roselli did not feel that Garibaldi could be reinforced. He already had some of the best troops at his disposal, and he did not hesitate to take others away from the duties they were performing under the orders of the man Roselli had appointed as engineer-in-chief, an insubordinate action which, constantly repeated, led to persistent disagreement with the Roman Command.

This disagreement between Garibaldi and the Command broke out into an open quarrel on the night of 21 June when, after a ferocious bombardment which had only stopped at dusk, French assault parties stormed through the breaches opened up in the Janiculum defences and captured the Central and Casa Barberini bastions. It all happened so quickly and the Italian defenders were so surprised and confused that it was feared the French would push on from the captured bastions to take the Villa Savorelli and San Pietro in Montorio from which they could have dominated the city. Garibaldi was ordered, therefore, to counter-attack immediately and throw the besiegers off the walls. Prompted by Manara and other officers, he refused. He was persuaded – and he was probably right to be persuaded – that his alarmed and discouraged men were in no condition to make a successful counter-attack; much better, his staff decided, that they should concentrate on establishing an inner line of defence along the walls built by the Emperor Aurelian as a protection against the barbarians from the north. It meant nothing to Garibaldi that the order to counter-attack came from his commander-in-chief. He believed it to be wrong. He ignored it.

The following morning Roselli arrived to repeat his order, accompanied by Avezzana, the Minister of War, a man whom Garibaldi respected. But neither Avezzana nor Roselli could induce Garibaldi to change his mind. He would not obey the order. And Avezzana, after making a personal reconnaissance, decided that it was now, in any case, probably too late to make the attack he had ordered the night before.[6]

Whether or not Garibaldi had been right from a military point of view, his failure to obey the Government's orders marked a new and critical stage in the antipathetic relationship between himself and Mazzini. The chances of a happy co-operation had never been hopeful. Both Mazzini and Garibaldi were stubborn men, unwilling to accept criticism, distrustful of guidance. They were, it was often suggested, jealous of each other: Mazzini of Garibaldi's influence and following, Garibaldi of Mazzini's acknowledged intellect. To the General the philosopher was 'a doctrinaire',[7] his followers 'learned academics accustomed to legislate for the world from their studies',[8] men who proclaimed 'themselves without a shadow of a reason, the party of action, and would allow no one else to take the initiative if they could help it'.[9] To the philosopher, the General was 'the most easily led of men', 'weak beyond expression', a man who hated it to be thought that he was under anybody's influence. If 'Garibaldi has to choose between two proposals,' Mazzini complained, 'he is sure to choose the one that isn't mine.'[10] 'You know the face of a lion?' Mazzini asked John Morley some years later. 'Is it not a foolish face? Is it not the face of Garibaldi?'[11]

It was certainly true that Garibaldi's character was the sort round which mischief-makers tend to cluster; and on this critical day in the history of the Roman Republic, Sterbini, the extreme radical who had played a leading part in the overthrow of the papal government, came forward as one of the General's champions, riding through the streets of the city, insulting Roselli and Mazzini and calling upon the people to make Garibaldi dictator. Garibaldi disowned his unpleasant advocate who was himself threatened with assassination by a sculptor in the Piazza Colonna; but Sterbini's action served to make the differences between the General and the Triumvir even more widely known than they were already.[12]

To Mazzini nothing mattered now but that the Republic should die in a holocaust of suffering and self-sacrifice, should provide an inspiration to Europe by the manner of its apotheosis. At the beginning of the siege he had thought it likely that a change of opinion in France or even an insurrection might make it impossible for Louis Napoleon to pursue the foreign policy he had adopted before the Assembly elections.[13] But now that faint hope had gone. By 22 June Mazzini considered 'Rome had already fallen'.[14]

But this was far from suggesting that she should surrender. 'God grant that the enemy will assault,' he wrote to Manara. 'And then we could have a noble defence of the people at the barricades. My mind is overwhelmed with grief that so much valour, so much heroism should be lost.'[15] In an excess of frantic enthusiasm he called upon the people to follow him to the walls and hurl the French back, so that the world might knew that the Romans had fought to the death, even, at the end, with their bare hands.

Garibaldi felt such hysterical demonstrations to be absurd. He had fallen back to the Aurelian Walls – these he would defend without interference from a confused mob. He could not expect to defend them successfully for long, but he could at least hope that before the French overwhelmed him, his view that the time had come to evacuate the city and carry on a guerrilla warfare outside it would prevail. In the meantime, having moved his headquarters to Villa Spada behind the Aurelian Wall and, supported by cannon amongst the pine trees on the high ground near San Pietro in Montorio behind him, he and his men faced the besiegers once more.

In front of him the Casa Merluzzo bastion on the outer walls was still in his hands, and a new battery was mounted between this and the San Pancrazio gate which he still held also. The Italian artillerymen in the re-aligned batteries continued to fight with their by now customary skill and bravery; and while buildings crumbled and collapsed in the dust on every side, fighting patrols went out by day and night to keep the French out of the commanding villas which separated the two armies.

On the other side of the Tiber, the fighting which before had seemed almost unreal to those who watched the smoke rising in the distance and heard the far-off boom of cannon from the safety of the Pincio, was now taken as a serious threat to the lives of the inhabitants.

A fortnight before the Marchioness Ossoli, who had been appointed supervisor of the hospital of the Fate-Bene Fratelli by Princess Belgioiso's Committee for the Help of the Wounded, had walked in the grounds of the Pope's palace on Monte Quirinale, which was used for convalescents.

In those beautiful gardens I walk with them [she told a friend], one with

his sling, another with his crutch. The gardener plays off all his water-
works for the defenders of the country, and gathers flowers for me,
their friend.

A day or two since, we sat in the Pope's little pavilion, where he
used to give private audience. The sun was shining gloriously down
over Monte Mario, where gleamed the white tents of the French light-
horse among the trees. The cannonade was heard at intervals. Two
bright-eyed boys sat at our feet, and gathered up eagerly every word
said by the heroes of the day. It was a beautiful hour. . . .[16]

But it was different now. The war had intensified and come
closer; and many of her friends and most of the foreigners were
preparing to leave a city falling 'with the hopes of Italy'.[17]

Arthur Hugh Clough was one of those preparing to go. Before
the assault on the 21st he had written to Thomas Arnold, 'We've
been bombarded, my dear, think of that: several shells have fallen
even this side of the river, and I actually saw two grenades, burst in
the air! Lots of killed and wounded, too, of course.' On the 22nd
'an immense number of bombs were thrown – they fell chiefly in
the Piazza di Venezia, P. Sant'Apostoli and Via del Gesu. . . . I
found a crowd assembled about 9 p.m. at the north-east corner of
Piazza Colonna, watching these pretty fireworks – Ecco un altro! –
One first saw the "lightning" over the Post Office, then came the
missile itself, describing its tranquil parabola, then the distant report
of the mortar, and finally the near explosion, which occasionally
took place in the air. This went on all night.'[18]

But although the explosions were increasing and getting nearer,
and so many foreigners were leaving, the Romans themselves,
Clough thought, were taking it all 'coolly enough':

I fancy the middle-class Romans think it rather useless work, but they
don't feel strongly enough on the matter to make them take active
steps against a government which I believe has won their respect alike
by its moderation and its energy – perhaps too they are afraid of the
troops, under which term however do not understand foreigners,
unless you choose to give that name to the levies of the Papal States in
general. Visiting the Monte Cavallo hospital the other day, where there
are I think 200 men, three Poles and one Frenchman were especially
pointed out to me, that I might say some words of French to them. All

the others I saw were Italians, from Bologna, Ferrara, Ravenna, Perugia and so forth. .... Nice fellows they seemed – young and mostly cheerful in spite of their hurts . . . one had lost an arm and a leg. Another had a ball in his hip yet to be extracted. 'And the like!' On the whole I incline to think that they will fight it out to the last, but *chi lo sa?*[19]

Certainly it seemed that the poorer classes were prepared to do so. In the Trastevere quarter which, standing as it does between the Janiculum and the Tiber, had been the most endangered part of Rome since the siege began, the people had been active in their support of Mazzini from the first. On the morning of 30 April they had been seen running out of the cramped and narrow streets down by the river with guns and knives to fight on the walls; and by 12 June, apparently, they were, although 'recently so Catholic', now 'cursing and blaspheming the Pope and clergy in whose names they saw this carnage and these horrors committed'. '*Ecco un Pio Nono!*' they would shout when a shell flew over; and when one fell amongst them and did not explode, women and children would run forward to pick it up and throw it into the river.[20] Towards the end of the month many of them had to abandon their ruined homes; but their spirit remained unbroken.

On the Aurelian Walls above them the hand-to-hand fighting continued; but Garibaldi was directing it in increasing anger and frustration. And when his renewed demand that Rome should be abandoned and the army taken out by the eastern gates to fight on in the hills was again rejected by the Triumvirs he refused to continue in command. On 27 June he came down from Villa Spada in a fury of resentment, calling off his Legion from their posts.

The Triumvirs were appalled; but nothing they said could induce him to change his piqued mind. Roselli took his place but, though a brave officer and far less hidebound than his critics suggested, he had little of Garibaldi's inspiriting personality. 'I tell you frankly, Colonel,' Hoffstetter said to his chief of staff as he took him round the position, '*Your* General is not popular enough to bring the defence to an honourable conclusion.'[21]

The situation was saved by Manara who managed to persuade Garibaldi that, however irrational the continued struggle on the Aurelian Walls might appear, it was his duty to his country as well as to the troops the Legion had deserted, to return. And so the General overcame his angry petulance and at dawn the following morning led his men back to their posts.

They were now all wearing the red blouses that he had ordered for them a month before, a uniform which Roselli thought was a waste of money for the Treasury as well as *'un inutile esibizionismo'*.[22] But as they came up once more from the Trastevere they were cheered loudly by people who, knowing nothing of the reasons behind their recall, believed they had left the front only to get new shirts and that Garibaldi had left his post only to be present when they changed into them. They were returning, in fact, merely to take part in the final catastrophe.

★   ★   ★

At dusk on 29 June candles were placed in the windows of the city, lanterns were hung up in the streets and rockets shot up into the sky as the inhabitants celebrated the Feast of St. Peter and St. Paul, encouraged to do so by the Government who felt that the red, white and green of the lights would provide a fitting symbol of the Republic's defiance of its enemies. The lights, though, did not burn for long. First, a sudden summer storm sent the rain pouring down in torrents on the city and afterwards a cold wind blew up, whining over the city like a passionless lament. And then, at about one o'clock in the morning, after a crushing bombardment that spattered cascades of mud over the ruins, the French began their assault.

One column, rushing into the breach by the Casa Merluzzo under heavy fire from a detachment of *bersaglieri* commanded by the seventeen-year-old Emilio Morosino, stormed into the bastion, while another column burst upon the Aurelian Wall and then fanned out towards Villa Spada on the right and the battery near the San Pancrazio gate on the left.

Woken by the urgent call, *'all' armi! all' armi!'*, Hoffstetter, without stopping to pick up his pistols, rushed out of the Villa Spada to find 'everyone was running. No shouting or clang of weapons. . . . My men whispered to me, *"I Francesi, i Francesi"* and wanted to fire at once. But I pushed the barrels of their rifles down with my sword, thinking it might just as well be some of our own people. Only when they were right on our bayonets did I see they were French chasseurs.'[23]

The skill and impetus of the French assault had driven some of the defenders to panic and as they rushed about wildly in the darkness, the voice of Garibaldi 'could be heard calling out, "*Orsù, Orsù!*" "Come on! Come on!" and then breaking out into a popular hymn'.[24] Encouraged by him and by Hoffstetter and Manara, and by others as brave and energetic, those already fighting struck out with increased fury and those formerly gripped with terrified panic returned to join them. The struggle became savage and bitter. Face to face, liked mediaeval knights, the enemies lunged at each other under the moonless sky, stabbing, swinging and hacking with any weapons that came to hand, shouting and screaming until the ground was thick with the dead and dying, sprawled in the ruins and the mud.

By dawn the Italians had recovered the defences of the Aurelian Wall, but with the French in the Casa Merluzzo and above the San Pancrazio gate, their position was tenable no longer. Medici was withdrawn from the Vascello Villa to the Savorelli, and at Villa Spada Manara and his *bersaglieri* were surrounded.

We shut ourselves into the house [Dandolo remembered], barricading the doors, and defending the windows. The cannon-balls fell thickly, spreading devastation and death, the balls of the Vincennes chasseurs hissed with unerring aim through the shattered windows. It is maddening to fight within the limits of a house, when a cannon-ball may rebound from every wall, and where, if not thus struck, you may be crushed under the shattered masonry; where the air, impregnated with smoke and gunpowder, brings the groans of the wounded more distinctly on the ear, and where the feet slip along the blood-soaked floor.

A musket ball, ricocheting from the wall, flew into his right arm, wounding him for the second time that month. 'My God,' said Manara, 'are you always the one to be struck? Am I to take nothing back from Rome?'

A few minutes later the Colonel fell back from an open window, shot by a ball which passed straight through his body. He was carried out of the house in a wheelbarrow and taken to Santa Maria della Scala where he asked to be treated by his friend Dr. Agostino

Bertani, a fellow-Milanese who had come to work in the Roman hospitals.

'Oh! Bertani,' Manara said to him, 'let me die quickly.' To Dandolo he entrusted the care of his children and asked to be buried in Lombardy with Dandolo's brother. Dandolo began to cry and the Colonel said, 'Does it hurt you then so much that I die?' But the young lieutenant could not answer him through his sobs, and so Manara added 'in an undertone, but with the holiest expression of resignation, "It grieves me also." '

He took the Sacrament and a little while later he pulled Dandolo towards him. 'I will greet your brother for you,' he said, and he closed his eyes.[25]

Garibaldi was still unharmed though he had been fighting furiously now for two hours and was covered with blood. 'His sword was like lightning,' Vecchi said. 'At every moment I feared to see him fall, but no, there he remained as immovable as destiny.'[26] After leading a last fierce but vain charge against the French, he had accepted – and he hoped that Mazzini would now accept – that there was nothing more that he or any of his soldiers could profitably do within the walls of Rome. Summoned to the Capitol to attend the last session of the Republican Assembly, he left the front determined to press his views yet again upon the Government.

His entry into the Capitol was predictably dramatic. His forehead sweating, his clothes covered with dried blood and dust, his bent sword sticking out of its scabbard, he walked slowly to the tribune steps, while the members of the Assembly stood up to cheer him. His servant Aguyar was dead, his friend Manara was dying, and he did not yet know how many others might be dying too.

The Republic was dying with them; and the Assembly had merely to decide the manner of its passing. Three plans had been proposed: a surrender, a struggle to the death in the streets, withdrawal to the hills. Everyone knew what the General's reactions would be. '*Ovunque noi saremo*,' he said, '*sarà Roma*' – 'Wherever we go, there will Rome be.'[27]

He wanted only volunteers to go with him, he said, and later when he spoke to these volunteers gathered in the Piazza of St. Peter's and surrounded by a shouting, swaying, cheering crowd, he told them how little they could expect from following him.

At first he could not quieten the crowd for there were many in it who screamed abuse at him for taking their sons away from them on a wild escapade that could achieve nothing, and there were others who did not want to hear him talk but only to shout his name. 'Citizens and women stormed him from all sides,' wrote the Dutch artist Jan Philip Koelman who was there. 'He only managed slowly and with difficulty to reach the Egyptian obelisk that stands in the middle of the Piazza. Here he stopped and turned his horse, and when his staff had joined him he gave a sign with his hand to stop the cheers.'[28]

But the cheering went on, louder even than before. When he began at last to speak, however, looking and sounding more than ever like the patriarch that Dandolo had described at Tivoli, a calm fell over the square.

'I am going out of Rome,' he said. 'Whoever is willing to follow me will be received among my people. I ask nothing of them but a heart filled with love for our country. They will have no pay, no provisions, and no rest. I offer hunger, cold, forced marches, battles and death. Whoever is not satisfied with such a life must remain behind. He who has the name of Italy not only on his lips but in his heart, let him follow me.'[29]

He told those who would come with him to meet that evening at the Lateran near Porta San Giovanni. And then he rode away, calm as ever, his features set in Olympian impassivity.

Mazzini could not share that apparent calm. After Garibaldi had left the Assembly on the afternoon of 30 June to return to the front, he had endorsed the General's views but had urged that the entire Assembly and army, and not just volunteers as Garibaldi had proposed, should leave the city for the Apennines to keep the Republican flag flying in the Romagna. But the Assembly out-voted him and passed this resolution:

In the name of God and the People –
The Constituent Assembly of Rome ceases from a defence which has become impossible and remains at its post.[30]

'Monarchies may capitulate,' Mazzini was later to complain, 'republics die and bear their testimony even to martyrdom.'[31] For him there could be no compromise; the Republic must fight on to the death in Rome with all its remaining strength or its example to the world would be tainted for ever.* In protest against the Assembly's decision he resigned, taking his two fellow Triumvirs with him. He wanted no part in the surrender, nor would he go with Garibaldi to wander about in the wilderness. He was not a man who could happily follow anyone and to follow Garibaldi would have been intolerable.

When the French entered Rome on 3 July he walked about in the streets in order, so it was afterwards said,[32] to offer himself to the knife of an assassin and so kill the lie of the Catholic press that the people wished him dead for having forced a tyranny upon them. Marchioness Ossoli who saw him that evening said that 'in two short months he had grown old; all the vital juices seemed exhausted; he had passed all these nights without sleep; his eyes were all bloodshot; his skin orange; flesh he had none; his hair was mixed with white; his hand was painful to the touch'. He had been walking about the streets 'all afternoon,' she said, 'to see how the people bore themselves'.[33]

How they did bear themselves was described in a letter received by F. T. Palgrave who might, Clough thought, like a commentary on the text which had appeared 'in the *Constitutionel,* that "on Tuesday, July 3rd our army entered Rome amidst the acclamations of the people" ':†

I stood in the Corso with some thirty of the people and saw them pass. Fine working soldiers, indeed, dogged and business-like, but they looked

* Mazzini's 'talismanic obsession' with Rome, as the Countess Martinengo Cesaresco called it, had blinded him to the fact that a city with so large a circumference, almost open on the left bank of the Tiber, could only successfully be defended by troops in position outside it. If the Republican troops had taken the road to Viterbo and threatened the enemy's flank, they might have retained the initiative. By withdrawing to the Upper Tiber they could have combined with other battalions in the Papal States and then successfully called to arms the people of the Romagna. This at least was Pisacane's opinion – *Guerra combattuta in Italia negli anni 1848–1849. Narrazione di Carlo Pisacane. Ripubblicata per cura del Prof. Luigi Maino* (Rome, 1906), 252-3.

† '*L'accueil de la population fut excellent et même enthousiaste dans les quartiers populaires. Les cris de "Vivent les Francais! Vivent nos liberateurs!" se croisèrent avec le cri de "Vive Pie IX!"* ' – Leopold de Gaillard, *L'expédition de Rome en 1849* (Paris, 1861), 262.

a little awkward while the people screamed and hooted and cried *Viva La Repubblica Romana*, etc. When they had got past, some young simpleton sent a tin pail after them: four or five raced down with bayonets presented, while my young friend cut away up the Corso double-quick. They went on. At this moment, some Roman bourgeois as I fancy, but perhaps a foreigner, said something either to express his sense of the folly of it, or his sympathy with the invaders. He was surrounded and I saw him buffeted a good deal, and there was a sword lifted up but I think not bare. I was told he got off. But a priest who walked and talked publicly in the Piazza Colonna with a Frenchman was undoubtedly killed. I know his friends and saw one of them last night. Poor man, he was quite a liberal ecclesiastic, they tell me; but certainly not a prudent one. To return to my own experience – After this, the column passed back by another street into the Corso, and dispersed the crowd with the bayonet point. . . . An English acquaintance informed me that in passing by the Café Nuovo, where an Italian tricolor hung from the window, Oudinot plucked at it, and bid it be removed. The French proceeded to do this, but the Romans intervened; Cernuschi, the Barricade Commissioner, took it down, kissed it, and, as I myself saw, carried it in triumph amidst cheers to the Piazza Colonna. I didn't follow; but on my bolder friend's authority I can state that here the French moved up with their bayonets and took it from Cernuschi, stripping him moreover of his tricolour scarf.[34]

P.S. The priest is not dead and perhaps will survive. But another I hear was hewed to pieces, for shouting *Viva Pio IX, a basso la repubblica*, etc.

The *Times* correspondent confirmed that the occupying troops were 'hissed and groaned at' as they passed up the Corso, 'particularly from the Café Nuovo, one of the strongholds of the Ultra-Liberals; and when General Oudinot and his staff came up in the evening . . . he and they were assailed by a group in and near the Café delle Belle Arti with repeated cries of "Death to Pio Nono", "Death to the Priests", "*Viva* the Roman Republic", "Death to the Cardinal Oudinot". The General's staff, who had borne with the good humour of French soldiers the first portion of these insults, became furious on hearing the Commander-in-Chief personally vituperated and without a moment's hesitation they charged the crowd'.[35]

But on the whole, as Clough agreed, 'the French soldiers showed excellent temper'. 'At the same time some faces I have seen,' he added, 'are far more brutal than the worst Garibaldian and we have hitherto seen nothing so unpleasing in the female kind as the vivandiere. . . .

'The American banker here tells me he was told in the morning the French were cheered. I rather doubt it, but I believe the bourgeoisie in part are very glad it is over.'[36]

Soon, indeed, the unrest died down. Before the Pope returned and the old sternly authoritarian clerical régime was restored under the influence of Cardinal Antonelli, the Romans were treated with careful restraint. The French behaved well, with far less severity than the Austrians in the provinces,[37] and were rarely provoked into retaliation. Gradually the insults decreased. At first the cafés patronised by the French were boycotted and at some, as at the big Caffè Nuovo, 'such unmistakable disgust was evinced that they had to be closed down'. But generally, as at the Bon Gout in Piazza di Spagna, the occupying forces were treated 'with polite indifference'.[38]

The search for what a French historian of the siege called 'the most deeply compromised of the revolutionaries' was conducted without either thoroughness or rancour. Certainly 'the greater part escaped, thanks to the complicity of the Consular Agents of England and the United States'.[39] The American Consul, Brown, thought it advisable to come downstairs with a sword in one hand and the stars and stripes in the other when the French came to search his house for political refugees. And the English Consul, Freeborn, issued so many hundreds of diplomatic passes that Lord Palmerston was constrained to reprove him. But the French search parties seem to have been more sympathetic than industrious. Mazzini, himself, helped by Lewis Cass, the American *chargé d'affaires*, got away to Civitavecchia and eventually to England without interference from the authorities.

Cass had also offered his services to Garibaldi, but although the General accepted an American passport he could not accept the shame of flight on a corvette. He was committed to go elsewhere; and by the time the French entered Rome he had already gone.

*   *   *

The volunteers, about four thousand of them in all, had gathered around the Lateran soon after six o'clock in the evening of 2 July. They were a very disparate collection: there were papal cavalrymen, and Bolognese lancers, *bersaglieri* riflemen, a few Poles who had fought in Rome with a detachment from the brigade formed by the poet Miçkiewicz, politicians such as Ciceruacchio, and boys such as Ciceruacchio's thirteen-year-old son, families seeking protection on their way home to the provinces, veteran Garibaldini wondered where next they would fight. Some, like Ciceruacchio's elder son Luigi, had come because the alternative might have been execution or a prison sentence; others in the hope of loot. So many of the best officers who had fought on the Janiculum during the siege were dead that Garibaldi could not but wonder how he would keep in control so large and ill-assorted a company. But the Swiss Hoffstetter was still with him, and Ugo Bassi, wearing a red shirt now as well as his crucifix, and he could hope that these two at least would help him maintain the strict discipline that would be so necessary on the march.

By his side there was a figure on horseback, a small figure in the red shirt of the Legion with hair tucked up under the band of a wide-brimmed hat.

Anita had arrived at Villa Spada on 26 June and, though her husband had forbidden her to come to Rome, he did not disguise his delight that she had disobeyed him. 'She was a woman of about twenty-eight,' wrote Hoffstetter who saw her now for the first time, 'with a dark complexion, interesting features and a slight delicate figure.' He could see how devoted to her the General was, and with 'what tenderness' he treated her.[40] When it was dark they rode out together through the Giovanni gate followed by their bedraggled army and a single cannon.

A week later *The Times*, reporting the departure from Rome of these 'worst enemies of the country . . . Garibaldi's brigands', added that they were hotly pursued by the 1st Division of the French army and would, therefore, 'probably be annihilated'.[41]

7

THE RETREAT TO SAN MARINO

After marching silently all night through the Campagna, first south-eastwards as though they were making for the Alban Hills and then northwards in the direction of Hadrian's Villa, Garibaldi and his followers reached Tivoli at seven o'clock the following morning.

Here amongst the olive trees on the slopes of the Sabine Hills the men looked back towards Rome. There was no sign of their pursuers. The French, in fact, had not yet left the city and when they did, believing that their enemies had made for the Pontine Marshes, followed Garibaldi's false scent as far as Albano.

The French, though, were only the nearest of their enemies. Farther south were the Neapolitans, to the north and east were Austrians, to the west were 6,000 well-equipped Spaniards who had landed in Italy at the request of the Church. Garibaldi could not hope to defeat any of these enemies if they found him; but he was determined that they should not find him – at least not until he was ready. And he still clung to the belief that he *would* one day be ready, for he thought that in Central Italy, in Umbria, Tuscany and the Romagna, despite the presence of the Austrians, he would be able to gather thousands of patriotic Italians round him and lead a people's army against their oppressors.

Before long, though, he was forced to accept a far less dramatic reality and to understand that the most he could hope to do was to lead his men to the help of Manin, still holding out in Venice. Already, indeed, he detected signs that most of his fellow-countrymen were tired and disillusioned in a way that he could never be, that they were not yet ready to fight – not yet even wanting to fight – a battle that he believed might be won by spirit and courage alone. Before they had proved their worth in the siege of Rome he had written to Anita: 'With what scorn must you not look upon this generation of hermaphrodites, on these countrymen of mine, that I have tried so many times to rouse to nobility, and with so little result.'[1]

Now they were relapsing again into their former indifference.

Reggio
Modena
DUCHY
OF
Romagna
MODENA
Bologna
Reno
Comacchio
Magnavacca
Reno
Mandriole
Sant'Alberto
Lugo
Ravenna
Faenza
Savio
Forlì
Cesenatico
Cesena
Sala
Rubicon
Savignano
Gatteo
DUCHY OF
Cerbaja
Santa
Lucia
Rimini
LUCCA
Vajano
S.Giovanni in Galilea
Verucchio
Prato
Scorticata
SAN MARINO
Lucca
GRAND-
Pietracuta
San Leo
Pesaro
Florence
Pisa
Arno
Empoli
Macerata
Leghorn
ARCHDUCHY
Pian di Meleto
Urbino
Metaurus
Borgo Pace
Mercatello
Sant'Angelo in Vado
Volterra
OF
San Giustino
Arezzo
Citerna
Cecina
Siena
Citta di Castello
Bagno al Morbo
Cortona
Macerata in
the Marches
Castelnuovo
Bocpetono Pass
TUSCANY
Piombino
Perugia
Follonica
Casa Guelfi
Assisi
Portiglione
Foligno
Salci
Grosseto
Orvieto
Todi
Spoleto
Elba
Terni
Viterbo
Rieti
Aquila
Civitavecchia
Rotondo
Sant'Angelo
Mentana
Vicovaro
Arsoli
Palo
Anio
Tivoli
Subiaco
Rome
Hadriano
Castel S.Pietro
Colonna
Palestrina
Frascati
Valmontone
Albano
Alban
Hills
Velletri
Frosinone
Arce
Anzio
Pontine
Marshes
Terracina
Gaeta

CENTRAL ITALY

0   10   20   30   40   50   60 Miles

Route of Garibaldi's retreat from Rome, 1849 ━━━━━

Route of his flight from Mandriole to Portiglione +++++

Hundreds of men had drifted away from the ranks in the first night of his march; many more were to follow them within the next few days. He compared these men bitterly with the hard, determined men he had led across the pampas and through the jungles of South America, ashamed to belong to these 'degenerate descendants of the greatest of nations', these 'unwarlike and effeminate countrymen' of his.[2]

His shame was unjustified, of course, for most of those who had left him, or were later to leave him, had never intended to stay. But he was not a man to sympathise with motives other than his own, nor indeed, a man to give praise to those who shared his motives and, because of this, who shared his suffering. They had agreed to come with him, to endure his hardships, to be hungry and tired with him, to fight with him, perhaps to die with him – they were doing no more than their duty, and nor, he felt, was he.

His retreat from Rome was more than a duty, though, it was a *tour de force* of astonishing and enduring brilliance. He had failed as a general in Rome, but by the time he reached the Romagna, his reputation as one of the greatest of guerrilla leaders had been triumphantly confirmed.

When he left Tivoli during the late evening of 3 July, his men, formed now into two regiments marching eastwards away from Rome, had appeared to be making for the Neapolitan territory of the Abruzzi. The following morning, however, they could be seen far on the other side of the mountain ridge moving back again towards Mentana. During the night they had pulled their carts up steep mule-tracks which the peasants said were impassable, through the echoing streets of mountain villages and then down again into the Campagna. For four weeks the gradually diminishing and constantly elusive army misled its pursuers and their informers in this way. Expected in one town it would suddenly appear miles away in another; leaving that in a north-easterly direction, it would next be found marching north-west towards a village believed to be far removed from its route. Before the first week was over the wagons had been abandoned, so that the men, using pack animals only, and existing on the flesh of the cattle that were driven before them, became more mobile and elusive than ever. A screen of cavalry fanned out in front of them, watching and misleading the enemy, spreading rumours and fear; while their leader himself, tireless and cunning, covered great distances, looking for new routes, inventing new ruses.

In the noonday heat, perhaps, or at night, the army would halt for a few hours' rest, and Garibaldi, quartering the men if he could in some monastery on high ground outside the walls of a town, would sit down with Anita and watch the great hunks of oxen turning slowly above the fires on the freshly cut spits.

Having only the now worthless paper money of the Roman Republic, he paid for this meat by raising loans from the towns and villages and convents on his way. Before its dissolution the Assembly had granted him full powers to act in its name and he made use of this authority now – as he was often later to make use of it – to lend some semblance of legality to actions which were in fact quite arbitrary. Occasionally a loan was willingly made, but more often it was only grudgingly allowed, or made from fear. The monks, in particular, upon whom the greatest burden fell, paid the money demanded of them with understandable reluctance and sometimes under duress. But although Garibaldi's hold over his ill-assorted followers was not as strong as it had been over the Italian Legion, there was little violence in these negotiations and less looting than was afterwards suggested. Indeed, nearly all the acts of violence and robberies committed during the retreat were the responsibility of small bands of men who had abandoned Garibaldi to become brigands in his name. Had they remained with him, he would have ordered them to be shot, as Hoffstetter said, 'without taking the cigar out of his mouth'. Even the smallest theft was deemed by him a capital offence, and at least one soldier was shot for stealing a hen.[3]

Garibaldi during these days was not a man any wary soldier would choose to disobey. Those who came into contact with him, silent and calm as he appeared, knew that the failure of the people to rise up around him and fight for freedom and unity filled him with angry bitterness. People in the towns would greet his approach with wine and flowers and the crashing noise of brass bands; they would sometimes offer to lend him money though they knew it was un-likely that they would ever be repaid; but 'well knowing what priestly vengeance meant', they would not act as guides for him, and they would not join him and they would not fight with him. When fighting was suggested the smiles became transfixed, the gestures more pronounced, the eyes evasive, and the conversation drifted away into the cautious pleasantries of the *gente montanara*. A few youths perhaps, more adventurous or disgruntled than the rest, would volunteer to join the little army, but when the town was left behind the numbers of those who had joined were always less than the numbers of those who had deserted.

At Terni on 8 July the dwindling numbers were, however, augmented, by about 900 men of a Republican regiment that had remained in arms after the fall of Rome. These men were commanded by a remarkable Englishman in a thin cotton suit and a white chimney-pot hat. Colonel Hugh Forbes, a forceful, rich, cantankerous officer of forty-one, had obtained a commission in the Coldstream Guards after coming down from Oxford and had married an Englishwoman by whom he had a son who was now with him at Terni. His second marriage, some years later, had altered his whole life. He had gone with his new wife, a beautiful Italian, to live in Tuscany and there became so deeply involved with the revolutionary movement that he was soon fighting for the Venetian Republic against the Austrians and later helping the revolutionary government in Palermo to organise resistance against King Ferdinand. After the return of the Bourbon forces to Palermo, Forbes left for the Roman Republic and had been given command of the troops north of Rome retreating before the Austrians in the Marches. He had managed to bring them back to Terni where the townspeople resented his sternly autocratic manner as much as his soldiers did, and were delighted to see him march away north again with Garibaldi on 9 July.

Not all of Forbes's soldiers followed him, however, and many of Garibaldi's men also stayed behind in Terni, so that the force which entered Todi two days later was not greatly increased after all. Nor, as he advanced north-east towards Tuscany, was Garibaldi able to hope that it ever would be increased. The going was harder than ever now, the route just as circuitous, the enemy armies closing in. At Orvieto the tired men were hurried out of the town as the French came in at their heels, and then, finding the most direct route over the mountains blocked in their faces by an enemy garrison, they moved west in the blinding rain through crumbling unfriendly villages to Salci and the Tuscan border. Once across the border they left the French behind, as they had already left the Spaniards and the Neapolitans behind; but the Austrians were still in front. And surrounded by the troops of Austria, the people of Tuscany were just as disinclined to join Garibaldi as the people of the Papal States had been. They greeted him with smiles and sometimes with cheers, they gave him money and food, and years later they remembered him with awe and admiration; but the recruits he had hoped to attract on his way to Venice did not appear. And he who did not know fear himself, could never forgive those less fortunate ones to whom it was a constant spectre, overshadowing their daily lives. He who would sacrifice everything for an ideal, could not understand the caution of those to whom their children or wives or parents or homes were more important.

At Arezzo this caution and this fear induced the inhabitants to close the gates of the town against him; and as Garibaldi halted outside, urged by his men to attack the place, the Austrians once more drew close. Knowing that he could not lead Italians to attack an Italian town which many of them would probably then loot, and that the delay had, in any event, now turned Arezzo into a possible trap, he was forced to turn aside at sunset and take his men up the mountain track beside the walls of the town.

He moved on only just in time, for the Austrians were now as close on his heels as the French had been at Orvieto – so close, in fact, that they caught up with the rearguard who had to turn round and fight.

There could be no illusions now about a new uprising in central Italy. Indeed, most of the peasants in the country around Arezzo regarded the Austrians as their friends and the Garibaldians as enemies, as bandits who should be handed over to their protectors. Several stragglers and some wounded men of the rearguard were, in fact, either taken prisoner by these peasants or shot out of hand. For this Garibaldi, knew, of course, whom to blame: it was the doing of the priests and friars, those 'traitors of the deepest dye', the 'very scourge of that Italy which, seven or seventy times they have sold to the stranger', those 'descendants of Torquemada', 'ministers of falsehood', the 'black brood, pestilent scum of humanity, caryatid of thrones still reeking with the scent of human burnt offerings where tyranny still reigns'.

Hunted by their own people as well as by the Austrians, Garibaldi's dispirited army could no longer consider itself a national force: it had become a band of fugitives. From the Scopettone Pass above Arezzo, these fugitives struggled down into the valley of the Upper Tiber and then up the mountainside again towards Citerna. At Citerna they halted for forty-eight hours while, in the valley below them, the white columns of the Austrian occupying army still moved along the roads looking for them in the cypress groves and the oak woods. And then, when it was dark they moved on again, winding their way down the mule-tracks on to the plain once more, splashing through fords, passing vineyards and fig trees and rows of poplars and the black shapes of shuttered houses. From San Giustino, up wandering mountain-paths to the Trabaria pass, through Borgo Pace and Mercatello to Sant' Angelo in Vado, through Pian di Meleto to Macerata, the exhausted volunteers made their way northeast towards the Adriatic coast and Venice. Sometimes a straggler lost his way and in the morning was picked up by an Austrian patrol to be flogged or shot as a rebel; sometimes a diversionary attack had to be made on the pursuing Austrians; once a squadron of Hungarian hussars galloped into the cavalry of the rearguard as they were resting in a town beside the banks of the Metaurus river, and cut them apart with their sabres; and every day, singly and in groups, men wandered off in the darkness, abandoning their leader who now seemed as doomed as his cause.

His officers began to leave him, too. At first Muller, a Polish Garibaldino, and then Bueno, the Brazilian leader of the cavalry, went over to the Austrians who could, at least, offer more to a mercenary than a friendless Italian revolutionary could. And after they had gone, several Italian officers decided to follow their example and, if not give themselves up to the Austrians, at least seek the protection of the little republic of San Marino, now within tempting reach.

And it was to San Marino that Garibaldi, faced by a strong Austrian column under General Hahne, was obliged himself to turn at dawn on 31 July. Colonel Forbes was with him still and the young Hugh Forbes, and Ciceruacchio with his sons, and Ugo Bassi and Hoffstetter. But of the men that they had led out of Terni less than 1,500 remained. Knowing that he could do no more now with these few tired and dispirited troops, he went up to the town of San Marino, perched on its high grey rock, to ask Belzoppi, the Captain-Regent, if he would take them in.

While he was negotiating with Belzoppi, General Hahne's advance-guard attacked his men who were too worn out to offer any resistance. Most of them dashed away up the slopes of the hill to be met by Anita Garibaldi rushing down towards the sound of the shots and shouting, 'Peppino! Where is Peppino?' The sight of the General's determined little wife and the presence of Colonel Forbes helped in rallying them, so that when the General himself came galloping out of the town the Austrian advance-guard had been held; and Garibaldi was able to lead his bedraggled men into the Capuchin convent which the friars had offered for their reception. Here, on the steps of the convent, Garibaldi sat down to write his last Order of the Day.

We have reached the land of refuge, and we owe the best possible behaviour to our generous hosts. We, too, have merited the consideration due to persecuted misfortune.

Soldiers, I release you from your duty to follow me, and leave you free to return to your homes. But remember that although the Roman war for the independence of Italy has ended, Italy remains in shameful slavery.

Garibaldi[4]

For his part he was determined not to risk remaining in shameful slavery in an Austrian prison, and taking advantage of a clause in the terms that the authorities of San Marino had negotiated with the Austrians – to the effect that the conditions of surrender had to be confirmed by the distrusted General Gorzkowski in Bologna – he informed his staff that he would march out of San Marino that night with a small force of selected volunteers and renew his attempt to reach Venice.

Leaving his men in the care of the San Marinesi, Garibaldi wrote a hasty and graceless note to the 'Citizen Representatives of the Republic':

The conditions imposed by the Austrians are unacceptable; and therefore we will evacuate your territory. Yours, G. Garibaldi.[5]

Then, having questioned three peasants as to the whereabouts of the Austrian forces on the plains below, he suddenly and dramatically announced to his staff in a café by the western gate, 'Whoever wishes to follow me, I offer him fresh battles, suffering and exile. But treaties with the foreigner, never!'[6]

Having made this characteristic and startling declaration, he jumped on his horse and rode out through the gate, without waiting to find out how many would follow him. Anita, he knew, would come. He had tried to persuade her to stay behind for she was now seriously ill, but she would have none of it and as he recorded later himself, she silenced him at last with the accusation, '*Tu voi lasciarmi*' – 'You *want* to leave me.'[7] Ugo Bassi came, too, and Colonel Forbes with the staff and about 230 men; and led by a San Marino workman who had agreed to guide them as far as the plain of the Romagna, they worked their way silently north through the Austrian lines towards the village of Gatteo. Here their guide left them and they went on alone towards the coast at Cesenatico, twenty miles north of Rimini.

It was night again when they arrived at Cesenatico; the fishing fleet had come home with their catch and the squat little smacks were lying with furled sails at anchor in the canal that ran through the middle of the town. It was very quiet, Garibaldi remembered; the fishermen were asleep in the houses by the canal; a few Austrian soldiers were playing cards in their guard house; some papal *carabinieri* were lounging about in their barracks.

Abruptly the silence was broken by Garibaldi and his followers who came galloping through the town, knocking up the fishermen, rounding up the Austrians and *carabinieri*, throwing food and rope into the fishing smacks; and then, having got the unwilling crews aboard, working hard to get the boats out through the breakers at the mouth of the port. But the breakers were so heavy that it seemed at first it would be impossible to get the boats out into the open sea. And the attempt would have failed, no doubt, had not Garibaldi, with the skill of a seaman and the strength of desperation, jumped from boat to boat, tying them to two kedge-anchors lashed together, and then, having forced a small boat out of the harbour with the kedge-anchors aboard, plunged into the sea to fix them so that the smacks could be hauled out of the port.

The operation took all night. The 'sleepy and unwilling fishermen,' so Garibaldi said, 'could only be made to move at all – let alone made to do the necessary work – by means of blows with the flat of our swords.' And once, after the kedge-anchors had been got into position by furious exertions, the rope snapped and the whole of the work had to be started again from the beginning. Anita, in great pain now, sat on the shore anxiously watching her husband shouting and hauling and splashing through the waves; while behind her Colonel Forbes, who had posted sentries at every entrance to the town, stood by a barricade to hold off the Austrians should they learn what was happening before the slow and exhausting operation was completed.

At last, about seven o'clock in the morning, the boats with their dyed sails flapping in the wind, were all out at sea.[8]

8

THE FLIGHT TO PORTIGLIONE

For Garibaldi it was a dreadful voyage. He was worn out, as he confessed himself, by the previous night's work, yet he could not sleep. Anita, 'tormented by a feverish thirst', and suffering agonising spasms of pain in her womb, lay beside him and he could do nothing to help her.

For the whole of the day the little fleet sailed north along the Adriatic coast, the red and orange sails of the smacks filled by a favourable wind, and by nightfall they had not been intercepted. But night did not bring security, and any hope there might have been of slipping past the Austrian naval squadron on watch by the mouths of the Po was dispelled when the bright full moon came up. Garibaldi feared that, as soon as they were seen and fired upon, the fishermen from Cesenatico would make no great effort to avoid capture. And he was right. By dawn most of the boats had been overhauled and captured, and the Italians aboard, together with Colonel Forbes, had been taken off to imprisonment at Pola on the opposite side of the Adriatic coast in what is now Yugoslavia.*

Three boats, however, with about thirty men in each, succeeded in evading capture and, pursued by long boats and pinnaces, sped through the rough sea for the lagoon district of Comacchio, north of Magnavacca. They plunged through the breakers to the shore and as soon as they touched ground, the Italians leaped out and dashed away across the sand dunes towards the tall reeds in the marshes.

On one of these boats was Garibaldi; but he could not run for he had Anita to carry, and when the others had all disappeared from view behind the sandhills, he could still be seen hurrying across the

* There they were imprisoned not executed as, having been taken at sea in Venetian waters, they were considered prisoners of war rather than Rebels. Colonel Forbes was released in October, after prolonged negotiations carried out on his behalf by his wife and the British authorities, the others – about 160 of them – soon afterwards.

sand with his wife in his arms and a single companion, Major Giam-battista Culiolo, who had been wounded in the leg at Rome, limping by his side. Already Austrian troops from Magnavacca had crossed the canal and were fanning out across the long, thin strip of sandy earth on which the fugitives had been seen to land. With the knowledge that anyone who helped the Italians or sheltered them was threatened with execution, and with the hope of sharing the large reward offered for their capture by General Gorzkowski, the Austrians could feel confident that they would soon round them up. Also, the strip of land they were searching – the Bosco Eliseo – was, in fact, an island; it separated the Adriatic from the lagoon, and was cut off from Magnavacca in the south by the canal and from the land in the north by one of the mouths of the Po. Certainly Garibaldi, Anita and Culiolo would have been caught had not they come, within a few moments of landing, face to face with a man prepared to risk his life to help them.

This man, Gioacchino Bonnet, an influential landowner in the district and a convinced liberal, had met Garibaldi eight months before at Ravenna when the Italian Legion was preparing to sail to Venice. One of his brothers, Gaetano, had been killed on 3 June at the Corsini Villa; and another, Raimondo, had accompanied Gari-baldi in the retreat as far as San Marino.

Gioacchino Bonnet was not on the Bosco Eliseo that morning by accident. He had seen the little convoy of fishing smacks sailing north the evening before, and having been told of Garibaldi's escape he knew who must be aboard them. Through the hours of darkness he waited for the sound of ships' guns and as soon as he heard them he jumped into his gig and drove fast to Magnavacca pier. Directed from there to the Bosco Eliseo by an old fisherman who judged more accurately than the Austrian officers what was happening out at sea, he sent his gig with a servant to a near-by farm and ran off himself to the sand dunes where the fishing smacks had beached.

Helped by a beachcomber, who was standing behind a sandhill watching the events that provided so exciting an interruption to the normal pattern of the days, Bonnet guided the fugitives first to a hut on the far side of the marsh and then to one of his farms where Anita was put to bed. Here they were safe for a few hours as the Austrians had gone hurrying off to the north on the track of another party of volunteers which they believed included Garibaldi in his red shirt and poncho, and his wife dressed as a man and riding a horse. In fact, Anita had abandoned her Garibaldino uniform some days before, and was now wearing a blouse and skirt; and Garibaldi had dressed himself as a peasant in some clothes which Bonnet had given him. But although the Austrians had for the moment gone off on a false scent, there could be no doubt that the fugitives would have to leave the farm soon and make for a place less likely to be searched.

Garibaldi was urged by Bonnet to leave Anita, for he could not hope to escape if she went with him; and he agreed to go on with Major Culiolo provided he could first take his wife to a house where she could be cared for. Bonnet suggested another of his properties, the Zanetto farm; and so during the afternoon, when all seemed quiet outside, the small party, pushing Anita in a cart, made for the northern end of the Bosco Eliseo where the Zanetto farm faced out on to the waters of the lagoon. Bonnet himself did not go with them. He had to return to his house in Comacchio and arrange for a boat to pick up Garibaldi and Culiolo from Zanetto and take them across the lagoon on the first stage of their journey of escape through the Romagna and Tuscany into Piedmont.

Without telling them who their passengers were to be, Bonnet sent the boatmen off across the lagoon and then returned himself to the farm by land. He narrowly escaped running into Austrian search parties as well as *carabinieri* on his way, and when he arrived back at the farmhouse he was disturbed to hear that Anita had become much worse since her arrival there, was intermittently delirious and, though she could not fully grasp what was happening any more, had begged Garibaldi not to leave her. Garibaldi no longer felt able to do so. 'Bonnet,' he said, 'you can't imagine all that she has done for me, and how much she loves me. I owe her too much and love her too much to leave her. Let her come with me.'

Bonnet protested that she would be well looked after at Zanetto, and that to try to escape with her would almost certainly lead to capture. But Garibaldi was adamant. He could not leave her; they must both go, or neither. Bonnet gave way. Anita was lifted into the boat and laid on the cushions in the stern, and the boatmen pulled away from the shore in the failing light.[1]

The flat surface of the lagoon was broken up, as it still is, by long thin banks of earth and by causeways stretching across it like the fin-spines of gigantic motionless fish. The main causeway, which carries the road from the island town of Comacchio to Ferrara, divides the lagoon into two, and to reach the southern shore at the far end of the lagoon the boatmen had to disembark at the causeway and carry the boat across the road. While they were helping their passengers back into the boat on the far side of the causeway, however, it suddenly struck one of them who these passengers were. Knowing that to be found helping Garibaldi to escape would end in his death, he became terrified, infected his companions with his fear and persuaded them to agree to abandon their dangerous cargo on the nearest bank of earth on which there was a hut.

Here it was, then, that Garibaldi, Anita and Culiolo spent the rest of the night, Anita in Garibaldi's arms, shivering in her feverish delirium, Culiolo at the entrance to the hut looking out across the still, moonlit water. But in the morning, it was not the Austrians that came out to fetch them, as Garibaldi had feared, but two Italian fishermen sent out by Bonnet who had heard by then of their plight. Garibaldi thankfully lifted his wife into the boat, but even now it was to be almost twelve hours before he was able to get her to a doctor. It took the two fishermen, Michele Guidi and his brother, all morning to row across the southern half of the lagoon towards the landing place near the Guiccioli dairy-farm at Mandriole which Bonnet had ordered to be prepared for her arrival; and then the boat had to be carried up the steep bank which divides the lagoon from the Po di Primaro before being rowed across the river. After that the brothers had to go to the farm for a cart, so that it was not until the evening that Anita was at last carried into the farmhouse. And by then she was close to death.

For a long time she had not spoken. Hours before she had murmured something to her husband about their children, but since then the only sounds he had heard were her quick, uneven breathing and the whimpers of pain. They had stopped the cart on the way to the farm to ask two young peasants standing at the door of a hovel for some soup, but when they had brought it she had had a violent convulsion and could not drink. She had relapsed into unconsciousness and had begun to foam at the mouth. Garibaldi wiped her lips gently.

The doctor from the near-by village of Sant' Angelo arrived at the Guiccioli farm in his cart and Garibaldi said to him desperately, 'For God's sake, try and save her.'

But it was too late. As they carried her up to a bedroom on the mattress that the Guidi brothers had put into the cart, her body shook in a final spasm. When Garibaldi laid her on the bed and looked into her face, he knew that she was dead. He felt her pulse but the veins in her wrist were still. He knelt down and suddenly burst into tears.

For a long time he knelt by her body, unable to control his sobbing, close to hysteria.

'No! No! She isn't dead,' he protested, 'it is just another fit. She has suffered so much, but she will recover. She isn't dead. Anita! Anita! It is impossible. Look at me, Anita! Look at me! Speak to me! Oh, Anita, what have I lost!'[2]

At length, when he grew quieter, Culiolo, who was also in tears, approached him and persuaded him to get away while there was still time. The Austrians were in Sant' Alberto and were bound to come to Mandriole soon. The doctor, and the two Ravaglia brothers who managed the Guiccioli farm, and the Guidi brothers and all the others who had helped him – or, at least, had not betrayed him – were in constant danger so long as he remained there. He knew they were right and that he must go at once; so, having in his own words 'directed the good people to bury the body',* he allowed a guide to

* The farm people obeyed Garibaldi's directions but, in their haste to get the body out of sight before the Austrians arrived, they had not dared to dig too deep. The shallow grave behind the farmhouse was soon excavated by an animal which, gnawing at a hand and forearm, left them protruding from the sand. A farmer's young daughter saw them, and her father called the police whose first suspicion was that they had a murder to investigate. The doctor confirmed this suspicion and, noticing that the eyes protruded, that the tongue was between the teeth and that the trachea was severed, concluded that the woman had died by strangulation. The presence of a six-month foetus in the womb led the police to report, that the body was that 'of a wife or woman who accompanied Garibaldi and who was reported to have landed in this district.

'The woman's height was approximately 1⅔ metres and her age between 30 and 35. The body was stoutish, the hair which had parted from the scalp and lay in the sand was dark, rather long and had been dressed *alla puritana....* The clothes on the body were a chemise of white linen, a petticoat of the same material and a burnous lead himself and Culiolo to Sant' Alberto. As they approached the village they hid in the doctor's cart and were taken to the cottage of a cobbler.[3]

*   *   *

Before dawn on 5 August, Garibaldi and Culiolo left Sant' Alberto for the pine forest north of Ravenna, walking along the bank of the Po di Primaro on a course mapped out for them by Bonnet. In the forest, hiding in the thick undergrowth beneath the juniper trees and the tall slender pines, Garibaldi and Culiolo evaded their pursuers with the help of several 'courageous Romagnoli', as Garibaldi described them, 'mostly young men, untiring in their care for my safety. When they thought me in danger in one place, I used to see them coming up with a cart to remove me to a safer situation many miles distant'.[4] Eventually they moved him and Culiolo out of the forest altogether and took them to a small thatched hut standing isolated on the lonely marsh between the forest and the sea. Then they were taken miles away to Savio between Ravenna and Forlì, and then north again to a suburb of Ravenna where they spent a week moving about from house to house, until Bonnet's friends had made all the arrangements for getting them across the Romagna plain to Forlì, and over the Apennines into Tuscany.

One day in the second week of August they were suddenly woken

of purple cambric with white flowers. The legs and feet were without covering and there were no ornaments on the fingers or neck; the ears, however, were pierced for earrings. The feet do not appear to be those of a person of the peasant class, as there were no callouses on the soles' – Report of the *Direzione generale di Polizia* in Ravenna, q. Guerzoni, i, 367.

The Ravaglia brothers, managers of the Guiccioli farm, were arrested and charged with murder. They were released, however, five days later when evidence was produced to show that Anita Garibaldi had been suffering from a malignant fever when she arrived at Mandriole. The police doctor then changed his mind, decided that death was due to natural causes after all, and that the trachea had been severed after death and probably during the course of burial. This verdict was eventually confirmed by the President of the *Tribunale collegiale* of Ravenna The story was, nevertheless, spread abroad by Garibaldi's enemies that Anita had been strangled and that it was he himself who had murdered her in his anxiety to escape.

up in a farm amongst the rice fields south-west of Ravenna, and told everything at last was ready. A few days later they were far away to the west, driving in an old country cart down the road that leads from Bologna to Florence.*[5]

*   *   *

While travelling along the road to Florence, Garibaldi and Culiolo stopped at a small inn at Santa Lucia for some coffee. The innkeeper's daughter who served them said to Garibaldi, 'The Tuscan and Austrian troops are out looking for you.'

'*What!*' Garibaldi said, 'You know me?' He seemed astonished that she recognised him. But although he had shaved his beard off, she said later that there was no mistaking him.

'You are Garibaldi.'

'When have you seen me before?'

'Don't you remember you came through here last November with your volunteers? It was the day of the fair at Gagliano.'

While waiting for the coffee, Garibaldi fell asleep at the table, his head on his arms. Culiolo woke him by gently tapping his hand. A group of Austrian soldiers had come into the inn and were sitting down at the other end of the long table. It was dark in the room for there were no windows, and the light from the door did not reach the corner where Garibaldi was sitting. But a lantern on the table shone in his face. The soldiers, however, were more interested in the innkeeper's daughter, a girl of twenty, than in the two dirty-looking peasants in the corner; and, while they watched her and spoke to her, Garibaldi had time to lean forward over the lamp,

* Not all those who had left Cesnatico with them were as fortunate. Most had managed to evade the Austrians after their dash across the sand dunes on the Bosco Eliseo; but Ciceruacchio and his two sons, after crossing several of the rivers north of Comacchio and reaching Venetia, were betrayed for the reward offered for their capture and all three were shot in the market square of San Nicolo.

Ugo Bassi, believing himself in no danger of his life since he had not carried firearms, had walked into Comacchio and had gone to bed in an inn. Here he had been arrested by an Austrian patrol and taken with a Garibaldino captain in an open cart to Bologna. General Gorzkowski had here condemned him to death, and, when the sentence had been approved by an ecclesiastical council in the palace of Cardinal Bedini, he and the captain, Livraghi, were taken to a hill outside the city and also shot.

light a cigar, and then turn the light away from him so that his face remained in shadow. He listened to the Austrians talking. The sergeant said to the girl that they were part of the advance-guard of a strong army coming up from the south with orders to find and capture Garibaldi. Garibaldi sat still, smoking his cigar in silence. As soon as the Austrians had left, he and Culiolo left too. They climbed the hill on the other side of the road and watched through a telescope as more troops from the Austrian army passed by the inn below. That night guides came up to them from Santa Lucia and they were taken over the mountains to Cerbaja.[6]

At Cerbaja they entered another inn and again found a friend, this time a young man who was out shooting and had taken shelter there from the rain. This young man advised them not to make for Piedmont by land as they had intended – all the roads were heavily guarded, he said – but to leave it to him to get them to the coast and then by boat to Chiavari. They trusted him, accepted his advice and allowed him to take them when it was dark to Prato, where in a quiet room at the railway station the details of the last part of their journey were discussed.[7]

In the early hours of the morning they were led out of the station and into a narrow side street where a closed carriage was waiting; and by dawn they had crossed the Arno at Empoli. For the whole of that day, 27 August, they continued on their journey in the guise of merchant farmers on their way to enjoy the curative waters of the small health resort of Bagno al Morbo. Whenever the carriage stopped to change horses a crowd of inquisitive onlookers would come to peer through the windows.

> Our halts in some places were rather longer than was absolutely necessary [Garibaldi remembered], some of the drivers being much less careful of us than others [not all of them knew the true identity of their passengers]. In this way time was given to the curious to surround the carriage. . . . In small towns our vehicle was, of course, turned into a sort of pillory by the idlers of the place who offered aloud a thousand conjectures as to who we were, and were naturally disposed to gossip about people whom they did not know. However, nothing took place beyond a few abusive epithets, which, as was to be expected under the circumstances, we pretended not to hear.[8]

So they arrived safely in Bagno al Morbo just before midnight, unrecognised, or at least unbetrayed; and on the morning of 2 September, when all arrangements for their embarkation had been made, they were taken to the Casa Guelfi, a tall, square house near the sea at Follonica, opposite the island of Elba. Here they were welcomed by several patriots who had undertaken to look after them during the last stage of their journey. From the Casa Guelfi, disguised now as sportsmen with double-barrelled shot-guns and dogs, they walked with four guides across the marsh towards the coastguard station of Portiglione, avoiding the station itself by going through a dark, thick forest of evergreens and then coming out on to a little sandy bay from which no buildings could be seen.

Garibaldi ran down to the water's edge, took off his boots and socks, and paddled with unconcealed excitement in the warm water. When the boat that was to carry them away beached on the shore, he and Culiolo stepped into it; and, as it drew away from the land, Garibaldi stood up to face the four men who had guided him from the Casa Cuelfi. They watched him silently. He raised his head and in a loud dramatic voice called out to them an epitaph on his adventure and on the death of the Roman Republic – '*Viva l'Italia!*'[9]

★   ★   ★

Four days later the Minister of the Interior in Turin received a telegram from the Royal Commissioner at Genoa. It read:

> Garibaldi has arrived at Chiavari. I intend to arrest him. What ought I to do? The best thing would be to send him to America.[10]

The Minister replied, 'Send him to America, if he will agree. . . . If he doesn't, arrest him.'[11]

Garibaldi's arrival in Piedmont was an obvious embarrassment to the Government. King Victor Emmanuel and his ministers were still struggling to overcome the consequences of their defeat by the Austrians at Novara. They had saved the integrity of Piedmont and the Constitution that Charles Albert had granted; but they had only been able to do so with the help of France (who had warned Austria not to extend the territories of her empire). Also, they had been forced to withdraw the Piedmontese fleet from Venetian waters, and to abandon for the moment the liberal parties in the rest of

Italy. To welcome Garibaldi as the hero of the hour was therefore, politically, impracticable; to leave him free to be elected to the Assembly in the coming elections unthinkable. And yet to arrest him was bound to arouse the hostility of the people. Indeed, the people's fury when he was, in fact, arrested, profoundly alarmed the Government and made it clear that, for the future, Garibaldi's popular appeal was a factor which could not be disregarded.

The protests were made inside Parliament as well as in the streets. A resolution was proposed that the 'arrest of General Garibaldi and his threatened expulsion from Piedmont are violations of the rights consecrated by statute, of the principles of patriotism and Italian glory'. One deputy, Valerio, in an impassioned speech, declared: 'Imitate his greatness if you can; if you are unable to do so, respect it. Keep this glory of ours in the country; we have none too much.' The resolution was passed by an overwhelming majority. There were four abstentions and only eleven 'noes'.[12]

The Government was compelled to release Garibaldi who was asked to relieve the tension that his arrest had caused by leaving Piedmont of his own accord. Offered a pension which he refused for himself but accepted at the rate of twelve pounds a month for his mother,[13] he agreed to go; and on 11 September he left for Tunis by way of Nice.

He was allowed to stay long enough in Nice to see his mother, now seventy-nine and growing very frail, and his three children. Menotti was nearly nine, Ricciotti two, and Teresa four. The little girl said to him as soon as she saw him, 'Mamma will have told you in Rome how good I was. Where is Mamma?'

This was the moment he had been dreading. 'When I first meet them again,' he had thought when his wife had died, 'they will ask me for their mother.' He held his daughter closer to him, but he could not bring himself to answer her question.[14] He left the two boys in the care of a cousin, and Teresa with the Deideris, and he sailed away for Tunis on board the *Tripoli*.

Tunis, however, would not have him, so he was brought back across the Mediterranean to the island of La Maddalena off the northern coast of Sardinia. After three weeks there he sailed for Gibraltar but the British Governor told him that although, he was, of course, free to go to England where he would be sure of a refuge, he could not remain at Gibraltar for more than fifteen days, since it was not a place for political refugees. He was, as he put it himself, 'cut to the heart'. 'The affection and just gratitude which I have always felt towards that generous nation,' he commented, 'made this proceeding seem all the more discourteous, futile and unworthy.'[15] He thought of going to Spain but asylum there was refused him also; and it was not until he had an invitation from the Piedmontese consul at Tangier that he was assured of a temporary home on the shores of the Mediterranean which he loved, and where he could feel himself not too far away from his children.

He spent seven months in Tangier, walking, fishing, shooting, riding hard until the sweat poured down his skin, gazing out to sea, often alone with the dog which he had brought with him, sometimes with Major Culiolo, who had joined him in his exile, with his host, Giovanni Battista Carpanetti, or with the British consul, Murray. In the evenings he would sit making sails or fishing nets, or even cigars. He began his autobiography, and in writing of his life in South America he found some relief from his loneliness in the memories of past happiness.* He made repeated efforts to return to his seaman's life as a captain in the merchant service; but pressure was brought to bear on those who would have employed him, and he decided to go back to America. He considered the possibility of returning to Montevideo, but on 12 June 1850 he said goodbye to his friends in Tangier and sailed for New York.

---

* This, the first version of his autobiography, was completed in America and published in 1859 in New York, in an English translation by Theodore Dwight, as *The Life of General Garibaldi Written by Himself*.

9

'A PLACE TO SETTLE'

Seven weeks later, on 29 July 1850, Garibaldi arrived in New York aboard the English packet ship *Waterloo*. He had been in great pain from his rheumatism almost throughout the crossing, and had to be carried ashore, so he said, 'like a bale of goods'.

The *New York Tribune* announced the arrival of the 'world-famed' Italian who, according to the *New York Herald*, was 'received with all the ardour of feeling, warmth of welcome, and republican enthusiasm which so peculiarly distinguishes the American character, in the generous and cordial welcome bestowed upon European republicans when driven from the land of their fathers by monarchical tyranny'.

He was asked to attend a banquet to be given in his honour at the Astor House Hotel, but he declined.* He also refused the offer of a home made to him by two American families; and feeling ill and depressed, he went to stay in the house of a fellow Italian in Irving Place. Afterwards he moved to the Pavilion Hotel in Richmond Terrace, Staten Island, then to the house of Antonio Meucci, who employed a number of Italian refugees in a small factory.

Garibaldi settled down with his fellow Italians to lead a new life of exile, quiet and withdrawn. Soberly, not to say sombrely dressed in a dark blue frock coat with a black scarf round his neck, he would sit in a corner of the room, almost forgotten, rarely speaking. Sometimes in the evenings he would go out for a game of bowls or to play dominoes at Ventura's café near the Park Theatre, but more often he stayed at home.[1]

He tried to get work in the Post Office Department but failed; and then, despite the rheumatism which had temporarily disabled his

---

* He pleaded ill health as an excuse. There was another reason behind the refusal, though, apart from his natural distaste for such functions – the strength of the Catholic opposition to any official recognition of his presence in America – Howard Marraro, *American Opinion on the Unification of Italy, 1846–1861* (New York, 1932), 167.

right arm as well as his legs, he went to work in Meucci's candle factory, 'bringing up barrels of tallow for the boiling vat from the old Vanderbilt landing'. But he soon tired of the dreary work and, sickened by the foul smells of the factory, he went down to the Staten Island docks one day to try to find more congenial employment as a sailor. He had learned a little English by now and when he saw some coasting vessels loading and unloading he went up to the nearest and 'asked to be taken on board as a common sailor'. 'The men I saw on the ship scarcely paid any attention to me, and continued their work,' he recalled later. 'I went to the second ship and did the same, with the same result. Finally, I went to a third, where they were busy unloading, and asked to be allowed to help in the work. I was told they did not want me. But I don't want to be paid, I insisted. No reply. . . . I was not wanted. I got the better of my mortification and returned to work at the tallow factory.'[2]

His time there was nearly over, however, for a short time later an old friend, Francesco Carpaneto, arrived in New York and he sailed with him on a business trip to South America. He contracted marsh fever at a Central American port where they called on their way; but by the time he reached Lima at the beginning of October 1851 he was well enough to accept command of the *Carmen*, an old sailing ship which was bound for China.

He would be away for at least a year, and that suited him well. He could see no immediate prospect of a new rising in Italy, and the thought of settling down on the American continent appalled him: 'This is a land in which a man forgets his native country. He acquires a new home and different interests.'*

For two years he sailed round the world with the *Carmen*, taking her to Hong Kong and Canton, to Australia and New Zealand, back to Peru, then round Cape Horn and across the Atlantic again for North America. He was accompanied by Giovanni Basso, a fellow exile whom he had known in the Merchant Service and had come

---

* He had filed his intention of becoming a citizen of the United States; but he could never bring himself to complete the formalities. Nevertheless he afterwards often claimed that he was, in fact, an American citizen – Howard Marraro, 'Unpublished American Documents on Garibaldi's March on Rome in 1867' in *The Journal of Modern History* (June 1944), xvi, 2.

across again in New York, a man who now became his devoted follower and was to remain with him through all the troubles and triumphs of the coming years. But Garibaldi felt lonely and sad, impatient to return to Italy, 'terrified at the likely prospect of never again wielding a sword' in her name. 'I thought distance could diminish the bitterness of my soul,' he wrote to Augusto Vecchi, 'but unfortunately it is not true, and I have led an unhappy life, restless and embittered by memory. Yes, I am athirst for the emancipation of our country. . . . But the Italians of today think of the belly, not of the soul.'[3]

Eventually, in January 1854, he was offered command of a ship, the *Commonwealth*, which would take him back to Europe. She was bound for England, with a cargo for Newcastle, and was then to carry coal to Genoa.

* * *

Garibaldi was welcomed at Newcastle as enthusiastically as he had been at New York. Here also he was offered a public reception, which, as in America, he refused. But he allowed a deputation, including several miners who paraded on the deck in their best suits and hob-nailed boots, to come on board to present him with a sword and a telescope 'purchased by the pennies of some hundreds of working men, contributed not only voluntarily but with enthusiasm'.[4]

In his by now 'tolerably fluent' English but with a strong accent, Garibaldi replied. 'As one of the people – a workman like yourselves – I value very highly these expressions of your esteem . . . Italy will one day be a nation, and its free citizens will know how to acknowledge all the kindness shown her exiled sons in the days of her darkest troubles.' Turning to Joseph Cowen, the leader of the deputation, he added dramatically, 'Should England at any time in a just cause need my arm, I am ready to unsheath in her defence this noble and splendid sword received at your hands.'[5]

It seemed, indeed, for the moment unlikely that he could hope to unsheath it for Italy. 'Many see Italian risings every day,' he had written a few months before. 'I see nothing.'[6] Certainly the recent Mazzinian conspiracy at Mantua and the revolt at Milan had been quickly and thoroughly repressed by the Austrians; and Mazzini himself, now living in London again, had long since been condemned both by the liberals of Europe and the moderates of Italy for refusing to accept the fact that the days of popular insurrection were gone. It might be that his blindly heroic agents, so ferociously punished by the Austrians when their wanton schemes were discovered, were serving to keep anti-Austrian feeling alive; but it was undeniably the case that these agents were arousing as much exasperation as admiration even amongst those who sympathised with their views.

'Garibaldi is here,' Mazzini wrote with irrepressible enthusiasm when he heard of his arrival in London from Newcastle. 'His name is all powerful among the Neapolitans since the Roman affair at Velletri. I want to send him to Sicily, where they are ripe for insurrection.'[7]

Garibaldi, however, was almost as disinclined to embark on what he called 'rash enterprises' as the Piedmontese Government itself. He doubted that Italy as a whole had much taste for the united republic of Mazzini's ideal and he was becoming increasingly convinced, despite his own professed republicanism, that it would be better to work with King Victor Emmanuel. For after all, his concept of a republic could be extended to include any kind of government to which the people consented; since the British people accepted Queen Victoria's Government, he considered that even that could be called republican.

It was a view which hardened during the month that he spent in London where he had an opportunity of talking once more with people who were closely acquainted with Italian affairs and could see them less myopically than Mazzini whose watch, Giuseppe Giusti said, had stopped in 1848.[8]

Some of these people he met at the Arlington Street house of Mrs. Emma Roberts, a rich and clever English widow who became extremely fond of him in what appears to have been a rather possessive and motherly sort of way. Though his feelings were not deeply stirred Garibaldi liked her, too; and one day, in an access more perhaps of loneliness than of love, asked her to marry him. She accepted, though neither of them considered the prospect of an early wedding. Garibaldi's doubts were emphasised by her riches, by the inordinately long time it took to eat dinner in her house where the footmen muddled him with their constant attentions, and by her eldest son who viewed with evident concern his mother's proposed marriage to this poor, melancholy, humbly born Italian.[9] Nevertheless, when Garibaldi obtained permission from the Piedmontese Government to rejoin his family at Nice, Mrs. Roberts and her young companion, Jessie White, the red-haired daughter of a Hampshire ship-builder, went with him. She rented a house where this 'quiet, thoughtful, unpretending gentleman', as Jessie White described him, became a frequent visitor. He did not talk much, but would sit quietly playing draughts or listening to his fiancée playing the piano, although he seemed to enjoy it only when she struck up a patriotic Italian tune. Sometimes when he was expected for dinner he would not appear at all, and hours later he would be found playing bowls 'in his shirt sleeves with some of the other *rompicolli di Nizza*'.[10] He seemed quite content to lead the quiet, simple, regular, unadventurous life he had led in Tangier before his departure for America. 'He will never begin anything himself,' Mazzini decided with some scorn. 'He needs to be presented with means already organised by others. He will follow the republicans if we act first, or the monarchists if they do so.' At the time it was close to the truth.

Occasionally he sailed along the coast in command of a small trading vessel; but the voyages were short, and most of the time he spent ashore living with Giovanni Basso in a little house by the Lazzaretto belonging to his cousin. Once he spent a month on holiday with Emma Roberts and Jessie White in Sardinia, where he spent much of the time shooting, killing hundreds of birds in a single day, or going on boar hunts; and a man who came across him then noticed how sad he seemed and how resigned.

His mother had died two years before while he was sailing across the Pacific to China, and on the night of her death he had dreamed of her lying on her bier and had tried to approach her, but he could not move. He had sent her his savings while he was away, asking her to keep them for the children, and since her death he had sent what he could to his cousin for them.

Menotti, now fourteen, was attending a military college; Teresa, ten, was still staying with the Deideris where he visited her each day; Ricciotti, eight, lived with him, and every morning when he was in Nice he would take the little boy from his bed and wash him under the pump with the same determination and thoroughness he employed when washing himself. In the afternoons he helped him improve his writing, making him go carefully in ink over the letters he drew for him in pencil in his own round clear hand. He believed the cultivation of an immediately legible script important and he was always prejudiced against those whose writing was untidy or difficult to read.

In the mornings he would get up at dawn and go down to the sea to fish, or climb up into the hills to shoot partridges as he had done when he was a boy, sometimes taking Giovanni Basso with him. And up there high above Nice he would tell Basso how he looked forward to having a small place of his own, far away from the world, where he could do as he liked. He did not know when he would be able to afford it, though, for he had never been able to save much from his earnings as a sea-captain. In the autumn of 1855, however, his brother Felice died, leaving him 35,000 lire. He said goodbye to Mrs. Roberts, whom he had perhaps already ceased to regard as a possible wife – though he saw her again the next year on a second visit to London and they remained good friends for the rest of her life – and he sailed away to find a new home and a piece of land to farm.

He went to Sardinia 'to traverse the Gallura where,' he wrote, 'I think it will be possible to choose a place to settle, either to pass some of the spring months there, or perhaps to stay permanently if I find something suitable.'[11]

He did not find anything suitable on the mainland, but at the end of December he discovered what he was looking for in the lonely little island of Caprera. It was a wild and rugged place, four miles by three, off the coast of the larger island of La Maddalena. It was covered with rock rose and lentisk, tamarisk and asphodel, juniper and myrtle, with uneven patches of smooth grass and groups of wild stunted olive trees, its rough surface broken everywhere by grey rocks. The sparse scraps of thin powdery soil had never tempted farmers to settle there, and the only permanent inhabitants were the wild goats from which the island got its name and three or four goatherds, one of whom, Battista Ferraciolo, descendant of an early-eighteenth-century bandit, agreed to sell Garibaldi part of the land that his ancestor had acquired on the northern half of the island. Ferraciolo's neighbour was a cantankerous Englishman named Collins, a man of perverse and aggravating eccentricities of behaviour with a charming and loyal English wife who was rumoured to have formerly employed him as a groom. But the Collinses, who lived in a villa on La Maddalena, rarely visited their property, leaving it to be managed by a goatherd, and so, like Ferraciolo, they were prepared to sell enough of it to allow Garibaldi, for the total price of £360, to become the owner of most of the northern half of the island.

Garibaldi moved into his land in the spring of 1856, taking Basso and Menotti with him. The nights they spent in a tent made out of an old sail which was frequently carried away by the fierce wind that springs so suddenly from the sea around Caprera to howl across the rocks, cutting the tender tops off the juniper bushes; the days were employed in building a little wooden house for Teresa and in trying to pick out from between the granite enough soil for a garden, a cornfield, an olive-yard and a vegetable patch. The wooden house was finished by the summer, but by then Garibaldi had come to realise that it would be years before he could make a farm out of that stubborn, stone-filled unresponsive earth; and perhaps, he sometimes feared, he never could. Eventually, however, he managed to grow some vines and figs, chestnuts and sugar canes as well as potatoes and beans. It was hard work, of course, and when the goats jumped over the dry stone walls with which he enclosed the cultivated spaces, and trampled down the stalks and ate whatever appealed to their voracious appetites, it all seemed scarcely worth while. And there was constant difficulty, too, with Collins who, infuriated by reports that the Garibaldi animals wandered on to his land to eat his grass, told his goatherd to take no trouble to ensure that his own animals did not stray over the boundary to eat some of the General's. Garibaldi finally decided to build a stone wall right across the island; but the animals still seemed to manage to find a way through.

At least, his own animals survived. They were mostly goats, a good strong breed brought over from Malta, a few sheep and donkeys and four or five cows; and later there were poultry and bees. He was going to be happy there, he told a visitor, and the constant struggle against the rock and the unremitting effort to fulfil the needs of the animals provided him with the sort of physical and emotional challenge for which he yearned.

When the wooden house was finished, work began on a more permanent house of stone. This, Garibaldi decided, was to be a handsome place with few but spacious rooms, tall windows and a flat roof, in the style of those South American farmhouses he had admired in his youth. By the autumn of 1857, helped by various friends who came to stay on the island with him from time to time, and by a mason and carpenter who had to go over his inexpert work and patch it up, Garibaldi had made part at least of it habitable, and he moved in with a maidservant, Battistina Ravello, a small, plain, swarthy young woman, a fisherman's daughter from Nice.

He was visited at this time by another woman, no less plain but far more sophisticated, whose equivocal relationship with him was an irksome tie which they were both on later occasions to regret. She was Maria Espérance, Baroness von Schwartz, a rich romantic novelist and travel-writer of twenty six, who had sailed to La Maddalena in the hope of obtaining permission to translate Garibaldi's memoirs into German.* Her father was a banker from Hamburg, but because she had been born in London where her father had settled, spoke English fluently and had an English passport, she liked to consider herself a 'delicate fair-haired daughter of England'. She had been twice married – her first husband had committed suicide; and three years before her visit to Caprera she had divorced her second. She was now living alone, a cosmopolitan, neurotic woman, clever, touchy and opinionated, but physically appealing.

Garibaldi was immediately and strongly attracted to her, and she to him. 'He immediately inspired me with such confidence,' she wrote afterwards, 'that it was as if I were meeting an old friend.' He

---

* These were eventually published in Hamburg in 1861. They contain variations both from the autobiography published in New York in 1859 and from the. French version edited by Alexandre Dumas and published in Brussels in 1860. Both Mme Schwartz and Dumas – also Franceso Carrano whose *Cacciatori delle Alpi* (Turin, 1860) was largely based on the same manuscript – had permission to modify the memoirs after discussions with Garibaldi.

Mme Schwartz used the pen-name of Elpis Melena – a literal translation into Greek of Espérance (Hope) Schwartz (Black).

asked her to stay with him; but she demurred, saying that she could not give him the trouble, that she would stay in the inn at La Maddalena, but would visit him the following day.

Early next morning Garibaldi crossed the choppy water that divided his island from La Maddalena in his little sailing boat and went up to the inn. Despite the rough seas, Mme von Schwartz agreed to accompany him back to Caprera and she returned with him to the harbour wall. It was kind of him to spare the time to come for her, she said, when they were in the dinghy. 'I have plenty of leisure,' he said. 'At the moment I am at war with nothing but stones. Look at the consequences. My hands are those of a labourer, aren't they?'

She could see his house from the sea – 'a white house against the granite cliff'. It stood high, a quarter of a mile from the water's edge, with an enclosed parterre in front. The rough path that led up to it was bounded by lentisk and arbutus, myrtle, heather and all sorts of aromatic shrubs growing in profusion amongst the rocks. 'There is sublimity here,' she thought, 'as though nature had predestined for the Cincinnatus of our age a solitude in harmony with his character.'

As they approached the house, the General's dogs ran out, barking excitedly as they bounded up to him. She noticed, as other visitors were later to notice, how strong was his affinity with these and all his animals. They were allowed to roam at will around the island and no one was allowed to use a stick on them, however stubborn they might be. All the cows had names and one day one of them, Brunetta, was 'seen coming down the hill. The General fetched some linseed cake, broke it and offered her a piece. The creature refused it but licked his hand like a dog. She had just calved and had brought her child to show it to him and when he had tenderly patted the little thing its mother ate the cake'.[12]

The donkeys also had names and most of these were christened by Giovanni Fruscianti, an odd, disrespectful but faithful servant who had fought under Garibaldi in 1849 and who, in memory of that year, had decided to call the two ugliest donkeys 'Pio Nono' and 'Antonelli'. Fruscianti lived with the family and had his meals with them. 'He hoes potatoes with me,' Garibaldi used to say, 'so why shouldn't he eat them with me?'[13]

It was not so much the presence of the rough labourer that embarrassed Mme Schwartz, however, as the behaviour of the maidservant, Battistina Ravello, whose relationship with the General she delicately described as 'not altogether straightforward'. 'She had no personal charms,' Mme Schwartz added, 'for she was small and rather ugly. She sat with us at table, and whenever the General showed me any particular attention, fell into a passion which she had difficulty in dissimulating. On these occasions she disdainfully refused to eat and drink; and Garibaldi's own discomfiture and conduct showed me clearly how matters stood.'

But the children were pleasant and well mannered – Menotti by now a 'young Hercules whose frank countenance and manly bearing' she confessed immediately excited her admiration, and Teresa 'a beautiful girl' with an olive complexion, dark chestnut eyes, fair hair and a 'supple vigour of movement' who was dressed up for the occasion of the German lady's visit in her best white piqué jacket and a muslin petticoat. And after the meal she was able to spend several hours alone with the General walking over his wild and beautiful land, and getting to know him so intimately that after her return to Rome he was able to ask her:

> How can I possibly convey to you all the gratitude and affection you deserve? If ever I wanted to lay all that I am and all that I have at the feet of a woman it is certainly now. . . . I am really happy and proud to occupy the thoughts, even for one moment, of so dear, so tender, so noble a woman.[14]

Their correspondence continued throughout the winter, maintaining, on Mme Schwartz's part, the emotional tone upon which Garibaldi had opened it.

> I hope [she wrote in January 1858], that the future will prove the sincerity of all my protestations of affection, of admiration and indeed, of adoration. . . . I beg you to continue to call me 'My Speranza, my Hope', because I am always that, and always want to be that. . . . My heart, my head, my mind, and my soul is full of you, because you are so much above every other man. . . . Farewell, my dearest friend. Don't forget me! Above all, don't forget the living and profound affection which the extinction of life itself will never quell, from her, who is with her whole heart, your, your, your Speranza.[15]

They met again in August that year when Speranza paid her second visit to Caprera. Garibaldi had promised to meet her at La Maddalena when the steamer from Genoa came into the harbour on its monthly trip to the island. He was waiting on the quay as the ship steamed in and he took her back to the house. It was as bare and sparsely furnished as ever; and the room to which she was shown had nothing in it but a table, a chair and a very hard bed with a yellow-and-white counterpane. There were no curtains or blinds at the open windows through which the General's cows stared at her with blank incuriosity.

Battistina was still there, sulky and distrustful; and Fruscianti with his strange manners and blunt talk. But Speranza was happy when she was out of the house, walking with her 'dearest friend' who looked so 'remarkably picturesque' with his poncho slung over his shoulders despite the heat of the August sun, listening to him as he talked to her about the wild life of his island, watching him bathe in the sea. One day while they were out walking, Garibaldi startled her by a sudden and, so she later maintained, unexpected question.

> We were on our way back to the house [she wrote], when he asked me to go more slowly as he wished to ask me something while we were alone together. We passed under the shade of a luxuriant fig tree. Garibaldi asked me whether or not I could decide to join my fate to his, and take the place of his Anita, by being a second mother to his children. A thunderbolt could not have startled me more than this overture, and I could only express the profoundest gratitude for the honour he did me, with, at the same time, an assurance that I would give serious thought to his proposal.
>
> We continued on our way home until we were in the vicinity of the house, when Garibaldi withdrew from mine the arm he had silently offered me a little while previously, and said, 'The women of the house are very fond of observing everything through a telescope.'
>
> Now Teresa and the maidservant, Battistina, were the only females on the whole island.[16]

Battistina was more than his maidservant, of course; she was his mistress. He did not love her – indeed, according to one of his officers, he never held her or any woman in his arms without dreaming of the dead Anita[17] – but he was a man with an urgent and impulsive sexual appetite, who believed in the free love preached by the Saint-Simonians of his youth. And Battistina had been ready to indulge him.

He saw no reason now to deny himself the pleasures of her body because he had found another woman who would make him a more suitable wife and a better mother for his adolescent children. Nor did he feel his obligations to his mistress need prevent him from making love to Speranza. 'How can I express all my love and gratitude?' he wrote to her after she had gone back to Rome. 'I can only say again that I am the happiest man in the world. This little room from which I write is dear to me since you shared it.'*[18]

Nine months after this letter to Speranza was written, Battistina gave birth to his fourth child.

*　　*　　*

Garibaldi, however, did not impart the news of Battistina's pregnancy to Rome; and the more matter-of-fact tone of his subsequent letters to Speranza was not due, he protested, to any desire on his part to make them less intimate but to a fear that they might be opened by others before she read them. They continued to discuss the arrangements for a trip to South America together which had been planned the previous year; and in a letter written in January 1859, in reply to one from Speranza which informed him that she had been ill, he wrote to say: 'How I long to be there to take care of you. We shall have to postpone our trip. But as soon as you let me know that you are fit, I will give you our departure date.'[19]

By then, however, plans had been made for his departure in a different direction and for a quite different purpose.

* In this letter, as in all those he wrote to her, he used the form of address *voi*. He reserved the use of *tu* for his children and for conversation with his oldest and closest friends. The only person he was ever heard to address with *Lei* was the King.

10

'VIVA LA FRANCIA!'

When Garibaldi sailed home to Nice from America one of the few deputies who had voted against the proposition that his arrest in 1849 was a violation of his rights, had become Prime Minister. This man was Count Camillo Benso di Cavour.

Cavour had been born in 1810, the younger son of the Marquis Michele, a member of the old Piedmontese feudal aristocracy. At the age of ten he had been sent to the military academy at Turin, and at the age of sixteen he received a commission which he held for five years. He did not like the army, though, and in 1831 he left it. Already he had developed strong liberal tendencies and had been led to believe, both by the July Revolution of 1830 in France and by his study of the British Constitution, that a monarchy need not necessarily be opposed to them. But prevented for the time being from taking any active part in politics by the repressive policies of the Piedmontese Government, he devoted himself to his father's estate at Leri.

The emotions aroused by the election of Pope Pius IX in 1847, however, had brought him for the first time into public notice. To publicise his ideas – first for constitutional reform in Piedmont, and then for war with Austria – he had founded a newspaper in Turin which he called *Il Risorgimento*. After the declaration of war, he had been elected to parliament; but, as a moderate liberal in a struggle between reactionaries and conspirators, he had made little impact. Gradually, however, his great gifts had been recognised and his ideas and influence had begun to spread. In October 1850, to keep him out of opposition, he had been offered the Ministry of Agriculture by Massimo d'Azeglio, who was at that time Prime Minister. Indeed, so strong had Cavour's influence become by then that for three days he remained in a state of 'painful hesitation' between the alternatives of 'joining the Ministry or of bringing it down'.

'Now I believe that this latter alternative,' he had told his bailiff at Leri, in whom he confided more than he felt able to do in those friends in public life who might betray his confidences, 'though it might have been more satisfying to the *amour propre* of its author, would have been highly detrimental to the interests of the country. In doing so I really believe that I am sacrificing a part, if not all, of my future to a sense of duty.'

It was not only the 'gravity of the country's situation' that had decided him, he added, not only the 'more than friendly explanations of d'Azeglio,' but also 'the pressure of the King'.[1]

King Victor Emmanuel and he had almost nothing in common, except a taste for country life; though even in this, whereas the King had an appropriately well-developed taste for shooting, Cavour did not bother with the snipe that swarmed in the ricefields at Leri.

Victor Emmanuel was a squat man with enormously strong, thick legs and an immense moustache which swept up towards his little, grey eyes in a ferociously intimidating crescent. He was untidy in his dress, blunt in his speech, coarse in his habits, with a passion for hunting and violent exercise, and the suspicious piety of a brigand. He detested official banquets, and an English observer once saw him sit through one without even removing the napkin from his plate. For more than an hour he 'neither tasted a morsel of food nor took a drop of water to drink but sat like a statue of marble, with both hands resting on the hilt of his sword'.[2] For his meals he preferred to eat huge peasant dishes of steaming ragout smothered in garlic and hot onions. His appetite for women – particularly for strong, wanton women like his mistress the Countess Rosina di Mirafiori – was equally voracious and untamed.

'The King appears to have lived more in camps than in courts,' the old Countess Damrémont observed after he had paid a visit to Paris. 'When writing to compliment the Empress, he said that *in her presence he suffered the tortures of Tantalus;* to Princess Mathilda that *she set him aflame;* that he had expected to be received behind *closed doors,* and that the open curtains *embarrassed him prodigiously.* One day in the Empress's circle he went straight up to Madame de Malaret, a lady-in-waiting, and said, "Good day, Madame. I like French-women, and have observed since my sojourn that they dress differently from the ladies of Turin. Here the approaches to Paradise are open."'

According to Lord Cowley, the British Ambassador, he was even more explicit with Madame Mallant. '*Il y a une bonne chose qui j'ai découverte à Paris. Les Parisiennes ne portent pas de caleçons. C'est un ciel d'azur qui s'est ouvert à mes yeux!*'

To Madame Walewska, next whom he sat at dinner, he said, contemplating her magnificent bosom, 'Oh, what a beautiful woman you are! Oh, I do love women.'[3]

During a performance at the Opéra, his eye alighted on a particularly attractive dancer and he turned to whisper in Louis Napoleon's ear, 'What is the price of that little girl?'

The Emperor said he did not know, so Baciocchi, the *maître de plaisir*, was consulted. Baciocchi, said, '5,000 francs' which Victor Emmanuel thought 'rather a lot' until his host – who confessed that he could not control his own sexual desires – said, 'Charge her up to me.'[4]

The activities of this irrepressible 'royal buffoon' with his fierce, half-defiant look and his handshake like the hard, rough clasp of a giant, were reported at length by Lord Cowley to London where his forthcoming visit was regarded with apprehension. To everyone's surprise, however, the English took to him. To be sure Charles Greville, unlikely to be drawn to so blunt and *outré* a personality, found him 'frightful in his person, a great, strong, burly, athletic man, brusque in his manners, unrefined in his conversation, very loose in his conduct, very eccentric in his habits'.[5] But the Queen was enchanted by him. He seemed like a bizarre relic of a bygone age when he told her 'he did not like the business of King and would much rather just be a soldier and go to war'. Proudly he showed the Prince of Wales his sword which could cut an ox in half at a single blow; and the Duchess of Sutherland felt sure he had the strength to wield it to this purpose. To her he seemed the only Knight of the Garter she had ever seen who 'looked as if he would have the best of it with the dragon'.[6]

To such a man, soon to be called the 'last of the conquerors',[7] the shrewd, calculating, devious and brilliant personality of Cavour could not be expected to make much appeal. But despite his excessive pride in his descent and in his coat of arms, despite his professed dislike of the limitations imposed upon his activities by the constitutional system, and his repeated irresponsible efforts to circumvent it, Victor Emmanuel was prepared to act as though he were a constitutional monarch; for he saw in Cavour the one man who could raise him in this capacity to the throne of a greatly extended Piedmont. And he was astute enough to understand well that he had no choice between rising to that eminence and falling to become plain 'Monsu Savoia'.[8]

Cavour's perseverance and skill in manipulating men and situations to his own ends, his instinctive flair for recognising the crucial and decisive moment after long periods of patient waiting, his cunning, not to say, unscrupulous opportunism, so carefully concealed behind the comfortable, frank, beard-fringed face and the small spectacles of a far less astute master of expediency, were all, at least in part, recognised by the King and valued by him. The contradictory complexities of Cavour's nature, his strong emotionalism, his romantic attitude towards women, his sometimes explosive passion, his willingness to take a sudden and unexpected risk, were either misunderstood or mistrusted; while the measures he took against religious orders and ecclesiastical properties, involving as they did a quarrel between Piedmont and the Papal Court, almost resulted in his dismissal. But Victor Emmanuel knew that in the last resort Cavour would always play his cards (which d'Azeglio said he kept permanently hidden in his sleeve) in the interests of the Kingdom of Piedmont with which his own ambitions were so closely allied.

Both men understood that their shared future depended upon the acceptance by the democratic and republican elements in Piedmont that an alliance with the monarchy and with France was their only hope of driving Austria from Italy. Both men understood, too, that only Cavour possessed the manipulative skill necessary to bring so improbable an alliance into existence, the right balance between the theories of liberalism and the practices of *Machiavellismo*; and it was, of course, this jealous recognition by the King of the greater subtlety of the man in whose company he never felt quite at ease which increased his personal dislike of him. Any fool, Cavour would say, could govern by force, as the King would like to have done; it took a statesman to govern by arrangement.

Cavour was helped towards his arrangement by two remarkable men: the Marquis Giorgio Pallavicino Trivulzio and Daniele Manin. Pallavicino was a rich Lombard who lived in Turin, an aristocrat who thought of himself as a democrat, a republican who wanted, in his own words, 'even more than the republic, *Italy*!' 'Republicans of Italy,' he entreated them, 'be Italians!'[9]

'To defeat cannon and soldiers,' he insisted, 'cannon and soldiers are needed. Arms are needed and not Mazzinian pratings. Piedmont has soldiers and cannon. Therefore, I am Piedmontese. . . . First I want to live; about living well, I will think later.'[10]

He was persuasive, determined and influential. Men listened to him, Vincenzo Gioberti responded to him, and wrote *Del Rinnovamento civile d'Italia* in support of his ideas for a resurgent Piedmont.* Daniele Manin responded to him and announced that the republican party should commit 'a new act of abnegation and sacrifice to the national cause. . . . I, a republican, plant this unifying standard'.[11]

From the alliance of these men a new national party was formed – a party dedicated to independence and unification and, eventually, to what it considered to be its greatest achievement – 'the marriage of the Italian insurrection to the army of Piedmont'.[12]

It was an essentially practical party believing, as one of its leading members put it, that 'in practical politics the impossible is immoral',[13] and that to be an effective force its appeal must range widely, capable of attracting such disparate men as Giuseppe La Farina (the Sicilian revolutionary who had once been Mazzini's principal agent in Paris and was now one of Cavour's most enthusiastic supporters), and Garibaldi himself.

'The adherence of Garibaldi to our principles is an event of immense importance,' Pallavicino told Manin, 'we must make the most of it. It secures for us the sympathies and, when required, the active assistance of all the youth of Italy.'[14]

Cavour, too, was anxious to secure the support of Garibaldi. The *'bravo guerriglero'* was known to have a personal regard for Victor Emmanuel and a personal dislike, aggravated by jealousy, of Mazzini. He was known to share Pallavicino's disdain of Mazzini's ill-planned and ill-executed insurrections, and to have a Saint-Simonian belief in the advantages of a popular national leader, the sort of

* It was noted at the time how attentively the King read this book and 'this seemed important, for reading books was not one of his usual occupations' – Luigi Salvatorelli, *Pensiero e azione del Risorgimento'* (Einaudi, Turin, 1960), 143.

benevolent *duce* that Victor Emmanuel might turn out to be. But Cavour knew him also to be a touchy, stubborn man with strange illogical ideas, a man who would need careful handling. When they met for the first time in August 1856, however, Cavour found him less difficult and suspicious than he had supposed, and soon succeeded in convincing him that he was, as Garibaldi himself confidently believed, 'his friend', and that they must work together for the good of Piedmont.

A year after this interview took place the national party, whose leadership had slipped from the hands of the sick Pallavicino and the dying Manin into those of La Farina, formed the *Società Nazionale Italiana*. Garibaldi was offered and accepted an honorary post as vice-president. And it was, thereafter, through this Italian National Society that the subsequent meetings between Garibaldi and Cavour were arranged, usually by La Farina, the Society's increasingly powerful Secretary.

The relationship between Cavour and the National Society had, of course, to be kept secret, for Louis Napoleon, whose help against Austria Cavour was striving to obtain, would interpret its policy as being directed – as indeed it was directed – not only against Austria but against the Pope, whom France protected, and against Ferdinand II of Naples, whose throne the French Emperor wanted for Lucien, the son of Joachim Murat, his uncle's brother-in-law.

The exact nature of the understanding between Cavour and La Farina is a matter still open to conjecture. It is traditionally supposed that it amounted, in fact, to a complete conspiratorial co-operation, though the evidence is circumstantial and not entirely convincing. What is at least certain is that Cavour knew, as he put it himself, that it was 'useful to make use' of the Society, just as it was useful to make use of Garibaldi.[15] And so although it was in the interests of La Farina, an ambitious man and an astute politician, to present himself as Cavour's close confidant,[16] La Farina's account of their first interview has, as Adolfo Omodeo observed, all the elements of *attentabilità*.[17]

This interview took place 'two or three hours before dawn' in Cavour's house in Turin. Cavour, so La Farina later said, expressed his faith in the ultimate possibility of Italian unity – though he had previously suggested that Manin's faith in it was nothing but 'foolishness',[18] and now warned La Farina that he doubted if the Italians were ready for it. 'Remember,' he continued, 'that among my political friends no one believes the enterprise possible, and that haste would compromise me and the cause. Come to see me whenever you like, but come at daybreak, and let no one else see or know.' If I am questioned in Parliament or by diplomats, I shall deny you, like Peter, and say, "I know him not".'[19]

Nothing must come in the way of Cavour's obtaining the help of France for his designs on Austria. He had taken Piedmont to war in the Crimea so that he could bring up the question of Austrian influence in Italy at the peace conference; he had urged his eighteen-year-old cousin, the beautiful and excitingly sensual Countess of Castiglione, to go to live in Paris and seduce the Emperor; he had spent and was continuing to spend large sums of money on getting Italian nationalist propaganda into French newspapers. But he had not yet persuaded Louis Napoleon to move to Piedmont's help. Intervention in the Crimean War had been justified, and the Italian question had been raised at the Congress of Paris. The Countess of Castiglione, 'Notre Dame de Cavour' (who had obligingly gone to bed with King Victor Emmanuel shortly before she left Turin for Paris), had succeeded in becoming Louis Napoleon's first *maîtresse-en-titre* and had patriotically carried out Cavour's instructions of filling the Emperor's mind with the problems of her previous royal lover. But although he listened sympathetically the Emperor gave no indication that he was ready yet to go to war or, indeed, that he would ever go to war. And in any event, what Lord Cowley, the British Ambassador, referred to as the 'decided liaison' between the Emperor and the 'beauteous Castiglione' soon drew to an end. For in the early hours of one morning in April 1857, as the Emperor climbed into his carriage outside the Countess's house in the Avenue Montaigne, three men ran out of the shadows and grabbed hold of the horses. The coachman had a struggle to beat the men off with his whip and drive away to the Tuileries. Next day three Italians were arrested and one of them confessed that he was acting on instructions from Mazzini. Shortly afterwards the Countess was advised to go home. Her indiscretions, and what the Emperor condemned as her constant need to be 'talked about', had ended her brief career.[20]

Louis Napoleon could not free himself so easily, however, from the indiscretions of the Mazzinians. Nine months after the attempt made outside the house in the Avenue Montaigne, three bombs were thrown at the royal carriage as it drove under the canopy outside the Opera. Ten people were killed and 140 wounded. A group of men ran forward to wrench open the doors of the splintered carriage and the Empress feared that they had come to finish with their daggers what their bombs had failed to do. But they were police agents. She climbed down calmly into the street, her left eyelid bleeding from a slight cut, and said 'Don't bother about us. Such things are our profession. Look after the wounded.' The Emperor, very agitated, seemed to want to turn back and see to the wounded himself; but his wife firmly led him into the foyer, whispering '*Pas si bête!*'[21]

Cavour was horrified. 'Let us only hope,' he prayed apprehensively, 'that this is not the work of Italians.'[22] But he felt in his heart that it must be. The Paris police were informed that a Mr. Alsop, a brewer's representative who had recently come to France from London by way of Brussels, would be able to help them. The man confessed that his English passport was not his, and that his real name was Felice Orsini. He had been a disciple of Mazzini with whom he had recently quarrelled. He believed that only Louis Napoleon stood in the way of a French attack on Austria. He lived long enough to see that he was wrong.

For the Emperor allowed Orsini's trial to be conducted as though it were a platform for Italian propaganda. Louis Napoleon's enemies naturally attributed his reaction to fear. Certainly he appeared far more shaken after the bombing than the Empress, and in an upsurge of the sort of rage that comes from fear he wrote a furious letter to Victor Emmanuel demanding the expulsion of the hundreds of emigrants who had flocked to Piedmont from other parts of Italy, and the suppression of the democratic press, especially the Mazzinian *L'Italia e Popolo* of Genoa.*

---

* Cavour replied that he could not suppress *L'Italia e Popolo* legally and to do so illegally would be very dangerous 'in the present circumstances'. He solved his problem in a characteristic way: he promised that it would be confiscated and prosecuted any number of times, even if it had to be absolved each time. The Prefect of Genoa was told to open 'a war to the death' against the paper, to

What was Napoleon up to now? Victor Emmanuel angrily demanded when he got the letter, cursing him with familiar crudity as an upstart and a parvenu. His written reply, though more dignified, was no less firm. His house, he reminded Napoleon, had 'carried its head high for 850 years'. No one would make him lower it. The Emperor had no right to treat him in this fashion. He wanted nothing but to be his friend.[23]

When he received this unaccommodating reply, Napoleon was feeling less overwrought.

'That's what I call courage,' he said when the Piedmontese Ambassador read the protest to him. 'Your King's a fine fellow. I like his letter.'[24]

The Emperor could find it in his heart to like Orsini too, to be moved by the brave self-sacrifice of a conspirator such as he himself had been many years before, and to believe that Orsini's plot had been a sign that the decisive moment for him to act for Italy had come. It was as though his former doubts and confused speculations, concealed as always behind an atmosphere of contrived mystery, had suddenly been dispelled by a brilliant vision of his ordained path. So when this would-be assassin wrote to him passionately appealing to him to help free his country from Austria, he not only permitted the letter to be read out aloud at the trial but caused it to be printed in the Piedmontese as well as in the French press. He would even have liked to reprieve Orsini; but when he suggested this course to Lord Cowley, the British Ambassador said that it 'would be construed as weakness and have the very worst effect'.

Napoleon was 'regularly bitten with this miscreant', Lord Cowley thought.[25] He had always remained a conspirator himself at heart and in Mazzini, Orsini's former master and his own antagonist, he recognised a fellow spirit, a man who represented one of his most troublesome preoccupations, yet whose dreams had curious affinities with his own. But he took the diplomat's advice; the 'miscreant' was executed on 13 March, shouting to the spectators before his head rolled into the basket, *'Viva l'Italia! Viva la Francia!'*[26]

confiscate it almost daily, 'even if the procedure seems scarcely legitimate'. The method worked: although the jury always acquitted it, the paper was eventually compelled to cease publication – Gaetano Salvemini, *Scritti sul Risorgimento* (ed. Piero Pieri and Carlo Pischedda) (Feltrinelli, 2nd ed. 1963), 17–18.

And so the bombs of Orsini which had so alarmed Cavour two months before had worked in the end to give him the opportunity he had been striving for. On 21 July 1858 he crossed the French frontier, wearing dark glasses and carrying a passport in the name of Giuseppe Benso, and met the Emperor at Plombières. And as the two men drove about in a phaeton in the hot sun they decided the fate of Italy.

Some excuse for war should be found and then 200,000 French and 100,000 Piedmontese troops would invade Lombardy and drive the Austrians out of Italy. Italy would then become a federation of allied states, as Gioberti had proposed, under the apparent leadership of the Pope and the actual protection of France. The Kingdom of North Italy would include Piedmont, Lombardy, Venetia and the Papal States east of the Apennines; Central Italy would be formed out of Tuscany and Umbria; the Pope would retain Rome; and the Kingdom of Naples would be reformed or else handed over to Lucien Murat. Victor Emmanuel would be asked to give his daughter, Clothilde, in marriage to the Emperor's cousin Prince Jerome. Savoy and Nice would be ceded to France.

The matter-of-fact, calculated simplicity of it all made it seem not merely practicable but almost ordained. There were serious difficulties in its execution, though, as Cavour well knew. Would the Pope agree to give up his temporal power in exchange for the rather nebulous title that was to be offered him? It soon appeared that he would not. Could the finances of Piedmont support so expensive a venture as a full-scale war? They could scarcely be expected to, without the help of the Rothschilds. Would the fifteen-year-old Princess Clothilde agree to marry Prince Jerome, the unattractive 'Plon-Plon', a fat and pompous satyr who was rumoured to horse-whip his mistresses and who was older than her father? She would surely not welcome the suggestion. And, indeed, when it was made to the poor girl she burst into tears.

This marriage was an important part of the secret pact, for the Emperor was not only concerned to link his family with so old and venerated a royal house, but he also envisaged a day when his cousin, with such a wife, might occupy the throne of the projected state of Central Italy. The reluctance of the Princess to oblige him and her father made him inclined to suggest that without a marriage there would be no war, and made Victor Emmanuel disinclined to order his daughter to marry a man she found so repulsive. She had not met him yet, though, her father reminded her, and perhaps when she did she would not find him so impossible after all. At length, to Cavour's intense relief, the Princess gave way. She told her father that she would agree to meet Prince Jerome and that if she did not find him actually repellent she would marry him. The marriage took place at Turin Cathedral on 30 January 1859.

Lord Cowley was disgusted. 'When one sees this child sacrificed, for it is nothing else, to the ambition of her father and Cavour what can one think of such men?' he asked after the Prince had taken his bride back to Paris. 'It is positively horrible to see that poor frail creature by the side of that brute (I can call him nothing else) to whom she has been immolated!'[27] It was a common enough opinion.

But Cavour could comfort himself that, although it was excessively unpopular both in Italy and abroad, the marriage had at least taken place; and on that issue, anyway, the Emperor was satisfied. By now, though, there were other problems.

A few weeks before the marriage, Louis Napoleon had said to the Austrian Ambassador in the hearing of all the other ambassadors in Paris, 'I regret that our relations are not so good as in the past'. And ten days later Victor Emmanuel had opened Parliament in Turin with a speech in which he referred to the '*grido di dolore*' – a phrase suggested by the French Emperor himself – 'the cry of pain' that came to him 'from so many parts of Italy'.

These two statements were taken as bearing only one interpretation: France and Piedmont were plotting a war against Austria. On 4 February an inspired pamphlet bearing the title *Napoleon III et Italie* appeared in the Paris bookshops and mentioned this war as a distinct possibility, thus increasing the growing concern with which the prospect of such a war was viewed all over Europe, and in particular by the English Conservative Government.

In England, Lord Malmesbury, the Foreign Secretary, referred privately to Piedmont as a 'mischievous, conceited little state' and professed that he thought it intolerable that 'Europe should be deluged with blood for the personal ambition of an Italian attorney and a tambour major, like Cavour and his master.'[28] The distasteful marriage that had seemed to be a prelude to this coming war, together with the fear that the war would, in its turn, be a prelude to a new era of Napoleonic conquest, had led to a cooling of enthusiasm for Italian nationalism throughout the country. Queen Victoria wrote that the conduct of the French Emperor and the Piedmontese King, with both of whom she had earlier felt herself to be on such good terms, produced 'universal indignation amongst all right-thinking people here'; and she believed, with due cause, that although English people generally liked the idea of Italian independence, they disapproved of the Emperor of the French attacking another Empire 'without rhyme or reason'.[29]

Elsewhere in Europe the fear that the war would endanger the Pope had roused the Catholics to determined protest; and with such powerful opposition raised against him, Napoleon began to back away from the undertakings he had given at Plombières.

But Cavour had gone too far to retreat. Helped by the National Society, he had done all he could to rouse his country to a fervour of patriotism. Italians from all over the Peninsula – and particularly from Lombardy where their evasion of conscription into the Austrian army caused particular offence – had been encouraged to come to Piedmont to enlist in the forces he was assembling for a war that was presented as a crusade. He could scarcely hope now to dampen the enthusiasm that he had created without destroying his reputation and career. There was, also, an additional complication: he had been warned by Odo Russell, the British Diplomatic Agent in Rome, that feelings in Europe were running high against him and that if he declared war on Austria, he would lose all the sympathy of his former supporters.

This was a matter which had been discussed at Plombières. Napoleon had insisted that the war must not appear to be a war of aggression, nor revolutionary in character. Austria must be provoked into the attack. Cavour was confident that she could be.

'I shall force Austria to declare war on us,' he told Odo Russell with disarming confidence, 'in about the first week of May.'[30]

By the middle of April, however, it appeared that Cavour's dangerous gamble had failed. Louis Napoleon, retreating in the face of opinion in England and France, recommended Piedmont to agree to a suggestion made by the English Government that there should be an agreed policy of simultaneous disarmament by all the countries involved. Cavour knew that to accept such a solution would mean the collapse of all he had been working for. In despair he locked himself in his room and contemplated suicide.[31]

For he knew that Piedmont could not flout the combined will of Europe; and eventually he came to the view that he must agree to disarm. Before this was known in Vienna, however, the Austrian government had made up their mind to act.

On 23 April Cavour was stopped on the steps of the Chamber of Deputies by two Austrian officers who handed him a note from their Emperor. Austria peremptorily demanded the demobilisation of the Piedmontese forces; and if a satisfactory answer was not received within three days the Emperor Francis Joseph would, 'with great regret, be compelled to have recourse to arms in order to secure it'.

'It is half-past-six,' Cavour replied hiding the gleam of triumph in his eyes by looking down at his watch. 'Come back at this time on 26 April and you shall have your answer.'

When the officers had gone, he turned to a friend rubbing his hands together as was his habit when he was excited. 'We have made history,' he said. 'Now let's have dinner.'[32]

11

WAR IN THE ALPS

In the middle of December the previous year, a Piedmontese ship had steamed into the harbour of La Maddalena to take Garibaldi back to the mainland. Cavour wished to see him on a 'matter of great importance'.

Garibaldi landed at Genoa in a state of high excitement. He spent the evening with friends, and when Luigi Mercantini, the writer of numerous patriotic poems, came into the room, he called to him eagerly, 'Write me a hymn for my volunteers'.

Early the next morning he was in Turin, talking to Cavour who told him most of what had been agreed at Plombières but carefully omitted any reference to what had been decided about the future of Nice. He was asked to enrol and take command of a volunteer force, and immediately he accepted.

He hurried back to Genoa to tell his friends the good news; and bursting into Agostino Bertani's surgery, he threw his arms round the doctor and said in a voice 'broken with emotion', 'This time we shall do it! I have been satisfied in high places. I am authorised to tell my friends to hold themselves ready.' 'In fancy's vision,' Bertani derisively commented, 'he already saw battalions of citizens rushing onwards with irresistible impulse; Italy redeemed by the prowess of her sons.'[1]

Bertani, as a convinced republican, could not share Garibaldi's enthusiasm. Mazzini also condemned the war since, if it were successful, it would lead to the prospective Kingdom of North Italy becoming 'a French dependency'. And this was a view Bertani felt inclined to share.

What about the French? he asked gloomily. But Garibaldi assured him that the important thing was not to worry about the French, but to enrol as many Italians as possible. Then, as excited as ever, he rushed out to pass the news on to Giacomo Medici and Nino Bixio, giving them instructions to get on immediately with the enlistment of volunteers. And soon, indeed, there were scarcely any of his old officers who were not caught up in his own eagerness for the coming war. Even the sceptical Bertani agreed to organise the ambulances and medical services as he had done in Rome.

In March Garibaldi was summoned again to Turin to discuss the formation of these volunteers in detail. At his previous interview he had presented himself dressed with incongruous respectability in a top hat and a frock coat; but on this occasion Cavour's servant came into his master's room to announce the arrival of a strange man, who would not give his name, with 'a big stick and a big hat'. Once again the interview was friendly and profitable, and when it was over Cavour took Garibaldi to introduce him to the King. Garibaldi liked what he saw of Victor Emmanuel who seemed to him 'sincere and natural', a man who might indeed become the military dictator, the 'supreme *duce*' that Garibaldi saw as a necessity to end the quarrels and hesitations of the politicians.*

Still nothing was said about the price agreed at Plombières for French intervention in the war. 'Be careful what you are up to,' Garibaldi warned the others with fatherly concern. 'The help of foreign armies always has to be paid for in some way or other.' Cavour and Victor Emmanuel maintained their silence.[2]

A few days later Garibaldi was granted a commission as Major-General in the Royal Army of Piedmont and given official command of the volunteers that Bixio and Medici were enlisting. They were to be called the *Cacciatori delle Alpi*.

* Garibaldi's belief in the efficacy of 'honest dictatorships', stemming, no doubt, from his contact with the Saint-Simonians and reinforced by his experiences in South America, was never to leave him. In *I Mille*, his autobiographical novel, he wrote: 'Our people lack discipline, discipline which made our fathers great, discipline from which they are dissuaded by a handful of doctrinaires for the petty glory of being called great. And this drives me further and further towards the idea of an honest and temporary dictatorship' – *I Mille* (Cappelli, Bologna, 1933. *Ed. naz. degli scritti di Giuseppe Garibaldi*, iii), 70.

Elsewhere he wrote, 'Having passed the better part of my life amongst the republicans of the New World, where I had the time to study the system, I always return to my conviction which is not new in me: that the conception of dictatorship by the people of ancient Rome was a propitious one' – see Carlo Tivaroni, 'Garibaldi e la dottrina della dittatura' in *Rivista Storica del Risorgimento Italiano*, ii, (1897) and Walter Maturi, *Interpretazioni del Risorgimento* (Einaudi, Turin, 1962), 248–9.

The *Cacciatori* were organised into three brigades, each consisting of two battalions with a strength of 500 men. The first brigade was given to Enrico Cosenz, a quiet, gentle-looking Neapolitan who had fought bravely for Manin's republic in Venice; the second brigade to Giacomo Medici; the third to Nicolai Ardoino who had fought in Spain as well as in the campaigns of 1848 and 1849. Nino Bixio was appointed to command one of the two battalions in Ardoino's brigade. In addition to these 3,000 infantry, there were fifty scouts (including Menotti Garibaldi) commanded by Francesco Simonetta; and forty snipers, one of whom was Stefano Canzio, within a few years to marry Teresa Garibaldi. These scouts provided themselves with their own horses and the snipers with their own rifles.

Indeed, the *Cacciatori* soon discovered that they could expect little in the way of equipment or stores from the regular army. They were provided with uniforms, but some units did not have enough boots, and others not enough cartridge belts. They were supplied with small arms, but these were for the most part limited to muskets of an antiquated pattern. They could get no artillery, no engineers, no horses for the ambulances. Their officers protested, first to the Army Command, then to the Government. The Army Command explained that they did not have enough equipment to spare for an irregular force of guerrillas whose leader had himself described their purpose as simply 'disorganisation of the Austrian Army by disrupting their lines of communication, blowing up bridges, cutting telegraph wires and burning stores'. And the Government, when appealed to, explained that it was the Army's responsibility, but said they would see what they could do.

They were determined not to do much. Ideally they had hoped to give Garibaldi an unofficial role, but the number of volunteers who came pouring into Turin, so many of whom asked to serve under him, had made it necessary for the Government to co-operate officially with Garibaldi – not so much, as Cavour told Nigra, because his help was needed to assure victory, as to 'inspire and maintain public confidence'.[3]

Cavour may not have completely understood, or indeed, have trusted the popular forces with which he had to work, finding comfort in the reflection that a democratic revolution had little chance of success in Italy, for the 'mass of people' were in general

The Bersaglieri resisting the final attack on the Villa Spada 30 June 1849

The Porta San Pancrazio after the fall of Rome

View of the ruins of the Vascello Villa from the grounds of the Pamphili Villa

'attached to the ancient institutions of the country'.[4] But he did understand that he could not afford to appear to be working against the 'elements favouring political change', and that, for the purposes of propaganda, the famous General was an essential ally. Garibaldi had a far shallower depth of thought and a less far-sighted vision than Mazzini, but he was much nearer to the people than Mazzini was. 'He understood them and was understood by them much better.'[*5]

A war in which Garibaldi fought would necessarily be a popular one, far more popular than one fought by the regular Army supported only by the French. His name was vitally needed, therefore, for the purposes of propaganda.

All this Cavour unreservedly admitted. But it would be folly, he believed, to allow Garibaldi too much of the credit for a victory which must, at all costs, reflect glory on Victor Emmanuel and strengthen the Kingdom of Piedmont. Garibaldi must be used as a magnet to draw volunteers to Turin, but he must not be allowed all the best of them; these must be reserved for the regular army; and, in any event, the total number of volunteers must be kept firmly in check. Later, when he completed his memoirs, Garibaldi understood this well enough himself. 'In 1859,' he wrote, 'I was kept as a flag to attract recruits . . . to summon volunteers in large numbers,

* It was, in fact, one of Garibaldi's greatest contributions to the national cause that he was able to persuade so many ordinary people that Italy was more than a word. As Denis Mack Smith has said, 'The making of Italy was to prove a victory for the intellectuals, the liberals, the middle classes; not for the uneducated, who hardly knew what the word *Italy* meant; not for the poor, who felt its presence only in higher taxes and conscription; not for those who lost a paternal, protective ordering of society to gain a more grasping competitiveness in which the weaker went to the wall; not for the Catholic masses, who saw the Pope deprived of his temporal power and the monasteries dissolved and Church property confiscated. There can be little doubt that Garibaldi's prestige among ordinary people helped to obscure what was really happening until they were too late to resist it.' Denis Mack Smith, *Garibaldi: A Great Life in Brief* (Knopf, New York, 1956), 67–68.

There can be little doubt, either, that although the monarchic and conservative parties were obliged by the revolutionaries to do things which otherwise they would not have done, 'the fact remains that the republicans never succeeded in carrying out a victorious revolution. The monarchic groups were never overcome.' – Gaetano Salvemini, *Scritti sul Risorgimento* (ed. Piero Pieri & Carlo Pischedda) (Feltrinelli, 2nd edn. 1963), 459.

but to command only a small proportion of them, and those the least fit to bear arms.'[6]

'The Government are frightened to death of Garibaldi,' Bertani confirmed to Panizzi. 'They hate to hear him acclaimed. They are afraid his troops will increase on the march and that his volunteer force will gain too much glory and too much sympathy, that it will distract attention from the Piedmontese Army and diminish its importance.'[7]

For the moment, however, despite his frustrations over the supplies of equipment, and despite his professed dissatisfaction with the quality of the majority of his men, Garibaldi was still happy and excitedly expectant. Indeed, he felt less concerned about the lack of equipment than did most of his officers, for he himself still believed that the bayonet was the best weapon a soldier could possess. And so long as there were enough fighters in the ranks as brave and spirited as those who had fought in Rome, this was all that really mattered to him.

The men might be untrained and for the most part far from fit enough to stand the vigours of an active campaign, but while they remained determined and confident and had a cause in which they believed, they could achieve great things. Many were professional men from Lombardy, many others were students anxious to escape the suffocating restrictions of their lives and hoping, no doubt, that their university would not dare to refuse them a degree just because they had missed their examinations to serve so noble a cause. But nearly all of them had some grudge against the troops occupying the towns from which they had fled, or some other reason to hate the Austrians. Garibaldi eagerly awaited his opportunity to take them into battle.

*   *   *

He was still waiting in Turin when Mme Schwartz, summoned by him from Rome, came to see him at the beginning of the third week in April. She found him in a cheerful mood. She had not been able to get past the guard outside his headquarters, but Garibaldi had come round to her hotel after Fruscianti, hearing her arguing, had gone into his room to tell him that she had arrived. He could not stay long, but promised to join her the following day for a midday meal.

In the morning, however, she had a note from him to say that the rheumatism in his knee was very painful and he could not get up and down the stairs. It was raining hard and went on raining all day. She felt miserable. It had been a long and exhausting journey from Rome, for she had had to take a boat from Civitavecchia to Leghorn and then wait fourteen hours for another boat to Genoa. And now Garibaldi, who had professed that he 'desperately' wanted to see her, said that he could not come. 'The recollection of that sad and wintry Sunday in Turin' which she spent in her room looking out at the rain pouring continuously from a leaden sky, she thought would never leave her.

Then, soon after half-past nine that night, there was a knock on her door. Twice she called 'Come in!' But there was no response, so she opened the door herself and saw her lover standing in the doorway. 'Is a visit to a lady so late at night permitted?' he asked her; and when he came into the room he apologised for not having come before. He had been so busy that day he had not had time even to wash or to eat. He washed his hands in her bathroom and when he had dried them she dabbed them with Blüthenthau. She offered to ring for a meal, but he said he would rather finish the remains of her tea which had not yet been cleared from the room. 'I want,' he told her, 'to drink out of your cup.'

Before he left he promised to come and see her the next day; but in the morning when she returned from posting a letter she found a note tied to the key of her room: 'My Speranza, at one o'clock I leave for Brusasco. I am depressed at not seeing you. Write to me there. Yours from the heart.'

She hurried to the railway station, hoping to see him for a moment before he left. She found him on the platform, surrounded by his staff and hundreds of soldiers and their friends who had come to wave them goodbye. She pushed through the crowd towards him, and gave him a box of chocolates, and then they went into the station-master's office where they could be alone.[8] Soon after one o'clock the train pulled out of the station. The soldiers leant out of the windows, waving, cheering, and singing above the noise of the engine Garibaldi's Hymn:

> *Si scopron le tombe, si levano i morti,*
> *I martiri nostri son tutti risorti!*
> *Le spade nel pugno, gli allori alle chiome,*
> *La fiamma ed il nome d'Italia sul cor!*

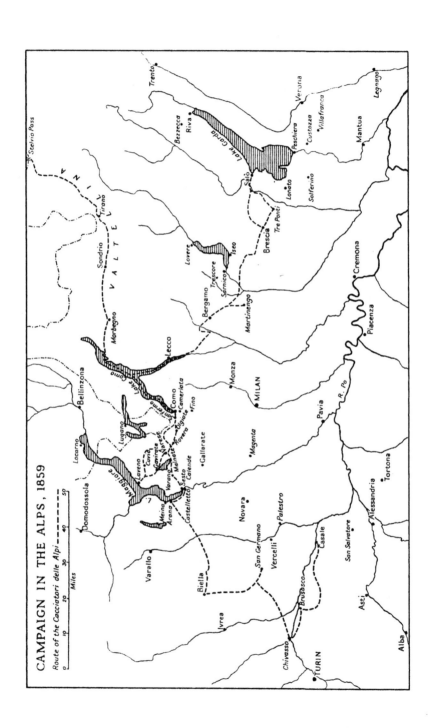

CAMPAIGN IN THE ALPS, 1859

Route of the Cacciatori delle Alpi - - - - -

Miles
0   10   20   30   40   50

Stelvio Pass

Trento

Bezzecca
Riva
Lake Garda
Salò
Peschiera
Verona
Villafranca
Costazza
Lonato
Solferino
Mantua
Legnago

VALTELLINA

Tirano
Sondrio

Lovere
Iseo
Tre Ponti
Brescia

Morbegno
Trescore
Bergamo
Sarnico
Martinengo

Lecco

Lake Como

Monza
MILAN
Camerlata
Como
Fino
Bellinzona

Locarno
Lugano
Lake Lugano
San Fermo
Laveno
Varese
Cuvio
Malnate
Varano
Rovera
Camerlata
Gallarate
Magenta
Pavia
R. Po
Cremona
Piacenza

Maggiore
Arona
Meina
Castelletto
Sesto
Calende
Novara

Domodossola
Varallo
Biella
Vercelli
Palestro
San Germano
San Salvatore
Alessandria
Tortona
Casale
Brusasco
Chivasso
Ivrea
TURIN
Asti
Alba

Veniamo! Veniamo! su, o giovanni schiere!
Su al vento per tutto le nostre bandiere
Su tutti col ferro, su tutti col fuoco,
Su tutti col fuoco d'Italia nel cor,
Va fuori d'Italia, va fuori ch'è l'ora,
*Va fuori d'Italia, va fuori, o stranier.**

     ★   ★   ★

The *Cacciatori delle Alpi* were still concentrated at Brusasco four days later when, on 29 April 1859, a huge Austrian army rumbled across the rain-swept Ticino into Piedmont.

The French did not declare war until 3 May and it would be many days after that before they could get their army across the Alps to link up with their Piedmontese allies whose forces numbered less than 60,000 men. The Austrians, however, did not take advantage of the opportunity offered them. Instead of sweeping forward round Turin to block the French advance, they wasted three weeks making clumsy reconnaissances in eastern Piedmont, giving the Italians badly needed experience of active service and the French time to concentrate in the valley of the Po.

The day after the Austrians crossed the Po, Garibaldi was ordered by General Cialdini to come up to Casale where the Piedmontese army had established a bridgehead. 'I do not intend to give you any orders', Cialdini wrote vaguely, 'but I shall be pleased to see you arrive.'[9]

Garibaldi moved off immediately, but at Casale he found no sign of Cialdini nor of his bridgehead. He remained in and around the town for four days during which the only enemy he saw were two Austrian hussars who galloped away at the sound of a shot; and,

* The tombs are uncovered, the dead come from afar,
  The ghosts of our martyrs are rising to war,
  With swords in their hands, and with laurels of fame,
  And dead hearts still glowing with Italy's name.
  Come join them! Come follow, o youth of our land!
  Come fling out our banner, and marshal our band!
  Come all with cold steel, and come all with hot fire,
  Come all with the flame of Italia's desire!
    Begone from Italia, begone from us now!
    Strangers begone, this is our hour!

then, exasperated beyond measure by his enforced idleness, he rode off to the King's headquarters at San Salvatore. On 9 May he returned from San Salvatore with this document:

> General Garibaldi, who is at present engaged in checking the enemy's advance on Turin, will in due course proceed to Biella by way of Ivrea where he will operate on Lake Maggiore on the Austrian right flank in any way he considers advisable. I, therefore, order all military and civil authorities and all municipal bodies to give him every facility for provisioning and accommodating his troops.
>
> General Garibaldi is authorised to command all volunteers at Savigliano, Acqui and elsewhere and to enrol further volunteers wherever they may present themselves if he considers he can make use of them.[10]

The King's order gave him more power and scope than even he could possibly have expected, and he rushed back to Casale to make use of it before the regular army or the Government interfered. The next day he led his men out of Casale in the still pouring rain towards Biella, up roads so deep in mud that the wagons stuck fast and the men had to put their shoulders to the wheel in an effort to dislodge them. He urged them on to more and more strenuous efforts, throwing his own weight behind the wheels and spattering his general's uniform with mud. Fearing political interference he was determined to get so deeply committed that it would be impossible for the Government to recall him. Two days later, however, the recall came. He was handed a letter from Cavour:

> General – I request you to set out with your brigade to San Germano. There you will place yourself under the command of General De Sonnaz, who has received instructions to drive the Austrians from Vercelli. When the town has been delivered, then you may act in accordance with the instructions given you by His Majesty.[11]

But Garibaldi was not to be put off. He obeyed Cavour's instructions and took his *Cacciatori* to San Germano, but when they arrived there, and Garibaldi found that the aged General De Sonnaz was quite unprepared to move against the stronger Austrian forces in Vercelli, he withdrew them and continued on his way to Biella, where he was greeted with just the sort of enthusiasm that, as Bertani had said, Cavour most feared.

At seven o'clock in the evening four days later, the *Cacciatori* moved down from the wooded hills towards Lake Maggiore. They were marching fast for they were without knapsacks now and carried all that they would need stuffed into their bread bags and into the big pockets which Garibaldi had had sewn on to their coats. Garibaldi himself had discarded the regulation kepi and was wearing a black felt hat with a broad brim, and when it was cold, he threw his poncho over the shoulders of his general's dark blue coat.

At the sight of the smooth water of the lake and beyond it the hills of Lombardy, his men gave a loud cheer. They were told to keep quiet, and they marched on down to Arona in silence.

They stayed on the outskirts of Arona for four hours, anxiously awaiting the news that arrangements had been made to feed them in the town. But although these arrangements were made – both at Arona and farther up the lake at Meina – when they moved on again, they advanced not towards Arona (as Garibaldi had led both them and the Austrians on the other side of the lake to expect they would) but farther south, towards Castelletto where the waters of the lake converge into the fast-flowing channel of the Ticino.

Here Simonetta, leader of the *Cacciatori*'s mounted scouts, had managed to collect several barges. And as the clock in Castelletto was striking midnight, the *Cacciatori* came down to the bank where these boats were moored and began to step into them under cover of an unusually dark night. By five o'clock next afternoon, the Austrian garrison in Sesto Calende had been captured and the whole of the *Cacciatori delle Alpi* were marching along the winding country roads of Lombardy towards Varese.

It was a beautiful morning, the sun shining brightly in a clear sky. Each village through which they passed was filled with people, cheering and shouting; and before midnight, when they entered Varese, the news that they had crossed the Ticino had spread all over Lombardy. In town after town revolutionary committees were formed, the Austrian police thrown out of their houses, and the people armed with what few weapons had escaped the searches of the occupying authorities. Many of these uprisings were premature and severely repressed, but in other places the Lombards could congratulate themselves that they had won their own freedom.

The *Cacciatori* were infected with the enthusiasm which their arrival had aroused. And when they were attacked in Varese on 26 May by General Urban they resisted with high-spirited determination.

Urban had advanced on Varese with a formidable force of cavalry, artillery and 3,000 infantry. But about a thousand of these infantry were detached to his right where they got lost in the hills; and so Garibaldi, who was occupying a naturally strong position in Varese, had only to contend for the moment with a force less numerous than his own. His outposts in a suburb of Varese were driven in, but when the Austrians followed an artillery bombardment with an infantry charge, the Italians counter-charged with the bayonet, cheering and screaming as they jumped out of their recently dug trenches, leaped over the garden walls, and dashed through the corn between the mulberry trees, driving the Austrians back. Garibaldi rode down to direct the advance, sending Cosenz out to turn the enemy's flank from the south, and prepared to pursue the retreating enemy. 'Gentlemen,' he said to his men with the cheerful yet heavy sarcasm that he felt inclined to use on such occasions, 'I am sorry you've been kept without your breakfasts, but you know it's not my fault. . . . We must go on a little and see what's become of our friends. It would be ungentlemanly not to see them a little farther on their road after they've come so far to visit us.'

His men followed him dutifully for two miles before being stopped by Urban's rearguard which repulsed the *Cacciatori*'s first over-impetuous attack. At a second attempt, however, the Austrian position was turned; but then Garibaldi, concerned that the flanking column which had been detached by Urban to his right would fall down on Varese in his absence, decided to withdraw. The *Cacciatori* returned to Varese 'all in the highest spirits', singing the song which everyone sang that summer: '*Addio, mia bella, addio.*'[12]

Garibaldi shared their optimism. He had successfully defended Varese; now he would attack Como. It was a decision of imposing and reckless grandeur, for Urban had been strongly reinforced by the Austrian command which felt acutely the danger of having to deal with guerrillas and insurrections on its right flank while threatened in front by the full and as yet uncommitted force of the French and Piedmontese armies. There were, in consequence, by now more than twice as many troops in the Como area as Garibaldi could bring against them. They were far less tired than the *Cacciatori* and far better equipped; but if Urban misplaced them or if he were attacked before he had had an opportunity of placing them at all, then Garibaldi had a chance.

At dawn he began the advance along the main road through Malnate and Rovera towards Olgiate; but with that suddenness to which those who had fought with him in earlier campaigns had long since grown accustomed, he swung off this road and changed direction north, leaving Cosenz to continue the easterly advance through Olgiate towards Camerlata. At Camerlata, the railway line from Milan stopped about two miles short of Como, and here Urban, his mind distracted by the numbers of reinforcements arriving almost hourly at the station, had concentrated the greater part of his force, sending relatively few battalions up to Como itself and detaching only one or two companies of Hungarians to watch the pass of San Fermo. And it was for San Fermo that the main body of the *Cacciatori*, through winding roads concealed behind the vine-covered hills, were heading.

On the afternoon of 27 May they came running up the narrow village street, bayonet in hand, ill-supported by covering fire from either side, too densely concentrated, too rash and too confident, losing men needlessly, yet still, as it seemed, irresistible.

Austrian reinforcements came struggling up the steep slopes from Como, but they came too late to prevent the Hungarians being thrown off the pass. For there was no stopping the headlong bayonet charges of the *Cacciatori;* they seemed infected by a wild euphoria as they ran from tree to tree and vine to vine, urged on by their shouting officers, and by Garibaldi waving his arms in a series of dramatic gestures. It was all magnificent, Nino Bixio thought, splendidly, unforgettably heroic. It was like living in 'a world of poetry,' he told his wife, 'our men cast themselves down like a torrent.'[13] And they forced the Austrians back.

Below them lay Como. They could see the little figures of the Austrian troops in their white uniforms crowding the Piazza d'Armi. They crouched at the top of the ravine, firing down into the town and towards evening they saw Garibaldi, with the brim of his hat pulled down low over his eyes, 'the only indication he ever gave of his thoughts being more intensely occupied than usual',[14] move closer down towards the enemy. Then evening came and they were ordered to tie up anything which might rattle, and to advance, in complete silence, down the steep and winding road. The suburbs of Como were reached, lights went on in the houses, people cried out *'Viva Garibaldi!'* and were begged to keep quiet.

The suburb is passed [wrote a man who was there]. At the entrance to the city is a dense mass of figures with torches. Lights rapidly appear in all the windows, and instead of a storm of Austrian bullets the troops are met with a deafening shout, *'Viva l'Italia! Viva Garibaldi!'*

The people were wild with delight. Men with torches marched on either side of his horse, and old and young rushed forward kissing his feet and clothes. Old men with tears streaming down their faces, and young girls threw their arms round our necks and greeted us as deliverers. The uproar was immense. The sound of the bells, which were ringing in all the *campanili,* and the music of the bands were drowned by the cheering of the crowds that were assembled in the large Piazza.[15]

The Austrians had gone. They had retreated, in fact, with such haste that they had abandoned in Como and Camerlata a great store of arms, equipment, food, and even money.

But with enemy troops still holding out at Laveno on the shore of Lake Maggiore behind him, and with Urban's large force reforming between Monza and Milan, Garibaldi could not stay in Como for long. So after a single day's rest, during which arrangements were made for the defence of the town by local patriots and a small force of volunteers, the *Cacciatori* were marched back towards Lake Maggiore to dislodge the Austrian force at Laveno which was threatening not only his communications but the passage of Piedmontese troops across the Lake.

The attack on Laveno was made during the night of 30 May. Garibaldi detached part of his force to outflank the town and sent in a frontal attack under Captain Landi. The result was disastrous. The flanking force got lost, as Urban's had done at Varese, and Landi's frontal assault was driven back with severe casualties. Garibaldi's bitter disappointment, after his triumphs at Varese and Como, turned to furious anger. When Landi, seriously wounded, came at dawn to report his failure, Garibaldi shouted at him 'You are lying!', and then accused him of cowardice.

'General,' said Landi, 'I am wounded.'

'Oh, go away!'

Garibaldi, who had been 'very stern and terrible throughout the campaign', turned his horse's head and rode off, giving orders for an immediate return to Varese. On the way he rode past Landi, feverish by now, being dragged along in a cart.

'I was in the wrong this morning,' he said, making his rough apology.[16]

He was well aware how dangerous a situation he was in. Behind him lay Laveno, still in Austrian hands, on his left were the mountains, to the south and in front were more Austrian troops. But when some officers suggested a withdrawal into Switzerland he turned on them angrily, demanding why they wished to fly from a temporary danger.

Already, in fact, although he did not know it until he reached Como again, the danger was past. For on 30 May Victor Emmanuel and General Cialdini had defeated an Austrian force at Palestro, and Urban had been recalled to the south. Five days after Palestro, the Austrians were defeated again in a savage and bitter battle with the French at Magenta.

Garibaldi could now move in relative safety. Though he had failed at Laveno, his brief and spectacular campaign had kept over 11,000 Austrian troops away from the main theatre of operations and had renewed the lustre of a world-wide reputation won at Rome. The Austrians spoke of him as the '*rötheufel*' – 'the red devil' – told stories of how he ate the flesh of his prisoners, raw, without salt, and of how they had seen the bullets bounce off his chest. By the Italians of Lombardy, he was treated, so one of Victor Emmanuel's Local Commissioners said, not so much like a victorious general as 'the head of a new religion followed by a crowd of fanatics. The women, no less enthusiastic than the men, brought their babies to Garibaldi so that he could bless and even baptise them. To these crowds that thronged him, Garibaldi would speak with that beautiful voice of his which was a part of the secret of his charm. "Come! He who stays at home is a coward. I promise you weariness, hardship and battles. But we will conquer or die." They were never joyful words, but when they were heard the enthusiasm rose to its highest. It was a delirium. The crowd broke up deeply moved, talking over what the general had said. Many had tears in their eyes.'[17]

When he left Como for Lecco, taking his men across the lakes in two captured steamers, the people dashed down to the shore cheering and waving frantically; and when he entered Bergamo they strewed flowers at his feet and rushed up to him to touch him.

On 13 June he entered Brescia; and here he was given orders which, for the moment, terminated this embarrassing acclaim. Unable to prevent Garibaldi's single-handed invasion of Lombardy, Cavour had been determined to make the most of it. 'Insurrection: General and Immediate', he had telegraphed to him and then sent the Marquis Emilio Visconti Venosta hurrying over the border to ensure that the liberated territories were administered by committees favourable to Piedmont. But now the time had come to take a more decisive action against the flamboyant leader whose forces were growing daily. At Brescia he was deprived of his independent command. And on 14 June he was ordered to advance on Lonato. Four regiments of cavalry and two horse batteries were promised him in support. But before they arrived, due to the rashness of one of his officers, the Hungarian Stefan Türr, his men became involved in a savage fight with far stronger Austrian forces, and suffered heavy casualties. Garibaldi surmised that the delay of the artillery and cavalry was intentional, a 'deliberate attempt to get rid of a man who had it in his power to become dangerous'.

And although the comment was made years later, when his distrust and dislike of Cavour had reached the point of paranoia, there could be no doubt that the orders he received on 20 June were, indeed, intended to get his *Cacciatori* out of the way. For they had by then become a serious embarrassment. They were sent well away from the theatre of operations to the Valtellina, supposedly to guard the Stelvio pass against a new Austrian advance from the north. It was precisely what Mazzini had foreseen. 'You will be shut up in some corner of the Tyrol or the Valtellina,' he had warned Garibaldi when trying to persuade him to stay out of the war, 'while the French Emperor does exactly what he wants without any possible intervention on your part.'

There were reasons, though, other than political ones, for the Government's action. The *Cacciatori* were far from being, as Garibaldi himself recognised, a perfect fighting unit. He had led them well, showing once again that he was a brilliant commander of irregular units, with an intuitive sense of tactics, a brain which came quickly to decisions which, however, unconventional or controversial, were then pushed through with single-minded determination. He was impressionable out of the field, but at war he made up his own mind without seeking advice, could not be persuaded to alter it, and was so self-possessed and self-contained that even his chief-of-staff was often in doubt as to what he intended to do or where to strike. Sometimes, indeed, he did not know himself until the very last moment; for he was a superb opportunist. One of his favourite sayings – most of them were nautical – was '*Bisogna approfittare dell' aura,*' – 'make the most of the breeze'. But he was by no means infallible, and his men even less so. They were – though the bravery of the majority could not be doubted – ill-disciplined, inclined to sudden panic and often unreliable. No one could deny that they had achieved much despite these limitations, and despite the inferior equipment with which they had been provided, but their victories had contributed a good deal less to the successful conduct of the campaign than their fame suggested. And now that their numbers had swelled to 12,000, most of whom had recently enlisted and were entirely untrained (but all of whom had to be supplied), they were a military as much as a political problem.[18]

*   *   *

Four days after the *Cacciatori* were sent to the Valtellina, the French fought the battle of Solferino in which uncounted thousands of men lost their lives. For ever afterwards Louis Napoleon was haunted by their screams as they died. It was a victory, his aide-de-camp General Fleury conceded, 'but what tears! What blood!' The Austrians were obliged to retreat; but the French and Italian losses were just as heavy as theirs. And the Emperor decided that the time had come to make peace. It was not entirely that he had lost his nerve, that his vigour had been impaired by the suffocating heat of the summer, nor that his performance as a general had shown so little of his uncle's decisive and wilful spirit that he felt compelled to destroy all his muddled and incoherent orders after the campaign was over. There were many good reasons for ending the war. Prussia was preparing to concentrate troops along the Rhine, Russia was becoming alarmed by the revolutionary character of the Italian uprisings, and in France itself the Clerical party were making protests which Napoleon could not ignore. Also, he had become increasingly aware of late how dangerous for France it might be to have a strong and unified country south of the Alps, of how much more Cavour was trying to get out of the war than their agreement had provided.*

On 10 July the French and Austrian Emperors met at Villafranca and, without consulting Victor Emmanuel, agreed to terms which seemed to Garibaldi just what one might have expected from that 'fox of a Bonaparte'.[19]

* Louis Napoleon was never, of course, a consistently purposeful man. He has been compared to a 'sleep-walker, who believed he was fated to follow the ghost of Napoleon wherever it might lead'. Having a romantic faith in his destiny, he would frequently adopt a demeanour of baffling and inscrutable silence. The words addressed to him, Tocqueville said, were 'like stones thrown down a well; their sound was heard but one never knew what became of them'. In these moods Moltke noticed that his features were not only immobile, but his eyes looked 'almost extinct'. (J. M. Thompson, *Louis Napoleon and the Second Empire* (Oxford, 1954)), 11.

As well as being a dreamer, he was a sentimentalist. He had, as A. J. P. Taylor has observed, 'that supreme characteristic of the sentimentalist of being attracted simultaneously to the most contradictory ideals. To be at once War Lord of Europe and the Guardian of European Peace; to be the friend of the Emperor of Austria and to expel the Austrians from Italy; to free Lombardy and to protect the Pope; to be more realistic than Bismarck and to be more idealistic than Mazzini; to restore order and continue the revolution; in a word to be at once democrat and despot.' A. J. P. Taylor, *The Italian Problem in European Diplomacy* (Manchester University Press, 1934), 7.

His feeling for Italian and, indeed, for European and human interests was, none the less, sincere; and because of this Luigi Salvatorelli has concluded that he was 'morally – and perhaps historically – a much superior man to Napoleon, "the Great", who never thought of anything except his career and his greatness (or at best of the material greatness of France)'. Luigi Salvatorelli, *Pensiero e azione del Risorgimento* (Einaudi, Turin, 1960), 161.

12

'LOVE AND DUTY'

Italy, Prosper Mérimée decided, was now 'in a worse mess than ever'. Piedmont was to be granted Lombardy, but Austria was to retain Venetia. And in Tuscany, Modena and the Romagna the provisional governments which had been formed during the anti-Austrian uprisings of the past three months were to be demolished and the old rulers restored.

'This treaty shall not be executed,' Cavour protested with a vehemence which was not merely impassioned but hysterical. 'I will become a conspirator. I will become a revolutionary. But the treaty shall not be executed. No! A thousand times no! Never! Never!'[1]

Recklessly he urged Victor Emmanuel to continue the war alone; and when the King refused to allow himself to be carried to such lengths by anger, Cavour lost his temper and with his lips trembling and his face 'as red as a furnace', threw himself into an argument which ended with the King's angry dismissal of him as 'no better than a *birichino* – a guttersnipe'.[2]

But although he resigned from office in disgust, Cavour did not lose sight of his aim. 'Ah well,' he said at last, resignedly accepting the fact that he would now have to reach some sort of alliance with the revolution, 'they will force me to be a conspirator for the rest of my life.'[3] And he continued to give help and advice to the moderate revolutionaries in Central Italy who had taken advantage of the war in the north to overthrow their governments.

The new moderate leaders in the Central States were as determined as was Cavour that the terms of Villafranca should not be passively accepted. And in the proud, patrician and sternly intractable Baron Ricasoli, Cavour found an ally in Tuscany whose great gifts rivalled his own.

In the month after Villafranca, Ricasoli helped to organise a military alliance between Tuscany, Modena and the Romagna to defend their independence, not so much against the signatories of Villafranca who were unlikely to fight for its observance, as against the Pope and any other Catholic power which he might induce to support him. Ricasoli invited Garibaldi to leave the service of Victor Emmanuel and to join the forces in Central Italy.

Garibaldi was delighted by the offer. His reputation had been greatly enhanced by his invasion of Lombardy and the subsequent fighting in the Alps; but he knew that his activities had, in fact, been entirely peripheral to the campaign as a whole which had been won by the regular army of Piedmont and by the 'brave sons' of the 'heroic French nation' whose sacrifices he was prepared to acknowledge more generously than could many others in their dismay at the news of Villafranca.[4] He got up from his bed in Lovere where he was suffering from a particularly painful attack of arthritis (which, until persuaded by Dr Bertani to submit to proper treatment, he had attempted to cure by 'his own favourite remedies of purging and sweating') and he wrote to Victor Emmanuel that he had been 'called to the command of the troops of Central Italy who intended to resist the installation of their former petty tyrants'.

He arrived in Florence to the excited acclamations of the people; and his journey from there to his headquarters at Modena was a triumphal progress. Although he was mistaken in believing that he had been 'called to the command of the troops', for he found himself a deputy to General Manfredo Fanti, an officer from Modena who had served in the Piedmontese army, it was Garibaldi whom the people looked up to as their military leader.

When he paid a visit to the Romagna in September, he was greeted with that frantic enthusiasm to which he had by now become accustomed. And in Ravenna, when the shouts of the people called him to the balcony of the Palace and he raised his hand for silence, 'the wind dropped, the flags drooped to their staves, and his audience seemed scarcely to breathe'. But as soon as he had finished, the cheering broke out again louder than ever, military bands struck up, processions made their way with flaming torches through the streets, and at the tops of their voices the crowds shouted the name of their hero, '*l'amato figlio del popolo*'.[5]

Garibaldi had written to the Deideris asking them to bring Teresa to share his triumphal tour with him, and he had asked Baroness Schwartz to come too. They all arrived while he was at Ravenna, and the day after their arrival they set out with him for a ride

The Pope blessing the victorious French Army from St Peter's

Cavour

Victor Emmanuel II

Louis Napoleon

through the pine forest to the house at Mandriole where Teresa's mother had died.

It was a beautiful morning with a gentle breeze stirring the leaves of the wild vines and the blackberry bushes as the party's two carriages and three *biroccini* bumped down the sandy tracks between the tall trees. The General was in a happy mood. He sat in the leading carriage next to Speranza talking of the adventures he had had since he had last seen her, and of the retreat in 1849.

The carriages and gigs came to a halt outside the farm and they all went inside the house where tables had been loaded with food and wine. Garibaldi made a speech. Perhaps it was a little too long, perhaps a little bombastic: 'For fourteen years without pay or reward I served the cause of liberty in other lands. What then will I not do for the land of my birth? . . .' But no one could object. He was so great a man; it was so great an honour to have him there.[6]

They cheered his departure; they watched him with silent sympathy as he went into the little church where Anita was buried to lay a garland of wild flowers near her coffin; they pushed forward to shake his hand; they crowded the road to Bologna along which, two days later, his carriage was unhorsed and pulled by hand through villages and small towns where the entire population seemed to be in the streets singing, shouting, ringing bells, waving scarves and ribbons, the men smoking cigars tied up with red, green and white streamers.

At Lugo, however, the happiness of Garibaldi's party was suddenly broken. In a room to which they had retreated 'to avoid the usual speeches', Signora Deideri told Mme Schwartz that she ought to marry Garibaldi and so 'save the whole family from disaster'. The curious phrase puzzled Speranza. She had been sitting at the piano playing Garibaldi's Hymn which had been set to dance music, and the tune had induced the excitable Teresa to grab Signora Deideri's ample waist and to try to dance with her. But Speranza left the tune unfinished.

'What do you mean?' she said.

And then she was told for the first time that Battistina had had a child by the General, and that he had promised to marry her as soon as he had got a copy of Anita's death certificate.[7] He would, in fact, have married her before, it seemed, had not the war broken out and had not the Deideris so strongly dissuaded him.[8]

The news, as she confessed, came as an appalling shock to Mme Schwartz. She resumed the journey to Bologna in a mood of wretched unhappiness. The wild welcome they received there and the presents that Garibaldi gave her – a ring, which she felt sure some other woman had given him, and a gold lizard which, he said, was a 'symbol of eternity' – only served to deepen her gloom. He seemed to treasure the welcome more than he treasured her; and when giving her the 'symbol of eternity' he never mentioned Battistina. She determined to go home.

The night before her departure the Deideris and Teresa arranged to go to the theatre, so that she would, at least, she hoped, have a chance to be alone with him before she went. When the others had gone to the theatre, she went to his room. He was lying on the bed reading newspapers. He was waiting until the others had left the hotel, he assured her without conviction, and had then intended coming to her room. Sadly she offered him her hand. He kissed it and she left.[9]

A few weeks later, however, she was back in Bologna. On her way to Rome she had received a message from him asking her to go to Sicily on a mission for him and she had now returned to give him her report. Once again she found him lying on his bed reading newspapers and magazines.

'See now, how these English concern themselves with me,' he said to her, apparently more pleased by the magazines than by her return. '*Per Dio!* All the history of my life, my fighting adventures, even those of South America, mine and my Anita's difficulties – it is all given on the stage of Astley's theatre, and now in these papers. What a people they are!'

And he handed her 'page after page of sketches and drawings'. He listened to her report without much interest, and teased her about her account of her arrest and brief imprisonment in Palermo with what she took to be a kind of 'contemptuous raillery'. She was almost in tears when she left him this time. 'Write to me,' Garibaldi called out to her as she hurried out of the room. But she thought to herself in anguish, 'How can a man, exalted by an entire nation as this man is, cause a lonely, devoted woman such suffering at heart?'[10]

Jessie White, who strongly disliked her and by now knew

Garibaldi well, thought Mme Schwartz's 'aggrieved wonderment' at Garibaldi's treatment of her and at his lack of gratitude for her services 'very funny'. Once a man had expressed devotion to the cause, Jessie White said, Garibaldi felt free to use him in any way he liked, and this equally applied to women. 'He had a special method of his own for pressing the juice from the grapes and throwing away the skins.'[11]

He had not meant to be unkind, though. The fact was, he was in love with someone else. He had met this 'dear creature' whose features, he decided, would remain for ever indelibly engraved upon his heart, for the first time five months before near Robarello. She had come from Como and had driven in her carriage through the Austrian lines with a message from the Marquis Visconti Venosta. She was Giuseppina, the seventeen-year-old illegitimate daughter of the Marquis Raimondi, who had a villa at Fino. And Garibaldi had conceived for her a passion of violent intensity.

Abandoning for once his usual forthright approach, he made his advances to her with a delicate, almost servile humility. One evening, after she had come to visit him at his headquarters in a lakeside inn at Como and they had spent part of the night together in the gardens by the shore, he had exclaimed, 'Oh, that I might belong to you in some way!'[12]

The thought obsessed him. 'I love you,' he wrote to her later. 'I love you. Oh! you with your angel face. . . . But when I told you that I might belong to you, I committed perjury. I spoke blasphemy. For I belonged to another woman. Those very words, "Oh, that I might belong to you in some way or another", I pronounced on my knees when I was neither physically nor spiritually free. Now, you must write to me – Madonna! – and tell me that my beloved still has a little friendship for me. I will content myself with that as if it were the longed-for love. . . . But, per Dio! Don't say to me that it is a matter of indifference to you. I should be driven mad by that.'

It did seem to be a matter of indifference to her, though. She was a sensual girl rather than an emotional one, and her lover despaired, so he lamented, 'of inspiring in her what I felt in my heart'.[13]

He never did inspire it. There were, however, for the moment other problems and other excitements to occupy his mind.

*   *   *

Several of Garibaldi's old comrades-in-arms including Cosenz, Bixio and Medici, had come with him from the Valtellina to join the army in the Central States, and their programme, Benedetto Cairolo declared frankly, was 'not local defence, but national war'. Mme Schwartz had seen the headquarters at the Palazzo Albergati in Bologna and it was impossible to mistake its *garibaldesco* air. Amidst the statues and clocks, cast down beside the looking-glasses and the thick damask curtains were 'troopers' hats with their feather plumes, sashes of different colours, pistols and pistol cases, red jackets, long and short sabres, all in the most motley confusion'. The headquarters was crowded with former officers of the *Cacciatori delle Alpi* as well as with new volunteers from the Romagna urging Garibaldi to continue the national war by advancing south into the Papal States, to take advantage of the national spirit before it cooled, supporting Mazzini's maxim 'that a revolution that stopped in one place was lost'.

There was much to be said for such a move. The French were still in Rome; but the Pope's forces in the provinces were limited largely to a few battalions of Swiss mercenaries who could not be expected to fight with the spirit of their opponents. And the chances of international intervention were not strong. After Villafranca the new Ministry in England had protested against the possibility of French or Austrian interference in Central Italy. 'The policy of Her Majesty's Government,' Lord John Russell had announced, 'is not to interfere at all, but to let the Italian people settle their own affairs.'[14] Also, there was the reluctance of Louis Napoleon, irrespective of British opinion, to restrain an attack on the Papal States outside Rome. Indeed, *Le Pape et le Congrès*, published in Paris at the end of 1859 and as much the work of the Emperor as *Napoléon III et Italie*, proposed that the Pope's temporal power should be limited to the Holy City itself.

The possibility of a quick settlement of the Roman Question appealed not only to Garibaldi, but also at first to General Fanti and to Luigi Carlo Farini, a friend of Cavour, who had been appointed Governor of the newly formed state of Emilia (consisting of Parma, Modena and the Romagna). General Fanti, indeed, gave Garibaldi permission to invade the Marches and Umbria in the event of a nationalist uprising there.

This permission, given to Garibaldi not only as an officer of the army of the Central States but as the new President of the reconstituted National Society, represented a danger which neither Rattazzi, Cavour's successor as Prime Minister in Turin, nor Baron Ricasoli could confidently face. Ricasoli's firm policy, hesitantly supported by the intriguing Rattazzi, was not to let Tuscany become involved in any such provocative adventure until an annexation with Piedmont had been achieved with the agreement of the interested European powers. But he was placed in an awkward predicament for, as Emilio Cipriani, the Governor of Bologna, warned him, 'In the Romagna the true master of the situation is Garibaldi. The Government which set itself against his powers would fall within twenty-four hours.'

Eventually, however, both Farini and Fanti were persuaded to come to Ricasoli's help. For neither of them, as representatives of the regular military and civil authorities, had been on satisfactory terms with Garibaldi since his arrival in the Romagna; and they both now recognised the danger, constantly envisaged by Cavour, of a successful expedition by irregular and revolutionary forces. La Farina, who had earlier recognised the importance of preventing a break with Garibaldi and his friends, now supported Farini and Fanti whom, he said, represented the attitudes of 'all the rich and intelligent classes' whose ideas were also shared by 'the immense majority of the population'.

To this opposition Garibaldi gave way. But a few hours after he had given his undertaking not to invade the Papal States, he heard that a revolution had broken out in the Marches and he decided that 'he must go to help it'. The report was, in fact, a false one; but he was actually on the march when orders were issued direct to his subordinates countermanding the operation.

He wrote an indignant letter to Fanti, complaining of the General's 'irregular proceedings and bad manners', and on 16 November gave notice of his resignation. The next day, on Cavour's advice, he was summoned to Turin where Victor Emmanuel offered him a generalship in the Piedmontese army which he refused and one of the royal shotguns which he accepted.

Although the King had been trying to use Garibaldi's activities as an excuse for annexing Tuscany, and was, therefore, as involved in the intrigues as (in their different and conflicting ways) Ricasoli, Farini and Fanti all were, he was the only one to escape the General's furious censure.

'I love and respect the King,' Garibaldi told the British Minister in Turin. 'He is a man of his word and his political situation is difficult and unfortunate. He has explained it to me.'

For the others, though, no words of condemnation were strong enough. He issued a resentful proclamation complaining of the 'cunning acts' which had been used against him. And then, having told the soldiers he had formerly commanded to remain at their posts, he took the train to Genoa to await the first boat for La Maddalena.[15]

Though Mazzini condemned him out of hand for giving way so submissively – 'the man is weak beyond expression'[16] – the period of Garibaldi's friendly co-operation with the Turin government was, in fact, over. He had now become a symbol of a programme in opposition to Cavour's, and to what he termed the 'miserable fox-like policy' of Fanti and Farini.[17] And soon, after a further interview with the King, in which Victor Emmanuel spoke of Cavour (who had by then returned to power) with obvious impatience and dislike, Garibaldi gained the dangerous impression that he would always be able to rely on the King's support when acting against his Ministers.[18] It was a misconception which was to cause more than one crisis in the future.

There were several days to wait before the next boat was due to sail from Genoa to take him to Caprera. And during this period of waiting he decided, for the time being, not to go back after all. Towards the end of the month, he left Genoa for Fino and while staying as a guest in her father's villa there he wrote an imploring letter to the 'adorable Giuseppina', stressing how deeply torn he was between the sentiments of duty and love – duty towards the woman on Caprera who had borne his child and to his national role of a self-denying popular leader, and love for his 'most beautiful *fanciulla*'. He was poor, he admitted; his health was bad; at fifty-two he was almost three times her age; but 'reply to me at once,' he begged her, 'I am in no state to be able to wait. . . . Yours for life – whatever may be.'[19]

A few days later he received her reply. Almost immediately he left for Fino, and there, so he said, 'I abandoned myself entirely to happiness and gave myself without restraint to the woman of my heart.'[20]

The wedding was conducted with the full rites of the Church. Teresa was a bridesmaid; several of his friends were present though few of them approved of the marriage; and when Garibaldi came out of the chapel he was looking serene and content. But he had moved only a little way from the door, when a man approached him and put a letter into his hand.

There are several versions, pieced together by hearsay reports, of what happened next; and several versions of the contents of the letter. It seems most likely that after Garibaldi had read the letter he took his bride aside into the shade of a tree, passed the letter into her hands and said harshly, 'Is it true?'

She read the letter, turned very pale and softly admitted that it was.

'Then,' Garibaldi shouted, 'you are *una puttana*, a whore!'

The young woman raised her head and said in a stronger voice, 'Listen to me.'

But Garibaldi would not listen, and he lifted up a garden chair, and made as if to hit her.

'I thought I was sacrificing myself for a hero,' the girl told him calmly, 'but you are nothing but a brutal soldier.'

Then she ran away and, for the rest of that day, no one could find her.[21]

The letter, according to Lorenzo Valerio, Governor of Como and Garibaldi's friend who had been his *testimone* at the wedding, was from the Marquis Rovelli, Giuseppina's cousin and her lover. Rovelli, overwhelmed with jealousy by the loss of his beautiful young mistress, had informed the General that his bride, who had only married him because her father had told her to, had spent the previous night 'in a younger man's arms'. Rovelli may also have added what he said later when Garibaldi was trying to obtain an annulment of his marriage – that since the age of eleven Giuseppina had had a succession of lovers and that the most recent one was a young regular officer, Luigi Caroli who (according this time to Madame Deideri) was the father of a stillborn child born to Giuseppina some months after her wedding.

Garibaldi (who may himself, of course, have been the father of this child) cared nothing for virginity in a bride; but the knowledge that Giuseppina had spent the night before their wedding with a man she loved more than himself, that she had married him reluctantly at the bidding of her father rather than from her own inclinations, and, above all, that he had been made a fool of in public, was more than he could stand.*²²

He told her father (with whom, however, he seems to have remained on the best possible terms) that he refused to accept her as his wife; and after three days he returned to Genoa, determined this time to get away to Caprera as soon as he could. Before he left Fino, however, he wrote to Bertani: 'You can assure your friends of South Italy that I am always at their disposition when they are really willing to act.'²³

If there could not be love there could at least be duty.

* Garibaldi never subsequently blamed her for what had happened. He may have believed, as many others did, that she was the victim of a plot by those who feared that his remarriage would entail his settling down and abandoning his plans for future action. Certainly he realised that she would not have married him at all had it not been for her father's persuasion.

Many years later, when she was over 70, Giuseppina Raimondi was quoted as having said sadly, 'It has been suggested that I should have persisted with my refusal of marriage to the very end. But although in those days, as a girl of eighteen, I was allowed sufficient liberty to go between Como and Varese as I pleased in troubled times, and was permitted to choose the men whom I would love, nevertheless the choice of a husband was jealously guarded. How can one expect so much courage from a girl who was abandoned by everyone? Even Caroli, who was certain of my love, left me on my own at the end.' – Giacomo Emilio Curàtulo, *Garibaldi e le donne con documenti inediti* (Rome, 1913), 295–9. After her marriage to Garibaldi was at last annulled she remarried. She died in 1919.

PART II
1860

1

'THE NEGATION OF GOD'

In the autumn of 1850 William Gladstone, then the Conservative Member of Parliament for Oxford University, concerned about the failing eyesight of his daughter Mary, had taken her on holiday to Naples. He returned to England some months later 'boiling and seething with indignation'. He had spent much of his time with Giacomo Lacaita, who was then legal adviser to the British Legation and who, later, after his exile and naturalisation in England, became Sir James Lacaita, private secretary in turn to Lord Lansdowne and to Gladstone himself.

Lacaita had talked with Gladstone about the appalling way in which the political opponents of King Ferdinand were treated, and suddenly and violently the English visitor 'erupted like Vesuvius'.[1]

It appeared that since 1821, when Ferdinand I with the help of foreign troops had put an end to the constitution he had been forced to grant the year before, Naples had been a state governed by the police to ensure the continuance of the privileges of the Church and the absolute power of the monarch. The police were composed, in the words of the British Minister in Naples, 'of the most brutal and reckless set of individuals', and had the power to imprison anyone without affording him the means of defence, to detain him year after year without trial, and even 'to supervise all the actions and control all the movements of all those – estimated at 50,000 of the most intelligent men of the country – who came under suspicion of being opposed to the régime'.[2] The corruption, as in all such states where so iniquitous a system is allowed to flourish, was not limited to the police. According to Luigi Settembrini, a provincial professor of Greek and Rhetoric, who gave up his career and freedom to oppose it, the tyranny had spread to the priests, the judges, the tax-collectors, to 'every employee of Government'. 'These men left us no hour of peace,' he wrote, 'but continually, daily, in the public square and in one's private house, stood by us, crying like robbers, "Give

or I strike." Such oppression corrupts a nation to the bones.'[3]
For speaking out against such oppression Settembrini was thrown
into one of those Neapolitan prisons which had all of the revolting
squalor and much of the revolting cruelty of an early-eighteenth-
century gaol, where 'time was like a shoreless sea, without sun or
moon or stars, immense and monotonous'.[4]

'Oh, my God, Father of the unfortunate, Consoler of those who
suffer,' Settembrini prayed while serving his long and agonising
term amongst the hopeless and degraded criminals in the island
prison of Santo Stefano, 'Oh save my soul from this filth, and if
Thou hast written that I must here end my sorrowful life, do let that
end come soon.'[5]

In another island prison on Procida, was incarcerated Sigismondo
Castromediano, Duke of Morciano, Marquis of Cavallino, who had
been sentenced to thirty-five years in irons for showing his approval,
as a local magnate, of the revolutions of 1848. He had no political
ambition, he wished only to live at peace in his castle, looking out
upon the crumbling wastes of Apulia. When Garibaldi later asked
him who were the judges that had sentenced him to so cruel a
deprivation of this contentment, he replied with distant pride,
'I have forgotten them'. He 'died on 28 August 1895 in the smallest
room of his vast, ruined castle a few miles from Lecce. He left no
heir to his poverty. . . . On his coffin were placed the chain of a
galley slave and the red jacket worn by Neapolitan convicts.
These, he used to say, were his decorations.'[6]

At the trial of one of those who shared the Duke's imprisonment
at Montefusco, Gladstone was present. He saw this man, Carlo
Poerio, a respected lawyer who had been one of King Ferdinand II's
ministers under the constitution of 1848, sentenced to twenty-four
years in irons on the evidence of a lying witness whose clumsy
incompetence the judges did their utmost to conceal. Later he
visited him in prison at Nisida; and at first he did not recognise him.
He looked exhausted and desperately ill and round the waist of his
coarse red jacket was a leather strap attached to two chains. One of
these chains was fastened to his ankle, the second to another convict.
They were never undone.

Gladstone returned home determined to do all he could to bring
the terrible things he had seen and the even more terrible things he

had heard to the attention of civilised Europe. He proposed writing an open letter exposing the cruelty and corruption to the Earl of Aberdeen.

Lord Aberdeen was sorely embarrassed. He asked Gladstone to delay publication until he had had an opportunity to write to Prince Schwarzenberg, the Austrian Chancellor, with whom he was on friendly terms, suggesting some sort of private representation to King Ferdinand. Schwarzenberg took a long time to reply and when he did so, his tone, as Aberdeen had feared it might be, was cold and discouraging. 'He showed that he resented the interference of a British ex-Foreign Secretary in such a matter. He said that he would bring Gladstone's views to the notice of King Ferdinand, but he informed Lord Aberdeen that the British treatment of political offenders in Ireland, in the Ionian Islands and in Ceylon had neither escaped his attention nor excited his disapproval.'[7]

Before this letter was received, however, Gladstone had decided he could wait no longer, and had published his letter which caused almost as great a sensation in Europe, and particularly in France, as it did in Britain:

It is not mere imperfection, not corruption in low quarters, not occasional severity that I am about to describe [he wrote], it is incessant, systematic, deliberate violation of the law by the Power appointed to watch over and maintain it. It is such violation of human and written law as this, carried on for the purpose of violating every other law unwritten and eternal, human and divine; it is the wholesale persecution of virtue when united with intelligence, operating upon such a scale that entire classes may be with truth said to be its object, so that the government is in bitter and cruel, as well as utterly illegal, hostility to whatever in the nation lives and moves, and forms the mainspring of practical progress and improvement. . . . The governing power, which teaches of itself that it is the image of God upon earth, is clothed, in the view of the overwhelming majority of the thinking public, with all the vices for its attributes. I have seen and heard the strong and too true expression used, '*È la negazione dio eretta a sistema di governo*' – 'This is the negation of God erected into a system of government'.[8]

King Ferdinand II, as head of this system of government, was left coldly unimpressed by the uproar which this passionate letter aroused. He instituted a new series of political trials in which over 300 prisoners were brought to face charges before judges who permitted condemnations on the evidence of a man found five times guilty of fraud. Many of the accused were sentenced to eighteen years in irons.

Despite his reaction, however, and his obvious contempt for European protests, Ferdinand was still widely accepted outside England as the lesser of two necessary evils in Italy. As Guizot wrote to Gladstone, emphasising what was taken to be the truth by many others of more liberal outlook than his, the only choice for Italy lay between tyrants like King Ferdinand and revolutionaries like Mazzini, and only tyrants could be expected to safeguard the existing order. Gladstone himself, in fact, like nearly all his colleagues in Parliament, did not yet believe that the attainment of eventual reform in Italy might lie only in the cause of Italian unity. He suggested that the idea of unity was nothing more than an abstract proposition and 'if there are two things on earth that John Bull hates, they are abstract propositions and the Pope'.[9] The problem was not to overthrow Ferdinand, but to reform him.

But was Ferdinand II capable of reform? He was known throughout the world as King Bomba – not, as his admirers insisted, because of the unwieldy shape of his tall bulging body but because the insurgents at Messina and Palermo had been bombed into submission in the revolt of 1848. He was epileptic, an energetic, practical yet superstitious man of forty-one, at once expansive, cunning and mistrustful, with a kind of perverse charm in his coarse geniality and with a strong Neapolitan accent. Except by his political opponents, he was more disliked outside his own country than within it, for he was adept at displaying those ostentatious forms of charity so dear, as Benedetto Croce has observed, to the Neapolitan heart. The offer of a half-smoked cigar to a beggar, the distribution of large sums from the royal treasury to poor people in cholera-infested slums (though he had a horror of infection) – these were the sort of gestures that endeared him to the *lazzaroni*. The liberals, of course, detested him – and with good cause, for although he was less of a monster than they liked to suppose, he was certainly 'proud of having been the first to dam the revolutionary flood'.[10]

But if he was a reactionary, he was not, as Pope Gregory XVI had been, an obscurantist.* He was determined to do all he could to make his country self-supporting – though this, no doubt, was due, at least in part, to his being one of nature's xenophobes, and while affable and courteous enough with diplomats and tourists, he became in his middle age, as Mr. Harold Acton has observed, 'morbidly suspicious of foreigners', distrusting even his Calabrian and Sicilian subjects.

In Giuseppe di Lampedusa's great novel, *The Leopard*, there is a brief, revealing, and entirely authentic glimpse of him in this light, as he grants a wary interview to the Sicilian Prince of Salina. The Prince, escorted by the Court Chamberlain through 'innumerable rooms of superb architecture and revolting décor (just like the Bourbon monarchy itself)' eventually reaches a private study where the King stands behind a desk heaped with papers.

He was already standing so as not to be seen getting up; the King with his pallid heavy face between fairish side-whiskers, with his rough cloth military jacket under which burst a purple cataract of trousers. He gave a step forward with his right hand out and bent for the hand-kiss which he would then refuse.

'Well, Salina, blessings on you!' His Neapolitan accent was far stronger than the Chamberlain's. . . .

The plebeian cordiality depressed the Prince as much as the police grins. Lucky those who could interpret such familiarity as friendship, such threats as royal might. He could not. And as he exchanged gossip with the impeccable Chamberlain he was asking himself what was destined to succeed this monarchy which bore the marks of death upon its face. The Piedmontese, the so-called *Re Galantuomo* who was getting himself so talked of from that little out-of-the-way capital of his? Wouldn't things be just the same? Just Torinese instead of Neapolitan dialect; that's all. Or maybe the Republic of Don Peppino Mazzini. . .?[11]

Unlike the sad, proud, vain Sicilian with the lazy desire of his race and kind to be left alone with his sense of superiority, the King

* He was the first Italian sovereign to take a serious interest in railways, and the line from Naples to Granatello which was laid in 1839 was the first in Italy. In 1840 Naples – the largest city in Italy and the third largest in Europe – was lit by gas. During his reign the capacity of the Neapolitan marine was greatly increased and two-thirds of the domestic produce was exported under the national flag – Harold Acton, *The Last Bourbons of Naples* (Methuen, 1961), 140–1.

was not, however, prepared languidly to consider the possibility of either the *Re Galantuomo* or Don Peppino Mazzini replacing him. Nor did he intend to rely on the help of Austria or France in keeping them out.

His ways and habits might have been vulgar in the extreme, as Alassio Santo Stefano, a revolutionary of 1848 justly said, 'but his was not a vulgar mind. He was as bigoted and superstitious as the greater part of his compatriots, but he was never a hypocrite. . . . He was a true Neapolitan at heart.'[12]

Indeed, his last instructions to his son, when he lay dying in agony in his huge palace at Caserta, were to keep the Kingdom independent of Austrian and Piedmontese influence. This son, dutiful and with a profound respect for his father's memory, did his best to do so. But he had none of Ferdinand's resilience and panache. Lymphatic and hesitant with a long head and nose, high brow, and dark sadly brooding eyes that lent to his face an expression at once wooden and lugubrious, he sought protection from the world behind a barrier of dismissive reserve. Dominated and disliked by his Austrian stepmother, the widowed Queen, he struck Henry Elliot, the newly appointed British Minister in Naples, as a very limp and characterless young man: .

> An entire want of sympathy or feeling for others was visible in a cold manner, unlike everything you could wish to see in a young man of twenty-three [Elliot thought], and it was painfully exhibited before his whole court on the day on which he received the homage of all the great people of his Kingdom. He stood on a carpet in front of the throne and as the lieges passed before him they kissed his hand, which he did not take the trouble to raise, allowing it, when they had kissed it, to fall back at his side as if it had been the hand of a doll, while he did not even look at the person who was doing homage; he peered about examining those who were coming next. One very infirm old man caught his foot in the carpet and fell flat on his face close to the feet of the King who neither stirred to help him nor allowed a muscle of his face to move while the poor old fellow, awkwardly and with difficulty, scrambled up and passed him without a word from the King of condolence for his mishap or of enquiry whether he was hurt.[*][13]

* His despondent and displeasing manner did not alter much for the better when he became used to being King. An English Admiral who was introduced to him at

Admiral Persano

Stefan Türr

Giuseppe La Masa

General Fanti

Rosolino Pilo

Francesco Crispi

Agostino Bertani

Giuseppe La Farina

Elliot had been appointed British Minister immediately on the death of Ferdinand II by a Government anxious to loosen the new King's ties with Austria. But neither he nor the French Minister, Brenier, could break the hold which Francis's stepmother still exercised over his mind. Nor could General Filangieri, Prince of Satriano, the most distinguished of his ministers, who advised him to grant a liberal constitution. When Francis continued to reject Filangieri's advice, the General offered to resign. The offer was refused and Filangieri went away to his villa in Sorrento and refused to leave it, protesting that he was ill.

Nothing was done. Ministers were sent down from Piedmont, first Count Salmour and then the Marquis Villamarina, to draw Francis into an anti-Austrian alliance. But King Francis would not have the alliance and he would not have reform.

And so the Government continued much as Gladstone had described it. Naples and Sicily were still 'entirely governed by an irresponsible police', Elliot wrote in his memoirs. 'Men by hundreds were arrested, exiled, or imprisoned for years, not only without going through any kind of trial, but often without being informed of what or by whom they were accused.'

The power of the Camorra had spread and seemed to be unbreakable since most of those who could have broken it were involved in it.

> There was no class, high or low, that had not its representatives among the members of the Society which was a vast organised association for the extortion of blackmail in every conceivable shape and form. Officials, officers of the King's Household, the police and others were affiliated with the most desperate of the criminal classes in carrying out

Naples in the summer of 1860 found a 'rather tall young man with dark hair, very closely cut, and a bronze olive complexion. The expression of his countenance was that of distrust and despondency, and in manner extremely formal and ceremonious.' He said to the Admiral that he understood he had just arrived from Malta (though he had been told a few minutes before that he had come from Palermo). When corrected, the King, who stood 'with both hands deeply ensconced in the ample side pockets of the peg top trousers of the period, then asked several questions in rapid succession'. The Admiral's replies were followed by a long, embarrassing silence – Rear Admiral Sir Rodney Mundy, *H.M.S. Hannibal at Palermo and Naples during the Italian Revolution, 1856-1861* (London, 1863), 204.

the depredations, and none was too high or too low to escape them. If a petition was to be presented to the Sovereign or to a Minister it had to be paid for; at every gate of the town *Camorristi* were stationed to exact a toll on each cart or donkey load brought to market by the peasants; and on getting into a hackney *carrosel* in the street, I have seen one of the band run up and get his fee from the driver. No one thought of refusing to pay, for the consequences of a refusal were too well known, anyone rash enough to demur being apt to be found soon after mysteriously stabbed by some unknown individual, whom the police were careful never to discover.'[14]

They were still careful, however, to discover those whom they regarded as conspirators. The numbers of these *attendibili* rose to 150,000; and often one of these men would be arrested and imprisoned on 'secret private denunciation, more especially on that of priests, who, when they wanted to get a man out of the way, sometimes with the most infamous object, accused him of blasphemy'.[15]

It was inevitable, of course, that Garibaldi should share the Englishman's indignation at these abuses. It was inevitable, too, that he should feel called upon to take up arms against them. He had, indeed, already agreed to take part with Medici, Bertani and Anthony Panizzi, the exile from Modena who became Librarian of the British Museum, in an abortive plot to rescue the Neapolitan political prisoners.[16] But when in 1857 he was asked to join another plot for the same purpose, a plot inspired by Mazzini, he said that he would not be a party to sending men to their slaughter to 'make the rabble laugh'.[17]

A leader to take these men to their slaughter was, however, found in the brilliant, fanatical Neapolitan Duke, Carlo Pisacane, General Roselli's chief of staff at the time of the Roman Republic. Pisacane sailed from Genoa with less than thirty men to perform his impossible task. He landed at Ponza, released all the prisoners (most of whom, of course, were ordinary convicts) and steamed away with his dangerous army south of Naples to Sapri where they landed with cries of '*Viva la Repubblica!*' He marched north into Basilicata, opposed not only by Neapolitan troops but by the Clergy, by peasants who were frightened by what seemed like a crowd of brigands, and by liberals who preferred the claim of Murat to the throne of Naples rather than those of Mazzini to a non-existent republic. Pisacane was killed; and his following destroyed; while in Genoa, where Mazzini had appeared in one of his improbable disguises, an extravagant attempt to seize the royal arsenals was prevented in a struggle in which a Piedmontese soldier was killed and after which Cavour was given the opportunity he had long awaited to have Mazzini condemned to death.[18]

Mazzini had been right about Garibaldi's probable fate in the war against Austria which ended in his being sent to the Valtellina; but Garibaldi had been proved right now. He was more than ever determined not to go to the help of the South, as he was so often being pressed to do, until he was given firm evidence that the people were willing to act to help themselves, to instigate a revolt which he could then support, and to rally round him when he arrived. But although these conditions might be difficult to fulfil in the Neapolitan provinces, in Sicily, he was assured, his presence might well lead to victory.

★   ★   ★

God first made the world, runs the Sicilian proverb, and then he made the Strait of Messina to separate men from madmen.

Those who inhabited this sun-scorched island felt themselves a world apart from the rest of Italy, as indeed they were. Geographically, racially, traditionally, they were different and they felt proud to be different. For centuries also, though, they had been subject to foreign masters – they had had Byzantine and Saracen rulers, Norman and Angevin, Spanish, French and English, and now Neapolitan. And perhaps the time had come at last for them to arouse their natures, at once languid and eruptive, to achieve a new identity within the Italian State.

The Bourbons had not found them easy to govern. They had resisted conscription, believing that it was 'better to be a pig than a soldier', and they had resisted even more strongly the deprivation of their liberties by the Neapolitan police. The resistance had increased their sense of insular solidarity, but had served also to increase their feeling that the poverty of the island might be due not so much to the inscrutable justice of God as to the far too scrutable injustice of Neapolitan tyranny.

Other apparent injustices that were inherent in Sicilian life might be accepted or disregarded, but injustices which were imposed upon them from without were increasingly resented. Up till 1848, however, the call was not for union with the rest of Italy, but for independence from the Kingdom of Naples. And it was only when the uprising of 1848 ended in such utter failure that men looked north for their deliverance.[19]

The northern calls, whether cried by Mazzinians for 'national unity' or by the more specific Cavourians for 'Italy and Victor Emmanuel', were still, though, not as attractive to Sicilians as the call for independence. And those Sicilian exiles who worked from the North against the Bourbon rule were soon made well aware of the difficulties they faced.

One of these exiles left London for Sicily in the summer of 1859. He carried a passport in the name of Manuel Pareda and he was wearing large mutton-chop whiskers and thick, blue glasses.[20] His name was Francesco Crispi.

A self-confident and strong-willed lawyer, Crispi had left his homeland ten years before and had striven ever since to bring his countrymen to work and fight for the future which Mazzini offered them. He had come at last to believe that the time was ripe for insurrection, and his conversations with revolutionaries in Messina and Palermo persuaded him to prepare with them a plan for an outbreak at Palermo for 4 October. The police learned of the plot, however. Several of those who were to have taken part in it were arrested and the rest dared not act alone.

Others of Mazzini's agents nevertheless urged the Sicilians not to despair. Why wait, Mazzini himself asked them. 'Wait? For what? Can you really believe either Louis Napoleon or Cavour will come to set you free? . . . Dare and you will be followed. . . . But dare in the name of National Unity . . . Garibaldi is bound to come to your help!'[21]

Garibaldi's advent, though, was far less certain than that.

★   ★   ★

Mazzini had asked him to go to Sicily as early as March 1854 when he had returned from his exile in America. Prompted by Crispi, the Sicilian conspirators had themselves asked him to go in September

1859. He replied that he would go 'with pleasure, with joy', but that the time was not yet ripe; he continued to insist that there must be an internal rebellion first.[22]

Confident, however, that once a definite plan had been proposed and an expedition organised, Garibaldi could be persuaded to 'fulfil his destiny', Crispi continued to discuss the proposed invasion with his friends. On 16 September he wrote from Sicily to Nicola Fabrizi, an exile from Modena who operated from Malta as another of Mazzini's principal agents for the South:

> The Neapolitan provinces must be stirred, or the Bourbon government at least so thoroughly alarmed, that they will not feel at liberty to send additional troops to withstand an invasion of Sicily. Should Sicily rise and Naples remain quiet, we should be ruined. An insurrection in the Abruzzi and in Calabria, an invasion by Garibaldi (whose name is greatly feared throughout this region) leading them to fear an invasion of the Kingdom, would ensure our success.[23]

In December the plan was discussed in greater detail and the proposition was put to Farini who was glad of an opportunity of finding employment outside Emilia for the Garibaldian volunteers that had been left there when their leader resigned his command in the army of the Central States. Farini gave his enthusiastic support to the proposal and asked Crispi to go to Rattazzi in Turin to secure the complicity of the Piedmontese Government.

Rattazzi seemed as eager to support the plan as Farini had been; but his days of power were drawing to their close. And when La Farina, Secretary of the National Society, who had already lent his influence to prevent a Garibaldian invasion of the Papal States, now raised his objections to the invasion of Sicily, the plan began to falter.

It was given a further setback by the activities of Garibaldi himself. Since he had come to realise that the National Society was now a supporter of the Cavourian group and the Cavourian policies which he opposed, he resigned from it to give his support to its rival, the *Liberi Comizi*, established by Angelo Brofferio, who was campaigning with Rattazzi against the return to power of Cavour.

And then on 31 December he announced an entirely new society of his own, *La Società della Nazione Armata* whose stated aims were far more actively military than those of either Brofferio's *Liberi Comizi* or La Farina's National Society. Within a week, however, Garibaldi's *Nazione Armata* was dissolved at the King's request; and the reputation of the founder suffered a severe blow.

'Poor Garibaldi,' Giacomo Medici commented sadly and appositely in a letter to Panizzi. 'He ruins himself in times of inaction; he talks too much, writes too much, and listens too much to those who know nothing.'[24]

The men who profited most from his activities were Cavour and La Farina. Cavour was now returned to power on a wave of public dissatisfaction with Rattazzi and distrust of Brofferio, while La Farina's National Society shared the fruits of a victory which it had helped Cavour to win.[25]

Cavour was generous in his triumph. 'Garibaldi allowed himself to be drawn into union with my personal enemies, Brofferio & Co., but I recognise in him nevertheless one of the greatest forces of which Italy can avail herself.'[26] And while Crispi was expelled from Piedmont as a dangerous Mazzinian agent, Garibaldi was allowed to collect contributions for a 'Million Rifles Fund' and to purchase arms on condition that the Government were told where they would be stored.

When or where these rifles would be used was still, however, in doubt. Mazzini's agents, working for an attack in the South, still pressed their views on Garibaldi, whose recent behaviour in Turin, while exhibiting his usual 'vacillation in the field of politics', had not, in the words of Nicola Fabrizi, diminished his stature as 'a very important factor'. But, Fabrizi went on in an exasperated letter to Rosolino Pilo (another of Mazzini's Sicilian agents), Garibaldi continued to be distressingly impressionable, as 'weak as any woman, allowing himself to be interviewed and hoodwinked by every newcomer'.[27]

Nevertheless, it was essential, Crispi agreed, to 'make use of him in every possible way'.[28] Bertani and Medici joined the others and set to work to persuade Garibaldi to act. But back came the familiar answer: 'You can assure your friends of South Italy that I am always at their disposition when they are really willing to act themselves.'[29]

Throughout the winter of 1859–60 the correspondence and

persuasion continued. By the end of February, however, little headway had been made with the obstinate General, always so suspicious of information he was unable to verify for himself. On 24 February Rosolino Pilo wrote to Crispi: 'I cannot make up my mind to go to Garibaldi, because before helping us, he demands that some decisive step be taken to prove that those in the interior are ready to act.'[30] But although he could not bring himself to go to see Garibaldi in person, Pilo wrote to him, telling him that he and his friends including Fabrizi (who was 'not easily deceived') were convinced that the 'bolder spirits in Palermo' were 'determined to have done with that despotism which opposes them and separates them from the rest of Italy. Mazzini no longer insists on a republic, so it is to you, most honourable friend, that this Italy of ours now looks for succour'.[31]

Garibaldi, who was now back on Caprera digging hard and doing his best to forget the young body of Giuseppina Raimondi, replied to Pilo a few days later. 'I do not flinch from any undertaking, no matter how dangerous, when it is directed against the enemies of our country,' he assured him. 'But at the present moment I believe any revolutionary movement, in any part of Italy whatsoever, would be ill-timed. . . . We must wait. . . . The time for action will soon come.'[32]

Later that month Garibaldi believed that the time for action had come already. The call did not come from Sicily, however. It came from Nice.

For on 24 March (in accordance with the secret undertakings given at Plombières) Savoy and Nice were officially ceded to France in consideration of her acceptance of the annexation of Tuscany and Emilia to Piedmont. '*Maintenant,*' said Cavour to the French delegate, smiling and rubbing his hands together in that excited, nervous way of his, '*maintenant, nous sommes complices, n'est-il pas vrai, baron?*'[33]

To Garibaldi the news came as a shock so profound that for the rest of his life he could never bring himself to forgive the detestable man who had so deceitfully sold his fatherland 'like a rag to the foreigner'.[34] Now, he, who had been born in Nice, had himself been 'made a foreigner'. He sent one of his officers to the King with instructions to ask if it were true and to answer him 'at once by telegraph yes or no'.

'Very well, then, yes,' said the King angered by the peremptory demand, 'but tell the General not only Nice but Savoy as well! And that if I can reconcile myself to losing the cradle of my family and my race he can do the same.'[35]

But Garibaldi could not do the same. His nationalism had always had that peculiar sensitivity of the man born on a frontier; and now that this frontier was to be moved to the other side of his birthplace, he felt that he had been personally insulted. He took the train to Turin to give vent to his seething anger and disgust at that 'flock of doctrinaires', those 'hired journalists, pampered pro-consuls and parasites of every description' who had allowed such a bargain to be concluded with 'that fox of a Bonaparte', representative of 'the worst evil ever conceived by the human mind – French diplomacy'.[36]

Words were no good, though: he must act. Encouraged by a committee of men from Nice he began to formulate a plan of action. While Crispi pressed him 'to think of nothing but Sicily', where a revolt, according to a wire received from Fabrizi in Malta, had broken out at last on 4 April; and while Sir James Hudson, British Minister at Turin and a close friend of Cavour, urged him to bend to the inevitable and not to feel encouraged by angry protests about Nice from London (where feelings about French encroachments were always tender and where, indeed, attitudes towards Italy were so often conditioned by suspicions of France) Garibaldi developed a hare-brained scheme to lead a raid on his birthplace.

He would take 200 men (armed with rifles from the stores of the 'Million Rifles Fund'), smash the ballot boxes in which the people of Nice were being asked to record their approval of annexation in a plebiscite, scatter the papers, and make it necessary for the Government to hold a new ballot. When the new ballot was held those who disapproved of annexation would have had an opportunity to change the opinion of those who were so actively canvassing in support of union with France. He was encouraged to believe in the success of this improbable plan by Laurence Oliphant, an eccentric and amusing English adventurer who promised to charter a coach in which a party of conspirators (who were to precede the sea-borne raid) could drive from Genoa to Nice.

On 13 April Garibaldi and Oliphant took the train back to Genoa,

They shared the same reserved carriage but they spoke hardly at all, for Garibaldi spent almost the entire journey reading a huge bundle of letters, which 'he tore up into small fragments as soon as he had made himself acquainted with their contents. By the time we reached Genoa,' Oliphant remembered, 'the floor of the carriage was thickly strewn with the litter and looked like a gigantic wastepaper basket'. Oliphant was curious to know what these letters were; but it was only later that he discovered.

On arrival in Genoa he went off to hire the coach and later 'repaired to the hotel which Garibaldi had indicated as his address and which was a rough, old-fashioned second-rate looking place upon the quay'. And here he learned that the pressure brought upon Garibaldi by the advocates of the Sicilian invasion had persuaded him at last to change his mind. The letters, given to him by Bertani in Turin and torn to shreds in the railway carriage, were from volunteers who wanted to fight in Sicily.

'*Amico mio*,' Garibaldi said to Oliphant when he arrived at the depressing Albergo della Felicità where the General and twenty or thirty men were sitting down to supper in a large private room. 'I am very sorry, but we must abandon all idea of carrying out our Nice programme. Behold these gentlemen from Sicily. . . . I had hoped to be able to carry out this little Nice affair first, for it is only a matter of a few days; but much as I regret it, the general opinion is that we shall lose all if we try for too much.'*[37]

The following morning Garibaldi left Genoa for Quarto, three miles down the coast, where his friend Augusto Vecchi, the lawyer who had fought under him at Rome, had a villa. Vecchi's coachman saw Garibaldi approaching the courtyard of the yellow-washed house and rushed upstairs 'four steps at a time', to his master's room, calling out excitedly, 'The General! The General!'†

---

* The voting in Nice and Savoy was overwhelmingly in favour of annexation to France, and although there was certainly much corruption there can be no doubt that a majority of the people did want the annexation to be effected. Of 26,003 votes cast in Nice there were only 260 '*nons*'. In Savoy 235 people voted '*non*', 130,533 '*oui*' – Paul Matter, *Cavour et l'Unité Italienne* (Paris, 1927) 321.

† Garibaldi was nearly always referred to simply as 'the General'. It was, an Englishman living in Italy decided, 'as though there were only one general in all the world'. – Thomas Augustus Trollope, *What I Remember* (London, 1887), ii, 222.

Vecchi hurried down, and saw his friend standing in the courtyard in the sunshine.

'Now that Nice belongs to Italy no longer, my dear Vecchi, I am like Jesus Christ – I have no longer a stone on which to lay my head. You are the richest of my apostles, that is why I come to ask for your hospitality.'

'The house and its master are yours, General. Do what you like with both.'

'Good, but Jesus Christ is not alone. He has with him his military establishment.'

'The house is large enough to receive his eleven associates.'

'Happily, for the moment, they are reduced to five.'

'Their names?'

'Fruscianti, Elia,* Stagnetti,† Gusmaroli,‡ and Menotti.'

'There is room for all.'

Garibaldi then crossed the courtyard, put his arms round Vecchi and they walked into the house together where the General's first action (as it invariably was at the end of a journey, however short), was to go into the bathroom to wash.[38]

For three weeks Garibaldi remained at the Villa Spinola, enjoying a game of bowls with Vecchi after their meals – 'one of his weaknesses being that he believed himself excellent at the game' – feeding the family's parrot with bits of fruit, getting up well before dawn and then, having drunk the cup of coffee that Fruscianti made for him, going for a strenuous walk in the hills to return to the villa wet with sweat and then to wash and to change all his clothes. Sometimes Vecchi accompanied him, and one day on their return they passed five or six children on their way to school. Garibaldi turned back to pick one of them up, a pale, sickly-looking little boy. 'Grow up to

---

* Augusto Elia: A seaman from Ancona, he was to command the *Lombardo*, the steamer in which Nino Bixio's men sailed for Sicily, and to be badly wounded at Calatafimi.

† Pietro Stagnetti: He remained on Garibaldi's staff throughout the coming campaign and drove with him into Naples. Subsequently he was a frequent visitor at Caprera.

‡ Luigi Gusmaroli: An ex-curé with a deep hatred of his former associates. He, too, remained on the staff to the end and drove with Garibaldi into Naples. He was also a frequent visitor at Caprera.

be a support for Italy,' he said earnestly to the surprised and nervous child. 'Seek to be its glory. You have a great country. Be yourself as great as she. And may God give you the happiness of turning out the vermin which devour it.' Then he put the boy down and gave him a coin.[39]

One of the vermin that Garibaldi would have liked to see turned out was, of course, Cavour. And one day he told Vecchi that he had said as much to the King. 'Sire,' he had proposed, 'if you wish, in six weeks you and I can make Italy. Rid yourself of this diplomat, who ties your hands, and then we will go forward.'

'And what did he reply?' Vecchi asked him.

'He did not reply,' the General admitted, 'and that is what maddens me.'[40]

The King, in fact, for all his supposed sympathy with the Sicilian invasion, for all Cavour's suspicions that 'his weakness for Garibaldi' was leading him to look 'for some excuse' to find a new Prime Minister, refused, at least for the present, to consider giving his personal and semi-official sanction to a venture of which his Government did not approve. According to Farini, now Piedmontese Minister of the Interior, the King told those of Garibaldi's supporters who urged this independent and unconstitutional course upon him that his Ministers were, with his approval, keeping 'a tight hold on policy', and that they were not prepared to allow the initiative to 'be taken out of their hands by Garibaldi or by anyone else'.[41]

Exactly what Cavour's policy was during these weeks when volunteers were arriving in Genoa by every train has long been open to conjecture. His official policy, of course, was to condemn the expedition; for the far-from-secret preparations at Genoa aroused vehement diplomatic protests which he obviously could not ignore. But was this official policy a blind for his secret collusion? It has been the orthodox view of Risorgimento historians that this was so.

'Certainly Cavour's help had to be given covertly,' Ida Nazari-Micheli wrote in 1911 in *Cavour e Garibaldi nel 1860*, 'and even to be concealed behind a pretended persecution. . . . But no one can deny any longer that Cavour helped the Sicilian insurrection from 24 March onwards, and the expedition of The Thousand from the time of its preparation.'

This is the point of view which has been supported by most of Cavour's biographers, and, of course, by fascist writers who liked to paint the Risorgimento as an essentially national and ideally romantic movement in which Cavour, Garibaldi and Mazzini acted together if not as friends, certainly not as the antagonists they were finally driven to be. Even those historians who have been unconvinced by the evidence of Cavour's active help, have suggested that he was at least prompted by an opportunistic anxiety not to prevent an action which he might be able in time to work to his advantage. G. M. Trevelyan, for example, 'ventured to suggest that Cavour was in some degree an opportunist waiting on circumstances, and unwilling to commit himself or his country till the latest possible moment'.[42] The argument, in fact, was, as Sir James Hudson commented at the time: 'if he fails we are rid of a troublesome fellow, and if he succeeds Italy will derive some profit from his success'.[*43]

This is an attractive interpretation and accords with many of the known facts. Cavour was not, after all, against the idea of active interference as such. It is true that in 1860 he did not want 'to push the Neapolitan question to a crisis',[44] since, apart from domestic problems, he did not want to risk the interference of France or Austria; and the interference of France – the withdrawal of whose troops from Rome he was trying to negotiate – could scarcely be avoided if Garibaldi combined an attack on Sicily with an invasion of the Papal States. But it is also true that if he were not to be given the 'much more time' he wanted, he professed himself willing to 'prepare plans'.[45] At the beginning of April, when news of the Sicilian uprising reached Turin, he immediately told General Fanti to ask General Ribotti, a Sicilian serving with the Piedmontese army, to resign his commission and to go to Sicily to organise the rebels. Ribotti agreed to go, but when he arrived at Turin a doubt had arisen as to the importance of the uprising and he was sent back to Rimini. A week later, when further news of the revolt suggested that it was more widespread than had been supposed, and when Government agents in Genoa had reported the increasing urgency of Garibaldi's

* This was certainly the impression his activities gave to his contemparies in England: 'Everybody believes that Cavour has covertly connived at it, though he pretends to oppose it.' – *The Greville Memoirs 1814-1860* (ed. Lytton Strachey and Roger Fulford) (Macmillan, 1938), vii, 477.

preparations, Cavour authorised the issue of 1,500 guns belonging to La Farina's National Society to Giuseppe La Masa, a theatrically enthusiastic Sicilian who had offered to lead an invasion of his fellow-exiles against their homeland.

The departure of a Sicilian expedition might well have forestalled the departure of a Garibaldian one; but if it was Cavour's intention to ensure that if any force had to go it must not be one that contained an uncertain number of Northern republicans, as interested in the Papal States as in Sicily, the intention was not realised. For La Masa agreed to combine his efforts with Garibaldi; and La Farina (who was also a Sicilian) agreed to issue his weapons to the joint expedition.

As it happened, the weapons were virtually useless, anyway. On their arrival at the Villa Spinola, Garibaldi discovered them to be not much better than a load of 'old iron'. They were antiquated, smooth-bore muskets, converted from flintlocks which had been sold by the army as obsolete. They were, in fact, worse than obsolete. It is 'no exaggeration to say that nine out of ten of them would not even fire'.[46] But at least they had bayonets – and Garibaldi's tactics were always to rest firmly on the bayonet charge – though even this advantage was not immediately apparent: for some of the muskets were so rusty that the bayonets could not at first be fixed.[47]

These ancient firearms had to be taken, though, for despite the encouragement and promises given to him by the Ansaldo armaments firm, they were the only ones that Garibaldi could procure. He had asked, through the Director of the 'Million Rifles Fund', for some of the 12,000 modern rifles in store at Milan to be released to him; and the Director had met with a definite refusal from the Governor of Milan. The Governor had afterwards written to Farini asking for the Government to confirm his refusal, and Farini had written to Cavour. And although Cavour did not wish personally and openly to commit himself, the refusal was confirmed by a Cabinet minute.[48]

The Governor of Milan at this time was Massimo d'Azeglio, the former Prime Minister, a man of most delicate scruple. His feeling, shared by Henry Elliot at Naples, was that the Government's under-hand methods and equivocal diplomacy were unpardonable. 'I should have preferred a more open conduct rather than the resort to so many artful tricks which have deceived no one,' he wrote later that year. 'Garibaldi went straight ahead, risking his own life, and all credit to him. Whereas we! . . . By deceit we might win something for the moment, but you lose far more in the long run when no one can believe you any longer.'[49]

And so d'Azeglio decided that to release a large stock of rifles to a force, whose known intention was to use them against a Kingdom with which the Government continued to maintain superficially friendly relations, was an action which he could not take. It would lay the Government open to the sort of charges which Henry Elliot was later to level against it when complaining of Victor Emmanuel's 'unscrupulous' and 'discreditable' methods.[50]

On the day before Massimo d'Azeglio's refusal to release the rifles, Victor Emmanuel, on Cavour's advice, had written to Francis II:

'We have now reached a time when Italy can be divided into two powerful states, one in the North and one in the South.' All that stood in the way of this friendly division was the matter of constitutional reforms in the Neapolitan Kingdom. This letter was not necessarily symptomatic, however, of what Elliot condemned as the Turin Government's policy of 'unscrupulous deceit'.

For Cavour was quite content, after all, to see Italy remain divided in this way for some time to come. He had always been more concerned that Piedmont should be made free and constitutional than that Italy should be made one; his sights were set lower than Mazzini's. And he was not yet ready, as he so often insisted, 'to push the Neapolitan question to a crisis'.[51] He was 'hostile to the idea of creating embarrassments for the King of Naples', and wished only to see Francis II 'reconciling the legitimate desires of his subjects with the conservative tendencies of his government'.[52]

Cavour's habit of saying one thing to one man and something else to the next, his willingness to contradict himself twice on the same day, his skill in persuading so many different men that he had as many different motives (and in persuading the Garibaldians, in particular, that he might give them the help that he was determined to deny them), his subsequent desire to rationalise his actions and idealise his motives make it impossible, of course, to reveal in a clear light any sort of consistent attitude. It is almost impossible, indeed, as Denis Mack Smith has written in *The Cambridge Historical Journal*, to summarise his activities at this time 'in any formula or pattern that is consistent with all the facts'. It can at least be argued, however, that such influence as he did have on events during these few days 'was used less to help than to deter and thwart Garibaldi'.[53] This was certainly the impression that many well-informed Italian observers formed at the time. 'Judging by what I saw and heard from the officers of the King's suite,' wrote Count Arrivabene, 'I have reasons to believe that Cavour, far from having encouraged the project, tried all he could to prevent it.'[54]

There were good reasons for this attitude, as Professor Passerin d'Entrèves has argued.[55] A man who had devoted his career to the Kingdom of Piedmont could not be expected to view with less than deep anxiety an expedition with so many Mazzinian undertones, an expedition which, if a failure, might result in his ruin, and if successful either in demands for a republic, or for Sicilian autonomy, or what was scarcely less to be dreaded, Victor Emmanuel having to accept the Crown of Naples from the hands of Garibaldi. And yet there was little Cavour could do to prevent the expedition sailing. He could take steps to ensure that it did not get the money which the Government could easily have supplied without the knowledge of the diplomatic world; he could endeavour to prevent it getting hold of the necessary munitions and ships; he could, as he did on 22 April, pay a personal visit to Genoa to emphasise the likelihood of failure; he could subsequently send various officers and confidential agents to the Villa Spinola – since Garibaldi refused to grant him a personal interview – to put further doubts into the General's mind; he could go to the King (though Victor Emmanuel was undoubtedly by now a Garibaldian at heart himself) and discuss with him the possibility of stopping the expedition and arresting Garibaldi. But Cavour had to face in the end the fact that he could not afford to arrest him.

The crisis had occurred at an unfortunate time. The surrender of Nice and Savoy, though officially approved by the inhabitants, had yet to be negotiated through Parliament. Cavour could hope that after the elections, due to be held on 7 May, his hand would be strengthened in that Parliament by a large majority; but by the time the results were in, the expedition might well have sailed; and in the meantime he had reason to believe that both Ricasoli and Rattazzi were being considered as alternative candidates for the premiership. And even if this expected strong vote of confidence were to be given him before the expedition started, could he defy public opinion which was wholeheartedly supporting Garibaldi? 'The Ministry,' Cavour told Costantino Nigra, 'is in no position to face the immense unpopularity which would have been drawn upon it, had Garibaldi been prevented.' Not now, nor at any time, could public opinion be ignored. *'Vous savez,'* he reminded Villamarina in Naples, *'que l'opinion publique est ma boussole* – my compass.'*[56]

And there was another consideration: if Garibaldi were to be forcibly held back, might he not become – as Cavour told Ricasoli he feared he would become – 'very dangerous in internal politics'?[57] That, at least, was one good reason for letting him go; and, if he were to go, he would take a lot of dangerous and undesirable men out of the North with him. But then if he were to be killed? Cavour would certainly be blamed for not giving him greater support. To let him go and to let him stay, he recognised as alternatives equally dangerous.[58] The only hope was that the revolt in Sicily would collapse, and Garibaldi would, of his own accord, cancel his dangerous plans.

★   ★   ★

There had been a time, indeed, when this cancellation had seemed more than likely.

It had been Garibaldi's original intention to sail for Sicily with only 200 men as soon as the rifles could be collected from Milan. The delay in the arrival of the rifles, however, prevented his departure for what would have been almost certain defeat. When La Farina's muskets arrived, he decided to sail with 500 volunteers on 28 April. Again he was prevented, this time by a telegram which arrived from Fabrizi in Malta on 27 April.

> Offer of 160 casks American rum 45 pence sold 66 casks English 47 in advance pounds 114 casks 147 Brandy without offer. Advise cashing of bill of exchange 99 pounds. Answer at once.

---

* Cavour always preferred to write in French. He had, after all, like Garibaldi and Mazzini, been born a French citizen in a Savoy-Piedmont which Napoleon's victories had made a colony of France. The Italian language had been unacceptable in Turin society and Cavour's knowledge of it was consequently always imperfect, as Garibaldi's was.

Garibaldi as a Piedmontese General in command of the Cacciatori Delle Alpi

Jessie White Mario

Anita Garibaldi

Francesca Armosino

Garibaldi at the time of the sailing of the Thousand

After this curious message had been decoded Garibaldi was shocked to learn its contents:

Complete failure in the province and city of Palermo. Many fugitives received on board English vessels that have arrived at Malta. Do not start.[59]

The uprising which had broken out at last in Palermo earlier in the month had, indeed, been a complete failure – and had, in fact, offered little chance of success from the beginning.

Planned by a brave and excitable plumber, Francesco Riso, and his nobly born namesake, Baron Riso, it had soon become the talk of the city. Long before the plumber and seventeen of his companions had charged out of a house he had rented opposite the Gancia Convent, the police chief, Salvatore Maniscalco, had discovered the plot. Within a few minutes of their eruption, Riso and his followers had been driven off the streets and into the Gancia Convent where they rang the bells to call the Palermitans to join in their revolt and threw bombs out of the windows to keep the soldiers off. The frightened Palermitans stayed indoors; the bombs, made by Baron Riso and his friends, did not explode.

The doors of the convent were blown open; Riso fell mortally wounded; the Baron was arrested. The latest Palermitan insurrection drew to its traditional close.

Outside the town, on the plain and in the mountains, however, bands of peasant rebels and bandits formed themselves into *squadre* under patriotic landlords or other chosen leaders, and wandered about between the villages, occasionally skirmishing with the Bourbon troops sent out from Palermo. But these Sicilian *picciotti* were rarely successful in their encounters and it seemed likely that here, too, the revolt would fail, even after Rosolino Pilo arrived in Western Sicily in the now desperate hope that he might keep the spirit of the rebels alive until Garibaldi came.

The depressing news from Sicily persuaded Garibaldi to believe that those who had advised caution were right. 'It would be madness to go,' he said to Crispi and La Masa with tears in his eyes.[60] They tried to get him to change his mind; but at length they came out of his room in Vecchi's villa gloomy and frustrated. Bixio stayed with him, continuing to argue, growing more and more heated until at last he too came out 'furiously angry; and the sad words passed round: *"Non si parte più."* '61

Bixio and La Masa said they would go without him; and next day a deputation of volunteers came down from Genoa and implied that Garibaldi was afraid, while they were ready for anything. But Crispi, while not agreeing with Garibaldi that it was madness to go at all, thought that it would be madness to go without him; and he advised that they should wait for a few days to see if 'new facts' turned up. On 29 April new facts did turn up; and according to Stefan Türr and Augusto Vecchi, Crispi himself had invented them.62 They were further messages from Rosolino Pilo in Sicily and Nicola Fabrizi in Malta declaring that the insurrection in Sicily was still going on.63 'Hereupon the General exclaimed, "Then let us start".'64

In Bertani's house in Genoa the next morning a council of war was held. Sirtori and Medici disapproved of the venture, thinking that it could not hope to succeed; but they were now the only two to speak out against it. And so, the final decision was taken: they would go.

Bixio, who had once been a sailor, was given the task of preparing the embarkation; Bertani was to continue his work of enlisting the volunteers. Many of these volunteers had left Genoa within the last few days, exasperated by the long wait and the uncertainty of departure; but there were others still arriving in the town from all parts of Italy, and it was hoped eventually to collect a thousand together within the next week. They were nearly all civilians. Garibaldi had asked the King to allow him to enlist those volunteers who had served under him in the *Cacciatori delle Alpi* the previous year, and who were now serving in the Piedmontese army, mostly in the 46th Regiment. The King listened sympathetically but, when he consulted Cavour, he was persuaded that the discipline of the army must come first and that if Garibaldi was allowed to take men away from it, the defence of Piedmont against Austria would be seriously weakened. Garibaldi accepted the decision; and in the event The Thousand included only five officers who deserted the regular army; and one of these, Giuseppe Bandi, became an aide-de-camp to the General with the King's knowledge and connivance.

The Thousand, when they reached Sicily, actually numbered 1,089 volunteers. Supported by contributions from towns all over the North, they were of all sorts and descriptions of men. In the *Istituto per la Storia del Risorgimento Italiano* in Rome, big albums containing photographs of them provide eloquent testimony as to the kinds of people they were – students, working-men, vagabonds and ruffians, tradesmen, civil servants, journalists, authors, university lecturers, barbers, cobblers, gentlemen of leisure, painters, sculptors, ships' captains, chemists, adventurers, businessmen, engineers, a hundred doctors, a hundred and fifty lawyers, and one woman, Crispi's mistress, a woman of peasant stock who worked as washerwoman and cook. They were of all ages – the youngest not yet twelve, the oldest a veteran of the campaigns of Napoleon I.

Most of them came from the towns of the North, the largest contingents from Bergamo, Brescia, Milan and Pavia, though only seven came from Turin. There were about a hundred Sicilians and Neapolitans, but only eleven Romans, and four Hungarians. By the evening of 5 May they had all been assembled at Quarto in the grounds of the Palazzo Spinola which stood between Vecchi's villa and the sea. For days, so Bandi said, the General had not had a moment's peace; there had been 'visit after visit, telegram after telegram, deputation after deputation'. But now everything had been settled; and all arrangements made. He felt, as he confessed later 'a harmony of soul . . . capable of attempting anything'.

He settled down to write one last letter: 'It is certain that we shall leave tonight for the Mezzogiorno.'[65]

Garibaldismo as a well-determined political movement was about at last to be born.[66]

2

THE SAILING OF THE THOUSAND

At half-past nine on the evening of 5 May 1860 Garibaldi left
Vecchi's villa and walked through the grounds of the Palazzo
Spinola towards the sea, accompanied by a number of his officers.
He was wearing his red shirt and baggy grey trousers with a silk
handkerchief round his neck. He carried his poncho, 'made of thick
Sardinian cloth, in bandolier fashion. He wore his sabre, his knife
in his belt, his revolver slung on his back, and his Colt's repeater
carbine on his shoulder.'[1]

Under the trees at the edge of the Palazzo's ground and on the
rocks by the sea, the volunteers were waiting, quietly watching the
cases of muskets being loaded into the boats. One or two of them
were in the uniform of the Piedmontese army, a few others in the
green uniform of the Genoese *carabinieri*; but most of them were in
their ordinary clothes. There was little evident excitement and
scarcely any noise. Even their friends and families who had come to
see them off stood in silence or whispering softly. It was a calm
evening, windless and cool.

When the moon came up, the long line of boats could be seen
moving out from the little bay to await the arrival of the two
steamers which a party of seamen and engineers were to seize in
Genoa harbour with the connivance of an agent of their owners.

All night long the volunteers waited, as the engines of one of the
ships, the *Lombardo*, were out of order and the other ship, the *Piemonte*, had to take her in tow before she could be got out of the
harbour. But at dawn both steamers hove into sight and the men
clambered quickly up the rope ladders while the boats went back
for other volunteers still waiting on the shore.

'*Presto! Presto! Sbrigatevi!*' the officers urged, for they had meant
to be well out at sea before daylight and there was the ammunition
yet to load. This was to have been rowed out in boats from Bogliasco
guided by some local seamen in a light skiff with a lantern in its
stern. But the seamen had not been able to resist the temptation to go

out smuggling on so propitious a night, and had rowed away into the darkness, leaving the men in the heavy ammunition boats to find the steamers as best they could. They never did find them. Instead of waiting off Bogliasco, they rowed west towards Quarto, passed by the steamers in the darkness and, when the sun came up, saw their trails of smoke on the horizon beyond Portofino.

Garibaldi seemed curiously undismayed. He had a feeling, he remembered years later, that he was destined to succeed no matter what the difficulties, a sense of elated confidence.

'We'll go on without them,' he said. 'How many of us are there altogether?'

'Counting the sailors more than a thousand.'

'*Eh! Eh!* What a lot!'[2]

Few of the men aboard the *Piemonte* felt as cheerful as he did. The decks were so crowded there was scarcely room to sit down; there was nothing to eat except a few pieces of crumbling biscuit; and the rolling seas had made most of them fearfully sick. More than one man said later that he had always expected to die when he got to Sicily, but that he had wished then that he could die on the way. There were over 400 miles to go.

They were not, however, to cover this distance in one voyage. For Garibaldi had already decided to call on the way at a port on the Tuscan coast, partly to land a detachment to make a diversionary invasion of the Papal States through Orvieto and Perugia, partly to join up with a party of Tuscan volunteers from Leghorn, but mainly so as to organise his Thousand into some sort of manœuvrable regiment and to give them some idea of military drill and tactics. Also he needed coal and food and water; and now, above all, he needed ammunition.

He found them all in the various small ports of the Gulf of Talamone, which he entered wearing the uniform of a Piedmontese general. At Orbetello, the commandant of the fortress was diplomatically persuaded by Colonel Türr to give up all that he had in his arsenal which included three antiquated field-pieces; at Porto Santo Stefano the official in charge of the coal store was roughly induced by Nino Bixio to hand over the keys of the shed; and at Grosseto, and in Talamone itself, the villagers were found willing to sell a little food.

There was trouble, though, in Talamone. The food was produced reluctantly, bargaining was ill-tempered, and there were arguments and fights which the officers were unable to control. Some volunteers got drunk and tried to force their company upon the girls promenading provocatively up and down the main street. When he heard of all this, Garibaldi was furious. He went ashore, glaring 'with the eyes of a wild boar', and in an intimidating rage ordered the entire army back on board the steamers. He himself stormed back into his cabin, slammed the door and no one dared approach it. When he learned that his commissary, Paolo Bovi, had still not returned with provisions from Grosseto he gave orders for him to be thrown overboard as soon as he appeared.[3]

Bixio was even more ferocious in his anger at these early displays of indiscipline. When he heard a volunteer give an answer which he took to be disrespectful, he threw a plate at the man's head, summoned all the other volunteers on deck and shouted at them: 'I command here. I am everything. I am Tsar, Sultan, Pope. . . . I am Nino Bixio. If you dare to think of mutinying or even to shrug your shoulders, I will come up to you in my uniform, sabre in hand, and I will cut you to pieces.'[4]

He was shaking with rage. They knew that he meant it. But instead of greeting his wild address with sullen silence, they broke into cheers.

He had little further trouble. Nor, indeed, did Garibaldi. His anger soon cooled. When the commissary at last returned with the provisions from Grosseto, he approached the General's cabin with nervous apprehension, tears in his eyes. But Garibaldi came out, nodded to him in the most friendly way, said 'Good morning, Bovi. You made me very cross last night,' and, having listened to his explanations, added, '*Eh! Va bene.*'

It was all over. Bovi wiped his eyes. Garibaldi's rage was terrifying; but his forgiveness as always was like a benediction.[5]

The time spent in the Gulf of Talamone was devoted to organising The Thousand. All the men (apart from the few artillerymen and scouts, the Genoese *carabinieri* and the headquarters staff) were divided into eight companies of infantry. Garibaldi appointed the company commanders who selected in turn their subalterns and non-commissioned officers. The companies, composed as far as possible of men from the same town, were divided into two battalions of four companies each. One battalion was given to Nino Bixio, the other to a Sicilian soldier, Giacinto Carini.

There were rather less men to dispose of than there had been at Quarto, for several uncompromising republicans had now left the ships in disgust at Garibaldi's announcement that the expedition's war-cry was to be '*Italia e Vittorio Emanuele!*' and sixty-one men, together with the seventy-eight Tuscan volunteers from Leghorn, had been despatched under Zambianchi on the diversionary invasion of the Papal States.*[6]

Many of those who remained behind at Talamone believed that the expedition to Sicily would prove no more successful than Zambianchi's was expected to be. But Garibaldi was not one of them; and when on the afternoon of 9 May the *Piemonte* and the *Lombardo* steamed out of the gulf of Talamone and set course for the north-west corner of Sicily, he was seen to be in a mood almost of gaiety. That evening he settled down in his cabin to compose a few verses which, he hoped, some of the more musical amongst The Thousand would set to music so that they might sing them while marching against the enemy in Sicily; and even when those to whom his aide-de-camp, Giuseppe Bandi, delegated this task made it clear what they thought of his embarrassingly bad compositions by lampooning them outside his door, he appeared not to mind.[7] He was at sea and sailing to war again. No one could stop him now.

* * *

Two days before, Cavour had sent this telegram to the Governor of Cagliari in Sardinia: 'Garibaldi has embarked with 400 volunteers on two Rubattino steamers for Sicily. If he enters a port of Sardinia arrest the expedition. I authorise you to employ, if required, the squadron commanded by Count Persano.'[8]

---

* This expedition was as foolhardy as it was ill-led. Even if the people in the Papal States had been likely to rise in support of it and had given Bertani and Medici, who had been left behind at Genoa, encouragement to send reinforcements after it, Zambianchi was the last man to lead it. He had shown himself in Rome to be a murderous ruffian, and now proved himself incompetent as well. The expedition, which indeed never seemed remotely likely to be a success, became, under his leadership, a fiasco – General Giovanni Pittaluga, *La Diversione* (1904), *passim*.

Next day he sent Admiral Persano a qualifying message: 'Do not arrest the expedition at sea – only if it enters a port.'[9]

All Europe was already in an uproar. Prussia protested; Russia protested; Austria protested; France countermanded the projected withdrawal of her troops from Rome; England expressed her fear that France would be paid for her protection of Italy against Austria by the cession of Genoa or Sardinia. Cavour, concerned to preserve his French alliance, felt obliged, as he told Ricasoli, to 'keep up appearances so as not to increase our diplomatic difficulties'.[10]

Admiral Persano later claimed to have felt sure that this was what was in Cavour's mind when the telegrams were sent. He replied by asking if the arrest were seriously meant, and when he was told that 'the Ministry has decided', he took this to mean that Cavour did not agree with his colleagues and that the Prime Minister hoped that he would not do anything. He telegraphed back, 'I understand'.[11]

But in a later message from Turin, where fears of the consequences of Garibaldi's activities had by then greatly increased, Cavour revealed that he was no longer merely concerned to keep up appearances. The Piedmontese fleet was ordered to arrest the expedition '*at all costs*'. The last three words were underlined.[12]

*   *   *

While these messages were crackling back and forth between Sardinia and Turin, the *Piemonte* and the *Lombardo* were drawing close to the Sicilian coastline. Garibaldi had at first intended landing on it close to Palermo, the capital; but he had changed his mind, thinking this would be too dangerous, and had decided instead to make for a point farther along the coast south of Trapani; the exact place would be determined by the movements of the Neapolitan squadron lying in wait for him. Eventually, on the advice of Castiglia, captain of the *Piemonte*, he decided to run ashore at Marsala after passing between the islands of Favignana and Marettimo. This would be dangerous enough, for there were four cruisers patrolling these waters, and when Marsala came into view what looked like two of them were seen to be in the harbour.

Garibaldi, however, after studying them through his telescope decided from their build that they were British, a view soon confirmed by the English crew of a sailing-boat which passed hard by

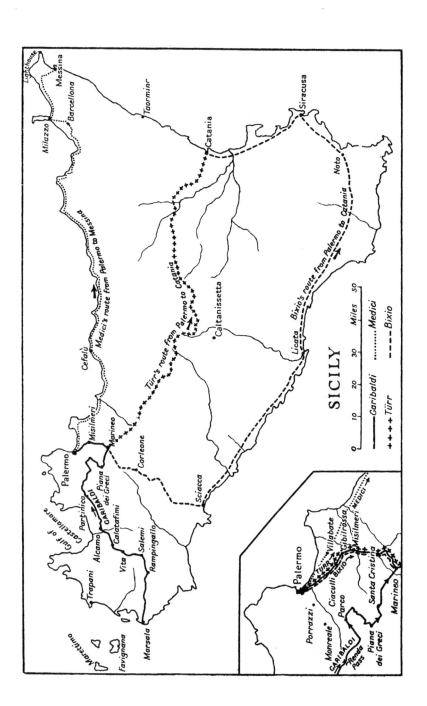

SICILY

——	Garibaldi
+++	Türr
········	Medici
– – –	Bixio

Miles
0 10 20 30 50

Lighthouse
Messina
Barcellona
Milazzo
Taormina
Catania
Siracusa
Noto
Cefalù
Medici's route from Palermo to Messina
Misilmeri
Türr's route from Palermo to Catania
Caltanissetta
Licata
Bixio's route from Palermo to Catania
Palermo
Marineo
Corleone
Sciacca
Piana
dei Greci
GARIBALDI
Partinico
Alcamo
Vita
Calatafimi
Salemi
Rampingallo
Trapani
Gulf of
Castellamare
Marettimo
Favignana
Marsala

Palermo
Porrazzi
Monreale
GARIBALDI
Renda
Pass
Parco
Ciaculli
Türr
Villabate
Bixio
Misilmeri
Medici
Santa Cristina
Marineo
Piana
dei Greci

the *Piemonte* on her way out of the harbour.* Some time later the nervous captain of a fishing-boat, which Garibaldi took in tow to help in the disembarkation, came on board to give the welcome news that the Neapolitan ships which had been at Marsala earlier on that morning had sailed away towards Sciacca. He said, too, that the Neapolitan garrison had also recently left the town of Palermo.[13]

Marsala, by one of those strokes of good fortune that were to characterise the campaign, was, then, for the time being unguarded. A few miles away to the south, however, the captain of the Neapolitan ship *Stromboli* had caught sight of the Piedmontese steamers and was turning back to intercept them. The *Piemonte* and *Lombardo*, steaming at full speed, raced through the waves to disembark their cargoes while there was still time.

Between half-past-one and two o'clock, the two Piedmontese steamers came round the lighthouse at the end of the mole and into the harbour. The British sailors on board H.M.S. *Argus* had a good view of them as they passed under her stern. Their decks were crammed with men, all armed but mostly in 'plain citizens' attire', packed together 'like herrings in a barrel'.[14]

The captain of the *Argus*, Captain H. F. Winnington-Ingram, had gone ashore with the captain of the *Intrepid*, Commander Marryat, to visit the British consul and to look round 'Mr. Woodhouse's wine establishment'. While talking to Mr. Harvey, the Woodhouse manager, Captain Winnington-Ingram saw the two ships steaming round the mole. The leading one, the *Piemonte*, got safely into the inner harbour, but the *Lombardo* grounded at its entrance.

Immediately shore boats began leaving the *Lombardo* to disembark men on the mole by the lighthouse. The first boatloads contained officers of the staff in red shirts; and this led the captain of the Neapolitan warship, the *Stromboli*, now rapidly closing on the Piedmontese steamers, to suppose that they carried British soldiers.

---

* The two ships were H.M.S. *Argus* and *Intrepid*. They had been sent to Marsala to protect the British colony which, like all the other inhabitants of the town, had been disarmed by a force despatched from the capital under General Letizia after there had been demonstrations in the streets in support of Riso's revolt at the Gancia Convent. The British colony were nearly all engaged in the trade for which Marsala is famous – the sweetening and fortifying of the local wine. A lighter type of Marsala is now known as 'Garibaldi',

Winnington-Ingram, who had feared that the *Stromboli* would open fire and that he would 'witness a fearful slaughter' as well as be struck himself by a ricochet shot, now saw that 'a doubt seemed to occupy the mind of the Neapolitan commander, for he brought his vessel to a standstill close to the *Intrepid*, and hailed that sloop to enquire if those were English soldiers landing. He, of course, received a reply in the negative, but was told that there were English officers ashore [they were eating ice-cream in a café] as well as the commanders of both English ships'.

In the meantime [Winnington-Ingram continued], the Sardinians were putting ashore men, stores and ammunition as fast as possible. . . . Presently a boat was seen to quit the Neapolitan war steamer and pull towards the grounded Sardinian. She had not, however, reached more than half-way to the vessel, when a panic appeared to seize those in her, and a retreat was hastily made to their ship which now opened fire upon the mole with heavy guns. Commander Marryat, Mr. Cousins [the British Consul] and myself embarked at once in a gig of the *Argus* and proceeded on board the Neapolitan to beg her captain to direct his shot and shell clear of the British wine establishments. To our surprise we found that officer to bear the name of a fine old English Roman Catholic family, to be complete master of our language. [He was Ferdinand Acton, a great nephew of Sir John Acton who had become Prime Minister of Naples under Ferdinand I]. He seemed much impressed with the responsibility of his situation, but promised not to injure British property. . . . We now left him and were pulling for the *Intrepid* when the Neapolitan sailing frigate came bearing down upon our boat, and her officers hailed and waved to us to pull faster. Hardly had they done so when a veritable storm of shot and missiles of all kinds, delivered from her broadside guns, passed over our heads, but fell short of the mole. One of her shot, however, entered Mr. Woodhouse's wine establishment and nearly killed Mrs. Harvey, the manager's wife. . . .

The Sardinian steamers being completely deserted, the Neapolitans sent in armed boats to take possession of them. They succeeded in bringing out the one that had entered the inner harbour, but scuttled the other that had grounded at its entrance.

The Neapolitan steamers continued, during this operation, to fire heavily at parties dragging guns and ammunition into the town, but we only saw one man knocked over [he was wounded in the shoulder]. The patriots stood fire splendidly and appeared to be altogether a fine body of men.[15]

Garibaldi stood outside the sea-gate which led through the mediaeval walls of Marsala into the town, encouraging the men as they filed through and teasing those who ducked and flinched at the whistle and crash of the shot. He had cause to feel cheerful, for the man Winnington-Ingram had seen knocked down on the mole was the only casualty that entire afternoon. If Captain Acton had opened fire sooner and placed his steamer closer to the *Lombardo* he could have 'raked her from stem to stern', as Commander Marryat said, 'and one may feel convinced that all landing by boats would have ceased'.[16]

As it was, by half-past four both the *Lombardo* and the *Piemonte* were cleared of all their men and stores, and Garibaldi and Crispi, who was now acting as his political secretary, were safely inside the town talking to the municipal authorities. Several of the leading citizens had already left the town but the others, assured by Crispi that their support would be 'the point of departure for the political transformation' of their country, agreed to sign a document to the effect that the Bourbons had ceased to reign in Sicily and that Garibaldi was now Dictator.[17]

The Dictator's followers spent the rest of that evening and night in Marsala. And they were disappointed by their reception. Expecting to be welcomed as liberators, they were greeted with nervous suspicion by a strange people whose language they could scarcely understand. Very few of them were willing to join Garibaldi, and several of those who did so during the evening ran away the following morning with the firearms which had been given them. At first the priests were blamed (quite unjustly) for the people's discouraging attitude; and Garibaldi, whose feelings nevertheless remained sanguine and content, had to send Sirtori, a former priest himself, round the town to prevent the more violent members of The Thousand from indulging their taste for priest-baiting. 'The priests might be enemies to modern ideas of progress,' Garibaldi said later, 'but they were enemies of the Bourbons as well.'[18]

And he needed all the allies he could find. The next evening he found some; for when his men, having marched all day over the dry, grey roads towards Palermo in the burning heat, fell down exhausted at Rampingallo, they were joined by the first of the bands of Sicilian *picciotti* which were soon to give the invaders the local support they so badly needed. These *squadre*, young peasants on sturdy horses with a variety of weapons from blunderbusses to pruning-hooks, came into Garibaldi's camp and the Dictator greeted them with arms outspread in welcome.

The next day they rode with his Thousand into Salemi, a hill town high above the thin olive groves of the upland plain, with the bells of the campanili pealing in their ears. At Salemi, after the ground had been prepared by La Masa and an enthusiastic friar, Father Pantaleo, who joined Garibaldi as a second Ugo Bassi, the Dictatorship was again proclaimed; and this time the proclamation – accompanied by the announcement of the abolition of various unpopular taxes imposed by the Bourbons – was cheerfully received. Garibaldi was delighted. 'I hope we shall become an avalanche,' he wrote that evening to Bertani. 'I have found the people better even than you said they would be.'[19]

Despite, however, the more encouraging reception that the Garibaldini were now receiving, few Sicilians could yet believe that the invasion could end in anything other than disaster.

When the expedition had sailed from Piedmont there were almost 25,000 regular Neapolitan troops in Sicily; and when news of the landing was received, three further battalions were immediately despatched to the island. Properly disposed and ably led, these troops would have wiped out their absurdly optimistic opponents within a few days. For although King Ferdinand, when a young man, had been gaily advised by his grandfather not to take so much interest in military uniforms, since 'however you dress them up, they will run away just the same',[20] the Neapolitan troops were then, and still were now, potentially good soldiers. The trouble was that their officers were not. Many of them had risen undeservedly from the ranks (the sort of families which provided officers in the North declined to do so in the South); some of them could not read or write; a few had criminal records, and nearly all were far too old for the duties they were expected to perform. They were, in fact, for the most part, as ill-equipped to lead their men into action as their superior officers were to direct their movements.

At Marsala itself the force under General Letizia, which had been sent into the town to disarm the inhabitants after Riso's revolt, was withdrawn on 9 May even though it was known that Garibaldi had sailed and might land there. To replace Letizia in the district General Landi was despatched from Palermo; but by the time Garibaldi had landed at Marsala, Landi's column, covering no more than thirty miles in six days, had only just lumbered into Alcamo.

Landi was seventy years old, quite as frail and almost as nervous as the antiquated Governor of Sicily, the Prince of Castelcicala. He moved on slowly from Alcamo on 13 May, following the troops in a carriage, and by 15 May he was at Calatafimi in command of about 3,000 men, including artillerymen with heavy field-pieces. He seemed quite at a loss to know how to deal with them. Anxious about his lines of communication back to Palermo, across which guerrillas had ridden to cut the telegraph wires and to build road blocks, he could not make up his mind either to advance or to retreat, or even to concentrate his forces in defensive positions round Calatafimi. He contented himself with sending out small detachments in different directions 'to impose morally on the enemy by marching about through the countryside'.[21]

One of these detachments, a light infantry battalion commanded by Major Sforza, was sent up on to a high hill outside Calatafimi known as the Piante di Romano. It was here that the first decisive battle of the Sicilian campaign was fought.

3

THE BATTLE OF CALATAFIMI

Garibaldi woke at dawn, called his aides-de-camp into the room and
said to one of them, 'Look out of the window. Is it raining?'

'It has been but now it is beautiful.'

'A good omen,' the General said and got out of bed. He drank a
cup of coffee, issued various orders, then began walking up and down
the room, singing at the top of his voice. When the bugles sounded
the reveille, he stopped to listen, standing quite still by the open
window. 'I *like* that reveille,' he said when the last note died away.[1]
He seemed more cheerful than ever: there would be fighting that
day.

Already his small army had been paraded in the outskirts of Salemi
and was preparing to march down into the valley to the north where
cypresses and poplars, prickly pears and aloes, stone-pines and lemon
trees threw their long shadows across the road to Vita. While the
air was still cool and fresh the march on Palermo began.

Garibaldi left his men in Vita and rode on towards Calatafimi,
turning off the road a mile north of Vita to climb to the top of a hill
from which he could see across the valley to the high, rocky summit
of the Piante di Romano where Major Sforza's light infantrymen
could be seen quite clearly in the bright sunlight. He gave orders for
The Thousand to come up from Vita to the slopes of the hill beneath
him. To his right amidst the jutting rock east of Monte Pietralunga,
and to his left on the other side of the road, the Sicilian *picciotti* sat in
the shade of grey boulders, overawed by the Neapolitan regular
troops in front of them and content to wait and to watch.

Major Sforza was a forceful officer, determined to interpret General Landi's orders as positively as he could. He decided that his men
could easily knock the rabble facing him back into Salemi, and gave
the order to his trumpeter to sound the advance. And as his men came
down into the valley and then began to climb the slopes of Monte
Pietralunga, where the Garibaldini were now gathered, they could
not but feel inclined to agree with their commander. For the ranks

opposed to them appeared to be not only ill-assorted and thin but, apart from a line of green-coated skirmishers – the Genoese *carabinieri* – there seemed to be no trained men amongst them. Most of the figures were in civilian clothes – some even wore top hats – and the red shirts of the others looked like the garb of convicts from the prisons of Naples.

Sforza's men approached this outlandish array firmly and purposefully, firing as they came. The Genoese riflemen returned the fire, and one or two Neapolitans fell, but the rest came on resolutely. Then, without orders but with an impulsive cohesion that made orders unnecessary, the Garibaldini rushed down the hillside at their enemies, threw the leading skirmishers back across the valley to the foot of the Piante di Romano and charged up its southern face with their bayonets flashing in the sunlight.

They were greatly outnumbered both in men and ammunition; their unreliable smooth-bore muskets were hopelessly inferior to the Bourbon rifles; and their antiquated artillery, held back on the road behind a barricade by a squadron of Neapolitan cavalry, could make no reply, until the very end of the battle, to the cannon firing down from the hill top.

The hill was steep and open, laid bare to the burning sun; but cutting across it were straggling terraces, built by the peasants to provide strips of flat arable land on the rocky slopes; and here, beneath the stone walls, the volunteers could shelter from the fire of the troops on the higher ground above them and recover their breath in the shade of the aloe and cactus bushes and the dusty fig and olive trees that grew between the rocks. Dashing from terrace to terrace, from one patch of shelter to the next, the volunteers moved up the hillside in small groups, sometimes driven back in one place, but then going forward again in another.

General Landi in Calatafimi reinforced Sforza, but his concern that the Sicilian *picciotti*, only a few of whom were taking part in the fighting on Piante di Romano, would cut across his line of retreat, led him to retain a third of his force as a reserve in the town. And by the middle of the afternoon it appeared to Landi that Sforza, in any case, had no need of any further men, for the Garibaldini appeared to be not merely held but wavering.

All of them were parched with a thirst that the oranges and

The embarkation of the Thousand at Quarto 5 May 1860

Twelve of the Thousand

lemons with which they had filled their pockets at Vita did little to allay; few of them were used to such violent exercise under so relentless a sun; many had been wounded; and some had wandered back to the safety of the valley. Türr and Sirtori and other officers ran from group to group, trying to restore the volunteers' flagging spirits. Bixio galloped across the lines on a white horse, exposing himself to the enemy's fire in an effort to encourage his followers to greater exertions. Garibaldi, wearing his poncho and surrounded by his staff, walked down from Monte Pietralunga and, with his sword in his hand, advanced towards the front.

His staff could not but see how close they were to defeat, how many men had been wounded – and how few doctors there were to care for them, since most of the medical staff were fighting at the front. But this was not a guerrilla's skirmish from which he could withdraw to come back to fight another day. It was an engagement which might decide the whole future of Sicily. And so when Bixio said to him, 'General, I think we should retreat,' Garibaldi turned on him with a flash of sudden anger and said with intensity, 'Here we shall make Italy – or die !'[2]

He moved on to the foremost terrace and there, while the voices of the Neapolitan officers could be heard quite distinctly above the noise of the firing beyond the top of the wall, he waited for his followers to prepare themselves for the final assault.

There were about 300 men with him and many of them were close to hysteria. 'What shall we do, General?' they kept asking him as he walked up and down in the shadow of the terrace wall, waiting for the stragglers to come up, trying to encourage the tired men to make one more effort, perhaps a final sacrifice. 'Italians,' he replied, stern and calm, 'here we must die.'[3]

Then, as he bent down to cross a gap in the wall, a heavy stone hit him in the back. Stefano Canzio, who was close behind him, heard the thud of the stone and then Garibaldi's voice shouting, 'Come on! They are throwing stones. They have run out of ammunition.' And immediately afterwards he saw Garibaldi clamber up the bank, waving his sword. Canzio followed after him.

But not all the Neapolitans had finished their ammunition and the Garibaldini ran up towards the crest of the hill under heavy fire.

Earlier that day Enrico Cairoli and a group of fellow-students from the University of Pavia had captured one of the enemy's cannon; but the others were still firing behind the clouds of smoke that masked the extent of the Bourbon position. Many more of the volunteers and several Sicilian *picciotti* who joined them were wounded in this final charge; but the rest rushed on, cheering and shouting, towards the ranks above them, knowing that they must fight hand to hand if they were to drive the enemy back.

When the clash came the fighting was ferocious. Garibaldi had never known a battle in Italy so fierce, he wrote later. The Neapolitans 'fought like lions', firing in disciplined volleys and then 'hurling stones like madmen', proving, as he wrote to Bertani with happy pride, 'what can be done with this family once it is united'.[4] But the courage and determination of his own Thousand 'and the few Sicilians who fought with them' was even greater.[5] And soon the enemy began to fall back down the valley and then up the hill towards Calatafimi.

Too exhausted to follow them, the Garibaldini sank to the ground on the crest of the hill amidst the bodies of the dead and wounded, panting in the heat, their mouths as dry as dust. They had lost thirty men killed and 150 more had been wounded – a total of sixty more than the Neapolitans – and amongst these were many boys not yet seventeen and one who had just had his fourteenth birthday. But the victory was theirs and it was decisive, and General Landi knew that it was. He wrote a despatch to the Governor of Sicily calling for 'help, immediate help'; and at midnight he withdrew from Calatafimi, setting out for Palermo by way of Alcamo and Partinico.[6]

★   ★   ★

Garibaldi (whom Landi claimed in his despatch to have killed) let the Neapolitans go; and, while the most badly wounded of his men were taken back in the carved and gaily painted carts of the Sicilian peasants to Vita, he wrapped himself in his poncho and prepared himself for sleep.

Early the next morning he moved on through Calatafimi to Alcamo where the people fell on their knees before him as if he were a saint, recognising in him, as Rosario Romeo has suggested, the 'incarnation of their ancient myth of a mighty warrior come to restore justice'.[7] And their priests, more inclined here than in the North to encourage desires for political liberty, did not discourage them from doing so. In asking Garibaldi to attend Mass, however, they admitted the desirability of presenting the hero to their flock as one sanctified and inspired by religion.

Garibaldi, anxious not to lose the support of the people by turning his back on their faith, accepted the priests' invitation to Mass. The acceptance seemed strange, even apostatical, to some of his officers; but Garibaldi, as an English secularist said of him years later, was 'never a philosophical atheist', though he was, in this man's opinion, 'a fierce sentimental one, from resentment at the cruelties and tyrannies of priests who professed to represent God. To disbelieve unwillingly from lack of evidence, and to disbelieve from natural indignation is a very different thing.'[8] In fact, though he detested the Church, Garibaldi was not an atheist at all. Instinctively he was deeply religious – 'I am Christian as you are,' he once told his Hungarian followers, 'it is the Pope who is anti-Christ'[9] – and he was irresistibly drawn to ceremonies of a mystical nature. Later on in Palermo he was to attend Mass in the Cathedral, listening attentively and appreciatively as the gospel was read, his naked sword in his hand. And now, as he knelt before the altar to receive the blessing of the Church from the priest who stood before him with crucifix in hand, he was seen to be profoundly moved. When he rode out of Alcamo and moved on north-east to Partinico, he rode in silence.[10]

At Partinico he saw with disgust how savagely the defeated Neapolitan troops had treated the Sicilians, and the ferocious reprisals which the Sicilians had taken against men who had thrown bombs, made out of wine bottles and gunpowder, into their houses and murdered their children. On either side of the long main street of the town the bodies of soldiers, many of them half naked and mutilated, lay outside the still smouldering houses, ignored except by dogs and flies.

As the volunteers wound their way westward up into the mountains, sickened by this welcome to the harbingers of national unity, it began to rain; and for three days, while they encamped on the *altipiano* of Renda, a narrow plateau surrounded by jutting grey rocks high above Palermo, the rain continued to pour down from a sky the colour of slate.

They had no tents, nor any other shelter. Their shirts were torn, their bandages covered in mud, their clothes as bedraggled as the scarecrows in the cornfields. But although ultimate victory seemed as uncertain now as it had before Calatafimi, at least they had done something by which they would be remembered and they were not defeated yet. They had helped Garibaldi convince the Sicilians that he was a man they could follow into battle, even if the only weapon they had was a nail on a stick. 'We shall soon be either in Palermo or in Hell,' Bixio told them. And they found it in their hearts to cheer him.

But between their camp and Palermo was Monreale, strongly held by three battalions of Neapolitan infantry; and in Palermo itself were over 20,000 troops with several warships behind them in the harbour. To attack so powerful a garrison with his own small and ill-equipped force was, of course, as Garibaldi knew, out of the question. The only hope of taking the town was to slip into it at its weakest point, helped by the Sicilian *picciotti*, and then bring about a revolution in the streets.

But first the troops in Monreale, half-way along the road between the *altipiano* of Renda and Palermo, had to be forced back towards the sea. This duty Garibaldi entrusted to Rosolino Pilo whose *picciotti* were occupying the high ground at Sagana three miles north of Renda. Pilo was ordered to close up on Monreale and to occupy the heights which commanded it; but before he could do so three columns of Neapolitans (each with a strength of a thousand men), sent out from Palermo to reinforce the outpost at Monreale, took the initiative from him. One column fell on the Garibaldian skirmishers, the other two attacked the *picciotti* and shot Rosolino Pilo as he was sitting behind a rock writing a message for help. He died with the pen in his hand.

This dispersal of the Sicilians from the higher ground to the north obliged Garibaldi to abandon his project of moving down towards Palermo along the Monreale road, and he decided to transfer his operations south-east and approach the port by means of the road from Parco (now known as Altofonte). In this area, around Monte Grifone, there were other Sicilians under the command of La Masa. Garibaldi left to join forces with La Masa late on the night of 21 May.

The wind howled between the grey rocks, hurling the rain into their faces as the volunteers filed along the bridle track that led to Parco. Alternately stumbling in their torn shoes over the rough stones underfoot, or sinking ankle deep into the patches of sticky marsh, they walked for hours in the darkness, cursing angrily their Sicilian guides and their foul Sicilian weather. When they reached the small white village of Parco in the early hours of 22 May, some of them were barefoot.

At Parco, however, Garibaldi decided to give them a respite and to hold his ground. 'I like the position well,' he told La Masa, and he disposed his men along the Cozzo di Crasto, a steep mountain spur which rises high above the roofs of the town.[11]

La Masa was instructed to fall on the enemy's flank as soon as the expected attack was mounted; and then Garibaldi would lead a frontal counter-attack. But when on 24 May Garibaldi saw two strong and converging columns approaching him, one from Monreale and the other from Palermo, he decided that he could not stay to be surrounded by a force greater than his own, and he gave the order to fall back on Piana dei Greci.

La Masa's Sicilians, who had already begun their attack on the flank of the Neapolitan column approaching the Garibaldini along the Palermo road, were outraged when they saw the Northerners disappearing down the mountainside behind them. And La Masa had to use all his powers of impassioned rhetoric to prevent them abandoning the fight and going home. Indeed, many of those Sicilians who were directly under Garibaldi's orders, infuriated by what they took to be his desertion of their fellow islanders in the moment of danger and by his detached calm – or as it appeared to them, his complacent indifference – during the subsequent retreat to Piana dei Greci, did, in fact, leave him there to return in anger to their villages.

They were not the only ones to suffer from this sense of disillusionment. In the ranks of The Thousand, too, the high spirits engendered by the victory at Calatafimi had by now been almost completely dispelled. Two attempts had been made to reach Palermo and both of them had been defeated. The feeling was widespread that Garibaldi had failed, that the revolution was over and that the invaders would soon be in a Bourbon prison. Indeed, had the two

Neapolitan columns pushed on hard to Piana dei Greci, no doubt all these fears would have been justified. But the column which had come from Palermo, having driven the invaders south from Parco, withdrew to the coast; and the other column, 3,500 strong, came on with such excessive caution, that when at last its vanguard did arrive in the town on 25 May the Garibaldini had gone. In which direction had they gone? the Swiss commander of the Neapolitan column, Johann Lucas von Mechel, asked the inhabitants, Albanian and Greek descendants of fifteenth-century colonists. South to Corleone, they replied. And so the column slowly continued on its way into the grey and ochre wastes of the Sicilian hinterland.

They were following a false trail. Garibaldi had sent his artillery, his wounded and sick, with an escort of *picciotti*, south along the road to Corleone under the command of Colonel Vincenzo Orsini, and at dusk he himself had led his ragged infantry after them two miles out of the town. But adopting the tactics he had practised so successfully in Umbria and Tuscany after the fall of the Roman Republic eleven years before and more recently in the Alpine campaign of 1859, he suddenly swung off the Corleone road and took his men across country towards Santa Cristina, Marineo and then north again to Misilmeri, only ten miles south-east of Palermo. From Misilmeri he sent a message on ahead of him to La Masa's headquarters at Gibilrossa: 'Dear La Masa, I hope to see you at three tomorrow morning (26 May) to make important arrangements.'

Promptly at three o'clock La Masa arrived at Garibaldi's headquarters in Misilmeri.[12]

4

THE CAPTURE OF PALERMO

On the afternoon of the day that Garibaldi arrived at Misilmeri, Admiral Sir Rodney Mundy, in command of the British Fleet in Sicilian waters, and Mr. Goodwin, the British Consul, went to the Royal Palace to enquire on behalf of the British Government what measures were being adopted for the security of the foreign property in the city. Their enquiries were addressed to Ferdinando Lanza, by now a frail and deaf old man, recently appointed Viceroy of Sicily in place of the even frailer Castelcicala.

Lanza had arrived at Palermo the day before General Landi's dispirited troops had returned from Calatafimi, and he had immediately sent back to Naples his report. 'The city is in great ferment. A rising seems imminent. All the villages round Palermo are in arms, and are only waiting for the arrival of the foreign invaders when they will break into the city.'[1] Lanza seems to have had little doubt, however, that the rising could be suppressed.

He had been undecided as to whether the forces at his disposal should remain concentrated in Palermo or should be withdrawn to the garrison at Messina. But now, from what Admiral Mundy had seen in the port, it appeared that Lanza had decided to bombard the town should the inhabitants show signs of breaking out into revolt. The Admiral asked Lanza if this was his intention; and Lanza, a man of 'benevolent disposition' whose manners were 'replete with dignity and courtesy', admitted politely that it was. He said that he intended to oppose the foreign invasion outside the city, that Garibaldi had, in fact, already been dislodged from his position at Parco and was in retreat, but that if the 'rebels should make the city rise, the fire of the artillery by sea and land would concur with the troops in the repression of revolt'.

'When General Lanza had finished his address I rose to depart,' Admiral Mundy recorded in his diary, 'thanking him for his candid statement, but at the same time, remarking that there was a vast difference between the indiscriminate destruction of the edifices of a great city, and the use of artillery against a people in revolt.'

The discussion then seems to have become somewhat heated, for Salvatore Maniscalco, the Minister of Police, who was also in the room, turned on Mr. Goodwin and asked him 'if he did not think a population deserved to be annihilated, should they rise up in insurrection against the constituted authorities. To this unexpected and ill-timed demand Her Majesty's Consul indignantly replied that he could not have supposed such a question would have been put to him; but that, as Signor Maniscalco had chosen to do so, he had no hesitation in saying that when a people were tyrannised over they had an inherent right to take up arms, and to fight against their oppressors.'[2]

The next day the Admiral and the Consul discovered that preparations for a bombardment were not the only precautions that the Government were taking. They had gone for a drive together in the Conca d'Oro, the lovely valley that surrounds Palermo, and there, amidst the orange and lemon groves, they saw 'several of the country palaces of the nobility who were supposed by the soldiery to be hostile to the Royal cause', being sacked and burned. In whichever direction the Admiral and his companion looked over this vast and richly cultivated plain they saw the 'smoke of ruin and devastation' and heard 'the constant report of musketry and the distant sound of cannon'.[3]

Despite the precautions that were being taken, however, General Lanza still comforted himself with the belief that Garibaldi was in full retreat. And while Mundy and Goodwin were listening to the sound of the cannon in the hills, he was telegraphing comfortingly to Monreale that 'Garibaldi's band is retiring in rout through the district of Corleone. He is closely followed.' Even when reports came to him that redshirts had been seen in the area of Gibilrossa, only six miles away, he declined to take the information seriously.

Had Mundy chosen to do so, he could have disillusioned the old Viceroy, for three of the Admiral's young officers had themselves actually seen the redshirts that morning.

These officers had been driving along the coast road from Villabate when a messenger rode up to them and invited them to pay a visit to Garibaldi's headquarters. They accepted the invitation and found the General 'standing in the middle of a large enclosure amidst a group of fifteen or twenty followers who were clothed in grey trousers and red flannel shirts, the Chief being himself in a similar costume. His principal companions at the moment were his eldest son Menotti, a stout and tall youth of nineteen, with his arm in a sling from a recent severe wound; Colonel Carini, a Sicilian; Colonels Turr, Talecki and Tukuri [Tükory], Hungarians; and the Priest Panteleo who, cross in hand, had fought bravely at Calatafimi. The soldiers around were mere boys of fifteen to eighteen years of age'.[4]

Also with Garibaldi was Ferdinand Eber, a Hungarian by birth, *The Times* correspondent in Italy. Eber had walked up to the camp some time before, with two representatives of a revolutionary committee in the guise of American naval officers from the U.S. steamship *Iroquois*. He found what seemed like a gypsy encampment – horses tethered beneath the olive trees, blankets and cloaks spread about amongst the boulders, and on a smoking fire an immense kettle containing the carcass of a calf and masses of onions. Beside the fire was a barrel of marsala and a basket of bread. The staff – amongst whom Eber had noticed Daniele Manin's son who had been wounded in the thigh – were helping themselves to the food with their fingers and sharing the single pot from which they drank the marsala.

As well as Pantaleo, a jolly man 'like the picture of a monk of the middle ages', and Gusmaroli, there were several other priests and monks who were 'amongst the most sincere and energetic promoters of the movement'. There were also a number of leading citizens from Palermo, and many scouts, most of them from 'good Lombard families'.

Garibaldi, answering questions and signing autographs with the greatest good nature, received his visitors with that 'charming quiet simplicity which characterises him'.[5] He asked the British officers to sit down and share some strawberries with him, spoke of his admiration of the British Navy and his 'affection and respect for the English people as a nation', and then moved to his tent which was composed of a worn-out old blanket, supported on pikes, before which 'a child, under the name of a sentry, was pacing to keep off the crowd'.

The officers learned that 'three or four thousand' of La Masa's Sicilian *squadre*, their confidence in Garibaldi restored, were also on the mountain – 'men, armed with old flink muskets, spears, scythes, and rusty cutlasses. They were told off in companies with innumerable tricoloured flags, green, white and red, displayed around their camp and were furnished with a host of musicians to incite them to martial deeds.'[6]

Ferdinand Eber and his friends on the revolutionary committee told Garibaldi all that they knew of the Neapolitan dispositions in and around Palermo. Parco was now heavily garrisoned, they said, and there were many thousands of other troops nearer Palermo on the roads leading into the town from Monreale and Porrazzi. On the outskirts of the town itself, particularly on the western and northern sides, there were still more concentrations of troops. But in the middle of Palermo, where the narrow streets and *angiporti* formed a maze of dark and dangerous passages, there were scarcely any troops at all. If the Garibaldini could force their way through to this part of the town, Eber said, they could get the inhabitants to join them and to throw up barricades to form a stronghold in the very heart of the enemy's position.

The route by which entry might best be effected, he thought, was through the Porta Termini, one of the south-eastern gates, and fortunately the one nearest to Garibaldi's present camp.

Breaking his usual habit of making his own unaided decision, Garibaldi called the Sicilians to a council of war. He told them that they could either withdraw to the mountains to collect and organise a larger army, or strike now. He himself favoured a *coup de main*, for the revolution might die unless he achieved another quick and marvellous victory; and after some discussion the Sicilians agreed with him.

The advance was to begin that night.[7]

★   ★   ★

As the moon came up, the long column of men, led by a small force of picked volunteers under the command of the Hungarian Tükory, began to move down through the steep and rocky gorge of a dried-up mountain stream towards the valley of the Conca d'Oro. Even by moonlight it was possible to see how tattered and ragged the volunteers had become since their landing at Marsala a fortnight before, and how sadly their numbers had decreased. The Thousand were now less than 750 strong and of these many were suffering from the effects of untreated wounds and unaccustomed exposure. Some of them were in rags, though many others were now in the clothes of monks which they had acquired by purchase or theft on the march.

They were supported by about 3,000 *picciotti*, who were leading the column behind Tükory's small vanguard. But these excitable Sicilian peasants, some armed with blunderbusses and shot-guns but many only with pikes or scythes, were an uncertain advantage, appearing to Eber, who had been granted permission to enter Palermo with them, an 'entangled mass almost impossible to unravel'.

By the time they had reached Ciaculli, half-way between Gibilrossa and the outskirts of Palermo, Nino Bixio had begun to wish they had not formed part of the column at all. Furious when they lost their way in the muddling labyrinth of paths around the crumbling Castello di Mare Dolce, and believing that the commanders of the various local bands were utterly incapable of maintaining any sort of military discipline, Bixio asked Garibaldi to allow him to replace La Masa with one of his own officers. Garibaldi, vowing 'never again to believe a Sicilian report on the state of any road', agreed to Bixio's request.[8]

Already, however, the men of the leading *squadre*, commanded by a village priest, had destroyed any hope that Garibaldi may have had of surprising the Neapolitan outposts that lay around the old Ponte dell' Ammiraglio over the Oreto river. For as they approached the bridge the excited *picciotti*, thrown into temporary panic by a bolting horse, began to shout and fire their shot-guns into the air.

Given this warning in good time, the Neapolitans were able to greet Tükory's advance-guard of Garibaldini with a concentrated fire as soon as they came into sight in the strong moonlight. Tükory's fifty men threw themselves to the ground, but the Sicilians behind them scampered away down the road, jumping for shelter into vineyards and leaving a dangerous gap between Tükory and the main body of The Thousand.

At such moments as these the General was at his most inspiring. The time for guile was over; it was courage now that mattered. '*Avanti! Avanti!*', he shouted at the top of his voice. '*Avanti! Avanti! Cacciatori!* To the centre of the town.'

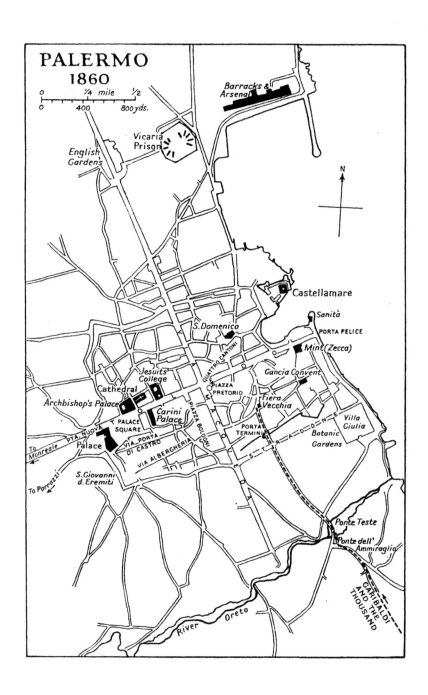

PALERMO
1860

0   ¼ mile   ½
0   400   800 yds.

English Gardens

Vicaria Prison

Barracks & Arsenal

N

Castellamare

Sanità

PORTA FELICE

S. Domenico

Mint (Zecca)

Jesuits' College

QUATTRO CANTONI

Gancia Convent

Cathedral

PIAZZA PRETORIO

Fiera Vecchia

Archbishop's Palace

Carini Palace

PIAZZA BOLOGNI

Villa Giulia

PTA. NUOVA
PALACE SQUARE

Palace

VIA PORTA DI CASTRO

PORTA TERMINI

Botanic Gardens

To Monreale

VIA ALBERGHERIA

To Porrazzi

S. Giovanni d. Eremiti

STRADONE

Ponte Teste

Ponte dell' Ammiraglio

GARIBALDI AND THE THOUSAND

River Oreto

At the sound of the words the two leading companies of Nino Bixio's battalion and the Genoese *carabinieri*, followed by some other Garibaldini and the few Sicilians who had not run off into the vineyards, came charging down the road, joined Tükory's men and sent the Neapolitans scattering back to Palermo. The line of the river was forced; a squadron of cavalry, which had come up to see what the firing was about, trotted away without firing a shot; and the long straight road that led to the Porta Termini was suddenly open. The Garibaldini ran down towards the gateway. The gate itself had long since been removed, but across the road the Neapolitan garrison had built a tall barricade which closed the entry to the town and now brought the charge of the volunteers to an abrupt halt. Several of them had been wounded at the Ponte dell' Ammiraglio, and several others, including Tükory, Benedetto Cairoli, Stefano Canzio and Nino Bixio, were wounded now as the Neapolitans caught them in an enfilading fire from either side of the gateway.

The survivors struggled to pull down the barricade, however, tearing at the boards and throwing the stones on to the road, while the Neapolitans maintained their furious fire upon them from both sides of the road. And although the aim of the Neapolitans was highly erratic, several more men were wounded now and Tükory was killed.[9]

Behind them Garibaldi and several of his officers at the Ponte dell' Ammiraglio, did their 'best to drive the *picciotti* forward'. But, as Eber said, it was 'not so easy, in the beginning especially, when the sound of cannon was heard in front, although its effects were scarcely visible. However, the *picciotti*, who reminded me very much of Bashi-Bazouks, can be led on after the first unpleasant sensation has passed away, especially when they see that it is not all shots that kill or wound, not even the cannon shots which make so formidable a noise. They could see this to perfection, for although the Neapolitan rifles are scarcely inferior to the best firearms, I never saw so little damage done by so much shooting.'[10]

So at length the Sicilians came forward and Garibaldi dashed on ahead of them to the front still shouting, '*Avanti! Avanti! Entrate nel centro!*' And as if in answer to his voice, the barricade gave way at last. The volunteers scrambled over its wreckage and ran down the long, straight street beyond it – the street that now bears the name of their leader – towards the Fiera Vecchia, the old market square beneath the iron balconies of whose tall surrounding houses the revolution of 1848 had begun.

Behind them the rest of the Sicilian *picciotti* had now come up to the cross-roads by the broken barricade at the Porta Termini (now the Porta Garibaldi); but the cross-fire was still strong here and they dared not cross the road. Eber and a Garibaldian pushed out one man to show the others how inaccurate was the Neapolitan firing, but it was not until a young Genoese placed a chair in the middle of the road and calmly sat down on it with his legs crossed, under a tricolour flag, that the *picciotti* were prepared to believe that they might survive the crossing. And then, first singly and afterwards in groups, they dashed across the road and over the barricade and on towards the Fiera Vecchia.[11]

Here Garibaldi, astride his horse, and Nino Bixio, who had himself cut from his chest the bullet that had wounded him at the Porta Termini, were now the centre of a wildly excited, cheering crowd.

'One must know these Sicilians,' Eber commented, 'to have an idea of the frenzy, screaming, shouting, crying and hugging; all would kiss Garibaldi's hands and embrace his knees.'[12]

But when the Garibaldini broke away from the crowds in the Fiera Vecchia and ran in small groups and in every direction down the numerous narrow streets that surround it, they were struck by a disappointing contrast. The streets were dark and empty and the noise seemed suddenly far away. Occasionally a face would appear behind a half-closed shutter and then quickly move out of sight; sometimes a young voice would cry out and then a door would bang and the cry would be muffled and die away.

The nervousness, though, was only momentary. When increasing numbers of peasants came in through the Porta Termini, more excited than ever now that they had been under fire and had survived, firing their shot-guns and blunderbusses in the air, cheering and shouting and waving their tricolour flags, giving the impression of great numbers and spreading exaggerated reports of the strength of the invaders from the North, the Palermitans began to believe that this was not, after all, another uprising that would soon be crushed as earlier ones had been by the Bourbon troops and the hated police, the *sbirri*. The more adventurous of them came out into the streets, joined in the celebrations which already seemed filled with a triumphant air, climbed the campanili and beat the great bells with hammers and pieces of pipe. It seemed as though the revolution had already succeeded.

Then the bombardment began. Both from the steamers of war in the port and from the batteries in the citadel and in the Palace Square at the western end of the town, the cannon opened up, as General Lanza had threatened they would, throwing shells and solid shot upon the congested city centre. Soon whole streets were on fire and entire families burned to death in the ruins. 'If the object of the Neapolitans was to inspire terror they certainly succeeded,' Eber told his readers. 'Everywhere you perceived ruins and conflagration, dead and wounded. . . . Whoever could took refuge in whatever he thought the most bombproof place, and those who could not you saw crying, praying and wringing their hands in the streets. It was a pitiable sight.'[13]

'A whole district near the Royal Palace, about a thousand yards in length by a hundred yards in width,' Admiral Mundy reported later, 'was a crushed mass of ruins, still smouldering in its ashes. Families had been burnt alive within the buildings and the atrocities committed by some miscreants of the Royal troops were frightful. . . . Mr. Herzell, the Swiss Consular Agent, remained examining the devastation till finally driven from the scene of horrors by the pestilential smell of the unburied bodies.'[14]

Mundy's verdict on the Neapolitan soldiers was confirmed by the Palermo correspondent of the *Morning Post* who wrote that in the Albergheria quarter 'a part of the town exclusively inhabited by the poorer classes, not even a single house is left standing, and one may fairly calculate the number of houses at about two hundred. The houses were not destroyed by the bombs or other projectiles, but by the soldiers themselves, who first entered and completely sacked them, and on leaving set fire to them, and heaven knows in each they could have found little more than the value of 2*s.* or 3*s.*'[15]

The behaviour of the Bourbon troops, who plundered churches as well as houses, was entirely to Garibaldi's advantage, throwing, as it was bound to do, the uncommitted poor unquestioningly on to his side. Also, Lanza's policy of bombardment instead of occupation enabled Garibaldi to overcome the disadvantages of fighting an army of 20,000 troops with a force largely composed of civilians, less than a fifth its size. Even when the bombardment stopped at about eight o'clock in the morning of 27 May, Lanza did not order his troops forward to occupy buildings, which might have enabled him to surround and contain the centre of the insurrection; but instead, as one of his own staff admitted, 'after two hours of bombardment and several more of plunder and arson, General Lanza thought he had done enough, and became almost entirely inactive, while Garibaldi occupied all the points which he needed'.[16]

Garibaldi himself, with his staff and about thirty men, advanced as far to the north-west as the Quattro Cantoni, the centre of the great cross formed by the Via Macqueda and the Toledo, the two long straight streets that divided Palermo into four segments. Here he turned west down the Toledo towards the Royal Palace, directing an attack which drove the Neapolitans back from the Piazza Bologni. Before noon he had returned to the Piazza Pretorio, at the south-eastern corner of the Quattro Cantoni, and had established his headquarters there.

He seemed quite unmoved by the day's events and by his initial triumph. When he was unsaddling his horse in the Piazza Pretorio, his pistol went off in its holster and the bullet narrowly missed his foot, tearing a hole in the wide bottom of his trouser leg. It was as if a pebble had been kicked against his ankle. And when Nino Bixio, his chest still streaming with blood, came up to him shouting that since there was no sign of an uprising in this part of the town they would all be killed before noon and that he would, therefore, attack the Royal Palace himself with any twenty men who would follow him, Garibaldi looked calmly at the wild, hysterical figure and told him gently to go to bed and have his wound properly dressed.

Throughout the next few days, while the fighting raged around him in the streets, Garibaldi maintained this imperturbable calm. Often he could be found sitting on the steps of the fountain outside his headquarters, smelling the flowers or nibbling at the fruit brought to him by admiring women. Sometimes while the shells fell on the buildings around him he would thoughtfully wind the strings of a little whip he carried round the fingers of his hands, and since he managed always to escape injury, the Palermitans, to whom the magical and the successful were inextricably entangled, attributed to that whip the properties of a divine instrument capable of averting danger.[17]

On the first day of the fighting, the General's impenetrable placidity seemed to the Sicilians to be fully justified. By early afternoon the *picciotti* and the Garibaldini had succeeded in forcing the Neapolitans out of all the streets east of the Via Macqueda and in containing them in their two strongholds on the seaward side, the Zecca and the Castellamare; while to the west they had succeeded in clearing all the buildings as far as the Jesuits' College on the northern side of the Toledo and as far as the Carini Palace on the southern side.

To prevent any signals from General Lanza's headquarters in the Royal Palace being seen by the ships in the bay a huge curtain was put up across the Quattro Cantoni. Barricades of rubble, furniture carts and carriages – soon to be replaced by neat structures of paving stones and sandbags – had been erected at intervals of a hundred yards in every street, radiating like the lateral strands of a spider's web from the centre at Quattro Cantoni. Women and old men waited behind closed shutters in the upper storeys of their houses, ready to throw iron bedsteads and pails of boiling water on to the heads of any Neapolitan soldiers who might appear in the streets below. The clanging of bells was incessant.

But although there seemed reason for confidence during that first afternoon, the situation of the rebels was, in fact, already growing desperate. The Neapolitans were strongly entrenched all round the Cathedral and the Royal Palace; and in the north, in the barracks by the Vicaria prison, were hundreds more troops under General Cataldo; while approaching the town from the south-west were the large garrisons from Parco and Monreale. Had the Neapolitan command, instead of concentrating all these troops in the area of the Royal Palace (where eventually 18,000 men were to be confined) used them to attack the insurgents on a wide front, there can be no doubt that Garibaldi would have been defeated.

He had been able to add few firearms to his stock of almost useless muskets, and his ammunition – maddeningly squandered by the Sicilian *picciotti* who could not be prevented from indulging their passion for shooting in the air – was almost exhausted. Even the best and most strong-willed of his Garibaldini found it as difficult to control these ebullient peasants as to maintain the enthusiasm and industry of the Palermitans, who in the midst of their activity would, without warning, give way to that lethargic resignation which periodically overcomes the Sicilian spirit like the enervating gust of a sirocco.

By 27 May, the third day of the fighting, Garibaldi's staff knew that the General was, behind that unruffled exterior, given now to moods of depression himself. The entrance into the town of the remnants of Rosolino Pilo's *squadre*, the release from the Vicaria of two thousand criminals and political prisoners, the isolated acts of heroism performed by some of the Sicilian aristocrats, such as the Di Benedetto brothers, as well as by many peasants and Palermitan citizens, had done little or nothing to improve his precarious position.

But he was, as always, ready to run to the point of danger whenever he felt his presence needed. And so when he was told, as he sat silently by the fountain in the Piazza Pretorio on the afternoon of 27 May, that the Neapolitans were advancing from the Cathedral and were likely to break through the Jesuits' College to the Piazza Bologni, he stood up immediately, said, 'I must go myself', and led a party of fifty men, mostly Sicilians, towards the oncoming troops. The man next to him was shot through the head and fell back into his arms; but, ordering his bugler to sound the charge, he led the rest on with such force that the Neapolitans were once more driven back to the walls of the Cathedral.[18]

Though in itself a minor engagement and no different in its essentials from scores of others fought in those three days amidst the dust and rubble of the city's upturned streets, it marked a turning-point in the battle. For to General Lanza it seemed an indication that the defeat of the insurgents would be a task beyond his resources. He had already lost 800 men wounded and well over 200 killed, and since the Palace was now a hospital (cut off from medical supplies, water and food alike), as well as a headquarters, he was made painfully aware of the suffering around him. Some hours after the failure of his men's determined effort to break through the barricades on the Toledo outside the Cathedral, he decided to end the fighting; and he stuck to his decision even when a messenger on the Palace roof reported that von Mechel's battalions, returning at last from their wild-goose chase south of Corleone, had been sighted coming to his relief only half a mile from Porta Termini.* Addressing the rebels' leader as 'His Excellency General Garibaldi', he suggested a conference on board Admiral Mundy's ship. The offer was accepted with well-disguised relief and a truce was agreed upon.

Von Mechel, however, knowing nothing yet of this agreement, came on slowly but purposefully through the Porta Termini and on towards the Fiera Vecchia. The few Sicilians behind their barricades, with little ammunition and less inclination to use it against four battalions of the best troops in the Neapolitan Army, ran away before them. Rallied at length by Sirtori, sitting uncertainly astride a huge horse which emphasised the frailty of his own emaciated frame, they held their ground for a time and prevented the immediate advance of the German troops of the 3rd Neapolitan Light Infantry on to the Piazza Pretorio.

While the Sicilians and Germans were firing at each other across the barricades, a young man in the uniform of an officer in the British Navy came out of a side street frantically waving a white handkerchief and pointing to his watch, a gesture which meant nothing to von Mechel's officers to whom it was principally directed.

I walked as quickly as possible up to the nearest officer of the foreign troops [the British officer, Lieutenant Edward Wilmot, afterwards reported]. He and his men were very much excited and seemed determined to push on and apparently intended to keep me with them.

A Neapolitan colonel, who had been sent from the Palace to Garibaldi at this moment came up and told me the whole affair was entirely a mistake, and he then apparently gave orders for the Bavarians to halt, but to hold the position they had gained.

* Von Mechel, skilfully misled by Colonel Orsini, had got within twenty-three kilometres of the southern coast before realising that Garibaldi had escaped him. He had received warning that the invading forces had been split and that Garibaldi had gone off to Misilmeri; but although his second-in-command, del Bosco, was inclined to believe the report, he still felt sure that he was following the real trail. Garibaldi was very lucky, Piero Pieri comments, in that 'four of the finest battalions in the Bourbon army and von Mechel and Bosco who were perhaps its two best officers had been out of the battle at the crucial moment' – Piero Pieri, *Storia militare del Risorgimento: Guerre e insurrezioni* (Einaudi, Turin, 1962), 668.

Not many minutes subsequently, Garibaldi himself reached the spot, accompanied by thirty or forty of his Italian band. He was *furious* and a very angry conversation took place between him and the Neapolitan colonel. Whilst this parley was going on, a shell fell close to us, thrown by a steamer which had been firing on the town in support of the Bavarians as they advanced.

Garibaldi, of course, had more reason to feel satisfied at the agreement to observe the truce than the Neapolitans had, for Palermo was now entirely at the mercy of von Mechel. In the Palace, Lanza's staff were desperately trying to persuade the old General that he had merely to give the order and Garibaldi could be defeated within the hour. But he would not give way to them. He had agreed to a truce, he said, and that was an end of the matter. His two representatives, Generals Letizia and Chretien, must go as arranged to the meeting with Garibaldi on board the British Admiral's flagship.

Garibaldi appeared on H.M.S. *Hannibal* in the uniform of a Piedmontese general officer. Admiral Mundy was struck by the 'great benevolence and intelligence of his countenance, without the least approach to fierceness'; yet there was 'not wanting a look of profound astuteness which would bespeak a more subtle temperament than which he is generally believed to possess. There is, at the same time, a simplicity and even a tenderness which is most captivating; whilst his general bearing is marked with dignity and composure.'

He was saluted by the guard of Marine Light Infantry according to his rank [Mundy wrote]. The same honours were paid to the general officers of His Sicilian Majesty.

The French, American and Sardinian Captains accompanied them into my cabin, and I was on the point of addressing a few words to the assembled party in a friendly way, relative to the object of their visit, when General Letizia stepped forward, and, in a manner which I thought quite uncalled for, interrupted me by an exclamation that he was not prepared to enter into communication with me, or to accept my mediation, in the presence of the captains of ships of war of other nations. He must therefore request that I would give directions for those officers to withdraw. He also desired to inform me that, although he had consented to meet General Garibaldi on board my flagship, he did not intend to recognise him in any official capacity or to confer with him personally on any subject whatever.

All mediation, Letizia insisted, must take place privately between Admiral Mundy, General Chretien and himself and then it would be for General Garibaldi merely to accept or refuse the terms.[19]

Mundy then turned to Garibaldi and asked him if he felt the same objection to the presence 'of the captains in command of the squadrons of these friendly Powers as that which had been notified by the Neapolitan General'. Garibaldi answered quickly and politely that any arrangement the Admiral thought fit to make would be perfectly agreeable to him and that he would be glad if they remained.

The reasonable answer seemed to anger Letizia still further. He repeated his determination not to allow the French, American or Piedmontese captains to attend the discussion and not to talk to Garibaldi at all. Then the French captain 'with great precision in his native tongue, expressed his astonishment at the conduct and language of General Letizia. He was seconded by Captain Palmer, of the United States frigate *Iroquois*, whose indignation was equally great, but, who not being so thoroughly acquainted with the French or Italian language, was necessarily unable to give the same force to his expression.'

The altercation had now become so unseemly and noisy [Admiral Mundy went on], that I deemed it absolutely necessary to stop further discussion by a decisive movement. I told General Letizia I was utterly unable to comprehend the meaning of the violent conduct he had exhibited, and I plainly intimated to him that, if he did not at once waive the objections he had offered, and consent to treat personally with General Garibaldi, and in the presence of the foreign captains, I should be obliged to re-land himself, his colleague, and General Garibaldi and declare the negotiations to be at an end. . . . General Letizia, perceiving I was in earnest in the matter, now gradually subsided into a calmer frame of mind, and eventually consented to the terms I proposed. Letizia then began to read the articles of the convention as drawn up by General Lanza. The first four articles were accepted by Garibaldi in silence but when the Neapolitan read out the fifth article: 'That the municipality should address a humble petition to His Majesty the King, laying before him the real wishes of the town, and that this petition should be submitted to His Majesty', Garibaldi burst out in a vehement and loud tone of voice, 'No!' Then drawing himself up, he added, 'The time for humble petitions, either to the King or to any other person is past, besides, there is no longer any municipality. *La municipalité c'est moi!* I am the municipality! I refuse my assent. Pass on to the sixth and last proposition!' Astonishment and indignation were depicted on the countenance of General Letizia on hearing these words. Folding up the paper which lay spread before him on the table, he exclaimed, 'Then, sir, unless this article is agreed to, all communication between us must cease'.

Garibaldi, who, previous to the consideration of the fifth point, had maintained a phlegmatic demeanour, now burst forth in reply with language that showed he also had completely lost command of temper. He denounced in unmeasured terms the want of good faith, indeed, the infamy, of the Royal authorities in allowing the foreign mercenaries, whilst a flag of truce was flying, to attack the Italian troops, who had orders to discontinue the fire. By this treacherous manœuvre they had wounded one of the bravest of his officers, the gallant Carini [whose leg was later amputated] and had acquired a position in advance which they still retained, in defiance of every principle of military honour. But perfidy, such as this, could not succeed; eventually it would recoil with terrific effect on the heads of the authors. General Letizia retorted with equal warmth.[20]

And so it seemed for a time that the conference would end in fierce and inconclusive argument; but Letizia knew that if General Lanza's wishes were to be observed, he must give way. Eventually and grudgingly he did so; and the articles providing for a cease-fire until noon the following day, the evacuation of the wounded from the Royal Palace and the free passage of provisions to it, were signed by both parties.

Before leaving H.M.S. *Hannibal* Garibaldi took the American Captain Palmer on one side and asked him to supply him with some powder. Garibaldi had already asked the Piedmontese captain and had been refused – a refusal which the General later attributed to the wilful obstruction of Cavour. But with Captain Palmer he seems to have had more success for a few weeks later it was 'a curious co-incidence that the American ship which was at Palermo during the siege was so short of powder when she arrived at Naples that she could not even fire a salute'.[21]

Despite his proud boast – '*la municipalité c'est moi!*' – Garibaldi's position, without ammunition, was little better after the truce than before it. And for a time he contemplated a retreat across the Conca d'Oro to the mountains. But on his return to the Quattro Cantoni an enormous crowd was waiting to receive him; and the encouragement which it gave him and the enthusiasm which he transmitted back to it persuaded him to change his mind. He made one of those heroic and emotional speeches at which he excelled, rather 'high-flown' the more matter-of-fact Mundy thought it, but though sounding 'bombastic and puerile in the ears of the more sedate Northman' was well adapted, it had to be admitted, 'to the fervid imaginations of the Italian people'. And Mundy was always to remember the 'clear silvery tone of his voice'.

His commands were to be up and stirring. Tomorrow would be a day of life or death. The whole population must work during the night – he and his handful of soldiers must have rest. The barricades must be enlarged, multiplied and strengthened. The *squadre*, now designated the Cacciatori dell' Etna, and every able-bodied man must be armed and at his post in readiness to renew hostilities at the expiration of the armistice, and the first act must be to drive the foreign mercenaries from the position they had treacherously gained under cover of the flag of truce.

At night the city was splendidly illuminated.[22]

The people were inspired to new and energetic activity; women, children and priests joined the men in working at the barricades; at the depots which had been set up for the collection and manufacture of arms, 'carpenters, bricklayers, stone-masons, ironmongers and artificers of every denomination were actively at work. . . . Thousands of pikes, pitchforks, swords and every imaginable rude weapon were placed out in the streets'.[23]

By the morning, in fact, so impressive was the continued spirit of determination amongst the people that the Neapolitan Colonel Buonopane, who had been discussing the arrangements for the movement of the wounded with Garibaldi's staff, reported to General Lanza that the revolt could not now be quickly crushed. And Lanza, who had given orders for a full-scale attack on the barricades to be made immediately the truce expired, now decided to ask for a further three days' armistice instead. Garibaldi and Crispi would have been glad to give their immediate approval, but they were shrewd enough to demand that the contents of the Mint, amounting to 134,000 ducats, be handed over to them in consideration of their agreement. To this Lanza weakly consented.[24]

For the Neapolitans the prolongation of the truce was an admission of defeat, for Garibaldi a triumph of propaganda. Within the last few hours he had managed to buy an additional supply of powder from a Greek ship that had recently entered Palermo harbour, but it was completely inadequate to replenish his depleted stock; and without a further supply, and with less than four hundred muskets left, he could not hope to resist the determined advance of the Neapolitans from the north and west and the German mercenaries from the south, however brave his followers and the Palermitans might prove to be. Nino Bixio, now on his feet again, doubted, in fact, whether the insurgents, even if they had all the powder and weapons they needed, would be capable of any sort of determined resistance. They were utterly unfit for prolonged military duty, he believed, and were quite capable of walking away when their inclination moved them to do so – as many of the *picciotti* had, indeed, already done, taking their captured Neapolitan rifles with them.

But neither Lanza in Palermo nor the King's ministers in Naples, after they had heard the gloomy reports from their army, could bring themselves to give the orders which would have assured them of victory. Concerned that a renewal of the fighting might involve them in difficulties with England and France, the Court and Ministry were content to suppose that General Lanza would have attacked without seeking advice from Naples if he had believed an attack would have quickly succeeded. And so, orders were given for the troops in Palermo to be evacuated.

On 7 June the withdrawal began. General Lanza led his troops out of the Palace Square towards a temporary camping ground on the northern outskirts of the city; and von Mechel followed him from the Fiera Vecchia.

'It was one of the most humiliating spectacles that could have been witnessed, and I turned from it with disgust,' Admiral Mundy wrote. 'At the entrance to the Toledo, the son of Garibaldi, mounted on a black charger, with a dozen red-shirted youths near him, took up a position in front of the principal barricade. This advanced post was supposed to be the guard of the main defence of the city from the seaward, but doubtless the Dictator placed his first-born in that marked locality in order that the vanquished hosts of disciplined men might defile before him, and their degradation if possible be made more apparent.'

Two days later a ship arrived in the harbour with a large cargo of arms and ammunition; and on 18 June, thirty miles to the west, Giacomo Medici arrived in the Gulf of Castellamare with the 'second expedition' of 2,500 well-equipped men. The next day, Garibaldi, confident now that Sicily was firmly his, moved into a small room in the north wing of the Royal Palace. The windows of this room looked down upon the Toledo and eastwards to the bay, where twenty-four ships were sailing out to sea, taking the last of the Palermo garrison back to the mainland.

'At sunset,' Admiral Mundy recorded in his journal, 'the last steam transport sailed for Naples, and the insurrection was everywhere triumphant.'[25]

5

THE DICTATOR OF THE TWO SICILIES

In Palermo certainly the insurrection seemed to be triumphant. It was undoubtedly welcome. 'Joy is written on every face,' Garibaldi wrote proudly, and it was scarcely an exaggeration. 'All is gaiety about us,' Count Arrivabene, the correspondent of *The Daily News* confirmed. 'All is smiling and beautiful.'[1] Even the Archbishop appeared to be pleased, and agreed to bless the liberators; while the nuns from the convents were 'one and all piously enamoured of Garibaldi. Not a day passed but offerings of candied fruits, preserves, syrups, sweetmeats, etc., arrived at the Dictator's residence, arranged in curiously wrought baskets, interspersed with artificial flowers, filigree work, embroidered handkerchiefs and banners, accompanied by inscriptions in gold letters on white satin of which the following is a specimen: "To thee Giuseppe: Saint and Hero! Mighty as St. George! Beautiful as the Seraphim!" '*[2]

And down at the harbour all classes of the people, were engaged in pulling down the Castellamare fortress, the symbol of Bourbon

* 'Frequent were the morning visits paid to the convents in which the city and its environs abound,' wrote one of the General's staff officers. 'One morning, in accordance with a previous invitation, we visited the famous convent of ——, outside the Porta Nuova. The Lady Abbess met us at the vestibule, and taking the General by the hand, led the way to the refectory, where the tables spread for breakfast resembled a fancy fair – sugar castles, cupolas, temples, palaces and domes; and in the centre a statue of Garibaldi, in sugar. As the General entered, the tress-shorn maidens clustered round him with timorous and agitated mien, but the benign and smiling countenance of the far-famed captain, the manners of the perfect gentleman which are so essentially his, reassured them at once.

' "How beautiful," exclaimed one. "He is the image of Nostro Signore," whispered another; while a third, in the heat of her enthusiasm, seized his hand and kissed it; he withdrew it, and she, springing on his neck, impressed a fervent kiss upon his lips. Her audacity proved contagious; it spread to her young companions, then to the middle-aged, to the venerables, and finally to the abbess, who at first seemed scandalised. We stood by, spectators'. – Alberto Mario, *Camicia rossa* (Turin, 1860, tr. London, 1865), 3-4.

power. So many red flags and streamers and lanterns hung from the windows that Alexandre Dumas felt it was 'like being in a vast field of poppies'.[3]

Dumas had arrived in Palermo on 10 June. He had met Garibaldi in Turin some months before and the two men had immediately taken to each other. To Dumas, Garibaldi appeared the perfect hero. 'There are some men who can achieve anything,' he thought, 'and Garibaldi is one of them. If he were to say to me: "I am setting out tomorrow on an expedition to capture the moon," I should doubtless reply, "All right, go on. Just write and tell me as soon as you have taken it, and add a little postscript saying what steps I must take to come and join you." '[4]

The novelist, then aged fifty-seven and as lively and virile as ever, had been on his way to the East in his schooner, the *Emma*, to write some travel sketches for a Parisian newspaper; but Garibaldi's forthcoming expedition to Sicily had deflected him. He had decided to write about that instead, and had now excitedly responded to Garibaldi's dramatic message: 'Rally to the sound of my guns!'

He arrived in Palermo accompanied by a suitably informal entourage – two young Parisian friends, one acting as his secretary, a doctor, a Greek youth whom he had befriended and educated, a well-known photographer and Emile Cordier, known as 'the Admiral', the pregnant, nineteen-year-old daughter of a bucket-maker, stylishly dressed in a velvet sailor suit and introduced by her lover sometimes as his son, sometimes as his nephew.[5] They were all enthusiastically welcomed by Garibaldi who had them lodged in the former governor's quarters in the Royal Palace. 'Make yourself comfortable there,' Garibaldi said to Dumas, 'and stop as long as you like. The King of Naples will be delighted when he learns that you are a tenant of his.'[6]

Garibaldi's apartments in the Royal Palace were far less splendid. And it was, in fact, this curious taste for simplicity that most intrigued the extravagant and egregiously self-indulgent Dumas.

Garibaldi's resources as Dictator were immense, yet he paid himself a salary sufficient only to cover his most modest wants; he had the entire staff of the Palace at his disposal, yet 'all he wants is soup, meat and vegetables'; he admired the *Emma* yet all he could find to say was, 'If I were rich I would have a yacht like that.'[7]

Like most abstemious and frankly disinterested men, however,

Garibaldi found it difficult either to refuse or even to recognise the self-seeker. 'He says *yes* to everyone,' one of his officials wrote in exasperation, 'and leaves me to sort everything out.'[8] Men and women would come to him with their petitions and applications for pensions and employment and they would find him combing his hair, or eating fruit, or even undressing and getting into bed, and he would listen to them, carry on with what he was doing, and unthinkingly grant their requests.*

It was more obvious than ever now that Garibaldi had neither taste nor talent for administration. 'Finance, taxation, police, law courts, bureaucratic machinery were alike for him artificial and oppressive accretions to the life of nature,' wrote one who knew him well. 'If he could, he would have swept them all away. As he could not do this, he resigned himself to submit to them, but in his heart despised and abhorred them. For one who holds these ideas, it is not easy to govern well or even to choose men to govern, and so it was with Garibaldi. One thing he saw with unerring vision, however, was that he must put off the annexation of Sicily to the Monarchy of Victor Emmanuel until the revolution, which was to lay the foundations of Italian Unity, had become an established fact.'[9]

Garibaldi made no secret of this ambition. 'I came here to fight for the cause of Italy, not of Sicily alone,' he declared. 'If we do not free and unite the whole of Italy, we shall never achieve liberty in any single part of her.'[10]

It was a view which Crispi supported, and although both he and Garibaldi, despite their republican proclivities, intended ultimately to hand over the island to Victor Emmanuel, they were equally determined not to do so until the rest of Italy had been liberated.

This, of course, was not a programme which could be expected to find favour in Turin. And Cavour now took active steps to alter it. There were, however, grave difficulties in the way of his doing so.

★   ★   ★

After the fall of Palermo, King Francis II had been 'seized with such a panic that he telegraphed five times in twenty-four hours for the

---

* They were often unconfirmed. Even Nino Bixio, anxious to provide for his daughters in the event of his death, was unsuccessful when, with Garibaldi's help, he tried to obtain an administrative post for his father-in-law. *Nino Bixio: Epistolario* (ed. Emilia Morelli, Rome, 1939), Vol. 1, 1847–1860, 113.

Pope's blessing', so Odo Russell the British Minister in Rome told his uncle Lord John. 'Cardinal Antonelli, through whom the application had to be made, sent the three last blessings without reference to his Holiness, saying that he was duly authorised to do so. The converts are awfully scandalised at this proceeding.'[11]

In appealing for help to France as an answer to his unnerving dilemma, Francis had been guided not so much by the reluctance of the more reactionary powers to help him but by their inability to give him the sort of support he needed: he needed naval help and he needed it at once.

But Louis Napoleon was not prepared to give it to him. There was a difference, the Emperor explained, between protecting the Pope and protecting the Bourbons. The French flag was flying in the Papal States. If there were an attack there he would be bound to intervene; but since French blood had already been spilt in the cause of Italian nationality in the North, he could not now fight against it in the South. There was only one solution: Francis must ask for the alliance with Piedmont which he had earlier rejected, and he must grant a constitution. 'We French do not wish for the annexation of South Italy to the Kingdom of Piedmont,' the Emperor told the Neapolitan envoys, 'because we think it is against our interests, and it is for this reason that we advise you to adopt the only expedient which can prevent or at least retard that annexation.'[12]

Francis was constrained to accept this advice; but it did not provide the answer for which he was looking. His grant of a constitution and the promise of a more liberal government merely revealed the fact that, with the exception of his still loyal army of 100,000 men, he had few friends left in his kingdom; while his plea for an alliance with Piedmont raised an uproar of protest in the North where several Neapolitan exiles were deputies in the Parliament at Turin.

Now Cavour was in a dilemma, too. It was difficult for him, as he said, 'to reject scornfully a settlement proposed under French auspices and by French advice [yet] if we consent to the alliance we are lost.'[13]

Cavour's problem, in the opinion of Henry d'Ideville, an attaché at the French Legation, was as terrible as any he had had to face.[14] He reacted to it in a characteristic way; while the newspapers he controlled attacked the Neapolitan alliance, he conducted diplomatic negotiations with the Neapolitan government with the professed aim of bringing that alliance about. And while maintaining this front of friendliness, he filled Naples with agents whose instructions were to incite a more conservative revolution than Garibaldi's, demanding immediate union with the Kingdom of Piedmont.

Henry Elliot, the British Minister in Naples, was horrified by this procedure. He admitted in his diary that the feeling in favour of annexation to Piedmont was 'certainly very universal'; but he added that this universal feeling 'springs from the belief that it is the best arm with which they can eject the Bourbons rather than from any real wish for it'.[15] Yet the deliberate encouragement of a revolution which no one could be sure of being able to control until 'it has spread ruin through half the Peninsula, while professing friendship for the victim all the time, is as discreditable as anything done by a Bourbon'.[16]

Cavour, of course, recognised the dishonesty and the danger himself. 'If we had done for ourselves the things we are doing for Italy,' he commented with wry concern, 'we should be great rascals.'[17]

Nor was it only his devious methods of dealing with Francis II in Naples which was earning him the condemnation of more scrupulous men; but also the activities of his agents in Palermo.

Garibaldi's immediate and triumphant success had forced him to lend his active support to the expedition. 'We cannot struggle with him,' he told Nigra. 'He is stronger than we are. Then what are we to do? There is only one thing to be done. Associate ourselves with him.'[18] Cavour, in fact, as Adolfo Omodeo said, was 'being dragged along by the current. He had become a machine whose gears are separated from the engine'.[19]

In return for an undertaking from Medici that the reinforcements in Genoa should make for Sicily and not for the Papal States – as Bertani, encouraged by Mazzini, had wanted them to do – Cavour had seen that money and arms were provided for them. He had also instructed Admiral Persano to give Garibaldi what secret assistance he could, believing now that it might even be to Piedmont's advantage to help Garibaldi to cross over to the Neapolitan mainland where he might waste his strength and make it possible for Sicily to be annexed behind him.[20] And so as to ensure that everything possible was done to bring about an early announcement of this annexation by Garibaldi, he had sent La Farina to Palermo with orders to use his influence as a Sicilian to create a popular feeling in its favour and to organise a 'regular' government on the island in place of the one run by Crispi.[21]

La Farina, an unfortunate choice for such a mission, had arrived in Sicily on 6 June and had soon professed himself satisfied that there was already a strong feeling in favour of annexation amongst the Sicilians, who believed that in this way a reconquest by the Neapolitans might be most surely prevented. The Sicilians were also, La Farina assured Cavour, hostile to Garibaldi's dictatorship and anxious to be given a settled and more efficient government.

'Garibaldi is greatly beloved,' he admitted. 'But no one believes him capable of running a government. In fifteen days these Sicilians have read Garibaldi as if they had known him for fifteen years. No one wishes to wound him, but all are determined not to tolerate a government which is the negation of all government. . . . The most unpopular among those in power is Crispi, who is not held in any consideration in this country, and who has already furnished proof of his utter incapacity.'[22]

Within a fortnight of his arrival the envious and tactless La Farina had placarded the walls ˙of Palermo with posters demanding 'annexation to the constitutional monarchy of Victor Emmanuel'. And before the end of the month he had succeeded in engineering Crispi's resignation.

'The battle of Calatafimi and the taking of Palermo,' Crispi commented in a letter to Mazzini, 'caused me less anxiety than does this mean and petty opposition. There are times when I long to fly from it all.'[23]

At the beginning of July, Garibaldi, warned by so many of his friends to beware of La Farina, had received him 'coldly and not without a touch of severity'.[24] Now he decided that the time had come to get rid of his unwelcome visitor. On 7 July he had him suddenly arrested and placed on board Persano's flagship.

It was announced in the *Giornale Ufficiale di Sicilia* that La Farina, 'by special order of the Dictator', together with two other men, had been expelled from Sicily, since the Government could no longer tolerate 'these individuals with their wicked intentions'.*

---

* The two other men were Giacomo Griscelli and Pasquale Totti. Griscelli, so he confessed, had been employed by the Bourbons and the Apostolic Delegate to

Cavour tried to turn the expulsion to his advantage, using it as further support for his contention that the Turin Government had no 'influence with Garibaldi'. Italian diplomats urged acceptance of this explanation in the capitals of Europe; but they were not always believed.[25] It had, though, by now become true, and Cavour had firmly decided that he could no longer wait upon events, but must put a firm 'brake on democracy', must do all he could 'to prevent the Italian movement from ceasing to be national and becoming revolutionary'. He professed himself ready to do 'anything at all to obtain this result'.[26] Fearful that the success of the revolution would leave serious after-effects of instability, he now made up his mind to use every means in his power to prevent Garibaldi crossing the Strait of Messina.

murder Garibaldi ('in the interests of God, the Church and Religion') while he was in Central Italy the year before. Luigi Carlo Farini had intercepted letters which revealed Griscelli's instructions but had not had him arrested. In fact, by the end of June 1860, when Farina had become Minister of the Interior in Cavour's Cabinet, Griscelli had become a double-agent working for the Turin Government as well as for the Neapolitans; and it was in the principal capacity of a Piedmontese agent that he had arrived at Palermo. Garibaldi believed that La Farina knew the full details of the unsavoury Griscelli's background and intentions, and although Professor Trevelyan thought that the circumstances of the insulting expulsion left 'a stain on the chivalrous conduct of Garibaldi', one may now conclude that only when the statement in the *Giornale Ufficiale* went on to condemn La Farina's National Society as 'rather a hindrance than a help to the cause for which we fought at Calatafimi and Palermo' did Garibaldi's abrupt reactions to the discovery of these spies in Sicily deserve to be called uncharitable. For the background to this duel for power between La Farina and Crispi see D. Mack Smith's *Cavour and Garibaldi 1860. A Study in Political Conflict* (Cambridge University Press, 1954).

In Crispi's opinion Cavour took the expulsions as a 'personal affront' and decided thereafter to ensure that Garibaldi received no further help from the Turin Government. Crispi never forgave La Farina, a man of 'immense presumption and puerile vanity', in whom Cavour had found a suitably 'pernicious ally' – Crispi, *I Mille*, 185–8, 233. He never forgave Cavour either; and although in later years he became reconciled to the monarchy, ranking Victor Emmanuel with Mazzini and Garibaldi as one of the three men to whom Italy owed most, he continued to dismiss Cavour as a man who had merely 'diplomatised the revolution'. When, as Prime Minister in 1895 he unveiled the monument to Garibaldi on the Janiculum it was clear from his speech that this opinion had not changed – Federico Chabod, *Storia della politica estera italiana dal 1870-1896* (Laterza, Bari, 1951), III.

La Masa and his staff

Calatafimi

And so, for the moment anyway, his objects were genuinely the same as those of the Neapolitan envoys still negotiating in Turin. On the day after La Farina's expulsion the King was persuaded to write to Garibaldi instructing him on no account to cross over to the mainland; two days later Cavour ordered that no further expeditions should sail from Piedmont; on 14 July Persano was told 'at all costs to prevent Garibaldi crossing to the mainland'; two days after that, the Neapolitan envoys were told that their army ought to 'go out and attack Garibaldi, catch him and execute him'.[27]

The Neapolitan army, however, seemed incapable of such enterprise. General Clary, the tall, arrogant and asthmatic commander at Messina, despite his advocacy of an aggressive movement against the invaders, appeared unwilling to put it into execution. Pressed to do so by King Francis and by many of his officers, he was hampered by the new Ministry in Naples which urged him to remain on the defensive in Sicily and gather his strength on the mainland. So pursuing neither the one course nor the other, he sent Colonel del Bosco and three thousand men to occupy the open country west of Messina, between Milazzo and Barcelona. Bosco's orders were vague and ambiguous but they permitted him, if attacked by the Garibaldini, to deliver a counter-attack. And this was something which Bosco, an aggressive commander, might at least be expected to do.

It was the opportunity for which Garibaldi had been waiting. Already he had despatched two columns, one under Türr and the other under Bixio, towards Catania where they united towards the end of July, having enlisted many recruits in the villages on the way and having imposed their authority over the brigands and counter-revolutionaries throughout the area of their march.* Now he sent

* Bixio's methods with counter-revolutionaries were predictably violent. On entering one town 'to trample out a small dash of communism' – for the rebels were both of the Right and of the extreme Left – he immediately imposed a fine on the commune of so much an hour so long as his presence was necessary. While he was having breakfast one of the ringleaders was brought in. His men were resting after their long march, so rather than disturb them he shot the man himself through the head. Thirty-two other ringleaders were shot before noon – C. S. Forbes, *The Campaign of Garibaldi in the Two Sicilies: A Personal Narrative* (London, 1861), 127. See Gramsci's *Il Risorgimento* for a criticism of the Garibaldini's failure to exploit this agrarian unrest.

This sort of firm action taken by the Garibaldians against the unruly Sicilian

Medici with his main force towards Barcelona where they would clash with the Bourbon troops under Bosco.

The two armies came into contact on 15 July; but Bosco, mindful of his orders, turned away towards Milazzo. Medici followed him, occupied an outpost which Bosco felt entitled to recapture, and so on 17 July the skirmishing began. It ended that day in Medici's favour. Bosco sulkily complained that his officers were useless, that he was left to do everything – '*tutto, tutto, tutto!*' – but that if he were reinforced by sea or by land he would enter Palermo on Medici's horse. General Clary, however, was already receiving telegrams from Naples condemning the action of his subordinate and ordering him to ensure that he did not get further involved.[28]

When Medici asked for reinforcements, on the other hand, Garibaldi immediately despatched them – a strong detachment under Enrico Cosenz, and the so-called 'English Regiment'.* Garibaldi followed these reinforcements himself, and on 19 July, while his official birthday was being celebrated in Palermo, he was surveying the wide, flat plain, enclosed by long beaches and by low, olive-covered hills, south of Milazzo.

peasants, disillusioned by now with a dictator who had not after all alleviated their social and economic distress, had the important effect of bringing the landlords round to Garibaldi's side. For they saw in him their only protection against lawlessness on their estates – Rosario Romeo, *Il Risorgimento in Sicilia* (Laterza, Bari, 1950).

* The 'English Regiment' was commanded by Colonel Dunne, a dashing officer who had trained Turkish levies during the Crimean War, and who enforced discipline with some of Bixio's violence. On one occasion he was seen riding up to a group of Sicilians who, under fire for the first time, were nervously sheltering behind a wall. He picked them up one after the other on to his saddle and pitched them headlong over the wall. The action was effective, apparently, for the Neapolitans ran away calling out, 'They can fly! they can fly!' –Count Charles Arrivabene, *Italy under Victor Emmanuel: A Personal Narrative* (London, 1862), II, 72–73. But apart from Dunne himself there were, in fact, relatively few English officers in the 'English Regiment'. Most of them were Sicilians, and nearly all the men – about 600 of them – were youths from the back streets of Palermo and boys from the 'Garibaldi Foundling Hospital', an institution run by a friend of Mazzini, Alberto Mario, who had married Jessie White in England in December 1857.

6

THE BATTLE OF MILAZZO

The Bourbon troops, concealed behind thick hedges of cactus and prickly pear, and in the shade of long white walls, were strongly entrenched on the plain south of Milazzo. There were 2,500 of them, mostly riflemen, well drilled and well equipped, supported by eight guns, sited to fire down the length of the straight, white roads, and by a squadron of cavalry. In reserve in the mediaeval castle on the rock behind the town, were a thousand more troops with forty cannon. Farther back still, on the narrow peninsula that juts into the Tyrrhenian Sea, were another 400 men posted as a reserve and as a defensive force against a possible landing from the sea in the rear of the position.

Colonel Bosco had reason to feel confident that his well-trained and well-sited force would prove more than a match for the irregulars who were threatening to dislodge him. For these irregulars, grouped into bands which were given the somewhat misleading title of battalions, had no cavalry and their artillery was limited to two carronades of dubious serviceability.

A more heterogeneous force never came into the field [Commander C. S. Forbes, an English traveller decided after inspecting them]. Northern Italians predominated, but English, French, Hungarians, Swiss and Germans of all shades were represented. Of our countrymen, many of them deserters from the Navy, there was a company of thirty-seven attachéd to Colonel Dunne's Palermitans, commonly called the English regiment, because raised by that officer. It also had an English Major Wyndham. In this company there were eleven cadets serving as privates until they had acquired the language, when they were to receive commissions. Dunne's regiment and another, also chiefly composed of Palermitan levies, represented the Sicilians – some of them so young and diminutive as to stagger under the weight of their own muskets. Generally speaking the entire force was armed with Enfields, but few knew how to develop the use of those deadly weapons, the sights being

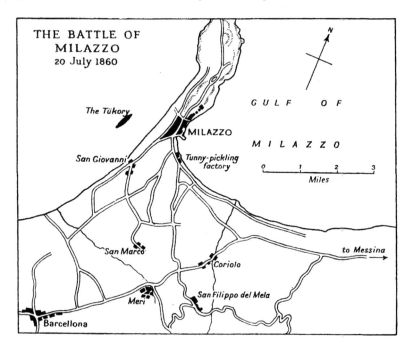

THE BATTLE OF
MILAZZO
20 July 1860

The Tükory

San Giovanni

MILAZZO

Tunny-pickling
factory

GULF O F

M I L A Z Z O

San Marco

Coriolo

to Messina

Meri

San Filippo del Mela

Barcellona

0 1 2 3
Miles

deemed a superfluity. Any martinet contemplating this army of liberation would have been heart-broken at the utter contempt displayed on all sides for those qualities which, on parade, are considered the *sine qua non* of a soldier; but these red-shirted, ragged-looking scarecrows, under this far from prepossessing exterior, were endowed with many of those sterling qualities which have often enabled impromptu levies to triumph over more elaborate organisations. A musket or rifle, sixty rounds of ammunition, a water bottle and, for the most part, an empty haversack, and you have the *impedimenta* of a Garibaldian.

Of commissaries in gorgeous uniforms there are none, yet of beef and bread there is an occasional supply – of discipline there is the merest shadow; all, however, are animated with unbounded confidence in their chiefs and especially Garibaldi who may be said to exercise an individual power over his followers wholly without parallel amongst modern commanders.[1]

In the early morning of 20 July, when they began their attack, the limitations of this mongrel army were immediately revealed. It had been Garibaldi's plan to direct the attack against the town by three converging movements – a frontal advance along the line of the main road from San Filippo del Mela, supported by two flanking attacks along the coast. But the left of these two flanking columns, led by its commander straight into a battery half a mile south of the town gate, was soon driven helter-skelter back through the vineyards where many men were killed.

Garibaldi sent Cosenz to assume command of his routed wing; and although this talented officer was able to restore order and some sort of confidence to the dispirited volunteers, he was unable to lead them forward in a resumed advance.

On the right, however, enthusiasm and wild courage made up for lack of experience and discipline. Repeated charges through the farms and vineyards, and then through the brakes of immensely tall canes that lined the beach, gradually pushed the Neapolitans back from one line of defence to the next until they were forced to withdraw towards a tunny-pickling factory just outside Milazzo harbour. But it was an advance which was as costly as it was slow and exhausting. Wounded men were continually being taken back to the makeshift hospitals in the villages to the south, while many other men, frightened by the strange sounds and sights and smell of battle, parched with thirst and dazed by the relentless heat, found it impossible to resist the temptation to go back to the hospitals too.

Many more would have done the same had it not been for the inspiration they derived from their apparently fearless leader, who exposed himself to the bullets of the enemy as though he had divine assurance that they could not touch him. Sometimes he would stand in the full glare of the sun as a squad of young volunteers filed past him on their way to the attack, repeating to each one in a low, confiding voice, '*Coraggio!*' Sometimes he would lead a charge himself, rushing headlong at the enemy with his sword in his hand, shouting words of encouragement.[2]

A young English volunteer in Colonel Dunne's 'English Regiment', A. B. Patterson, remembered one such charge. He was standing at the edge of a cane-brake into which the Bourbon troops were firing, the bullets snapping the canes all round him and wounding many of his companions. Garibaldi galloped up, jumped off his horse and rushed up the narrow ride towards the wall behind which the enemy riflemen were kneeling. 'He did not once look round to see if his men were following, but he knew that none who saw him would linger.'[3]

Later the dashing and ubiquitous General found himself and one of his aides-de-camp, Giuseppe Missori, surrounded by about a dozen cavalrymen. Missori shot the horse of their leader who stood up in the stirrups as it fell and lashed out at Garibaldi with his sword. Garibaldi parried the blow, then, grabbing hold of the horse's bridle, brought his sabre down on the officer's neck and almost severed his head from his shoulders. Meanwhile Missori had shot two more of the horsemen; and the rest, frightened by the sudden death of four of their company, galloped away towards the bridge which carried the coast road over a culvert in front of the town gate.

This bridge was the scene of furious fighting. Colonel Bosco had already decided that if his lines on the plain were to be forced, he would make his final stand here. His guns on either side of it could be supported by the cannon in the castle, and his riflemen could fire on it both from the houses on either side of the town gate and from the buildings by the harbour wall.

The defensive strength of the position was indeed formidable, and so many men were eventually lost here that Garibaldi decided that no immediate attack could be made on the town. He gave orders for the position to be held but not extended, and for the men to get some rest in the tunny-pickling factory and in the buildings around it.

Garibaldi himself, as though the battle had already been satisfactorily decided, calmly took off his shirt 'washed it in the brook near by, and hung it up on the bushes – ate his lunch of bread, fruit and water – smoked his cigar barebacked – and, wrapt in thought, sat contemplating the drying of his garment'.[4]

Then, as soon as the shirt was dry, he went across to the other beach to find out what progress Cosenz had made against the right flank of the Bourbon position. On his way he saw a paddle-steamer standing some way off shore between the town and the south of a dried-up torrent bed that took the winter rains down to the sea through Meri. It was the *Tükory*, formerly the *Veloce*, a ship carrying ten guns, whose crew had deserted from the Bourbon service and had just arrived to offer the Dictator their help.

Garibaldi got into a small boat that had been dragged up on to the beach, and rowed out to her to give the captain instructions to take her closer inshore and bombard the Neapolitan troops who were holding up Cosenz's advance.

This action was wholly successful. The Neapolitans, under fire from the sea and in danger of being cut off from the town by the volunteers fighting at the bridge, withdrew into Milazzo, making it possible for Cosenz to join Medici and so continue the Garibaldian line right across the neck of the peninsula.

At four o'clock the order to advance into the town was given, and the volunteers went forward. At first they wondered at the weakness of the enemy's fire, and then found to their amazement that Milazzo was deserted. For Colonel Bosco, feeling that his discouraged troops were incapable of holding it against such determined opponents, had withdrawn to the castle on its granite precipice three hundred feet above the sea. By nightfall Garibaldi was in full possession of the town below and its streets were barricaded against a counter-attack from the castle.

But Bosco's men, far from being capable of a spirited counter-attack, seemed not even prepared to withstand a siege. There was little food in the town and no fresh water, and when they were placed on half rations they threatened to open the castle gate. They paid no attention to the sanitary regulations drawn up by their doctors, even declining to bury the corpses that were left to putrefy in the appalling heat.

Bosco semaphored to Messina with a catalogue of complaints, warning that the morale of his men was 'destroyed'. But the morale of the senior officers at the army headquarters was not much better than that of the men at Milazzo. General Clary, who had in the past strongly recommended offensive action against the rebels in Sicily, now that the opportunity to take this action presented itself, seemed hesitant and unsure. The orders he had given Bosco never envisaged a full-scale battle at Milazzo, he afterwards complained. The expedition had been sent against Medici on the understanding that no compromising action would be taken farther west than the heights above Messina where Clary had intended to make his stand.

Now that Bosco had allowed himself to get shut up in Milazzo, Clary did not know what to do. At first he insisted that Bosco must immediately be relieved, but then allowed himself to be persuaded that the lack of land transport, and the presence of a column of about a thousand Garibaldini marching north from Catania, were sufficient reasons for keeping his 15,000 men in Messina. The day after he reached this decision he changed his mind, and ordered three regiments to go to Milazzo by sea. A few hours later this order, too, was countermanded.[5]

General Clary was not entirely to blame for his indecision. At Naples the arguments about the Sicilian problem had still not been resolved. The War Minister, clinging to his view that Sicily should be abandoned, believed nevertheless that Bosco must be rescued and gave orders for an expedition to set sail for Milazzo. The Neapolitan navy, however, had other ideas, and encouraged by Admiral Count dell' Aquila, the King's liberal uncle, they refused to take the troops on board. The Ministers met to discuss this new crisis, which several of them welcomed as a way out of their predicament, and gave way with evident relief to Count dell' Aquila's urging that Bosco should be evacuated, not reinforced, and that not only Milazzo but Messina also should be surrendered.

On 23 July Colonel Anzani arrived in Milazzo harbour aboard the *Fulminante*, with instructions to arrange these capitulations; and a treaty was soon signed by which the Neapolitan troops were to march out of the castle with their arms and half the battery mules, the rest of the mules and all the horses, together with the cannon and ammunition in the castle, being left behind for Garibaldi.[6]

Colonel Bosco regarded the terms as a personal insult. He marched out of the castle at the rear of the long file of his troops, 'a fine, ugly man with a good deal of hair and swagger',[7] pulling at his immense and extravagantly curled moustache, while the townspeople hissed and insulted him. He had said that he would enter Palermo in triumph on Medici's horse, and now it was to be Medici who would ride into Messina on his.

This horse and the others that Bosco had had to leave behind in the castle were running round the outer enclosure when Garibaldi came up from the town.

'Nothing could exceed the filthy state of the castle,' wrote an English observer. 'Men and mules seemed to have pigged it out together; how they held out so long as they did astonished me, as the stink of the dead horses lying about was intolerable and the water perfectly undrinkable.'[8]

Garibaldi seemed unconcerned, however, and gave his companion a demonstration of his skill with the lasso that delighted them. Admiral Persano was with him and Jessie White (who, with her husband Alberto Mario, had come to Sicily with the reinforcements under Medici), and the Countess Della Torre, a strange woman whom Garibaldi had met in London in 1854 and who had now come out to join him on the field of battle wearing a hussar tunic, a big plumed hat and a sword of improbable length.

They all congratulated the General on his great victory. It had been an expensive victory, though, at a cost of 800 men killed and wounded, casualties over four times as heavy as those suffered by the enemy.[9] And the Marios, unable to join in Persano's expressions of happiness that it had been won for the King of Piedmont, soon left the General to visit the religious houses in and outside the town where several of the boys who had run away from the 'Garibaldi Foundling Hospital' lay wounded.

These temporary hospitals, like nearly all those to which the wounded Garibaldini had been taken in the past and were to be taken in the future, were ill equipped, with no proper bandages, no means of deadening pain, and as few surgical instruments as men qualified to use them.

Jessie Mario had brought a supply of mattress covers with her from Palermo for the wounded, but there was not enough straw in Milazzo with which to fill them; and she had to content herself with walking round the crowded rooms with her husband. They were both overcome with emotion.

As I passed down the left corridor [Alberto Mario recalled], I heard a young voice crying, Signor Comandante, and saw three lads lying on the floor, their once white uniforms stained with blood and dirt.

'They are your boys; they deserted to Dunne,' said my wife. 'Come and see another.' And she led me into a room opening out of the corridor, where on one of the beds abandoned by the monks, lay a little fellow asleep, an ice bladder on the stump of his lost left arm.

'It was amputated this afternoon,' said my wife. 'Poor little mite, he is only twelve. He said, "I'll be good if you hold me, Signora. If it hurts I won't scream. I'll only cry a little". I held him on my lap; he kept his word, and told me afterwards that I cried more than he did, which was quite true. Then he fell fast asleep, as they nearly all do after an operation.'

'Are you angry with us, Signor Comandante?' asked one of the elder lads, taking my hand and stroking it as I returned to them. 'Such lots of our brigade are wounded or killed; our Colonel says that after the battle of Milazzo no one can say again that Sicilians never fight.'

I felt choking. I could not speak. I kissed their pale brows, put some money into their hands, and rushed out into the open air.[10]

*   *   *

The next day, Giacomo Medici left on Bosco's horse to negotiate with General Clary for the capitulation of Messina. Clary had protested that he would refuse to obey the humiliating orders to surrender which had come from Naples with Colonel Anzani; but, in fact, on 28 July he signed a treaty which provided for the complete suspension of hostilities, the occupation of the town by the Garibaldini and the withdrawal of the royal troops into the citadel where they were to remain passive spectators of whatever future action Garibaldi might take.[11]

*   *   *

The form of that future action had already been decided. The day before Clary and Medici signed their treaty, a messenger, Count Litta Modignani, arrived in Milazzo with two letters for Garibaldi from Victor Emmanuel. The first, official letter was unequivocal: it forbade Garibaldi to cross the Strait of Messina to invade the Kingdom of Naples.[12]

Cavour, at whose suggestion this personal letter had been written, was now more than ever concerned by Garibaldi's continuing success. The volunteers' victory at Milazzo had made it seem likely that they would repeat their triumphs on the mainland. And it was 'most important that the liberation of Naples should not be due to Garibaldi,' as he urgently reminded the Marquis Villamarina, Piedmontese Minister in Naples, 'for if that happens a revolutionary system will take the place of the monarchist national party'.[13]

He expressed the same fears to Nigra in Paris: 'King Victor Emmanuel will lose nearly all his prestige. He will become, in the eyes of the majority of Italians, no more than the friend of Garibaldi. He will probably keep his crown, but it will shine only with such reflected light as a heroic adventurer will judge willing to throw upon it. The King must not have to accept the Crown of Italy from the hand of Garibaldi: *elle chancellerait trop sur sa tête!*'[14]

It might be difficult now, if not impossible, to prevent Garibaldi crossing over to the mainland; but he must, as Cavour instructed Persano, be delayed 'by indirect methods as long as possible'.[15] And in the meantime it was essential that the Piedmontese agents succeed in provoking a movement in Naples, a movement which 'must take place', as Cavour insisted to Villamarina, 'before Garibaldi arrives there' – the movement which would give Victor Emmanuel the excuse he needed to march into Neapolitan territory himself.[16]

Victor Emmanuel, however, appears once again to have been acting on a line of his own. Openly he supported Cavour in his determination to prevent Garibaldi crossing the Strait, but in his heart he hoped he would do so, and secretly encouraged him to do so. The second, unofficial letter that Count Litta carried with him contradicted the formal instructions contained in the first and advised the General how to reply to it. Whether or not this second letter was handed to Garibaldi, there can be little doubt that he was given to understand the gist of it, for he was never a man, as Nino Bixio said, to disobey a royal order. Certainly he wasted no time in replying to it.[17]

He left Litta, went into his bedroom, told his staff not to make so much noise, and sat down to write. Litta waited for the reply, feeling, so he confided to his diary as if he were 'in the midst of one of those numerous bands of brigands who at one time infested certain parts of Italy'.[18]

Sir [Garibaldi wrote]. Your Majesty knows the high esteem and love I bear you. But the present state of things does not allow me to obey you. . . . If now, in face of all the calls that reach me, I delayed any longer I should fail in my duty and imperil the sacred cause of Italy. Allow me then, Sire, this time to disobey you. As soon as I have fulfilled what I have undertaken, by freeing the peoples from a hated yoke, I will lay down my sword at your feet and obey you for the rest of my life.[19]

The laying down of his triumphant sword at the grateful King's feet was exactly what Cavour was determined to prevent, but the difficulties of preventing it grew with every day. The Piedmontese agents in Naples showed no signs of being able to provoke the sort of incidents he required; the Neapolitan army was proving far more loyal to the King than he had hoped;* the reports of enthusiasm for Garibaldi in the South were increasingly alarming. Yet to take military action against the revolution might prove even more dangerous than allowing a foreign country to do so.

Louis Napoleon was at least willing to interfere. Since Piedmont had now finally refused the Neapolitan offer of alliance, there seemed no other means of preventing the annexation of South Italy to the North and the consequent creation of a new state in Europe which, strong enough to be independent of France, would turn away from her. But to interfere might lose him the friendship of England.

Ever since Villafranca the leading British Ministers, Lord Palmerston, Lord John Russell and Gladstone, had been pursuing a pro-Italian policy against the wishes of the Queen and the Court, of the Conservative opposition and, indeed, of many of the members of their own Cabinet. The general feeling in the country was behind them, however, and so now was *The Times*.† They did not yet believe in either the possibility or the desirability of Italian national

* On a Sunday evening in the middle of July hundreds of soldiers had run loose through the streets of Naples, forcing everyone to cry '*Viva il Re!*' The British Consul Bonham, 'found himself in the middle of it before he knew where he was, and was surrounded and made to show his loyalty like the rest, which he did without being invited twice; but, not having taken off his hat at the sacred name of royalty, it was knocked off by a neat cut from a sword' – *Some Revolutions and other Diplomatic Experiences of the late Right Hon. Sir Henry G. Elliot, G.C.B., edited by his daughter* (London, 1922), 31.

† In Europe, indeed, and particularly in Germany and Russia, there was a widespread belief that Garibaldi's whole expedition was underwritten in England. And it was true that many well-known English people, from the Duke of Wellington to Lady Byron, had contributed to his funds. It was also true that workmen in Glasgow had given up their afternoons off to make munitions for him, and that a collection at the Athenaeum had realised £300 in a single night. Duke Ernest of Saxe-Coburg thought that 'the mystery of how 150,000 men were vanquished by

unity, but they did believe that the policy of the Government should be 'not to interfere at all, but to let the Italian people settle their own affairs'. And gradually they had been persuaded by Hudson and Elliot – themselves late converts to the idea – that unity might come, however impracticable such a solution appeared, and that it was in the interests of Britain to allow it to come.

This was not to say, of course, that they believed that they ought to encourage it to come. Indeed, Lord John Russell – although, as he told Palmerston, he 'could not stomach defending Bombino' (Francis II) – wrote to Henry Elliot at the end of June to say, 'If you have any means of communicating with Garibaldi, you may tell him that the British Government think he ought to be content with the whole of Sicily and not stir any further the fire of Italian insurrection. Perhaps the captain of a man-of-war might carry this private message.'[20]

Russell was prepared to accept a *fait accompli* – and, in the event, the British Government recognised the new unified State of Italy more quickly than any other – but for the moment there were still strong doubts in his mind and in the minds of his colleagues. National self-determination was, after all, a revolutionary doctrine. And to smile upon a principle in Italy made it all the more difficult to frown upon it in Ireland.[21]

While advising restraint, however, the British Government stood by their declaration not to intervene to ensure it. So when Louis Napoleon requested a 'joint naval blockade' they were ill disposed to the idea. So, indeed, was Cavour, 'since any such intervention was bound to be to some extent at Piedmont's expense, and would emphasise Italy's servile status'.[22] Therefore when Sir James Lacaita, on behalf of Cavour, pointed out the 'dangerous complications which must arise if a stop was not put to them', the negotiations were abruptly ended. And without British support Louis Napoleon felt unable to act alone.[23]

Spared a confrontation with an Anglo-French fleet, Garibaldi was nevertheless still faced with immense difficulties. A contested passage of the Strait had always been notoriously hazardous, and to get across with his single warship, the *Tükory*, to answer the guns of the

a thousand Red-shirts was wrapped in English bank-notes!' – Martinengo Cesaresco, *op. cit.*, 266.

powerful Neapolitan Navy, seemed to many of his officers an impossible undertaking.

Garibaldi appeared now to be infected by their foreboding. Alberto Mario, whom he had recently commissioned and appointed to his staff, said that 'preoccupied by serious cares', he had 'grown taciturn. His brow, hitherto so open and serene, was often clouded.' Always once, and sometimes twice a day, he went up to the lighthouse outside Messina 'to superintend the mounting of the batteries, the fitting up of gunboats, or the organisation of his troops who occupied the wretched village or bivouacked along the scorching sandy beach.'[24] Mazzini wrote to Crispi to complain that any delay might prove fatal, that he could not understand Garibaldi, for, once an enemy had become demoralised, then was the time to follow up one's advance.[25] But, Garibaldi retorted, Mazzini was far away, quite out of touch with the military difficulties which he did not understand anyway.

Once Mario went with the General to the lighthouse and they climbed to the top; Garibaldi remained there for more than an hour with his telescope turned to the opposite coast. 'Not a word was spoken either in going or returning.'[26]

On the beach behind the lighthouse the waiting volunteers, often hungry and thirsty, exposed to the heat of the day and the mists of the night, were beginning to grow restless in their evil-smelling camp. Many of the Sicilians had already gone home, and more were following them every week, having little interest – now that their island was free – in the cause for which the others were going to fight, and being disillusioned by Garibaldi whom they had expected would support them against the landlords and give them land of their own.

As well as losing men, Garibaldi was running out of money; and when one day Alexandre Dumas came to Messina to tell him that the Municipio of Palermo had refused to honour a letter of credit because the General had omitted to write the word 'Dictator' beneath his signature, the tears poured down his face.[27]

On the night of 8 August, encouraged by another message from the King urging him to go on to Naples and then into the Papal States,[28] he made his first attempt to invade the mainland. It was a failure. A force of 200 shock-troops were packed into rowing-boats near the lighthouse and sent across to capture the fort on the opposite side of the Strait. They managed to evade the Neapolitan warships and get ashore near Altifiumara, but their attack on the fort was repulsed, and they were forced to retreat into the mountains. Here, under the command of Giuseppe Missori, they roamed about, evading the Bourbon troops sent out to capture them and lighting huge bonfires at night to show the volunteers at Messina that they were still alive and waiting for them to join them. But for the moment no more Garibaldini could join them; and their only reinforcements were Calabrian peasants who came into their camp wearing what seemed to one of Missori's officers a kind of outlandish uniform – fustian knee-breeches, goatskin sandals and cone-shaped hats decorated with narrow streamers of black velvet. With their sunburned skin and 'masses of raven black hair', their almond-shaped eyes and vigorous limbs, they seemed to be 'one of the finest types of the human race'. But there were few enough of them, for the presence of 16,000 Bourbon troops in Southern Calabria made a widespread uprising impossible; and although in Upper Calabria and in Basilicata revolutionary committees were being formed, the advent of Garibaldi was needed as a rush of air is needed to set glowing embers aflame.

Garibaldi, however, had begun to believe, now that so many Sicilians had left him, that he could not make another attempt at invasion until reinforcements came from the North; or at least until a diversionary attack was made by the men that Bertani's revolutionary committee had collected in Genoa. Already, on 30 July, he had told Bertani to 'push on with all possible vigour with the operations in the Papal and Neapolitan territories'.[29]

Bertani, however, was forestalled by Cavour who sent Farini to Genoa to advise Bertani that an invasion of the Papal States by a revolutionary force would be bound to lead to French interference and that, in any event, the Government had decided to come to Garibaldi's help. Bertani must, therefore, divert his volunteers to Sardinia and then on to Sicily. They could attack the Papal States from there, if he liked, but not from Genoa. Bertani agreed to accept the compromise and sailed to Messina to persuade Garibaldi to come back with him to lead the new invasion.[30]

When the two men arrived in Sardinia on 14 August, however, they discovered that most of the ships which had brought the volunteers to the island from Genoa had been forced to sail on to Sicily by the Piedmontese fleet in accordance with the agreement which the Turin Government had induced Bertani to make with them.

Bertani, who had hoped Garibaldi would invade the Papal States from Sardinia despite this agreement, was furious, but Garibaldi himself seemed not in the least concerned. He called at Caprera to see his mistress and his baby, to feed his cows and taste his melons, and then he sailed back to Sicily, knowing now that he could, with these 6,000 extra men that Cavour had removed from Bertani's control, cross the Strait with confidence.

Leaving the main part of his force at Messina, he collected 3,400 men at Taormina, thirty miles to the south, and gave orders to Nino Bixio to cram them into two steamers – the *Torino* and the *Franklin* – which he had sent all the way round the island to meet them there.

Men of The Thousand raiding a farm for their breakfast

The capture of a Bourbon spy outside the American Consul's house in Palermo

A skirmish during the battle of Milazzo

Garibaldi fighting at Milazzo

The surrender of the Neapolitan troops at Soveria-Mannelli

Garibaldi leads the final attack during the battle of the Volturno

THE MAN IN POSSESSION
Victor Emmanuel: 'I wonder when
he will open the door'

RIGHT LEG IN THE BOOT
AT LAST
Garibaldi: 'If it won't go on,
Sire, try a little more powder!'

7

CALABRIA

Soon after dark on 18 August, the *Franklin* and the *Torino*, with their bulwarks, paddle-boxes and rigging all clustered with troops, steamed out from below the rock of Taormina and set course for the Calabrian coast at Melito. It was a dark and quiet night and not a single ship of the Neapolitan fleet was sighted. At dawn the men, many of them suffering from fever brought on by their days of exposure on the beach at Messina, gathered in the stern of the ships and saw the dim coastline come into view; then, more clearly, a long, desolate, sandy beach and the cupola of an old chapel surrounded by a hedge of prickly pear. Here they were rowed ashore in the ships' boats and marched up the beach to wait for Giuseppe Missori and his men to come down to join them from the mountains.

For the whole of that day and the next night they camped near Melito, without food or water. Meantime the rumours, and then the confirmed news, of their landing were debated in Naples and eventually telegraphed to the various regiments stationed in Lower Calabria.[1]

These regiments numbered 18,000 troops, but not a single one of them was stationed south of Reggio. Nor, indeed, after the news of Garibaldi's landing had been confirmed, did any of them move down there, despite the advice and protestations that were telegraphed at regular intervals from Naples. In command of the garrison in Reggio itself was an old General, Gallotti, who denied the possibility that Reggio could be taken from the landward side. He remained in the castle, itself in a dangerous position, for it was only half-way up the hill on which Reggio stood; and, though its defences were formidable, they were overlooked by the houses in the upper part of the town. His more capable field commander, Colonel Dusmet, was ordered to bivouac his men in the confined space of the Cathedral Square.

Shortly after midnight on 20 August, suddenly and violently, the Garibaldini erupted into the Square. There was a sudden and

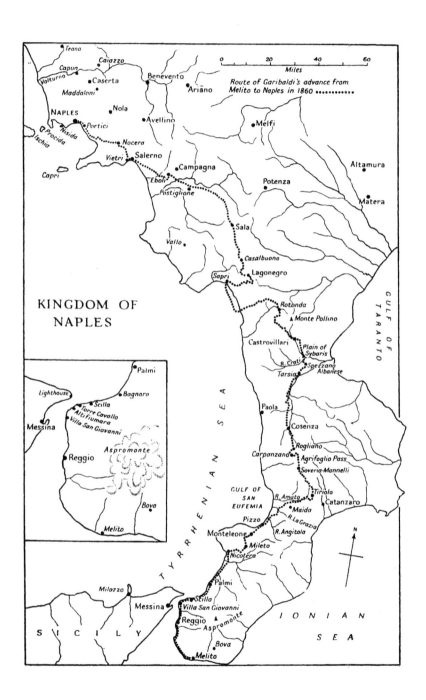

Teano
Caiazzo
Capua
Volturno
Maddaloni
Caserta
Benevento
Ariano

Route of Garibaldi's advance from
Melito to Naples in 1860 ••••••••••

Nola
Avellino
Melfi
NAPLES
Nisida
Portici
Procida
Ischia
Nocera
Vietri
Salerno
Capri
Campagna
Altamura
Eboli
Postiglione
Potenza
Matera

Sala

Vallo
Casalbuono
Sapri
Lagonegro

KINGDOM OF
NAPLES
Rotonda
Monte Pollino

GULF OF
TARANTO

Castrovillari
Plain of
Sybaris
R. Crati
Spezzano
Tarsia
Albanese

Palmi
Lighthouse
Bagnara
Scilla
Torre Cavallo
Altafiumara
Villa San Giovanni
Messina
Aspromonte
Reggio
Bova
Melito

Paola

Cosenza

Rogliano
Carpanzano
Agrifoglio Pass
Soveria-Mannelli

GULF OF
SAN
EUFEMIA
R. Amato
Tiriolo
Catanzaro
Maida
R. La Grazia
Pizzo
Monteleone
R. Angitola
Mileto
Nicotera

TYRRHENIAN SEA

N

Milazzo
Palmi
Scilla
Villa San Giovanni
Messina
Reggio
Aspromonte
Bova
SICILY
Melito

IONIAN
SEA

0   20   40   60
Miles

ferocious fight in which Dusmet and his young son were both killed and in which Nino Bixio's horse was wounded nineteen times. Bixio himself was shot twice in the arm, but he refused to retire from the fight until Garibaldi sent him to bed with the cheerfully sardonic comment, 'I suppose the balls that hit *you* are made of puff-paste.'[2]

The General seemed happier than he had ever been since the landing at Marsala. For the complications, the political arguments, the delays, the importunities of the 'crowds of adventurers that infested his table',[3] were all over now. He had not discussed his military plans with anyone for the past few weeks; he had taken the decision when and where to cross the Strait entirely by himself; and he had been successful. A month before, Admiral Mundy had described him as being 'thin and careworn, evidently harassed in mind and devoid of his usual composure'.[4] But now he was on the move again. Sicily lay conquered behind him. Naples lay waiting deliverance in front. His duty was clear, and his guiding star, Palinurus, which he had pointed out to his staff the night before the attack on Palermo, was sharp and bright again. He had marched to Reggio with his sabre over his shoulder, singing cheerfully. Outside the town the outposts manned by the National Guard had challenged him in the darkness:

'*Chi va là?*'
'*Garibaldi!*'
'*Avanti!*'

He needed no permission. He was going forward anyway; but it had been good to know that even the National Guard were prepared to welcome him.[5]

The fierce fight in the town with Colonel Dusmet's infantry had cost him over a hundred men; but he had never doubted the outcome, and by morning all the troops in Reggio had been driven back into the castle. When reinforcements for the garrison at last arrived from the north, Garibaldi led his men out of the town and into a furious bayonet charge. The reinforcements quickly retreated and then, after a desultory rifle duel, withdrew altogether. Turning back towards the castle he ordered an officer and thirty of his best marksmen to pick off the Neapolitan gunners who were still firing from the ramparts.

'March separately,' he said, 'and, if needs be on all fours, to avoid the bombs. I absolutely forbid anyone to get wounded.'[6]

Within two hours, according to the proud officer whose skilled riflemen succeeded in killing or wounding 'nearly all the gunners as they stood at their pieces', the garrison hoisted the white flag and the town surrendered. That night the General's entire staff were promoted.[7]

The capture of Reggio, after so short a battle, was the first of a succession of triumphs that helped to support Garibaldi's cheerful mood. On 22 August he moved up north into the hills above Villa San Giovanni, and by the evening he had joined forces with Cosenz who had been able to get across the Strait from the lighthouse north of Messina with 1,300 reinforcements in a flotilla of rowing boats while the Neapolitan fleet was away from its usual station making a belated attempt to prevent Garibaldi's landing at Melito.

Garibaldi now had about 5,000 men under his command, a force slightly larger than his enemies had so far been able to muster in Villa San Giovanni. And by the night of 23 August he had cut off the Neapolitans' line of retreat along the coast road to Scilla, and had completely surrounded them.

Their two commanders, Generals Melendez and Briganti, could have escaped the day before from the net that Garibaldi had drawn around them; but they waited where they were, believing that General Vial, their commander-in-chief in Lower Calabria, would be sure to send at least some of his 10,000 troops to their rescue. They waited in vain. Vial, a young dilettante who owed his command to his family's influence at King Francis's court, declined to move from Corleone until forced to do so by telegrams from Naples. And his eventual arrival by boat at Villa San Giovanni did nothing to improve the perilous situation of his elderly subordinates: he had brought only one battalion with him. And although he promised to land it at Scilla and break through the Garibaldian perimeter from there, high seas gave him an excuse for changing his mind and he took it back with him to Corleone.

One of his deputies, General Ruiz, who commanded the troops that had pursued Missori over the upper plains of Aspromonte, came down again to the coast at Altifiumara. But at Villa San Giovanni, which he entered alone, leaving his men behind on the coast road to

Scilla, Ruiz saw how unlikely it was that the trapped troops there would put up any sort of fight should he succeed in driving his own battalions forward against the Garibaldian lines that encircled them. They were standing at street corners, sitting on the pavements outside cafés and wine shops, while several of Garibaldi's officers walked about unchecked from group to group, assuring them that the great General was invincible and that to fight against him was, in any case, an act of treachery against Italy.

There was little enthusiasm for this sort of talk amongst the royal troops, but few of them were moved to protest. They listened, for the most part silent and sullen, smoking their cheap cigars and spitting into the gutter. They had been prepared to fight well in the Bourbon uniform for the royal flag; but this new tricolour that had replaced it since the recent grant of a constitution by King Francis seemed a poor substitute, an admission almost of defeat. Down here in these dry and dusty Calabrian wastes it was difficult to believe in the cause they were supposed to be defending. In some villages the peasants in their strange, high conical hats and their wives in their long, black, shapeless skirts seemed loyal enough; they would sometimes even smile, murmur a '*Viva il Re*', tired and spiritless, like an *Ave Maria* repeated too often as a penance, but a symptom at least of a loyalty not yet dead. Many of the townspeople, though, appeared to have lost their faith, to have no interest in being defended from sedition, to be prepared even to welcome these heathen brigands from the North. So why die fighting for a cause that seemed as doomed as the corroded Calabrian hills above them?

General Ruiz left Villa San Giovanni with his mind made up. The troops there would not fight. He would not take his own men to join in their surrender. He went back to Altifiumara, turned his battalions about and sent them marching away on the road to Bagnara. And at dawn the following morning, the Garibaldini came down from the hills into Villa San Giovanni.

They advanced in mass and in silence. A few Neapolitan cannon opened up on them, but the volunteers neither halted nor replied to the fire. They came on slowly and calmly through the cannon shot and the rifle fire; and before they had reached the outskirts of the little town, the firing stopped. General Briganti had decided not to fight. He asked to be allowed to surrender with the honours of war.

Garibaldi gave him and his colleague until three o'clock that afternoon to surrender unconditionally.

By three o'clock no answer had been received and the silent advance began again. The Neapolitan troops, utterly broken in spirit by now, threw down their rifles and knapsacks and ran away along the coast road towards Scilla. They were stopped by the Garibaldian outposts, who opened fire on them from behind their road blocks, and then they ran back again towards the town like frightened animals.

Garibaldi rode down amongst them. 'Soldiers,' he called out in that clear, silvery voice which Admiral Mundy had so admired in Palermo. 'You, as well as my companions, are the sons of Italy – remember that. You are at liberty. Whoever wishes to remain with us may apply to General Cosenz, your countryman, who has authority to enlist you. But whoever wishes may go home'.

This sudden, unexpected, reprieve was too much for some of them who rushed at him and tried to kiss his legs and feet. Few of them, however, chose to seek out General Cosenz; and the great majority wandered away to begin their long walk home.[8]

There were still 10,000 troops farther north, but there were good grounds now for hoping that they would follow the example of the battalions at Villa San Giovanni. And as the march on Naples began, this hope seemed about to be fulfilled.

On 24 August the garrison at Altifiumara surrendered to Garibaldi, then the garrison at Torre Cavallo, then the castle at Scilla. The batteries in the captured forts were turned on the Neapolitan warships in the Strait, and Medici was able to bring over fresh battalions from Messina.

Once it was clear that Garibaldi's hold on the toe of Italy was securely established, the people showed their relief and happiness. 'The population are frantic in their demonstrations of joy,' Commander Forbes, who was himself to be hugged and kissed far too much for his taste, had written from Reggio on 21 August. 'All the men appeared to be armed, and are joining. To understand many is impossible; they still preserve the Hellenic tongue. . . . Garibaldi's reception, and that of his troops, far surpasses anything met with in Sicily – there is not near so much noise and demonstration, but much more reality.'

Garibaldi was welcomed, in fact, as though he were divine. Men knelt down to kiss his feet and women pushed their babies into his arms so that he might bless them. Indeed, Forbes was frequently assured by the peasants that Garibaldi was the brother of the Redeemer. ' "*Il nostro secondo Gesu Cristo*" was the constant ejaculation with these simple people – a strange contrast to the opinion of the Neapolitan soldiers, who, in obedience to a very common suspicion in South Italy, say that Garibaldi has sold himself, body and soul, to the devil. In proof of this, they appeal to his apparently charmed life, adding that the rifle balls merely lodge in his red shirt, and he shakes them out after he has done fighting.'[9]

* * *

Before the month was out, several thousand Calabrians had taken up arms in support of the invaders. Baron Stocco, an influential landlord from Catanzaro, who had sailed with The Thousand, returned to his family's estates and gathered together about 6,000 farmers and shepherds armed with shot-guns, axes and scythes, at the bridge across the Angitola north of Pizzo. Here Stocco intended to stand and prevent the withdrawal of General Vial's troops from Monteleone to Naples. Vial himself escaped with some of his men by boat from Pizzo; but the rest were left behind under General Ghio to make their way back to Naples as best they could by land.

With Stocco's armed *contadini* in front of him, and Garibaldi's followers coming up behind, Ghio concluded that this was impossible. He sent back an officer to Garibaldi's headquarters with a flag of truce and a request for a passage to Naples with the honours of war. Garibaldi refused the request and demanded, as he had done of General Briganti at Villa San Giovanni, unconditional surrender.[10]

Garibaldi was at Nicotera on the sea coast when General Ghio's offer of surrender reached him; but the following day he had turned inland and entered Mileto, a town half-way up the mountainside. And here in the middle of the main street, he noticed a long, wide stain of dried blood and the charred remains of an animal. The blood was that of General Briganti. Some of his disgruntled soldiers had recognised him, as he rode through the town towards Naples, wearing civilian clothes with a hat pulled down low over his eyes. They had rushed at him, shouting '*Traditore!*' and firing their rifles. When he was dead they had stripped his body, and cut off his head and genitals. Then they had killed and burned his horse. Their officers stood by, muttering weak protests.[11]

Garibaldi moved on to Monteleone. He was travelling in a *carrozzella* now, well ahead of the main body of the army. The Marios were still with him and Commander Forbes, with some other English adventurers who had come along as one of them put it 'for the ride'. It was a hard ride, and even some of the staff found difficulty in keeping up with him.

When their sweating horses panted into Monteleone, the towns-people came out in their hundreds to greet the marvellous General and he climbed up on to a balcony to talk to them. The cheering died away as they stood in the piazza, silent and expectant, their heads raised towards him. He looked down at them, his arms crossed, and his head bent low in his tall Calabrian hat. For a long time he did not speak. It was an impressive performance which a later demagogue might well have envied, and for years afterwards his audience remembered it.[12]

From Monteleone the fast pursuit of the Neapolitan troops was continued, past Pizzo and then over the Angitola bridge, which Ghio's battalions had been allowed to cross in the mistaken belief that they had joined the revolution, and on towards Tiriolo.

After the passage of the Angitola, the pace of the pursuit increased, for Ghio's battalions must not be allowed to join their companions in Upper Calabria and occupy a mountain position which would bar the way to Naples. And so Garibaldi, still well ahead of his main force, drove on faster than ever: across the bridge over the La Grazia, and past the Plain of Maida where the white, rocky beds of dried-up rivers cut through the brushwood into the Gulf of Santa Eufemia; then across the Amato Valley, and up 2,000 feet above the sea to Tiriolo where a man can stand and look across the whole Italian peninsula from the Tyrrhenian Sea in the west to the Ionian in the east. And then, five miles beyond Tiriolo, the enemy were sighted at last.

They were encamped in and around the village of Soveria-Mannelli, without outposts or guards, sitting and cooking stolen sheep in the morning sunlight. As before at Monteleone, so now at Soveria-Mannelli, they had been trapped between two converging forces – Garibaldini behind them and five miles in front of them (by the pass of Agrifoglio on the road to Cosenza) thousands of armed *contadini*.

This time, Garibaldi was determined the Neapolitans should not escape. And as Baron Stocco's men came up, followed by a few of Cosenz's companies, exhausted by their hard march, he set them up into the hills around the village where the Bourbon troops still sat, impassively watching the carcasses turn on the spits over the crackling fires. They remained unconcerned even when the Garibaldini and Calabrians came down the hill, as at Villa San Giovanni, in a wide semi-circle, slowly and silently. They looked up at them sullenly. There was no resistance, nor was any expected. A few waved their hats and cheered listlessly. Without argument the infantry gave up their rifles, the artillery their cannon, the cavalry their horses; and then the men wandered away, troop after troop, battalion after battalion, disconsolately over the mountains.[13]

The pace of the drive to Naples could still not be slackened, though, for Garibaldi was determined to get there before Cavour contrived to put an end to his Dictatorship or otherwise prevent his invasion of the Papal States. So for hours on end he rode along without speaking in his bumpy *carrozzella*, his head nodding in the shade of his Calabrian hat, through Carpanzano and Rogliano, and through other towns where church bells rang in greeting, bands struck up in his honour, squibs exploded in the streets, and streamers and garlands, banners and flowers were waved and thrown at his feet. Then, at nightfall on 31 August, he came into the brilliantly illuminated streets of Cosenza.

Bertani joined him here with the news that he had brought 1,500 men in transports to Paola. These reinforcements Garibaldi placed under Türr's command and sent on by sea to Sapri Bay; and then, at three o'clock in the morning, after a few hours' rest in Cosenza, he jumped into his carriage and rattled off with Bertani and Cosenz on his way to meet them there. Through Tarsia he went and on to Spezzano Albanese, high above the Plain of Sybaris through which the tributaries of the Crati River wind their way down into the Gulf of Taranto; then up again to Castrovillari beneath the towering limestone heights of Monte Pollino; then through the wild mountain passes that lead out of Calabria to Basilicata; and on to the hill town of Rotonda and down at last, off the main road and on mule back, to the coast where he took a boat to Sapri and there found Türr's troops waiting for him the Bay.

Behind him the main body of his army, and those Calabrians who had been persuaded to stay with it, toiled on by forced marches in the suffocating heat of the day and the darkness of the night. Hungry, for there was still no organised commissariat, exposed, for there was so little shelter, sometimes sick and always tired, they hurried northwards over the rough and winding roads.

Discipline was sternly maintained and men found looting were shot out of hand. Once near Villa San Giovanni, Commander Forbes had found a man dying in the road.

> He had been shot for taking grapes [Forbes said]. On mounting the bank I saw sentries in all the vineyards. A corporal immediately ordered me down, unless I wanted to be killed. I told him of the man in the road. Oh, they are thieves. Warnings have been of no avail, so sentries are posted in the vineyards with orders to shoot all they find stealing. You know we can't disgrace ourselves by allowing the poor to be robbed; besides, it might ruin the cause.'
>
> When I remember the plundering propensities of my own countrymen, I shudder to think what may be the consequences should many of them join the army.*14

* In fact, nearly all the Englishmen who had joined and had fought at Milazzo had now been disbanded, being 'excessively insubordinate' and refusing to submit to the rigours of the campaign without either pay or the opportunity to plunder. 'This is not the place for Englishmen,' Forbes decided. 'One of the great features of this army is its sobriety. I have never seen or heard of a Garibaldian the worse for liquor, consequently discipline is easy. What our countrymen would be under the great temptations of a cheap wine country, is not quite so certain.' Forbes, *op. cit.*, 274.

Forbes's opinion was confirmed some weeks later when the British Legion – or the Garibaldian Excursionists, as they had called themselves in England – arrived in Naples. There were about 600 of them, and although some of them behaved well and fought bravely in the few minor engagements in which their late arrival permitted them to take part, there were too many hooligans amongst them for the Legion as a whole to be welcome. 'Last night,' the British Minister in Naples commented the day after their arrival, 'they immediately distinguished themselves in a truly national manner by getting drunk and disorderly, and in sleeping on and

Sometimes the Calabrian peasants would beckon the men of the rearguard into their cottages for a meal; and the offer was gratefully accepted. The hungry men would enter a little hovel where the smell of animals and stale wine was stronger than the smell of cooking, and they would watch the gnarled fingers of their hosts pick out lumps of greasy flesh from the pot on the scarred table. They were surprised to see so much meat in so impoverished a household; and then they remembered the corpses of the Bourbon soldiers being taken away in the peasants' carts – but not, apparently, for burial.[15]

★ ★ ★

On 4 September Garibaldi, now ten miles north of Sapri Bay on the road to Casalbuono, was overtaken, while having a meal in an inn, by a Piedmontese naval officer. This man carried a message for him from Agostino Depretis (La Farina's successor as Cavour's representative in Sicily) who had been appointed Garibaldi's pro-Dictator. Depretis urged Garibaldi to agree to the immediate annexation of Sicily to Victor Emmanuel's Kingdom. Both Türr and Cosenz felt convinced that the time for annexation had now come, and advised Garibaldi to give his consent on condition that Depretis remained in Sicily, and that the island continued to support the Garibaldian army. The General listened to their advice in sympathetic silence and then began to dictate a complaisant letter: 'Dear Depretis, let the annexation take place as soon as you like . . .'

under the tables in the principal cafés which have today been closed in consequence.' – Elliot, *op. cit.*, 99.

'With the exception of their gallant Colonel [John Peard] and Lord Seymour [son of the Duke of Somerset],' wrote Count Arrivabene, 'they were assuredly not very manageable fellows.' Arrivabene, *op. cit.*, ii, 72 – Their colonel himself agreed with him and in a letter to a friend asked to be defended from 'ever again commanding a brigade of English volunteers in a foreign country. As to the officers, many were most mutinous and some something worse.' – Thomas Adolphus Trollope, *What I Remember* (London, 1887), ii, 223.

Unlike the Irish volunteers who fought for the Pope, few of them were sincere enthusiasts for the cause in which they were being paid to fight. Most of them no doubt shared the feelings of the adventurer whom an English tourist met in a train that summer. He did not 'care a button for one side or the other'. He merely wanted 'at all costs to have a lark' – Francis Galton (Ed.) *Vacation Tourists and Notes of Travel in 1860* (London, 1861), 3.

At this point Bertani came into the room where the discussion had taken place, 'gave a start of amazement', and immediately began to do all he could to change Garibaldi's mind. 'General,' Bertani protested, 'you are abdicating. Yes, General, you are hampering the revolution, and relinquishing all possibility of carrying out your programme.' It would be better, he advised, to retain the Dictatorship of Sicily, and be sure of assistance from there and from the Neapolitan provinces for a drive into the Papal territories. Garibaldi listened quietly, as he had listened to Türr and Cosenz, with that 'penetrating, questioning glance of his', and he allowed himself to be persuaded again. He told his secretary to tear up the letter he had just begun and dictated another in its place, asking Depretis to delay annexation for a little longer.[16]

As soon as this letter was written, he set off again on the road to Casalbuono.

On the way he overtook a column of 3,000 Bourbon troops under General Caldarelli who offered no resistance; and then, passing through Casalbuono, he rattled on in his carriage towards Eboli and Salerno.

Ahead of him a small and incongruous scouting party was racing north at a speed even greater than his own, galloping through forests of oak and beech, past little towns and villages perched on the side of mountain ranges where at night, far away above them, the fire of charcoal-burners glowed in the darkness. In this party were Nicola Fabrizi, Antonio Gallenga,* who on Eber's joining Garibaldi's army had been appointed *The Times* correspondent, Commander Forbes and Colonel John Peard whose commanding figure and great beard led the people to mistake him for Garibaldi.†

---

* 'Antonio Gallenga was an Italian rolling stone, now aged nearly fifty, who had spent much of his life in exile, but had also been a deputy in the Sardinian Parliament and correspondent of the *Daily News*. After an abortive essay in regicide, he became a supporter of Cavour, and was hated by Mazzini, who suspected him of being a police agent' – *The History of The Times* (London, 1939), ii, 284.

† Colonel Peard, the famous 'Garibaldi's Englishman', had offered his services to the Piedmontese Army the year before. They had been declined and he had gone on to enlist as a volunteer in Garibaldi's *Cacciatori delle Alpi* where he fought throughout the campaign with a rifle he normally used for deer stalking. He was a first-class shot and was said to make notes of the numbers of Austrians he killed or

'It was thought that it would do good to yield to the delusion,' Peard wrote in his diary. But he had to admit that it became a fearful nuisance, 'for deputations arrived from all the neighbourhood to kiss my excellency's hands, and I had to hold regular levees'. At Postiglione, which he entered accompanied by hundreds of people from a neighbouring town, by National Guardsmen, boys waving flags, girls throwing streamers, and brass bands blowing their trumpets and crashing their cymbals above the cheers, everyone 'went mad with excitement', and one of the priests fell to his knees and welcomed the supposed Garibaldi, with the now almost customary welcome – 'the second Jesus Christ!'

At Eboli, the entire population, so it seemed, was in the streets to welcome him and within half an hour, Commander Forbes said, the whole town was brilliantly illuminated with 'brass bands banging away in every direction, and the crowd roaring themselves hoarse and calling on the General to appear'. Peard was not the General, Forbes insisted, but the people of Postiglione, where they arrived next day, knew better. 'Oh! you're right to try to keep your secret,' they told him, 'but you know it won't do. We know!'

Whatever scruples Forbes may have felt about encouraging the deception, Peard did not share them; but rather saw in the people's wounded in a little black notebook. 'I have a great respect for Italian independence,' he once said in reply to a question about his motives in fighting for it, 'but I am also very fond of shooting.'

He wore his well-cut civilian clothes in the field, until he was warned he ran the risk of being shot as a spy, and then he changed into the uniform of the Duke of Cornwall's Rangers.

On joining Garibaldi in Sicily he was given a company of riflemen equipped with the novel 'revolver rifle' supplied to The Thousand by an American supporter. But when he was not chosen to take part in the first expedition across to the mainland he threw up his command and joined this independent group of Garibaldi's followers. Later, as previously mentioned, he was given command of the British volunteers.

An extraordinarily powerful man, six feet tall and weighing fourteen stone, he could swallow the contents of a two-quart loving cup without a heel-tap. But he was as versatile as he was tough, a barrister, a talented artist and an expert linguist – See 'Garibaldi's Englishman: The Story of Colonel John Peard' by W. Baring Pemberton in *History Today* (December 1959); and G. M. Trevelyan, 'The War Journals of Garibaldi's Englishman', *Cornhill Magazine* (Jan., June 1908).

mistake an opportunity of securing a useful advantage. It was clear to him and to Fabrizi and Gallenga that if Naples were to be defended at all, the Neapolitan army could not fall much farther back. Either a battle would have to be fought on the plains of Eboli or a holding action on the mountains behind Salerno. Peard, Fabrizi and Gallenga decided to set about frightening the Neapolitans into the belief that the battle could not be won and the mountain range could not be defended against the vast strength of the Garibaldini and the revolutionaries they had aroused.

The official in charge of the Eboli telegraph was summoned and instructed to send a telegram to the Minister of War at Naples, informing him that Garibaldi had arrived at Eboli with 5,000 men and that a further 5,000 Calabrese were expected. 'Disembarkations are expected in the Bay of Naples and the Gulf of Salerno tonight,' Peard dictated. 'Strongly advise your withdrawing garrison from latter without delay before they are cut off.'

While the message was being written down, an incoming telegram arrived from Naples. 'Any news of the division Caldarelli?'

The nervous official, 'trembling like an aspen leaf', was told by Peard and Gallenga to reply that Caldarelli with his whole division had gone over to Garibaldi. An agitated telegram from General Scotti, commanding the troops at Salerno, received a similar reply.

Forbes said to Peard, 'What on earth is the good of all this? You can't imagine they will be fools enough to believe it?'

'You will see,' Peard said. 'It will frighten them to death, and tomorrow they will evacuate Salerno.'

He was quite right. Eight hours after the telegrams were despatched the General in command at Salerno was ordered to retreat to Nocera.

The next day Peard, still mistaken for Garibaldi, was welcomed into Salerno by wildly enthusiastic crowds; and on the day after that, the General himself arrived. While the people laughed and cheered around him, he deferentially took off his hat, bowed low to his impersonator and called out '*Viva! Viva Garibaldi!*'[17]

8

NAPLES

A fortnight before, Alexandre Dumas, who was acting as Garibaldi's ambassador in Naples and had anchored his yacht just opposite the Palace, had looked up to the window of the King's room and had seen the thin figure, standing in the shadow cast by the awning, scanning the horizon through a glass. 'He probably thinks,' Dumas commented derisively, 'that he can already see the avenger coming.'[1]

King Francis knew by now that his cause was lost. The army was still, for the most part, loyal to him; the Neapolitan nobility continued, waveringly, to support him; and in the country many peasants refused to be provoked into a break with the traditions of their past. But Francis had few other friends; and he had many enemies. He distrusted his Ministers – and, in particular, the most powerful of them all, the wily and designing Don Liborio Romano who controlled the *Camorra* as well as the police and the National Guard – and he suspected his own citizens of Naples as much as the agents that Cavour had sent from Piedmont in his efforts to rouse them to active revolution. As it happened, the King had little to fear from the citizens, however disillusioned with him they might have been; for few of them, as Türr was later to complain, had either the inclination or the energy to risk their skins while the Garibaldini were prepared to risk theirs for them.

In the plausible Don Liborio Romano, though, the King had a more justifiable object of mistrust, for this shrewd and calculating schemer had long since accepted his master's downfall as inevitable and he was working hard to ensure that it did not entail either his own ruin or that of the society in which he prospered.

As soon as the news of Garibaldi's landing at Reggio had been confirmed, Don Liborio handed the King a memorandum in which he suggested that His Majesty should withdraw from Neapolitan territory for the time being, and leave as regent a man capable of inspiring public confidence and of preventing the otherwise inevitable horrors of civil war. But this the King, backed by the more reactionary of his advisers, refused to do. Despite the frail insipidity of his appearance and his despondent, distrustful manner, he was not without courage. He had always been indecisive, certainly; and he found it difficult to make up his mind now whether to lead his army south and prevent the further advance of Garibaldi on Naples, or to withdraw from the capital and gather a faithful army round him north of the Volturno. But he was determined not to give way submissively, nor to abandon the fortunes of his dynasty.

On 4 September he made up his mind at last; he would withdraw north to Gaeta and make his stand there. None of his Ministers showed any desire to accompany him, but when he took leave of them and committed his capital to their care, he showed neither anger nor bitterness. He seemed, indeed, quite cheerful, as men do when they have reached a firm decision, however painful, after days of worry; and he left them in no doubt that it was his intention to return. 'Don Libò,' he warned, 'look out for your head.'[2]

He had already taken his last ride through the streets of Naples with his Queen; and the people, as they took their hats off to them, had noticed with surprise how calm and relaxed he looked. For a moment their carriage had been brought to a standstill by the busy traffic beside the shop of a chemist, whose business had been patronised by the Royal Family. They saw the Bourbon lilies, for years displayed so proudly over the front door, were being hurriedly removed by a workman. The King had pointed this out to his wife, made some remark in her ear, and they had both laughed.[3]

Now, as they moved out of the Palace – already deserted by the courtiers who had wandered so complacently through its glittering rooms in times that put no strain on loyalty – and as they walked arm-in-arm down towards the dock where the *Messaggero* lay waiting to take them to Gaeta, they maintained their cheerful composure.

'We shall be coming back,' the Queen had assured her maid who wondered why she was leaving most of her clothes behind. But as the *Messaggero* steamed out of Naples harbour, it did not seem to those who watched their sovereigns go that the Queen's hope could ever be fulfilled. The *Messaggero* signalled for the other ships in the port to follow her; but none moved from its anchorage and the *Messaggero*

Garibaldi in Naples 1860

Garibaldi on Caprera

steamed out into the bay alone. When she came into Gaeta harbour the following morning, she was still alone.[4]

★ ★ ★

A few hours after the King's departure Don Liborio signalled to 'the invincible General Garibaldi, Dictator of the Two Sicilies', assuring him with unlimited respect that Naples awaited 'his arrival with the keenest impatience' in order to salute him 'as the redeemer of Italy', and to place in his hands 'the power of the State and her destinies'.[5]

After receiving this effusive telegram Garibaldi was surprised to be told by the Mayor of Naples, and the commanding officer of the National Guard who had gone out to Salerno to meet him, that he could not enter the capital just yet. There were still strong garrisons in the city's four castles, he was warned, as well as several contingents of Bavarian mercenaries still retreating slowly north to Capua along the Vietri–Naples railway line. Besides, adequate preparations had not yet been made for his welcome; it would take at least a day, for instance, to erect triumphal arches.

Garibaldi refused to be deterred. He said he would enter the capital at once. And nothing either his staff or the emissaries from Naples could say had any effect on his determination to do so. Neither the cannon of the Bourbon garrisons, nor the rifles of the Bavarian mercenaries, neither the lack of triumphal arches, nor even the continued absence of Türr's 1,500 men, his nearest troops, still forty-eight hours' march away, could induce him to change his mind.

'Naples,' he said, dismissing the protestations of his more cautious advisers in one of those flamboyantly purposeful declarations with which he silenced argument, 'Naples is in danger. We must go there today, at once, this minute.'[6]

And he did. Having sent a telegram ahead of him announcing his arrival for noon, he left immediately for the terminus at Vietri where he boarded a special train which was to take him to the capital. His staff were with him, several of the National Guard of Salerno, and hundreds of others with real or assumed rights to share his triumph. They crowded the compartments and the corridors, they clung to the sides of the carriages and the roofs, and they all seemed as boisterously excited as those who had cheered his departure for

Salerno where an English tourist, W. G. Clark, the Public Orator of Cambridge University, drawn to the window of his room by the roar of *vivas* in the street, had seen one of the crowd 'while cheering in the most frantic manner, suddenly fall to the ground in a kind of convulsive fit'. Clark had asked his landlady if the man was drunk. 'No,' she had said, 'it is joy. Ah,' in a tone of reproach, 'you English, who have always been free, cannot imagine the delight of deliverance.' And she made 'a gesture as if she were about to fly'.

Clark had immediately driven to Vietri station to join the people in the crowded train. He forced his way into a third-class carriage, already containing about thirty or forty people who, during the whole of the journey, 'did not cease shouting and singing'.

> Some were in uniform of the National Guard, and almost all were armed in one way or other. The most conspicuous figure was a priest on the podgy side of forty, in the usual long black gown and broad-brimmed hat, with a musket and wide tricolour scarf. His bass voice was loudest of all in the choruses, and in the cheers as we passed each successive station. In the intervals he was smoking regalias, which he brandished with the left hand, as he brandished the musket with the right. The songs were interminable. . . .
>
> At every station a mob of curious people were gathered who exchanged cheers with the occupants of the train, but it was evident that they scarcely believed Garibaldi himself to be present. . . . The demonstrations of welcome came from all classes; from the fishermen who left their boats on the beach, from the swarthy fellows, naked to the waist, who were winnowing corn on the flat house roofs as well as from the National Guards.[7]

Outside Portici the train was stopped by a naval officer who frantically pushed his way into Garibaldi's compartment and shouted to him above the deafening noise made by his fellow-travellers, 'Where are you going to? The Bourbon troops have trained their cannon on Naples station.'

'*Ma che cannoni?*' the General replied calmly from his seat by the window. 'When the people receive us like this there are no cannon.'

The train moved slowly on again, and Garibaldi turned once more to gaze contemplatively out of the window.

At half-past one, an hour and a half late, the train puffed

laboriously into Naples station; and within minutes its passengers
were surrounded by a surging crowd that swept across the platform,
knocking down the barriers, pushing past the guard of honour,
drowning with their shouts and cheers Don Liborio's grandiose
speech of welcome.

Garibaldi and some of his staff managed to force their way
through to an open carriage, which was borne along by the crowd –
not, however, towards the centre of the city as had been planned, but
down towards the Castle of the Carmine where the Bourbon troops
looked out at the street along the barrels of their loaded cannon.

'*Ma che cannoni?*' Garibaldi stood up in the carriage, folded his
arms on his chest and looked steadfastly at the fort in the scorching
sunlight. He was wearing a black wide-awake hat, a black neckcloth
and the coloured silk handkerchief which, knotted round the neck,
fell loosely down the back of his red, purple-stained shirt. The
troops, who had been ordered by the King not to open fire, obeyed
their instructions and remained inactive.

The Dictator sat down again and the carriage moved on towards
the quayside. He was as calm as he had been in the train – placidly
unconscious, it seemed, of the riotous welcome the Neapolitans
were giving him. Occasionally he took off his hat and inclined his
head slightly, benignly, almost condescendingly, but he did not wave
and he did not smile. When his carriage reached the quayside, however, where the countless thousands of people lining the walls, and
peering out of the windows above them, and where the sailors,
clinging like monkeys to the masts and rigging of the ships in the
port, all broke out into an ecstatic cheer at the sight of him, Garibaldi stood up, took off his hat, and acknowledged the cheers at last,
lifting up his arms as if in benediction. In the great square, known
today as the Piazza del Plebiscito, the slow progress of the carriage
was halted and the Dictator climbed out and entered the Foresteria,
an annexe of the Palace, and from one of its iron balconies, he held
up his hands for a moment's silence. Gradually the shouts and cries,
'not like the rolling cheers of an English crowd,' Clark thought, 'but
confused and inarticulate', died away at last and Garibaldi spoke.

'You have a right to exult in this day,' he said in his clear voice, the
most beautiful voice that Maxime Du Camp had ever heard.[8] 'It is
the beginning of a new epoch not only for you but for the whole of

Italy, of which Naples forms the fairest part. It is, indeed, a day of glory and a holy day – a day on which a people passes from the yoke of servitude to the rank of a free nation. I thank you for this welcome, not only for myself, but in the name of all Italy which will be made free and united with your help.'⁹

His voice fell into silence and then once more the people began to shout and cheer and sing. They followed him to the Cathedral where he had decided to attend a Mass to demonstrate to the Neapolitans, as he had demonstrated to the Sicilians, that although he fought against the Pope he did not fight against God. And after he had been shown the dried blood of St. Januarius, due in a fortnight's time gratifyingly to repeat the miracle of its liquefaction, Fra Pantaleo, 'a Sicilian version of Friar Tuck, leapt into a pulpit in vestments bristling with weapons and delivered an impromptu sermon, the gist of which was that God first delivered the law to Moses, then sent an improved version of it by his Son Christ the Redeemer and now fulfilled it in its final perfection by means of the new Redeemer, Garibaldi.'¹⁰

When Mass was over, the crowds followed him to the Palazzo d'Angri where his headquarters were to be; and for three days and for most of three nights they filled the streets with the din of their impromptu *festa*.

'Night and day,' Commander Forbes wrote home on 11 September, 'the entire population were in the streets. Not only was all business suspended, but the people roused themselves into a state of frenzy bordering on madness.'¹¹

The noise was indescribable [Clark reported]. The hero's name was repeated in all manner of forms, as if it were a declinable noun – Garibaldi, Garibaldo, Garibalda – nay, it was metamorphosed into Garribar and Gallipot and Galliboard; at last the two first syllables were suppressed, and 'Viva *Board*' was the favourite cry, the sound of the last syllable being prolonged to the utmost. You heard too, 'Viva Vittorio Emmanuele,' and still more frequently, 'Viva l'Italia unita' which at length was shortened into *una*, and when people got so hoarse that they could not articulate any longer, they held out the forefinger and shook it as they passed, indicative of their desire for unity. Men, women and boys crowded the carriages and clung to them like swarming bees – I counted thirteen persons in a small vehicle drawn by one horse. Some waved flags, some brandished daggers, holding them occasionally in an unpleasant proximity to one's throat, and shrieking with menacing scowls, 'Viva Garibaldi!' Others danced frantically along waving torches over their heads. I have never seen such a sight as the Strada di Toledo presented as you looked up it, the long lines of stationary lights converging in the distance, and the flags drooping from the windows, and down below the red movement of the torches, and the waved banners and gleaming arms. Here and there an excited orator addressed the crowd about him in wild declamation; little bands of enthusiasts, headed sometimes by a priest and sometimes by a woman, went dancing through the streets and burst into the *cafés*, compelling all present to join in the popular cry. . . . When I was in the Café d'Europe a priest rushed in with frantic gestures, with eyes starting from his head, with a banner in one hand and a knife in the other, uttering horrible and inarticulate howlings. . . . An unfortunate man who did not cry 'Viva Garibaldi!' when he was bidden was ripped open by another enthusiast and died on the spot.[12]

There were flags everywhere, but there seemed as much doubt as to what the Italian tricolour actually was as to the name of the man who had inspired this sudden enthusiasm for it. Everyone knew that its colours were red, white and green, but whether they should be placed, like the French, parallel to the staff, or like the Dutch at right angles to it, no one seemed certain. Nor was there any consistency in the arrangement of the colours, though the white was usually put in the middle and often adorned with a portrait of the hero.

On the second night there was a performance of the ballet at the San Carlo – 'an excruciating performance,' Commander Forbes thought it, 'executed by a very wooden-legged corps' – and the audience seemed to take more pleasure in shouting *'Viva!'* in reply to Garibaldi's *'Viva Vittorio Emmanuele!'* than in listening to the music.

'Viva Venezia!' was also by now a popular cry, and when he first heard it Garibaldi was seen to 'smile grimly'. Towards the end of the ballet, a man in a shooting-coat jumped on to the stage shouting *'Viva!'* and the dancers gave up the performance, joined in his cheers and lifted their arms towards the General's box. Garibaldi had to be escorted to his carriage by a body of National Guardsmen with drawn swords.[13]

For most of them, no doubt, it was the mood of the *festa* that excited their capriciously responsive natures, rather than the joy of liberation or the promise of unity.

Naturally, Garibaldi's reception was enthusiastic [the English Minister in Naples commented with some disdain], and the Neapolitans had an opportunity of showing what a base calumny it had been to accuse them of want of courage; for as soon as it was quite certain that the soldiers were irrevocably gone, and that there was not a chance of their having an enemy in their neighbourhood, arms were dragged out from every hole and corner and paraded and brandished in the most heroic manner; red shirts were mounted, as spotless and bright as the first day of a hunting coat, their owners proudly feeling that their possession entitled them to all the glories of Sicily and Calabria.

However, while the town was running mad with flags, daggers and red shirts, the thinking portion of the public was in the most gloomy and despairing humour, for it was understood that Garibaldi had thrown himself entirely into the hands of the extreme party, and that he would not hear of annexation until 'both the Roman States and Venetia had been conquered'.[14]

Indeed, even those who saw in the departure of the Bourbons the dawn of an era of freedom and self-fulfilment were soon disillusioned by the mistakes and miscalculations of the new provisional Government.

Garibaldi's difficulties were immediately apparent. He had expected – as the Government in Turin had also expected – that once the Bourbon King and his supporters had been overthrown the army would come over to the side of those who were fighting for unity. But although a few Bourbon officers showed signs of being willing to do so, scarcely any of their men seemed prepared to abandon the cause for which they had been trained to fight. Unity meant little to them, the white flag and the white uniform of the royal Neapolitan army meant much. Since they had been taught to feel separate and aloof from civilians, even in Neapolitan territories, they could scarcely be expected to feel any closer to these strangers from the North. So when the four castles, which they had been left behind to garrison, were handed over to the new Government, the invitations to desert which were so urgently pressed upon them were coldly ignored or angrily rejected. Half of them went home or formed gangs of bandits in the hills, while the other half – about 40,000 men – marched north to join the reinvigorated army of King Francis which was growing fast behind the Volturno.

It was moving to see how these soldiers, barefoot and in rags, worn out by their long journey to avoid the places occupied by Garibaldini, were heartened as soon as they had joined their comrades [one of their officers wrote]. Shouting *'Viva il Re!'* they asked for rifles even before asking for bread, of which they had greater need. 'But why did you come here instead of going to your home?' they were asked. 'Because it is our duty,' they replied.[15]

The threat from this royal army in the north, encouraged by frequent visits from the King, was complicated by a royalist uprising in the east, where the peasants, encouraged by Bourbon troops, had attacked the houses of liberals who were prematurely celebrating the downfall of the old régime. And when Türr's 1,500 men arrived at last in Naples on 9 September, Garibaldi felt obliged to send them immediately to the Ariano district, where the worst disturbances had occurred. He was once more left in Naples without an army to support him.

At first such support seemed unnecessary. He persuaded a battery of Piedmontese artillery and a battalion of *bersaglieri* to come ashore from their transports in the harbour and garrison the town; and he had no difficulty in getting several of the King's former ministers, including, of course, Don Liborio, to remain in office. But a fortnight later the entire Ministry resigned in protest against the highhanded manner with which Garibaldi's Secretariat treated them; and by the end of the month both the military garrison and the ordinary police had shown themselves incapable of protecting the population from the depredations of professional criminals who had been released from prison together with the political prisoners.

Garibaldi's Secretariat, dominated by Bertani and Crispi, gave further offence by ignoring the susceptibilities of the Neapolitan people who watched with concern these outsiders issuing decrees which went far beyond the scope of a temporary government, advancing to places of trust those 'who can boast of having acted with the most notorious treachery and bad faith',[16] giving a pension to the mother of a man who had attempted to assassinate King Francis's father, and appointing an unqualified Frenchman, Alexandre Dumas, to the honorary Directorate of the National Museum.

No small disgust has been created by the nomination of Alexandre Dumas as the Director of the Museum and of Pompei, etc. [Henry Elliot told his brother], and people fully expect that, with such a black-guard there, some of the greatest treasures will soon be missing. The said Alexandre Dumas is lodged at one of the Royal Palaces, drinking the King's wines and feasting at the public expense with the choice company that he is in the habit of keeping about him, among which there is a very charming midshipwoman, who does duty in a yacht in a dapper jacket and trousers.

Some days later Elliot decided that Francis II's former subjects were 'fast getting as anxious to be out of Garibaldi's hands as they had been a few weeks before to get into them'.

To the despair of his real admirers, he unfortunately considers himself a great administrator [Elliot went on], and issues decrees, of which some are good, but others as monstrous as anything that was issued by the Kings, his predecessors. He loves to come down upon the priests, and, though I have little enough sympathy for all that fry, I must confess that they have good right to grumble a bit. He began by confiscating the property of the Jesuits, then he laid hands on that of the Bishops, who are to have an allowance of not more than 2,000 ducats, or £330 a year; and now there is a thundering decree by which priests who preach 'censure upon the institutions or laws' are to be fined and imprisoned and, though the minimum of these fines and imprisonments are prescribed, the maximum are not, so that the culprits are liable to anything short of death, and the reverend padres had therefore better mind their Ps and Qs. . . .

The poor people complain that there is no work, that food is much dearer, that plundering is going on in every department, and nothing but confusion everywhere – all of which is perfectly true, and will go on increasing till the direction of matters is got out of the hands of the people who now conduct them. . . . In truth the state of the country is as bad as possible and all the old abuses are continued and sometimes exaggerated by the new officials, who imprison and flog on suspicion or on slight proof of political misdemeanours, while crime is left totally unpunished. . . . Within the last six weeks there have been three or four murders within earshot of our door and there is not a talk of anyone being taken up or tried; and the same thing is going on all over the country, so that it is high time that some sort of government were established. Of course, I do not include among the murders the killing of the old policemen and spies, which took place some time ago and was looked upon as a matter of course.[17]

The growing feeling against the new Government was as strong in the outlying provinces as it was in Naples itself. Some of the governors of these provinces, so Aymé d'Aquin, the French minister, reported to Paris, behaved 'not as agents of a free government but as veritable tyrants. For instance the Governor of Chieti in the Abruzzi inflicts the penalty of flogging as in the worst days of absolutism.'[18]

These harsh opinions of Garibaldi's Government were ones which nearly all outside observers shared. They could not but agree that the Dictator's heart was in the right place; his plans for social reform, for free education, for the extension of railways, were praiseworthy enough. But his attempt to abolish gambling, his sending the Archbishop into exile for refusing to sing a Te Deum, his evident determination to push on with his revolution, seemed quite unnecessarily provocative.

In three weeks [W. K. Clark wrote in his diary], I have seen the extinction of a popularity that seemed boundless. The people who were wild with delight at the arrival of Garibaldi would now be equally delighted to get rid of him. The reasons for this change are obvious. His refusal to declare at once the annexation of Southern Italy to Northern has alienated the moderate party and generated suspicions of his intentions which his violent language on several occasions has tended to confirm. . . . A feeling has been created that he is dragging Naples on, not towards a peaceful union with the rest of Italy, but towards an abyss of anarchy and war. Again many of the decrees issued by him far outstep the limits of a confessedly temporary and transitional power. . . . Add to these causes of complaint the bullying and insolent demeanour of many of Garibaldi's officers, and the natural reaction and discouragement which could not but follow such a fever of excitement, and we shall see enough to account for the decline of his popularity.[19]

Most Neapolitans were principally concerned by the continued reluctance of the Secretariat to take any steps towards the announcement of annexation, and they complained that the direction of affairs was falling into the hands of the most extreme republicans. It was true, they admitted, that Garibaldi had immediately after entering Naples issued a decree handing over to King Victor Emmanuel the whole of the Bourbon fleet (most of whose officers had, in fact, already been won over by Persano), and that he subsequently sent a steamer to Genoa with the offer of the pro-Dictatorship to the Marquis Pallavicino, a good servant of Victor Emmanuel; but he had made it clear that he would not hand over the country until he had crossed the Volturno and taken Rome. It was true, too, that Garibaldi's feeling for Rome was a romantic one; that once there, once he had marched up to the Capitol in triumph and avenged the defeat of 1849, he would then surrender his powers to Victor Emmanuel. But he was surrounded by men whose ambitions were quite different from his. Cosenz, Sirtori, Türr, Medici and Bixio, his companions-in-arms, were not regarded as politically dangerous, but these men seemed to have less influence with him the more he saw of Bertani and those other radicals in a cabinet which (though it admittedly had contained a fair proportion of conservatives) now seemed to be dominated by the men of the Left.

Bertani, in particular, rarely let Garibaldi out of his sight. Constantly urging him on to Rome, refusing to allow him to doubt that, having got so far he could fail to succeed in his final endeavour, Bertani, usually so calm and self-possessed, but now with his dark eyes flashing, played on the General's weaknesses and vanities, his obsessive dreams. Bertani wanted nothing for himself. He was not interested in bringing down Cavour to profit personally by his fall, like so many others in the North; but he did want, it seems, to discredit the King, to delay annexation until the House of Savoy was manœuvred into a position in which the only way to obtain the crown of Italy would be by bending down to pick it up from the feet of the revolutionaries. And so Cavour, too, must be discredited, blackened in the eyes of Garibaldi, repeatedly denigrated as 'the man who had sold Nice'.

Garibaldi rose to Bertani's tauntings of the complacent aristocrat who had waited behind a screen of evasions to profit by the blood of The Thousand; and less shrewd than his mentor, he went so far as to write to Victor Emmanuel demanding the instant dismissal of the Prime Minister, and of the man who supported him in his 'infamous conduct', Luigi Carlo Farini.[20] Garibaldi was not encouraged to do this by Bertani, who feared that the unequivocal request could only strengthen Cavour's hand, but by what he took to be the wishes of the King himself.[21] For Victor Emmanuel, who had privately admitted that he would prefer Garibaldi to Cavour as his Prime Minister, was still secretly encouraging the General to defy the Government in Turin, to press on farther north so that, provided failure did not make it necessary for him to deny responsibility, he could profit by success.

Nor was it only the King's supposed wish which induced Garibaldi to demand the dismissal of Cavour, for he was also prompted to do so by the more direct urgings of Mazzini.

* * *

The news of Mazzini's arrival in Naples, and that of the Milanese federalist Carlo Cattaneo, had been passed on to Turin by the Cavourians in tones of the greatest alarm, and had been received in Turin with foreboding. Cavour confessed himself deeply disturbed and he renewed his efforts to find men capable of counteracting the influence that Mazzini and Cattaneo might have – and Bertani and Crispi did have – over the Dictator's impressionable mind.*

Conscious now that any personal intervention was impossible and any warning a provocation, Cavour turned in desperation to anyone who could still exercise influence over Garibaldi and dissuade him from a course of action that would inevitably result either in civil war or in war with France. Men as disparate as Kossuth and

---

* Cavour also apparently took steps to have Mazzini removed from Naples by force. According to Augusto Vecchi's son, who was told the story by one of Cavour's secretaries, a plan was made to have Mazzini seized and chloroformed by two police agents as he walked home one night to his room. While unconscious, Mazzini was to be carried aboard a Piedmontese warship and held a prisoner there, while the ship sailed between Sardinia and Sicily, until the crisis in Naples was past. Mazzini left Naples, however, before the police agents received their final instructions from Turin – Jack La Bolina (A. V. Vecchi) *Cronachette del Risorgimento italiano* (1920), 67-68.

Lord Shaftesbury were induced to write to the General and to beg him not to jeopardise his hard-won gains by attacking the Pope and dragging France into a quarrel from which she would otherwise hold aloof.

But it was no good. Garibaldi was determined to march on Rome. At a meeting which Admiral Mundy (at the request of Admiral Persano) and Henry Elliot (on instructions from Lord John Russell) attended on Board H.M.S. *Hannibal*, he listened with quiet patience to the Englishmen's arguments and then reiterated his unalterable plans – a march on Rome, the coronation there of Victor Emmanuel, to be followed by an Italian attack on the Austrians in Venezia. He insisted that, in advising him against an attack on Venice, Lord John Russell was 'not acting in accordance with the wishes of the English people'.

'I was quite ready to admit that the whole of England was with him at heart,' Elliot noted in his journal, 'but that nevertheless we were a practical nation, and if he was believed to be pushing things to such an extremity that would lead to a European war, he might be sure that he would very soon forfeit the sympathies and good wishes of the English.'

But Garibaldi would not admit that either an attack on Rome or on Venice was 'in the least likely' to provoke a European war.*

* Denis Mack Smith's assertion that a march on Rome was militarily a legitimate speculation and politically less dangerous than is usually believed, contradicts the whole tradition of Anglo-Saxon historians of the Risorgimento. But although it is true, Italian historians have argued, that there was a widespread expectation that the Pope was about to leave the Vatican and that the hour for ending his temporal power had come, the Bourbon army of Naples was one thing, French troops were another. Garibaldi's heroic defence of Rome in 1849 had demonstrated that he was capable of acting bravely against the French, too. 'But it also demonstrated that he could not have continued the unequal struggle for long' – Walter Maturi, *Interpretazioni del Risorgimento* (Einaudi, Turin, 1962), 678. 'The duel between Cavour and Garibaldi was not only the duel between conservative Italy and radical Italy, between monarchy and revolution,' as another Italian historian has put it. 'It was also a duel between reality and dreams, between the real Italy and idealist Italy. . . . In Sicily Garibaldi had knocked against the fragile, crumbling edifice of the Bourbon kingdom; whereas in Rome and in Venice, there was the Pope, there was Austria, there was Europe' – Franco Valsecchi, 'Garibaldi e Cavour', in *Nuovo Antologia di Lettere, Arti e Scienze* (1960), 300–1.

'I'm not afraid, I assure you, of this M. Napoleon,' Garibaldi insisted. 'It is because Cavour was afraid of him that he allowed Piedmont to be dragged through the mud, and consented to the cession of Savoy and Nice which I never should have allowed, for I should have made Napoleon afraid of me.'

'From anyone else this would have been rodomontade,' Elliot decided, 'but one has certainly no right to apply such a word to Garibaldi. The real truth is that he is an enthusiast, pursuing his Italian unity to its utmost extent, and determined to risk all that has been won rather than stop one step short of the accomplishment of the whole.'[22]

There was, however, still hope for Cavour that what he feared would be the cataclysmic effects of the spread of Garibaldi's revolution might be prevented by means other than his own so far unrewarding diplomacy – for satisfying reports were now coming in of the growing strength and encouraging morale of the Neapolitan troops which had concentrated north of Naples between Gaeta and Capua.

* * *

These loyal Bourbon troops, well over 40,000 in number, were occupying a position of great natural strength in a highly reactionary district. On their left was Capua whose defences designed by Vauban had been modernised only five years before, and on their right was Gaeta, a secure base many miles behind the Volturno. The river itself, deep and muddy, afforded few crossing places; while the open land to the south of it, well suited to cavalry and field artillery, provided an ideal battlefield for disciplined troops to out-manœuvre the sort of army that their enemies would be likely to bring against them.

The revolutionary army had an official strength as great as that of King Francis. But Garibaldi himself was obliged to admit that less than 20,000 of them would ever come anywhere near the firing; for, apart from the thousands of men on garrison duty in Sicily, Naples and the provinces between, there were almost as many who would perform no service at all, preferring to lounge in the streets and cafés in a variety of exotic uniforms, feeding each other ice-cream on the tips of their swords.

Of the 15,000–20,000 who did come into the firing line – mostly Northern volunteers, with 3,000 men from Calabria and Basilicata,

3,000 from Sicily, and, according to Türr, exactly 80 from Naples –
there were very many whom the Bourbons were quite right to
describe as the dregs of Italy. 'Never, surely, was there such a motley
army as this,' W. G. Clark commented. He had seen Türr's troops
arrive in Naples on 9 September and had been amazed at the contrast
between

> these filibusters and the well-fed, well-armed and well-clothed royal
> troops. Of the Garibaldians, no two men were armed or clothed alike:
> some had only one shoe, some no shoes at all; there were boys of twelve
> and thirteen years old in the ranks, side by side with grey-bearded
> veterans; there were the most bizarre contrasts as to personal stature,
> and they made no pretence of keeping line or keeping step. Many of
> them carried loaves stuck on the end of their muskets or bayonets. ·

Later he saw them in their outposts facing Capua

> all apparently in high spirits and good health, more like jolly beggars
> than a regular army. . . . They take their work easily, leaning against a
> vine-clad poplar in any attitude they may fancy. Provided they do their
> work, Garibaldi and his officers do not seem to care how they do it. A
> martinet would be sorely out of place here. . . .
> [The army contains] men of all ranks and of all characters. There are
> men of high birth and gentle breeding, there are also outcasts and vaga-
> bonds; there are generous and chivalrous enthusiasts, there are also
> charlatans and impostors, and unhappily it is not always the former who
> fill the highest places.[23]

A few of those who had sailed with the original Thousand had
been vicious enough, but the proportion was far greater now, since
the reinforcements who had filled the gaps in Garibaldi's ranks had
almost invariably been of worse quality than those whom they
replaced. And this process of adulteration had been accentuated by
Cavour who, anxious to make it impossible for Garibaldi to attack
Rome, had put an effective stop to the supply of volunteers from the
North.

★   ★   ★

Garibaldi established his headquarters in the vast palace at Caserta
which had been built by Vanvitelli in the style of Versailles for King

Francis's great-great-grandfather before the French Revolution. Here Garibaldi lived the simple, regular life that had become traditionally associated with him, going to his room at dusk and getting up so early that he sometimes discovered his staff had not yet gone to bed. Much of the day was spent visiting the outposts in Santa Maria and in Sant' Angelo, a village at the foot of Monte Tifata built out of the ruins of Roman villas. And often he would climb to the summit of the mountain and watch through his telescope the movements of the Bourbon troops in the valley below.

Sometimes in the early evening he would stroll in the long gardens behind the Palace, between the pools of water and the broken statues, the grottoes and the avenues of ilex, and up to the great cataract where the water, carried across the valley by Vanvitelli's aqueduct, plunges down from the rocks; or he would walk in the courtyards of the Palace surrounded by a bodyguard of redshirts armed with immense halberds that they had removed from the walls of one of the state apartments. And whenever he approached one of the brass bands, with which his force was now liberally supplied, the trains of 'Garibaldi's Hymn' would fill the air and loud voices would sing the so familiar words.

'Foreign tourists were constantly visiting Garibaldi at that time,' wrote Count Arrivabene, who, as the *Daily News* correspondent, had been given quarters with the General's staff. 'They had no difficulty in getting at him, for almost everybody was at liberty to join the staff of the General, and survey the line. There were, of course, a good many English and these were perhaps the most welcome guests. . . . Even English ladies visited us every now and then. All these tourists met with the most cordial reception at our headquarters, where they stopped even for some days, and became guests of the General's table.'[24]

One of these English ladies was enchanted by Garibaldi's charm and easy manner. She had seen him some days before in Naples and had written home to her father to say: 'I have today seen the face of Garibaldi; and now all the devotion of his friends is made clear as day to me. You have only to look into his face, and you feel that here is, perhaps, the one man in the world in whose service you would follow blindfold to death. . . . One could love the cause without seeing him, but in seeing him you seem to be suddenly gifted with the power of seeing it as he sees it, and you love it better for his sake.'

Now when she met him face to face in his little room in the Palace, 'reached by a poky side stair', she was not disappointed. 'He was sitting behind a plain, green-baize table but left his writing and came forward and shook hands heartily with us all. He has a cheerful, simple way of saluting everyone – not that high society knack of appearing to be intensely listening and anxious for your answers, when you know you will fade utterly out of that person's mind in five minutes. There is no affectation or overdoing.' While he was complaisantly signing autograph books and writing messages with as much concentration 'as he would have given to a plan of attack', his admirer walked up close to him to look down at his hair. Several of her friends had got what they swore were genuine locks of it, but of different colours; and this was 'well-nigh causing a civil war'. She noticed, though, that while the ends were tawny, there were, in fact, quite dark patches at the top of the head, and several white strands – 'so now we can all set our minds at rest'.[25]

*   *   *

Despite the impression of calm and confidence he gave to his visitors, however, Garibaldi understood well enough the dangerous position in which his out-numbered army was placed. General Ritucci, the Bourbon commander-in-chief at Capua, appeared to be content for the time being to remain on the line of the Volturno, knowing that a Garibaldian attack could be defeated, hoping there might soon be help from the Pope or the Austrians, and expecting that, in any event, merely to block Garibaldi's advance to the north would eventually be enough to wither the remaining power of his already uncertain political control over the Neapolitan territories to the south. But if Ritucci decided to attack in force, Garibaldi's slender forces might well be thrown back out of Caserta and their hold on Naples destroyed.

And then, there came startling news from the North that rendered the continuation of the stalemate impossible.

*   *   *

Cavour, who had successfully put a stop to Victor Emmanuel's underhand approaches to Garibaldi by threatening to resign and expose them, had by now seized the initiative, and finally accepted once and for all the idea of unity.[26]

Realising that it was no longer possible to 'rule the revolution at Naples', he had decided that the time had come to prevent its further advance by advancing himself to meet it, 'whatever the consequences'.[27] Informing Louis Napoleon that his only reason for doing so was to check Garibaldi, he gave orders for the invasion of the Papal provinces of Umbria, and the Marches. Napoleon had approved, saying only to the Italians, '*faites vite*'.[28]*

The Piedmontese army crossed the frontier on 11 September, under the Command of General Fanti, with Cialdini and Della Rocca as his two corps commanders. They were opposed by the French General Christophe de Lamoricière, commanding an international army of Papal crusaders – mostly Austrian, but including many Irishmen and several companies of Frenchmen and Belgians as well as Italians. These dedicated men fought bravely and often heroically, but at Perugia, at Spoleto and on 18 September at Castelfidardo they were defeated; and Lamoricière with the remnants of his force was driven back to Ancona.[29]

---

* In Rome, the French Ambassador, the Duc de Gramont, 'an amiable humbug', in Odo Russell's opinion, who 'like all French diplomatists in Italy, affects the greatest contempt for Italian aspirations', wishing to hang Cavour and shoot Garibaldi, suggested to the Pope that France would oppose 'any aggression on the Papal Territory, with force of arms'. When the Pope, alréady 'painfully surprised' that Austria had not come to his rescue, realised that the French were not going to live up to this promise, he condemned Louis Napoleon's policy so strongly in the presence of General de Goyon, commander of the French garrison in Rome, that Cardinal Antonelli felt obliged to apologise to the Duke de Gramont. Antonelli explained, so Gramont told Russell, that 'the Pope who had suffered formerly from epilepsy, when threatened with an attack of that disease could not be held responsible for all he said; that the approaching symptoms of the attack were visible in the eyes and hands, and that when he, Cardinal Antonelli, perceived them he avoided many subjects in conversation with His Holiness. He had been led to expect by Monsieur de Gramont that the Emperor Napoleon was going to war with the King of Sardinia for the purpose of driving the Piedmontese troops out of the Holy See and he was now beginning to fear for many reasons that the Emperor would not fulfil his promise'. Noel Blakiston (ed.), *The Roman Question: Extracts from the despatches of Odo Russell from Rome, 1858-1870* (Chapman and Hall, 1962), 129.

9

THE VOLTURNO

The day after Lamoricière retreated into Ancona, Garibaldi returned to Caserta from a visit he had felt compelled to make to Sicily in order to quieten demands for the immediate annexation of the island. On his return he discovered that in his absence Türr, who had been left in command, had committed an act of dangerous provocation.

Before leaving for Sicily, the General had sent a small force of a few hundred men across the Volturno to threaten the Bourbon communications behind Capua, and by so doing to discourage Ritucci from the full-scale attack which the volunteers might not be able to contain. Türr decided, however, to extend these operations behind the Volturno on a far more ambitious scale; and gave orders, in the General's absence, for the taking and holding of the hill town of Caiazzo and, at the same time, for a diversionary attack on Capua.

The attack on Capua, as ill advised as it was badly led, cost the Garibaldini 130 in killed and wounded, and its easy repulse gave the Bourbon headquarters at Gaeta confidence to order Ritucci 'to march forward, to find and destroy the enemy and to advance on the Capital'.[1] Before doing so Ritucci decided to retake Caiazzo, whose garrison of 300 Bolognese Garibaldi had unwisely reinforced with a further 100 men.

Ritucci moved to the attack on 21 September, sending 7,000 men against Garibaldi's 900, and after a short and bitter fight, throwing them back across the river with a loss of well over a quarter of their force.

If Ritucci had attacked Garibaldi's main position the next day, it is impossible to believe that he would not have broken through to Naples. Very little had been done to strengthen the position by earthworks. Apart from a single sandbag battery in front of Sant' Angelo, another at Santa Maria, a third on the railway line farther to the left, and a rather feeble breastwork connecting the Capua gate in Santa Maria with the amphitheatre, no artificial barrier had so far

been created. The War Minister in Gaeta and the King, both recognising that the fighting of the previous week had greatly improved
the confidence of their army, were anxious that Ritucci should, in
fact, attack. For after the Piedmontese victory at Castelfidardo it was
essential to get back to Naples before Victor Emmanuel reached it.
For a week, however, while the Bourbons elaborated plans of quite
unnecessary complexity, and while King Francis unsuccessfully tried
to replace Ritucci with a French general, no movement was made.
Garibaldi took advantage of the delay to strengthen his lines and to
make new batteries for several cannon which had recently arrived
from Naples. He was also given the opportunity to instil fresh confidence into his tired and hungry and increasingly dispirited men.
One of these men, a young Milanese noble, described a fortnight
later how he did so, giving a revealing account of the strangely
emotive power of Garibaldi's personality. What had induced him, the
young man was asked, to give up ease and luxury for the life of a dog
'in a camp without commissariat, pay or rations?'

'You may well ask,' he said. 'I tell you a fortnight ago I was in
despair myself, and thought of giving up the whole thing. I was
sitting on a hillock, as might be here. Garibaldi came by. He stopped
– I don't know why. I had never spoken to him. I am sure he did
not know me, but he stopped. Perhaps he saw I looked dejected, and
indeed I was. Well, he laid his hand on my shoulder and simply said,
with that low, strange, smothered voice that seemed like a spirit
speaking inside me, "Courage! Courage! We are going to fight for
our country." Do you think I could ever turn back after that?'[2]

It was well that there were men like this in Garibaldi's force, for
many others had, in fact, turned back, or were ready to do so when
the fighting began; and of those who remained, there were scarcely
any who felt that confidence in victory which had enlivened the
exhausted army on the hills above Palermo.

At least, though, the army was now well placed and well commanded, with Bixio on the right near Maddaloni; Medici and Count
Milbitz, an old Polish officer, on the left around Sant' Angelo and
Santa Maria; and Türr in reserve at Caserta, where the railway line
could be used to bring up reinforcements to either flank. Whereas
the Bourbons, when they did at last move into the attack, operated
on lines so extended that von Mechel on the left, approaching

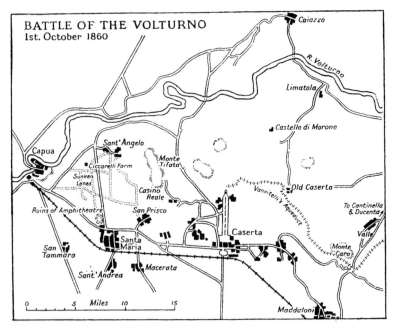

Maddaloni by way of Ducenta and Cantinella, was for a long time out of touch with Ritucci who was advancing on Sant' Angelo and Santa Maria from Capua. The delay caused by this breakdown in communications was, as Ritucci sullenly complained to von Mechel, 'likely to prove fatal' to the Bourbon cause.

'I free myself from all responsibility for the wisdom of the action,' he warned the Minister of War at Gaeta from whose office his ill-contrived orders had emanated; 'nor am I responsible for what disappointments may occur owing to von Mechel not acting in unison with me.' But though the operations were not being conducted at all as he would have wished, he was prepared to do his best, and he confirmed that the attack would take place 'the day after tomorrow – October 1st – at dawn'.[3]

All night long before that dawn his troops were moving into position, coming out, column after column, through Capua's southern gate in a dense fog, filing down the deeply sunken lanes between Sant' Angelo and Santa Maria towards the very heart of Garibaldi's position, the sound of their movements muffled by the heavy air.

But although they could not be seen or heard, Garibaldi knew that they were coming. Earlier on in the night he had been standing on the terrace of the church of Sant' Angelo, looking across the valley toward Capua and he had seen a rocket shoot up into the darkness and then a bright flare slowly descending. 'Gentlemen,' he had said, 'we must not sleep too heavily tonight.' And he had laughed as he jumped on his horse to gallop back to Caserta.[4]

By dawn he was back at the front again, talking to Milbitz at Santa Maria. The Bourbon troops had approached Santa Maria in strength during the night, and were now driving the frightened men in Milbitz's outposts out of San Tammaro and the cemetery to the north of it, and sending them running back to Naples where they spread news of a terrible disaster. Had Garibaldi not been there a disaster it might have become; but his invigorating presence, and the orders he sent back to Türr to send out some of his reserves by train from Caserta station, soon restored confidence and enabled him to leave the sector and drive north in his carriage to Sant' Angelo where he believed the main attack was being made.

As he approached Sant' Angelo the noise of battle grew louder. The carriage hurtled up the road, across two bridges that spanned the sunken lanes in which the Bourbon troops had crept the night before, and on towards another bridge that took the road across a lane near the Ciccarelli Farm. But before the carriage reached the bridge a platoon of Neapolitan infantry clambered up on to the road and opened fire on the General's staff.

The carriage rattled on; the driver was hit in the chest and an officer behind him was also mortally wounded; one of the horses stumbled and fell; and as the carriage skidded to a halt Garibaldi jumped out, sword in hand. Waiting only for a few of Medici's infantry from Sant' Angelo to join him, the General charged down the road at the astonished Neapolitans and sent them scampering back down into the lane.[5]

It was the first of numerous charges he led personally that day. During the whole of the morning, in fact, he was seen hurrying about the streets of Sant' Angelo and in the outskirts of the village along the lower slopes of Monte Tifata, forming and reforming groups of infantry, leading them at the enemy, repelling countercharges, giving orders, shouting encouragement, with an energy astonishing in an arthritic man of fifty-three. Heedless of danger and miraculously impervious to it, there was something unreal about him, something not quite human, an unearthly light in those flashing eyes which shone so brilliantly that one of his soldiers afterwards told the French traveller, Louise Colet, '*on voit le feu des yeux dans la nuit. Ses yeux dévorent l'ennemi, ils le consument, ils le terrassent. Garibaldi est foudroyant et beau dans la mêlée, comme l'archange Michel, de Raphael, piétant sur le démon.*'[6]

He was wonderfully encouraging to most. But to some of the older men, of course, those who had been hardened by war and suffering, those whose instinctive romanticism had been deadened by the sight of too much hysterical bravery, he appeared '*piuttosto bizzarro*' – rather quaint.

'Victory! Victory!' he kept shouting as he hurried about in his wide trousers, and great red flapping shirt. 'Victory! Victory! All along the line!' And these veterans muttered quizzically in response. 'Victory? *What* victory?'[7]

It was certainly difficult to see any signs of victory yet, here or on either flank. In Santa Maria the struggle still continued, without advantage to one side or the other, as the cannon roared at each other beside the ruins of the amphitheatre, and the infantry charged at each other, slashing and jabbing with their bayonets. On the right, where Bixio's force defended the approaches to Caserta from the south-east, several Garibaldian officers and their men fled at the sight of von Mechel's columns storming up the slopes of the valley. Bixio was saved, however, as Garibaldi himself was ultimately saved, by the mistakes of his opponent.

Von Mechel had chosen to divide his force, attacking Bixio's 5,600 men with rather less than 3,000 Austrian and Swiss mercenaries, and sending his subordinate, Ruiz, with 5,000 men but no clear instructions, round his right flank. He had hoped, so he suggested later, that Ruiz would sweep down from Monte Caro on Bixio's left to support the frontal attack, but the only orders he gave him were to occupy old Caserta and to keep up communications with the left and right flanks of the Bourbon army. Ruiz was not an imaginative soldier, likely to act on his own initiative, and von Mechel was, therefore, unable to follow up his initial success in dislodging Bixio's right. For without the help of Ruiz, who remained in the hills far away to the north, he had not the strength to throw the Garibaldians back. By noon von Mechel had recognised this and had decided to withdraw to Ducenta. He had lost 200 men, including ninety prisoners.

Bixio's losses, however, had been heavier, and even these were less than those suffered by the Garibaldini on the other flank where the most costly fighting had taken place. Here, and in particular in Santa Maria where the town band, playing with loud and remorseless determination in the main street, endeavoured to spur the Garibaldini on to further efforts and to restore their flagging spirits, the casualties had been horrifying. By three o'clock in the afternoon all the remaining reserves from Caserta had been brought up by Türr into the almost surrounded town where the bodies of six hundred men lay dead and dying in the narrow, smoke-filled streets beneath the shuttered houses.

Ruiz now had his chance to take his 5,000 uncommitted men down from the mountain into the deserted heart of Garibaldi's position in Caserta. But he did not take it. On his way to Old Caserta from Limatola he had turned aside to attack 300 men from Cosenz's brigade defending the mediaeval ruins of Castel Morrone; and after what he described himself as 'four hours of fierce fighting' with men who, when their ammunition was exhausted, stood their ground defiantly hurling rocks of limestone down the smooth open slopes of the mountainside, his troops captured the castle and bayoneted its gallant defender, Pilade Bronzetti, whom they found lying wounded inside its broken walls. But though the Garibaldian headquarters and rear now lay open to him, Ruiz stayed where he was in the mountains.

Now Garibaldi was given his opportunity and he took it. He gave orders for the last reserves which Türr had just brought up from Caserta to follow him in a bayonet charge out of Santa Maria towards Sant' Angelo, and so relieve the pressure on Caserta and clear the enemy off the road where his carriage had been ambushed that morning.

As he formed up his men, the faithful Jessie Mario came up to offer him a glass of water and some figs. She was followed by a group of English sailors from the *Hannibal* who were trying to persuade her to ask someone to supply them with muskets. 'What, Jessie,' Garibaldi said cheerfully, his mouth full of figs. 'Don't tell me you're helping these sailors desert their Queen.' 'No,' she replied. 'They have only come for fun.'[8]

A few moments later Garibaldi was dashing up the road towards Capua, while Colonel Eber, the former *Times* correspondent and now one of his best officers, was leading a simultaneous charge up to Sant' Angelo across the Ciccarelli bridge.

It was the turning point of the battle. These two determined charges (backed by 200 wild Hungarian cavalrymen mounted on horses captured from the Bourbons) were decisive against troops who were now exhausted and disheartened. By four o'clock the battery astride the road, which had been firing with devastating effect all day, was abandoned, and the Garibaldini from Santa Maria rushed out to the dismounted guns and, with the help of the English sailors from the *Hannibal*, remounted them and brought them back. Four hours later all the Bourbon troops south of the Volturno, except Ruiz's 5,000 at Old Caserta, had been withdrawn into Capua. The following day Ruiz, having discovered at last what had happened to his colleagues, gave the order to follow their example and retreat across the river; and although over 2,000 of them refused to obey him while Caserta lay so invitingly open to attack and plunder, all of these men were soon captured in the net which Garibaldi and Bixio were able to draw around them.

Excluding 2,253 prisoners of war, the Bourbons officially admitted losses of 991 killed and wounded. And although Ritucci dismissed it as 'a missed opportunity', he had suffered, in fact, a severe defeat, a defeat inflicted upon him by a man who had previously been considered incapable of conducting a pitched defensive battle.

The Garibaldian losses, however, totalling over 2,000 killed, wounded and missing, showed at what price this victory had been won.[9] And Garibaldi's army was hopelessly ill-equipped to deal with so large a number of wounded, let alone the hundreds of men who had fallen sick through exposure and hunger.

Many of these men were sent back to Naples where the conditions in the hospitals horrified an English resident who volunteered to nurse in one of them. 'It was a barrack turned into a hospital,' she wrote, 'and the horrid arrangements that satisfy the dirtiest of all animals, the Neapolitan soldier, were still existing. At this end of the ward you enter the second room from the large salon, and the room runs along to your left. But the first room of the row, which is on your right, is the public place for all the floor. Don't imagine, however, that it has any sanitary arrangement whatever; no pipes nor drains; simply the open floor of the room. It is what you could not imagine unless you saw it. . . . Accustomed as I am to come across the dirt and smell of the streets here, I never imagined the possibility of such an odour.'

She could not prevail upon the staff to do anything about it and went out herself to buy chloride of lime from the English pharmacy. She could not persuade the staff to do anything about the food either. It consisted mostly of soup that looked like washing-up water. 'The meat for the broth is passed through hot water which is given to the soldiers; the meat itself being taken home by the cooks to feed their families.' She and her sister-in-law protested to the Governor and demanded that he 'scold the cooks'. But he 'only shrugged his shoulders, spread his hands, made ill-used eyelids, and left *her* to scold the cooks'.

'Baskets full of provisions come in at one door and go out of the other and are re-sold,' she went on indignantly; 'and the money goes into the pockets of the hospital staff. The same with donations of linen.' Even the shirts of the wounded were stolen and the men left to lie on mattresses on the floor without sheets or pillows. Occasionally a visitor would pass through the wards, look at a badly wounded man, exclaim, 'Oh! How ill he looks!' and dump sugared almonds on to his bed without any enquiry as to whether or not he was capable of eating them.

The visits of Garibaldi were eagerly awaited. The men, when they knew that he was coming, sat up excitedly in bed, shouting '*Papa nostro!*' and sometimes they jumped out on to the floor, opening up their wounds. But when he had gone, the hospital returned to its squalor and its attendants to their thieving and indifference.[10]

Would you conceive it possible [Henry Elliot indignantly asked his brother], that the Neapolitans who pretend that a great national movement has been going on in their country, have not moved a hand for the reception of the sick and wounded from Capua, some of whom, amounting to many hundreds were left for twenty-four hours after being brought to Naples without persons being found even to give them a glass of water, and the authorities have now summoned to the work the French Sœurs de Charité from Castellamare. It is a literal truth that of all the Neapolitans I am acquainted with, most of whom profess the hottest patriotism, not one single one that I have heard of joined Garibaldi, or risked the tip of his nose, and now they do not even stir to save the sick and wounded.[11]

And even those who remained behind in the field hospitals at Caserta and Santa Maria, despite all that Garibaldi's few doctors and Jessie Mario could do for them, fared little better. 'The wards were tolerably clean and airy,' a visitor thought, 'and the wants of the poor sufferers seemed as well attended to as circumstances permitted, but it was a sad sight.'[12]

* * *

It seemed, indeed, to many of those who had fought with Garibaldi in the battle of the Volturno that their efforts and sacrifice had availed them nothing. The enemy had been forced to retreat into Capua, but that fortress and Gaeta still held out against them; and there was no longer any opportunity of marching on Rome with an army so exhausted and so badly mauled. Mazzini urged Garibaldi to do so, but the General knew that he could not. 'I have long been thinking of it,' he said to Alberto Mario with Mazzini's letter in his hand. 'But I cannot advance on Rome leaving behind 60,000 men entrenched in Capua and Gaeta, who can march into Naples the moment my back is turned.'[13]

Cavour, too, knew this. For weeks he had been afraid that there might be a clash between the royal troops and the Garibaldini, and he had felt compelled to give orders to the Piedmontese high command to launch a full-scale attack should this occur. There might be war, '*guerra tremenda*', but that, he said, 'must not worry us'.*[14]

---

* On 12 September Cavour had confessed to Nigra that he would not have stopped short of civil war if he had felt sure of having public opinion on his side: '*J'ai poussé l'audace jusqu'au point où elle pouvait aller sans courir le risque de voir éclater la guerre civile; et je n'aurais pas même reculé devant cette extrémité, si j'avais pu espérer d'avoir pour moi l'opinion publique*' – Carteggi di Camillo Cavour: Il Carteggio Cavour-Nigra (Zanichelli, Bologna, 1929), iv, 202.

Now, however, Garibaldi's army was no longer in a condition to fight, and in any case Garibaldi had averted the possibility of civil war by sending word to his commander on the Neapolitan frontier in the Abruzzi, 'If the Piedmontese enter our territory receive them like brothers.'[15]

But although Cavour no longer had cause to fear civil war, he was still concerned lest Garibaldi should 'obstinately retire to Caprera' before his soldiers had fulfilled his instructions to 'receive the Piedmontese like brothers', and before he had gone out personally to welcome King Victor Emmanuel and thus demonstrated to Europe that there was no fundamental conflict of interests between them.

As soon as news of the battle of the Volturno had been received in Turin, Cavour asked Garibaldi's old and trusted friend, Augusto Vecchi, to call on him, and he spoke to him for two hours. 'At the end of our interview,' Vecchi told Garibaldi, 'he told me to accompany you to meet the King. And he ended by saying that Venice would be ours six months sooner, if you did not separate yourself from Victor Emmanuel – or, to put it quite plainly, if you did not obstinately retire to Caprera. . . . Invite the King personally by telegram to come quickly to Naples. And go to meet him. I ask you this in the name of Italy, our mother, for whose greatness we both swore many years ago to make every kind of sacrifice.'[16]

Garibaldi had already decided that he would agree to meet the King. He felt that there was nothing more that he could do now. Once he had recognised that he could not go from Naples to Rome and Venice, he saw no point in any further delay in announcing the annexation. 'The political importance of the problem was for him obscured by the territorial.'[17] But there remained one question of great importance which was undecided: whether to obtain the agreement of the Neapolitan and Sicilian people to the annexation to Piedmont by a quick and simple referendum in which they would be asked to vote 'Sì' or 'No', or by the far slower method of electing representatives to an assembly which would discuss the conditions upon which annexation might be arranged. Ideally, of course, the election of an assembly was much to be preferred, for care could then be taken to ensure that the South was not precipitated into a hasty, and subsequently regrettable acceptance of the laws and customs and administrative systems of the North, so alien to its traditions and so incompatible with its temperament. But there was no time, the Government in Turin insisted, for an ideal solution. The idea of unity had too many enemies both within Italy and abroad; the existence of a united country must be presented to Europe as quickly as possible as a *fait accompli.*

Cavour's supporters, and in particular Pallavicino, the recently appointed pro-Dictator in Naples, did all they could to persuade Garibaldi to agree to an immediate referendum which would end this period of danger and uncertainty, while Cavour's opponents urged the impressionable General to demand an election. Some of these opponents, like Cattaneo, were anxious to ensure the development of a separate administrative system for the South; and others, like Crispi and Mazzini, to prolong the life of the Dictatorship for the sake of the revolution. But they all condemned with equal warmth the idea of the referendum.

The arguments and counter-arguments which poured into Garibaldi's ears during this angry duel between the rival parties confused and saddened him. Reminded that the inhabitants of Savoy and Nice had been invited to vote in a referendum by Napoleon III, he decided to support the election of an assembly. But when Pallavicino resigned and the people of Naples loudly protested their dissatisfaction with Garibaldi's decision, his mind began to waver. Türr took the opportunity to present him with petitions calling for a plebiscite signed by hundreds of officers of the National Guard and thousands of Neapolitans. Garibaldi, always susceptible to emotional appeals of this sort, was persuaded that he ought to change sides. And during a long meeting held in the Palazzo d'Angri at Naples, he looked up from these documents and his expression betrayed the relief he felt that the muddling discussions could now be ended. 'If this is the wish of the Neapolitan people,' he announced, 'it must be satisfied.' And turning to Pallavicino added, 'Dear Giorgio, we need you here still.'[18]

A few hours later Pallavicino took back his resignation and Crispi handed his in; and on 21 October the referendum was held.

The voting was not secret and Admiral Mundy recorded in his diary his opinion that the apparently decisive vote in favour of the proposition that 'the people wish for Italy one and indivisible with

Victor Emmanuel as constitutional King, and his legitimate descendants after him', could not, in fact, be considered a 'correct representation of the real feeling of the nation'.

Yesterday I visited a few of the polling places in the city whilst the election was going forward [Mundy wrote]. More than 100,000 people took advantage of the opportunity of recording their opinion, yet a stranger passing through the streets would have discovered no excitement, not even a crowd collected at any particular spot. Perfect order reigned everywhere; but I think, considering the general temper of the inhabitants, it would have required strong moral courage for anyone to publicly announce himself as an enemy to the sacred watchword of '*Italia Una*'.

Every man privileged to the franchise had first to produce his paper from the mayor, showing that he was entitled to vote; he was then admitted through a file of the National Militia up to a platform on which the urns were fixed. The urns to the right and left of the central vase, and several feet distant from it, had the words '*si*' and '*no*' painted on them respectively in large type. Up to one of these the man had to walk beneath the gaze of a dozen scrutators, and thrust in his arm and draw out a card. . . .

I only saw three individuals who, after a few moments of apparent reflection, advanced to the left and fished up a '*No*'. I must, however, observe, that no offensive remark was made either by the overseers or by the bystanders at this open manifestation of preference for the Bourbon dynasty; but as voters had to deliver up their papers for identification, their names and calling were, of course, known.[19]

There were far more abstentions than there were votes cast, and many of those who voted were not quite sure what they were voting for; while many others only did so, in the opinion of the British Minister, 'to escape from the present anarchy'.[20] But since of the one-and-three-quarters of a million cards counted in Sicily and on the mainland less than 11,000 were *No's*, it could be reported that the people of the Neapolitan Kingdom had given their overwhelming support to 'one and indivisible Italy'.

*   *   *

Four days after the announcement of the poll, Garibaldi left Medici to protect his lines around Caserta, and crossed the Volturno with the rest of his army under a scattered and perfunctory fire from the Bourbon garrion in Capua. He was on his way to meet Victor Emmanuel.

The meeting took place near Teano on the morning of 26 October. It was a damp day, overcast and threatening. Garibaldi and his staff, all wearing their red shirts, waited for the arrival of the King outside a little inn at the junction of the two roads along which the regular army was marching. Above them rose the hills of Vajrano and below them the wide expanse of the plain, broken here and there by ploughed fields, isolated poplars and the faded autumn vines. The General was wearing his poncho and 'under a little pork pie hat he had tied a handkerchief to protect his ears from the morning dew'.[21]

Soon after dawn the first regiments of the royal army appeared on the road from Venafro, and as they approached the cross roads where Garibaldi stood, their bands marched off the highway into the fields to play stirring martial music while the men trooped by them; they then fell in again at the rear of the columns. When the commanding officers of the various battalions reached Garibaldi, they gave the prescribed salute, some making it less formal with a wide and friendly smile, but most of them keeping their faces set as if, one of Garibaldi's staff thought, 'they were unconscious of or indifferent to the presence of the Liberator of the Two Sicilies'. Indeed, this officer added, an impartial observer of their respective expressions would have taken them for the liberators and him for the liberated.[22] It was certainly an attitude which their commander-in-chief, Fanti, was anxious to encourage, though Della Rocca had greeted Garibaldi earlier with friendly courtesy.[23]

While Garibaldi was talking to one of the generals, his staff heard the music of the royal march and then 'a group of carabinieri on horseback, forming the bodyguard, armed with swords, handcuffs and thumbscrews, announced the presence of the Monarch. The King, in General's uniform, rode a piebald Arab, and behind him came a long train of guards, chamberlains and orderlies. . . . All were alike adverse to Garibaldi, to this plebeian donor of a realm'.[24]

Both they and the Garibaldini behaved politely, however, and when he caught sight of Victor Emmanuel, Garibaldi rode up to him and lifted his hat from his head. The King held out his hand.

'*Ah, caro Garibaldi,*' he said, '*come state?*'

'*Bene, Maestà; e Lei?*'

'*Benone.*'[25]

Count Arrivabene noticed that they shook hands cordially.[26] Then Garibaldi turned round in his saddle, waved his hat to his men behind him and called out, 'Hail to the first King of Italy!' And the men responded, '*Viva, il Re!*'[27]

So far there had been no dispute, only coldness between some of the rival officers and a certain embarrassment; and the sight of the King and the former Dictator talking beside the road, while the rest of the regular army marched on past them towards Teano, seemed to promise hope of a friendly future. Alberto Mario, sitting in his saddle close to Victor Emmanuel and Garibaldi, strained his ears to catch what they were talking about. He was anxious, he confessed, to hear for the first time in his life a King's discourse, to judge for himself whether lofty sentiments would correspond with the grandeur of this truly epic occasion, arousing thoughts of Hannibal and the Roman Consuls.

'The King talked of the fine weather and the bad roads, interrupting the conversation to administer gruff reproofs and manual checks to his fiery and restless horse. Then they rode on, Garibaldi on the King's left and a few paces behind, the Sardinian and Garibaldian staff pell-mell. But soon they broke up into two groups again – in one line the modest red-shirts, in the other the splendid uniforms shining with gold, silver, crosses, medals and the *Gran Cordone*.'[28]

The King and Garibaldi were still together, however, riding side by side and continuing their awkward conversation. But soon they, too, separated; for the noise of the marching and the music, and the sight of the glittering uniforms, the swaying plumes and helmets had attracted all the peasants of the neighbourhood who gathered round Garibaldi to cheer him. He pulled in his horse and held it back a few paces behind the King's, and shouted at the excited people clamouring round him as he pointed to the figure in front, 'This is Vittorio Emanuele, the King, *your* King, the King of Italy. *Viva il Re!*'

The peasants stared at him uncomprehendingly and, after a moment's silence, burst out again, '*Viva, Viva, Galibardo!*'[29]

The King, thinking it best to dissociate himself from so unflattering a demonstration, spurred his horse into a gallop and so escaped the further attentions of these tiresome new subjects.

Garibaldi galloped after him and their conversation was resumed. The King talked now, though, of less mundane things and he broke the bitter news that the regular army would immediately take over the war that the volunteers had begun. The Southern Army, as it had come to be called, must no longer consider itself an independent force.

The King did not trouble to speak too gently: Cavour had succeeded in persuading him at last that Garibaldi was not just a political opponent of the Prime Minister but had been a potential rebel against the King.[30] 'Your troops are tired,' he said, 'mine are fresh. It is my turn now.'

Garibaldi listened in silence; and then at the bridge which crosses the stream before Teano he raised his hat in farewell and trotted sadly away down a side road towards Caserta.[31]

*   *   *

Garibaldi dismounted at a little village 'and led his horse into an outhouse by the road'.

> Entering the outhouse [Alberto Mario wrote], I found the General standing by a barrel, on which his orderly had laid the breakfast, a piece of bread and cheese and a glass of water which as soon as he had drunk he spat out, saying—'There must be a dead animal at the bottom of the well'.
>
> Slowly and silently we retraced our steps to Calvi. Garibaldi's countenance was full of melancholic sweetness. Never did I feel drawn to him with such tenderness.[32]

'Jessie,' he said next morning to Mario's wife with a weary sadness, less bitter than resigned, 'they have sent us to the rear.'[33]

Della Rocca took over the operations at Capua, while Fanti and Cialdini conducted the siege of Gaeta.* For a time the Garibaldini were unaware of the transference of command, for Garibaldi had

---

* Capua fell after a heavy bombardment by Victor Emmanuel's army on 2 November; and Gaeta, after a long and stubborn resistance, inspired by Francis II and his heroic wife, on 13 February, the following year.

Garibaldi welcomed in London in 1864

At a reception given by the Duchess of Sutherland at Stafford House

arranged for Della Rocca's orders to be issued to his men as though they emanated from himself.[34] Grateful for this assurance that they would be obeyed, Della Rocca went to visit the volunteers' headquarters in the Palace and found Garibaldi ill in bed in a little room above the powder store.

I begged him to move immediately [Della Rocca wrote], and smiling he promised to do so. Propped up with little pillows, he was wrapped in a military cloak, a little cap on his head and a silk handkerchief knotted round his neck. As I entered he held out his hand and seemed quite touched when I told him I had only come to ask how he was. He was still more pleased when I told him how well I got on with his generals, Cosenz and Sirtori, notable personages and most excellent men, and how I regretted the enforced absence of Bixio who had been sent to hospital in Naples owing to a fall from his horse. Mine were no idle compliments. I meant what I said, and I saw Garibaldi was pleased that I appreciated his friends.[35]

But pleasant as were the relations between Garibaldi and Della Rocca, there was no such feeling of mutual sympathy, nor could there ever be, between Garibaldi and Fanti, a man whose influence was so much greater than that of his good-natured subordinate.

The fault was not Cavour's. Indeed, Cavour had always insisted that if the Garibaldini welcomed Victor Emmanuel, they must be treated well, whatever the regular army thought of them. 'Reasons of State of the first importance demanded firmness' when dealing with Fanti and the other diehard officers of the General Staff, Cavour wrote. 'Woe to us if we show ourselves ungrateful to those who have shed their blood for Italy! Europe would condemn us. In the country there would be a great reaction in favour of the Garibaldini. I have had a warm argument with Fanti on this point.'[36]

The argument may have been warm, but the point was not taken. Fanti was disposed not merely to condemn the slovenly attire and lack of discipline of the Garibaldini, but to dismiss their service as unworthy of gratitude. And when it had been agreed, with some hesitation and demur on both sides, that the King would come to Caserta to review the Garibaldini and that their principal officers should be presented to him – when all the arrangements had been completed and the day of the review arrived and the various regiments were drawn up outside thc Palace, the King did not come. Fanti and his colleagues had persuaded him to remain at his headquarters without sending any explanation for his absence.*[37]

Garibaldi did not blame the King, though Victor Emmanuel had not, it seems, needed much persuasion to stay away; but he virulently condemned Fanti and, even more virulently, he condemned Cavour.

The King, however, was still to be respected; and when Cialdini asked Garibaldi to enter Naples in the royal carriage on the very next day after the volunteers had paraded in vain beneath the high walls of the Palace, the disgruntled man, after an outburst of abuse levelled at Fanti and Cavour, agreed to do so.

It was a day far different from that on which Garibaldi had entered Naples alone two months before. The welcome was swamped by rain which fell heavily and steadily throughout the time of the procession, destroying the triumphal arches and emphasising the glum mood of the two silent figures who sat side by side in the principal carriage, Garibaldi looking sadly at the rows of dutifully cheering faces under the dripping umbrellas, the King with his uniform streaked by damp blue lines where the dye had run in the rain that dripped from his beard.

'A poorer affair could not be imagined,' Elliot thought, 'for the weather was atrocious, and none of the preparations being complete, the whole thing was completely *manqué*, so much so that I should not wonder if it were to be encored as though it had not taken place.'[38]

Nor was the situation improved when Victor Emmanuel made a speech and, talking of the supreme power which had been con-

* Fanti's attitude towards the volunteers was mentioned by the King in a letter to Cavour dated 22 November 1860. Victor Emmanuel in a sour mood wrote of Garibaldi that 'ce personnage n'est pas si docile et si honnête homme de ce que on le fait et de ce que vous le croyez vous même. His military talents are very feeble, as the affair at Capua well shows. . . . He is surrounded by *canaille* whose evil counsels he follows and he has plunged this unhappy country into *un état epouvantable*.' All the same it had to be admitted that he and his followers had fought bravely, and yet Fanti treated them 'in public with supreme contempt', going so far as '*maltraiter des mutilés qui demandaient l'aumône*' and even ridiculing their bravery – Luigi Mondini, 'Vittorio Emanuele, Cavour e Garibaldi: Cinque lettere inedite del Sovrano', in *Nuovo Antolotia di Lettere, Arti e Scienze* (1960), 485-502.

ferred upon him by universal suffrage, referred to Naples and Sicily as those two noble 'provinces', a word which, in the circumstances, was peculiarly ill-chosen.

Later there was a presentation in the Throne Room of the Palace and Garibaldi remained in the background with his hat on. 'A court functionary wonders at this,' Crispi noted in his diary, 'and is told that the grandees of Spain had the right to stand before their King with head covered, and that Garibaldi is a grandee of Italy, and perhaps something more.'[39]

The General was thinking, so he said later, about the future of his volunteers, who he now felt sure were about to be disgracefully treated by an ungrateful government. Both his concern and his subsequent anger when he believed his men had been betrayed were entirely understandable. They were not, however, wholly justified.

Cavour had originally intended to form a division (to be called the *Cacciatori delle Alpi*) from the best of the men, to disband the rest with gratuities, and to give some of the officers, who were not in the *Cacciatori delle Alpi*, the chance of a commission in the regular army. That these intentions were never realised was not the fault of Cavour, nor altogether even the fault of Fanti and his fellow generals. The fact was that many of the Garibaldini who offered themselves for service in the regular army and the *Cacciatori delle Alpi* did not afford the sort of material to justify Garibaldi's complaint. Most of the best volunteers went back willingly and happily to civilian life when the fighting was over, and those that remained, while not predominantly the 'outcasts and vagabonds' that W. G. Clark described, were, nevertheless, of sufficiently questionable quality to make it unwise to risk the formation of such a volunteer division as the *Cacciatori delle Alpi*.* Also it was unreasonable to expect, as Garibaldi did expect, that the ranks of all his numerous and arbitrarily promoted

---

* After Garibaldi had left Naples many of these followers who remained behind did, in fact, act in a way to justify Clark's complaint. 'There was a disturbance in San Carlo last night at the conclusion of the ballet,' the Naples correspondent of *The Times* wrote in a far from uncommon report. 'The Garibaldini called for "The Hymn! The Hymn!" But the call was not at first responded to. The Redcoats then drew their swords and prepared to march on the orchestra which fled, as well as the actors and a great part of the audience.' – *The Times*, 15 December 1860.

officers should be recognised. There were over seven thousand of them, many of whom had been commissioned for some isolated act of courage which bore little relevance to their capacity to lead and manœuvre a platoon of men; and some of whom had had only a few weeks' experience of military life or none at all. Even so, over half of them remained in the reorganised army and sixteen survivors of The Thousand eventually became generals. But to Garibaldi, who had set his heart on the formation of a permanent division of his supporters to lead the march on Rome, the manner whereby his army had been dismembered was an outrageous act for which the Turin Government could never be forgiven. He complained with bitter fury – and this was certainly true – that many of the volunteers who had sacrificed so much for Italy were treated less favourably than even the Bourbon army.

Garibaldi himself was granted a commission as full General of the Piedmontese army; but when Cialdini came to hand it to him, he screwed the paper up and threw it to the ground. There was nothing left for him to do now but to go home. He had asked to be appointed Lieutenant-General for the Southern provinces and the appointment had been refused him and given instead to Farini who thought (as Victor Emmanuel did) of the Neapolitans and Sicilians as an inferior and unattractive race, and who was to govern them no more success-fully than Garibaldi had done, without any of Garibaldi's sympathy.

'The country here is not Italy but Africa,' Farini told Cavour, 'and the Bedouin are the flower of civil virtue when compared to these people.'[40] Garibaldi had reason to believe that Farini thought of the volunteers in the same way. Personally, he told Persono self-pityingly, he felt like an orange which had been squeezed to the last drop and whose peel had been thrown into a corner.[41] It was very like the simile that Jessie Mario had used when speaking of him.[42]

On 9 November he sent Major Missori with a message to Admiral Mundy telling him that he intended to leave next day for Caprera and would like to go aboard the *Hannibal* on his way home to say goodbye to him. Garibaldi stepped on board at six o'clock when the Admiral was still in his bunk.

> He was dressed in his usual costume [Mundy said], the red flannel shirt and grey trousers, but was without a sword. Looking out of the stern verandah windows, and pointing to an English merchant vessel blowing

off her steam at a cable's distance, he said in a melancholy tone. 'There is the ship that is to carry me to my island home; but, Admiral, I could not depart without paying you a farewell visit. It is the last which I make before leaving Naples. Your conduct to me since our first meeting in Palermo has been so kind, so generous, that it can never be erased from my memory'.

Mundy replied that he had merely fulfilled his duty as any British naval officer would have done; and then they spoke of other things. Garibaldi's mood was sadly dejected, the Admiral thought, but when he asked Munday to visit him at Caprera and the Admiral replied that he had another eighteen months of service in the Mediterranean and at the end of that time, he 'could hardly expect to find him at the same little spot', Garibaldi's mood changed immediately.

Within five months, he said excitedly, he would be in the field again.[43] He had already said as much in his farewell address to his army when he had promised his men that they would soon meet again to 'march together to new victories'.[44]

'I shall never rest satisfied,' he told Mundy, 'till emancipation from foreign rule has been effected throughout the entirety of the Italian kingdom. Rome and Venice are not French and Austrian cities. They are Italian cities. They belong to Italy alone.'

He spoke with passionate vehemence, and Mundy's diffident attempts to point out the dangers of any action unless undertaken with the sanction of the King and Parliament served only to arouse him to greater excitement. All the old grievances were aired once more, and the traditional enemies again condemned: the French Emperor, the main opponent of Italian freedom; and the Italian Prime Minister, 'who had acquiesced in the degradation of his country, by yielding to the will of the spoliator'.

Rome, the Empress City of the world, and Venice, the Queen of the Adriatic, could not be allowed to remain in the hands of the alien. It was an intolerable humiliation, and they must be rescued at all risk.

The Admiral was 'not altogether astonished at the vehemence of his language on this particular head'; but he was at a loss to understand the inveterate hatred he seemed to cherish for every act of the

Chief Minister, and of the general distrust of everything Pied-montese'.

Suddenly Garibaldi's outburst ceased; and when he rose to take his leave 'his previous animation had departed and his whole manner was that of a man who was suffering a poignant grief. . . . He slipped into his little skiff and, rowed by four boys, returned to the *Washington*. In a few hours the steamer rounded the Island of Ischia, and turning her head to the northward steered a direct course for Caprera'.

Aboard the *Washington* Garibaldi's possessions took up little space. He was going home as lightly burdened as he had been when he had sailed from Quarto six months before. He had been offered an estate, a dukedom, the Collar of the Order of the Annunziata, and enough money to support these honours, but all of them he had refused. He took, instead, two horses whom he had named 'Calatafimi' and 'Milazzo', the portable bath he always carried with him on his campaigns, a few little bags of coffee, sugar and dried beans, a sack of dried fish, and a case of macaroni.[45]

PART III
1861–1882

1

'ROMA O MORTE!'

The house at Caprera to which Garibaldi once again returned was rather less uncomfortable now than it had been in 1857 when Mme Schwartz had paid her first visit to the island.

The General's room, however, though better furnished, was as damp and disorderly as ever. As well as his small iron bedstead, draped in muslin to keep out the mosquitoes, and a big chest of drawers placed in front of a window that faced north, he now had a walnut writing table with bookcases on either side of the fireplace. But the stone floor was always wet since the drain pipes which carried the precious rain-water from the roof discharged into a cistern beneath it, and the room was always untidy since the General rarely put anything away. His clothes – red shirts, underpants, trousers and socks, many of them neatly mended by himself – hung on a clothes-line which stretched from one end of the room to another; and on every available piece of furniture were stacks of newspapers, countless bundles of letters and documents, books and the more or less useless oddments with which he found it difficult to part. Over the fireplace hung a picture of his daughter Rosita who had died at Montevideo; and above his bed, in an ebony frame, a lock of her mother's hair, and a portrait of his own mother – 'a very sad, sweet, yearning face', Jessie Mario thought it. Beneath this were portraits of three of his officers – Colonel Vecchi and two others who had been killed in the last campaign. On the opposite wall were two swords and a Brazilian whip.

On the other side of the little entrance hall was Teresa's room and behind, approached by a small dark passage, two other rooms and the kitchen. On the northern side of the asphodel-lined parterre there was now a range of more recently constructed buildings – one of them an iron house given to him by English admirers – and in these buildings various of the General's friends were able to find some sort of accommodation on their regular and often prolonged visits to the island.

These friends included Giovanni Basso and Luigi Gusmaroli; Giovanni Battista Carpanetti, the Sardinian who had welcomed the General into his house at Tangier; Eliodoro Specchi and Pietro Stagneti, two veterans of the fighting in 1849 who had followed him into exile in the United States; and Augusto Vecchi. Giuseppe Deideri never stayed long, for the climate did not suit him, but his wife still looked after Teresa. Menotti was usually there too; and soon there was also his brother Ricciotti, who had been taken to England by Mrs. Roberts to be cured of a leg infection and had stayed on to go, at her expense, to New Brighton College near Liverpool.

'Each had his particular task – hoeing, watering, pruning, wall-building, stone-carrying, writing letters – many, many letters; and rarely one without an answer. Each steamer brought sacks of mail for Caprera.'[1] Often they were not stamped, and he made unavailing complaints about this in the newspapers, and eventually took to leaving his own letters unstamped.

Work on the island began early. Garibaldi himself was usually awake at three o'clock and sometimes even earlier, reading the letters and the newspapers that he had not finished the night before by the light of the lamp by his bed. At four he would call Basso or another of his friends into the room to suggest answers to one or other of his numerous letters.

A few of them came from cranks – a priest who believed Italy to be possessed and called upon Garibaldi to drive Lucifer's representative, the Pope, from Rome and all his devils with him; or an inventor who had perfected a machine capable of destroying an army of 200,000 men. A few were begging letters, but most of them came from admirers (by far the greatest number of these were romantic Englishwomen) begging for his autograph or a lock of his hair. He rarely disappointed them.*

---

* Cavour managed to collect several well-authenticated tufts, and sent them to England with a sardonic covering letter. At Naples, according to an English-woman who lived there, Garibaldi was besieged at the Hôtel d'Angleterre by women who came asking 'that each might cut off a lock of his hair. General Türr was with him, and looked quite out of patience, standing guard over him with a comb, and raking down his head after each operation' – Josephine Butler, *In Memoriam Harriet Meuricoffre* (London, n.d.), 65.

Sometimes a more important letter worried him, such as one he received in February 1861 from Lord John Russell asking him in very firm tones 'seriously to reconsider' his declaration that he proposed to begin a war in the spring, since no 'individual, however distinguished has a right to determine for his country the momentous question of peace or war'.*[2]

He would spend a long time wondering how best to answer such letters as these, and would even wake one of his friends in the middle of the night to help him. It was not irksome to be so disturbed, but an honour, Augusto Vecchi thought.

Vecchi was once called after he had gone to bed and summoned to the General's room to decipher an ill-written letter.

The writing was really illegible [Vecchi recalled], and I had never seen it before, but I succeeded in making out the contents of the letter and wrote the answer. The General read and signed my answer, and said 'You have guessed my thoughts; I should have expressed myself exactly the same. Bravo! But I was born in a land where they do not speak Italian, and I have lived so long in countries where men have other languages on their lips. Do me the kindness to send me a dictionary from Genoa in which the words are all given with the explanation of their proper use. It will help me in my difficulties when you are gone'.

I returned to my room to write, confused at the kindness of this excellent man, and wondering at his unaffected modesty. . . . If he had lived in the age of heroism, he would have been deified as the most perfect work of the Creator. . . .

Some hours later, he came in to me with some more letters which he placed on my table. Seeing several pieces of granite and pumice-stone

* Queen Victoria persuaded Palmerston to prevent Lord John Russell sending as friendly a letter as he had originally intended. She had, indeed, not wanted a letter to be despatched at all, since it implied 'a recognition of the General's position as a European power' and since it also might lead to a prolonged and embarrassing correspondence, and create the feeling in the General's mind that 'when in future the disapprobation of the British Government was not expressed it gave its consent to "his aggressive schemes" ' – *The Letters of Queen Victoria*, 2nd Series III, 431–4; Brian Connell, *Regina v. Palmerston: The Correspondence between Queen Victoria and her Foreign Secretary and Prime Minister 1837–1865* (Evans Brothers, 1962), 300.

and quartz arranged along the edge of the table, he said, 'Have you turned geologist, Augusto?'

'No, General,' I replied. 'I have picked up some bits of stone in my walks about the island to send to those who love you, and who ardently desire to possess something from this place. Surely, you're not sorry that I should clear off some stones from Caprera?'

'Please yourself,' he said. 'I shall be sure to have too many left.' And he went away laughing.[3]

When his correspondence had been attended to, Garibaldi had a cup of coffee and then went out to work in his garden before breakfast which was at nine o'clock. He was joined in the garden by Fruscianti (who had taught him what he knew of gardening and farming and the art of building) and in the summer of 1861 by an English gardener, Robert Webster, who had been sent out to him by a rich admirer with a present of seeds and plants.*

The General was a diligent gardener and a persevering farmer, keeping a careful account book and diary of his various activities. But, according to Fruscianti, he was a very bad mason. He seemed most happy when hoeing in the garden or tending his plants for which he developed an almost mystical attachment.

Once when he and a guest were working in the vegetable garden together, the guest accidentally knocked a beanstalk down and was embarrassed to catch his host's eye and see the angry expression that flashed across his face. For the rest of the morning he felt Garibaldi's gaze directed at him as he worked, dreading a repetition of his carelessness. But at length he was forgiven. Garibaldi came up to him and said, 'Bravo! Come and wash your hands in my room.' And throughout the meal the General was particularly attentive to him, helping him from the dishes on the table until, as he confessed, the friendly hospitality quite confused him.[4]

The midday meal, like the supper in the evening, was simply cooked

---

* When the gardener had gone home to England Garibaldi, who had grown fond of him, wrote him a kind and characteristic letter:

Mio caro Robert, Among these granite rocks we used the same tool – the hoe. I am happy only when I am using it. Your country is free and therefore you are not obliged to change the hoe for the sword – *sempre con affectto, vostro* G. Garibaldi. – Curàtulo, *Garibaldi e le donne,* 36.

but the food was always good. The General himself did not eat much, and scarcely ever ate meat, on which he had lived for too long in South America, where, as he once told an English guest, an animal would sometimes be killed merely for its tongue. There was usually meat for others, though, and on occasions the food on the table was abundant. One winter afternoon in 1861 the guests sat down to macaroni, followed by fish, roast partridge and wild boar, and then Calabrian dried fruits with coffee. They had Capri wine to drink, but their host preferred water, drinking it from the spout of an earthenware jug which he kept beside him on the table covered with a piece of paper. Sometimes when meat was short, a more exotic dish would be served, and once an English nobleman who had sailed to Caprera in his yacht sat down to a meal of young blackbirds, some salted and others minced and fried in butter, served with beans cooked in oil. One of the other guests asked the Englishman if he had ever tasted such a dish in his life.

'Oh, no, never. But it was really excellent.' Many of his friends 'to have such a dish would pay its weight in gold'.

The General pressed him to eat more of both sorts of blackbird and he did. He seemed delighted, but his neighbour could not tell 'whether it was the meal or the host that delighted him so much'.

When the Englishman took his leave, 'he asked Garibaldi for a keepsake, intimating that he would like to have a pair of strong nailed shoes that he had seen under the bed.

'"I understand your wish," said the saviour of Italy, very good-naturedly, "but I happen to have only this pair, and the shoemaker lives on that shore on which it has pleased others to make me a foreigner. They are a souvenir of my native land." And, turning to a clothes line on which hung some red shirts, he continued with a pleasant smile "If one of these shirts would do instead. . . .?'

'"Certainly, thank you!" said my lord: and away he went delighted.'*[5]

The General was always being asked for souvenirs by the tourists who came to the island so regularly to see him; and he never failed

* Several of Garibaldi's red shirts were made for him by Messrs. Thresher and Glenny, 152–153 Strand, London. The directors of this firm believe they were presented to him and to other members of The Thousand as a contribution to the fund opened in London for the Sicilian expedition.

to find them something to take away, even if it was only his auto-graph or a peculiarly attractive piece of red granite or quartz. The hairs from his comb and his nail parings were greatly prized; and one Englishwoman was lucky enough to find one of his labourers digging potatoes in his general's uniform. The General had given it to him for working in, the labourer said, so the visitor bought it and took it home with her.

Garibaldi was at once so affable and so dignified, another English visitor decided after being favoured with a signed photograph to take away with him, that one could not fail both to love and to respect him. He must have some defects of character, this English-man, Sir Charles McGrigor, reflected after spending a few memor-ably happy days with the General to whom he had presented on behalf of various subscribers in London a 'well built and fast sailing yacht of fifty tons'; but what these defects were, it was impossible for Sir Charles to say. Garibaldi's character 'in a world of prevailing meanness and selfishness, appears as rare as the existence of flowers and verdure in the centre of a desert'.[6]

It was, in fact, an almost universal opinion. For the power of his personality and the gentleness of his manner successfully concealed his defects from his visitors whose flattery, indeed, and the flattery of those who saw more of him, concealed these defects from himself. But the flaws in his character were obvious enough, of course, to the women who knew him intimately. Jessie Mario, for example, came to realise that he could be unjust and vindictive, even deceitful, and that his self-importance never allowed him to laugh at himself or others to mock him. If she herself teased him about a particular phrase he had picked up and used frequently, he would refuse to speak to her for the rest of the day. But his guests rarely saw this aspect of his character. To them he appeared as the ideal patriarch, tolerant yet commanding, whose benign features, soft voice and air of unemphatic authority inspired immediate and lasting devotion. He could disappoint them on occasions, but he rarely disillusioned them. They took their moods from him, respecting his long silences and recurring melancholy, happy when he recovered his usual placidity.

After the evening meal he was occasionally downcast, eating and drinking in gloomy silence and rising to go to his room as soon as he had finished, leaving his companions to worry that one or other of them might have offended him. But more often he was, or at least appeared, to be content; and then he would light a strong cigar, drink a cup of tea, of which he was extremely fond, and begin to talk of the past. Often there would be singing. Garibaldi had a pleasant voice and Specchi had been a professional singer. Neither of them ever tired of Rossini, and 'almost every night in which there was singing' during Sir Charles McGrigor's visit, the General would say *'noi termineremo col Barbiere'*.[7]

Sometimes there would be a recital of patriotic poetry instead, and Garibaldi joined in the verses he knew by heart in his richest declamatory style. And one evening, Augusto Vecchi remembered, they were all assembled in Madame Deideri's room when Teresa said:

'Do they dance much in la Maddalena?'

'Oh dear, yes!' Vecchi said. 'They dance their legs off'.

Teresa thought of Menotti who was in Milan. 'He will be dancing there,' she said gloomily. Everyone was enjoying themselves except herself.

Garibaldi looked tenderly at his beloved daughter, and Madame Deideri interpreting his glance said, 'Never mind, Teresa. Papa will dance with you.' The General did not answer her, but got up and left the room. Teresa looked sad and she said, 'Oh yes, see how much Papa wants to dance!' Her usually contented, cheerful aspect changed into such a dismal expression that I can compare it to nothing but the expression to be seen on the people's faces in London on Sunday.

Suddenly, however, the door opened and the General appeared in full dress. 'Here I am, Teresa,' he said. 'Specchi, be so kind as to play us a waltz.' And he danced with her. He is a capital dancer.[8]

In the summer evenings when the sea was calm, they would go down to fish by torchlight. The sea was full of fish – lampreys, soles and mullet, sprats and whitings, and shoals of them would swim to the surface attracted by the light of a flaming torch of resinous wood. Garibaldi's aim was certain and he would rarely fail to bring one of the larger ones up at the end of his spear.

When they got back to the house with their catch Garibaldi would go immediately to his room, for he disliked sitting up late. He did not often read a book though there were a number in the house, as Baroness von Schwartz had noticed in the 1850's, mostly presents from admirers and several of them in English – Shakespeare and Byron, together with works on navigation and the art of war. Later another friend noticed Plutarch, La Fontaine and Voltaire, books on Greek and Roman history, and a worn copy of Saint-Simon's *Le Nouveau Christianisme*.

'I read few works of fiction,' he admitted to Sir Charles McGrigor, 'but I do like Sir Walter Scott. He is a grand *romancier*, and much to be preferred to Dumas.' He enjoyed poetry, particularly patriotic poetry, but mostly he read newspapers which came to the island in great bundles from La Maddalena. He was anxious to keep in touch with the outside world, he said. He lived a secluded life; but he could not think of himself as a man whose public life was over and whose duty done.

★   ★   ★

'Here I await the fresh call to arms.' The familiar phrase was contained in a letter to the Neapolitans who had asked him to stand for election to the Piedmontese Parliament. He used the excuse to decline the offer, explaining that his place was not upon parliamentary benches but in the field of action. Later, however, the growing dissatisfaction in the South with the rule of the North and the appalling inefficiency of the officials who had taken over the government in Naples, induced him to change his mind. He arrived in Turin at the end of April 1861.

He had been able to bear no longer the thought that his redshirts were being treated with shameful and humiliating contempt by the Government, that they were being ungratefully disbanded by a 'gang of parasites'. Influenced by Brofferio and Rattazzi and by malcontents of all sorts who came or wrote to Caprera to stir his wounded pride, he was persuaded that Cavour was personally to blame – Cavour who had, in fact, done his best to soften the hard, high-handed attitude which the King and General Fanti had adopted.[9]

Soon after Garibaldi's arrival in Turin, Cavour was given due warning of the sort of attacks which were about to be made upon him. Already the General had been reported as having referred to

Garibaldi's house and outbuildings on Caprera

The front of Garibaldi's cottage on Caprera in 1861

The back of the cottage in 1861

Garibaldi with his animals

Garibaldi working on his land

Garibaldi in his last years

Cavour's supporters as 'a crowd of lackeys, men without heart and without patriotism'. He reiterated these charges, and others, now. The King sent for him but, on this occasion, failed to subdue him. Baron Ricasoli called him to account in Parliament, and in a moving, brilliant, gently sarcastic speech (a speech which so impressed Cavour that afterwards he said, 'Now I know what true eloquence is. If I die tomorrow here stands my successor') the Tuscan baron suggested to the Deputies that it was impossible to believe that the great patriot had used the words imputed to him.

A week later, however, when Garibaldi himself appeared in the Chamber, it was easy enough to believe that he had, in fact, used them. He came in through a side door, half an hour after the sitting had begun, wearing his red shirt and his grey poncho, looking, Henry d'Ideville, an attaché at the French Legation, acidly commented, 'like a prophet, or if you prefer it, an old comedian!'[10] He was helped by two friends to a seat where he stood with flushed face – yet, as a more sympathetic spectator put it, 'supremely dignified'.[11] He waited for the cheers to subside. Then he took the oath of a Deputy and sat down slowly, clutching his stick between his rheumatic knees.

This was the first time, d'Ideville sardonically remarked, that this 'demi-god had deigned to sit amongst the simple mortals who were his colleagues'. Everyone had been awaiting the occasion with impatience, 'feeling with good cause that it would be the signal which would bring into the full light of day the suppressed yet violent struggle between the party of action and the Government'.[12]

As soon as Garibaldi was seated, the debate which his entrance had interrupted was resumed. He listened to Ricasoli repeat his belief that the remarks attributed to him had surely been misreported; and he listened to General Fanti, the War Minister, calmly and lengthily insist that it was impossible to maintain in peace-time, and in a country where military service was compulsory, a corps of volunteers.

Garibaldi was seen to grow restive, and when he rose to reply with a sheaf of notes – written for him it was believed by Rattazzi – a huge magnifying glass in his hand and his spectacles on his nose, the Deputies and the spectators in the galleries and the 'Ministers at the green table just below the President's chair, knew that the storm, which had been visibly gathering, was about to break'.[13]

Henry d'Ideville watched Garibaldi closely, thinking how like a lion he looked, how expressive his small eyes were. He began to speak slowly and confidently, his sonorous, vibrant voice ringing through the Chamber, his strange costume giving to the scene a 'sort of theatrical interest'. But then, '*hélas!* the actor forgot his lines, and was soon hesitating and muttering as he tried to regain the thread of his ideas'.[14]

Unable to read his manuscript or to hear the whispered promptings of the two 'acolytes' who had helped him in, he cast the notes aside and threw himself with increasing vehemence into what developed into a violent attack upon the Ministry, which he accused of having provoked 'a fraticidal war' in the South.[15]

Soon the Chamber was in uproar. Shouts of protest from the Government's supporters, cheers from Garibaldi's friends on the Left, the frantic ringing of the President's bell, the enraged shouts of Cavour, as he pounded his fist on the Minister's table, filled the air with a tumult of noise. When, in desperation, the President put on his hat to indicate that the sitting was suspended, the Deputies rushed down the aisles, one of them to swing his fists at Cavour, another to shout at Crispi who was seen 'bawling, gesticulating like a maniac'.[16]

At length order was restored. But when Garibaldi, who appeared stolidly unperturbed by the uproar he had caused, returned to his theme, he advocated not merely the maintenance of a corps of volunteers, but the formation of a whole army of volunteers, greatly outnumbering the regular army and dedicated to a march on Rome or Venice, with himself at their head. Fanti vehemently protested against such an idea, and once more it seemed likely that the debate would end in uproar. Then Nino Bixio stood up to make an impassioned plea for the ending of personal and party quarrels in the interests of national unity. He would give his life and even his family, he said, to see the mischief-makers, who had embittered the relationship between Garibaldi and Cavour, 'grasp each other's hands'.[17]

Immediately Cavour responded. Controlling his seething passion with evident difficulty, he made a conciliatory speech, though without giving way in the least to Garibaldi's demands and when he had finished it, he was loudly cheered.

The Times correspondent saw Garibaldi make as if to get up and walk down the aisle to shake hands with the Prime Minister, but

one of his friends 'forcibly prevented him'; and when, as if in agreement with this friend, he spoke in reply, not refuting the Government's arguments but bringing up old grievances, he did not allow
a note of propitiation to enter either into his remarks or into his
tone of voice. Continuing to insist that the volunteers should be
organised as he wished them to be organised, he concluded as though
the comment should end the discussion, 'That is my desire'.[18]

'Arrogant towards the Government, insolent towards Parliament,' d'Ideville commented when the debate was over, 'he treated
the King with familiarity. And in Turin where monarchial sentiment is very strong, Garibaldi has a very different reputation than he
enjoys elsewhere. He is very unpopular and regarded as a man
dangerous for Italy. Tribute is paid to his courage and to his honesty;
but no one is ignorant of the fact that his character is weak and his
understanding limited.'[19]

> You are not the man I thought [General Cialdini wrote in an open letter
> to the Press, expressing a widespread disillusion]. You are not the
> Garibaldi I loved. With the disappearance of the spell, the affection that
> bound me to you has been dispelled. . . .
>
> You dare to put yourself on a level with the King, speaking of him
> with the affected familiarity of a comrade. You mean to place yourself
> above custom, presenting yourself in the Chamber in a most outlandish
> costume; above the Government, branding its ministers as traitors
> because they are not devoted to you; above Parliament, heaping with
> vituperation the Deputies who do not think as you do; above the
> country, desiring to drive it where and how suits you best. Very well,
> General! There are men not disposed to tolerate all that, and I am one
> of them.[20]

At the end of the long letter he wrote in reply, Garibaldi threw
down the challenge to a duel.

Once more the King intervened. But although Garibaldi and
Cialdini were reconciled, the interview at the Palace with Cavour
was less friendly. Garibaldi was polite but would not retract any of
his demands or accusations, and since he had sworn to chop off his
hand rather than allow Cavour to shake it, neither of them made any
advances.[21] 'I never saw his hands at all,' Cavour told Ricasoli. 'He
held them under his prophet's mantle all the time.'[22]

Cavour remained placatory. He felt, one of his most distinguished biographers has said, 'a noble pity for Garibaldi, a man so heroic of stature in one field, so dwarflike in others', a man 'whom someone described as having, "the heart of a child and the head of a buffalo" '. Excuses could be found for 'this misguided and ill-advised' man who was prepared to 'make the interest of the few thousand volunteers paramount to the welfare of Italy'; and Cavour did find them.* Cavour's biographer, however, found only one:

> The best excuse we can find for Garibaldi is that, like the small boy who does a great injury, he did not realise what he was doing. His obsession of hatred for Cavour, his innate megalomania, his inability to reason from which came his lack of historical perspective, his accessibility to flatterers, his unwavering devotion to whatever plan he adopted, and his certitude that whatever he planned was the final evangel of patriotism, predestined him to threaten the very existence of Italy in 1861. If it be argued that he served Italy by goading the reluctant forward and by enabling Cavour to hasten unification by scaring diplomacy with the spectre of the Revolution, then the reply is yes, but Garibaldi might have done this service without adopting the policy of hatred which so greatly impaired his achievement. Much more was involved than the explosion of his personal wrath. The Party of Action made him their tool. They hoped, under cover of his immense presence, to shape the foreign policy of the new kingdom; as they might have done, had this move for the enrolment of a half-million volunteers, to be led by him, been successful.[23]

Cavour never recovered from this final quarrel. 'If emotion could have killed,' he said, remembering the agonising debate in the Chamber, 'I should have died during that hour.' And ever afterwards, so he confessed to a friend, he 'never felt well'. The efforts to stifle his indignation when Garibaldi 'so unjustly attacked' him, had

---

* Even at the height of their quarrel in August 1860, he had admitted that public opinion would not have been with him in a fight with Garibaldi and 'public opinion would be right. For Garibaldi has rendered to Italy the greatest service that a man could render her: he has given the Italians confidence in themselves: *il a prouvé à l'Europe que les Italiens savaien· ·· battre et se mourir sur les champs de bataille pour reconquérir une patrie*' – *Carteggi di Cavour. Carteggio Cavour-Nigra* (Bologna, 1929), iv, 144–5.

struck him in a vulnerable spot. His pallor when he said this 'was ghastly, his eyes lustreless, their whites very yellow'.[24]

On 29 May he went home from the Chamber and admitted to his devoted butler that he was completely exhausted. 'But I must go on working,' he said. 'The country needs me. Perhaps I will get away to Switzerland, though, this summer.'

That night he was very sick, and in the early hours of the morning the butler ran out to fetch the doctor, who advocated bleeding. For three days he was bled intermittently until there was no hope of recovery; but he would not give up working, even going so far as to hold a Cabinet meeting by his bedside, until his brain clouded over and he could not even concentrate sufficiently to read a book.

On Sunday, 2 June, his beloved niece, Countess Alfieri, was horrified to discover that his left hand and arm were cold as ice, while his brow was feverish. There were more bleedings and he became delirious, though when the King came to see him and grasped his hand, deeply moved by his weakness, he spoke earnestly of Italy's needs and of the 'poor Neapolitans' corrupted by 'that rascal Ferdinand'; and when one of Italy's most distinguished specialists arrived he managed a last, sad joke: 'I've sent for you a little late because up till now I wasn't ill enough to be worthy of you'; and when at last Countess Alfieri told him that she had sent for Fra Giacomo, who had promised to be with him at the end, although he had been excommunicated by the Pope, he understood, pressed her hand and said, 'Have him come in'. At five o'clock Fra Giacomo administered extreme unction; Cavour then stretched up to pull his niece's face down to his lips, kissed her twice and whispered, 'Goodbye, dear little one.' He turned to Fra Giacomo and, reaching out to touch his hand, he murmured, '*Frate, Frate, libera Chiesa in libero Stato.*'

For an hour he lingered, while Countess Alfieri moistened his lip and wiped the sweat from his forehead, and the last intelligible words she heard him say were, 'Italy is made – all is safe'.*[25]

* * *

* Cavour's true motives and the measure of his achievements are matters still in debate. Early idealistic interpretations of his career gave way, first to those which revealed in his work the methods and emotions of the *Realpolitiker* (a man, in Giovanni Gentile's words, 'prepared to lose his soul for his country') then to the

For Garibaldi, however, Italy was not yet made, could never be whole until Rome and Venice were joined to her. 'Brave Garibaldi!' Cavour had muttered during one of those long rambling monologues which had characterised the last hours of his illness. 'Brave Garibaldi! I bear him no grudge. He wants to go to Rome and Venice. So do I.'[26]

So did almost everyone else in Italy, radicals and conservatives more sympathetic interpretation of Adolfo Omodeo who, while admitting Cavour's 'machiavellico' diplomacy and politics and his occasional mistakes, presented him as a man dominated by 'l'ideale liberale'. To accusations, for example, that Cavour installed in Piedmont not a parliamentary régime so much as a dictatorship, Omodeo replied, 'It is not at all contrary to the spirit of liberalism that a political situation should be summed up in a significant personality, within the limits of respect for the forms and conditions of liberty. . . . Who would consider English history with its Walpole, Pitt, Peel, Gladstone, Salisbury, Lloyd George, Churchill, etc. as a chain of dictatorships?' – Adolfo Omodeo, *Difesa del Risorgimento* (Einaudi, Turin, 1951), 275.

Omodeo's view of Cavour is in strong contrast, of course, to the earlier view of the democratic propagandists and to the portrait presented by those who saw in Cavour's dealings with Garibaldi an attempt to preserve his personal position. And it is also in contrast to the more recent interpretation of Denis Mack Smith, who in his *Cavour and Garibaldi 1860: A Study in Political Conflict* blames Cavour and his colleagues for suffocating the germs of Italian democracy and for many of the flaws in the original creation of the Italian Kingdom, particularly the adoption of a parliamentary system subservient to vested interests and designed to perpetuate the problems of the South. The publication of Mack Smith's harsh opinion of Cavour induced many historians to come to his defence. In England Cecil Sprigge defended him warmly in the pages of *The Manchester Guardian* (14 May 1954) and A. J. P. Taylor writing in the *New Statesman* (24 April 1954) said that if Cavour had not existed, Garibaldi would either not have succeeded or would have had to end up playing Cavour's part. As it happened, Cavour perhaps made the greater sacrifice by remaining in power while Garibaldi, by returning to Caprera, could 'remain an idealist until the end of the chapter'. Martin Braun in *History Today* (October 1959) concluded that if one had now to choose between Cavour and Garibaldi, one would choose Cavour for 'have we not had a surfeit of charismatic leadership, of dictator-intoxicated ideology, of mass acclaim and mass enthusiasm? What we hunger for is solid, reliable, unpretentious, statesmanship.'

A survey of these and other attitudes to Cavour and Garibaldi has recently been provided by Walter Maturi in his *Interpretazioni del Risorgimento: Lezioni di storia della storiografia* (Einaudi, Milan, 1962).

alike. The only real question was when and how – there could be no doubt who would lead such expeditions. And so, once more, Garibaldi became the subject of rumours and the centre of intrigue.

No one could be sure, however, in what way the unpredictable hero might act. It even seemed likely, at one time, that he would go to fight for the northern states in America, as, a few years later, it seemed likely that he would go to fight for the Mexican revolutionary, Benito Juarez (after whom Alessandro Mussolini was to name his elder son).

Abraham Lincoln offered Garibaldi command of an army corps and permission had been obtained from the King for him to accept it. But in writing to accept Lincoln's offer, Garibaldi had characteristically demanded not an army corps but supreme command, and an undertaking that slavery would be formally abolished. He did not want to risk the chance of being let down by indecisive politicians prepared to trim their sails.

He did not want to run this risk in Italy, either. And he continued to storm in word and print against the cautious and the cowardly who would not strike out to cut the Gordian knot.

Meanwhile the rumours varied and multiplied: he was going to capture Fiume; he was preparing an attack on Venice; he had been promised a million lire by the Government to attack the Austrians in the Balkans.

And then it was learned for certain that he had left Caprera, that he had seen the King in Turin and that he had also seen the new Prime Minister, Rattazzi, who had recently succeeded the more scrupulous and less accommodating Baron Ricasoli.

It seemed certain that Rattazzi, who had a strong taste for conspiracy, would involve Garibaldi in some plot. But no one outside the intrigue was sure – no one is sure – what exactly had been agreed. It was clear at least, though, that when Garibaldi embarked on a Government-sponsored tour of northern Italy, making inflammatory speeches, encouraging students and schoolboys to practise fighting as part of their homework, instructing his agents to enrol volunteers and to collect money and arms, the Government took fright at the wild enthusiasm he aroused. He was not impressive as a speaker before cultivated audiences – he had failed in Parliament and was inclined to dislike those who had succeeded – but before a crowd, speaking in simple generalities, yet with intense concern and sincerity, he was inspiring and masterful. The 'sort of intimate communion of mind' that existed between himself and the masses was, one foreign observer thought, 'perfectly electrifying'.[27]

At the end of April, at a secret meeting with his officers at Trescore, he put forward a plan for the capture of Venice by means of a landing in Dalmatia, a plan which he assured them had the collusive support of the Government; and Rattazzi, alarmed by his indiscretions as to Government complicity, felt compelled to act. On 15 May, one of Garibaldi's principal staff officers, Colonel Francesco Nullo, and a hundred volunteers were arrested at Sarnico. Some of them were later shot as they tried to escape from prison.

Garibaldi was overwhelmed with anger and resentment. Speaking at the funeral of the volunteers whom the police had killed, he was beside himself with emotion. Convulsively crumpling his hat in his hands, words failed him and he broke down. He wrote to Parliament protesting furiously that the Government had called him from Caprera and had then abandoned him. The Opposition took up his complaint and demanded an enquiry, which the Government resisted, merely releasing the imprisoned volunteers in the hope that the uproar would die down.

Rattazzi, protesting in public that the million lire supplied to Garibaldi had been intended 'to encourage emigration', confessed in private to Sir James Hudson that he had been trying to push the volunteers into the Balkans – Cavour himself had smuggled arms into the Balkans for use in a war against Austria – but that when it had been discovered that Garibaldi was planning an assault on Venice he had to be publicly disowned. Rattazzi did not admit that Louis Napoleon was a party to the Balkan plot, a plot that would have appealed to the Emperor since trouble in the Balkans might make it easier for him to seize the Rhineland provinces. Nor did he suggest that before it became necessary to abandon Garibaldi, he and the King had been in close collusion with him.

But when, the next month, Garibaldi arrived in Sicily, Sir James Hudson had no doubt that he was again being secretly supported by Rattazzi and once more encouraged to strike at Austria in the Balkans. Some of his companions on the voyage, however, and, in particular, Giuseppe Guerzoni, believed – or at least later suggested

– that Garibaldi's original intention was merely to use his popularity and authority in the island to reconcile the Sicilians to their new Government, and to persuade them not to press for independence from Italy.[28]

But having arrived in Palermo he seemed once more to be carried away by the enthusiasm of his reception, believing that the shouts in the piazza were manifestations of public opinion. Soon he was making fervent speeches in which he spoke of his impatience and his enforced idleness, of the need to win Venice and Rome, of Louis Napoleon as 'the chief of brigands and assassins'.

He left Palermo for a tour of the battlefields of The Thousand, and everywhere he went he was welcomed with an excitement that was close to hysteria; the Sicilians recognised in him again, as they had done in 1860, their own simplicity of spirit, a man who shared – even if all his followers did not – their own desires and sorrows. Bands played, crowds screamed, men ran forward to grasp his hand, women wept at the sight of him, flowers and streamers were thrown at his feet. He stood up in his carriage to speak, imposing a mood upon his audience and then abandoning himself to it – in a style that D'Annunzio and Mussolini were more self-consciously to perfect – until his speech became not a speech at all, but a dialogue, a kind of unrehearsed litany. And in this litany the urgent cry of 'Roma o morte!' became a dominant theme, repeated in the streets of Palermo, and in the cathedral at Marsala before the altar during Mass.

Volunteers flocked to him, many of them hungry outcasts in rags but others thrilling to the magnetism of his personality. And he, persuaded to believe that the whole of Sicily was with him, and encouraged in his belief by members of the *Partito d'Azione* into which the various democratic groups had formed themselves, prepared to lead them for a second time across the Strait of Messina.[29]

On 20 August he led 3,000 of them over to Catania, where the royal garrison made no attempt to interfere with his arrangements. Indeed, the Government seemed anxious to help rather than to hinder him. Few people took the King's proclamation condemning his activities as anything other than a necessary protection against diplomatic protests: Garibaldi had plenty of money – and where did that come from, if not from the Government? Also, carefully preserved in an important-looking metal box, he had a document with a red seal which was shown to any official who questioned his activities – and what could that be but a mandate from the King? Garibaldi's rifles were landed in Catania docks without protest by the customs; and the warships in the harbour quietly steamed out to sea without attempting to prevent his seizure of two packet boats into which his volunteers were crammed.

They landed in Calabria without opposition and marched on Reggio. But now that their destination had become obvious to the world, they were treated with less accommodation. Marching north along the coast road, they were fired on by a royal cruiser; and outside Reggio they were advised to make a detour into the mountains as the garrison had orders to resist them.

Up till now Rattazzi's Government had been prepared, as the King had been prepared, to do nothing positive, to give vague and ambiguous instructions, or no instructions at all, until it became clearer whether or not Garibaldi would be successful. The Government had, for instance, ordered the fleet in Sicilian waters to 'do anything the occasion warrants, always keeping in mind the good of your King and Country'.[30] And the King had agreed in private that, 'to a certain extent', Garibaldi was acting on his orders.[31] In any case, Garibaldi could scarcely be held back with safety; the force of public opinion in the South was too strong for the unpopular Government in the North to withstand. Already, the year before, strong repressive measures had had to be taken against the threat of a counter-revolution in the South. Resentment against Turin was, in fact, widespread all over what had formerly been the Kingdom of the Two Sicilies: there was bitter feeling – later to grow so bitter that the whole conception of the Risorgimento was condemned – that the North had stripped the South of its riches, ignored its claims and abandoned it to poverty.

Now that Garibaldi was on the mainland and marching north, however, another voice was heard – that of Louis Napoleon. Rattazzi had tried to persuade him that revolution in the South could only be prevented if Italian troops were allowed to move into Rome; but the French Emperor, anxious to get the burden of Rome off his shoulders but determined not to do so at the expense of the Pope's security, had not been susceptible to such crude persuasion, lacking as it did all the subtleties of Cavourian technique. Louis Napoleon insisted that the Italian Government must take a decisive step.[32] Both Rattazzi and the King were anxious enough to do so, for by now they had begun to fear, as Garibaldi approached Naples, that there was greater danger of rebellion in the South in allowing him to continue than in preventing him. It was General La Marmora's view, indeed, that Garibaldi's march on Rome was nothing but a pretext. 'I am absolutely convinced,' he wrote, 'that the intention of Garibaldi and his followers is to undermine – *scalzare* – the monarchy, and to destroy the army.'[33] General Cialdini was accordingly told to put an immediate stop to Garibaldi's adventure.

Cialdini instructed Pallavicini, a colonel of *bersaglieri*, to 'leave with a column of six or seven battalions, to make every effort to overtake Garibaldi, and to attack and destroy him if he offers battle'.[34]

Garibaldi still hoped that, if he were careful to avoid the King's troops, they would take steps to avoid him. On 27 August, however, he was disillusioned. On that day his rearguard were attacked by the regular forces under Colonel Pallavicini. Still, he went on, astonished by the action of the royal troops, but hoping that a forced march would give Pallavicini an excuse to lose him. His guide led him astray in the mountains – or his own sense of direction was not as reliable as once it had been – and by the time the forced march was over, his exhausted followers had been taken back almost to the place from which they had started several hours before. They were desperately hungry as well as exhausted, for all that they had found to eat since landing had been a few sheep and a small crop of potatoes which they had pulled out of the earth and eaten raw. Most of them were young, many of them boys from the towns; few of them were of the same type as the best of those who had landed at Marsala with The Thousand. By the time Garibaldi came out of the pine forest and reached Aspromonte on 28 August, 500 of them were missing.

Next day the remainder of them were drawn up in a strong position which they could well have defended. But Garibaldi could not bring himself to defend it, in what might then have become the first battle of a civil war.

The *bersaglieri* came up the slope towards him, firing as they

advanced. Some of the volunteers on the left flank, commanded by
Menotti, and some of those on the right under Giovanni Corrao,
returned the fire. Garibaldi, however, walked out in front of the
men in the centre shouting, 'Don't fire! Don't fire! *Non fate fuoco!*'
He kept on shouting while messengers ran over to Menotti and
Corrao with his orders, and while a bugler blew the 'Cease Fire'.
Suddenly he was seen to clutch at his left thigh with his crumpled hat,
and then he fell to the ground.

The wound in his thigh was not serious; but a second bullet had
lodged beneath a bone in his left foot. He was carried away and
laid under a tree next to Menotti who had also been wounded. An
officer lit a cigar for him and put it in his mouth.

A doctor knelt beside him and took off his boot and sock. There
was a swelling on the foot and Garibaldi said, 'If that's the ball take
it out straight away.' The doctor cut into the flesh but he could not
find the ball and he dared not probe too deeply.

The firing had stopped now; and abruptly, without the sound of a
bugle or any other warning, an army officer galloped up, and,
remaining in his saddle and declining to salute, demanded Garibaldi's
surrender.

'I have seen thirty years of warfare,' Garibaldi answered him in a
voice choking with indignation, 'thirty years – a good deal more
than you. And let me tell you that negotiators never present themselves like this.'[35]

He refused to discuss the surrender with such a representative;
and told his officers to disarm him.

Colonel Pallavicini then arrived himself and approached the
General with his hat in his hand. He knelt down beside him and
whispered softly in his ear that he had orders to ask him for his
unconditional surrender, but that he would do all he could to meet
his wishes. He asked after his wound, and added in a 'tone of the
deepest regret, "I have to fulfil a very painful duty" '.[36]

He was afterwards criticised for taking his humble respect too
far, a respect which Garibaldi ever afterwards remembered with
gratitude. But Giuseppe di Lampedusa understood his feelings well
enough and, introducing him as a character into his great novel,
puts words into his mouth which provide a fitting epitaph to this
sad day:

They were all genuine acts of respect. You should have seen him, that poor great man ... the only really decent person in that whole wretched countryside ... stretched out under a chestnut tree, suffering in body and still more in mind. A sad sight! He showed himself plainly as what he's always been, a child, in spite of beard and wrinkles, a simple, adventurous little boy; it was difficult for me not to feel moved at having had to shoot at him.[37]

★   ★   ★

Garibaldi was carried down the mountainside to Scilla in great pain on a stretcher. For a time he was imprisoned at Varignano on a charge of treason; but there was never a question of his being brought to trial when it became clear that the King's earlier collusion might be revealed; and he was granted a free pardon, though some of his volunteers were executed.[38]

Sympathy for him had swept not only across Italy but across the whole world. Telegrams and letters, poems and presents, cigars, flowers and books were heaped beside his bed. Over twenty doctors from all over Europe came to his bedside to offer their advice as to how the ball in his foot might best be extracted; a thousand guineas were raised in England towards the cost of two visits by an English surgeon; and Lady Palmerston, appalled by the Irish who ran through the streets of London shouting 'No Garibaldi! The Pope for ever!' sent him an invalid bed.

At last Professor Zanetti, the great Tuscan surgeon, enlarging the orifice of the wound by inserting cotton-wool steeped in gum, felt prepared to make an attempt to extract the ball [Jessie Mario wrote]. Garibaldi held my hand during the whole of the operation, and as soon as the forceps entered the aperture he exclaimed 'Per Dio! c'è!' A few seconds later Zanetti produced the sharpshooter's bullet, which, striking first against a boulder thence rebounding into the ankle, had assumed the perfect form of a cap of liberty.

It was a supreme moment of emotion when Zanetti held it up to view. Garibaldi embraced the surgeon, then all of us: the news spread – spread like magic and rejoicing was universal. Sheets and bandages, stained with the blood of the martyr of Aspromonte, were eagerly sought for, and torn to ribbons for distribution, to be treasured as sacred relics. Menotti, the General's son, kept the bullet, refusing to part with it, though an Englishman offered a fabulous sum for its possession.[39]

A month later, on the afternoon of 20 December, he sailed home to Caprera. But he was not left there in peace, and a succession of visitors came to the island throughout the following year. He avoided the least welcome ones by pleading illness; and he was, indeed, for most of the year far from well.

For weeks on end he was obliged to stay in bed; his foot gave him a great deal of pain; and his right hand became so stiff and swollen with rheumatism that he could no longer write. In the autumn, however, he began to improve and though he had still to rely on his crutches, at least he felt the need and desire to move about. One of his more persistent visitors, Mrs. Chambers, the representative of an English committee who wanted him to come to England, pressed him to make the trip. At first he was reluctant to go; but gradually he began to change his mind. He liked the English and he knew that they liked him: and, although his demeanour was always modest, there was no doubt that he enjoyed flattery and public adulation. Besides, he might do some good: he was always conscious of his responsibilities as a symbol of Italian unity; and lately he had become interested in the cause of Denmark struggling against Austria and Prussia for the possession of Schleswig-Holstein. England, the 'constant friend of the weak and the oppressed' would surely join him in the championship of the Danish cause.

And so on 3 April 1864 Garibaldi entered Southampton Water aboard the *Ripon*.

2

LONDON, 1864

No one seemed quite sure why Garibaldi had come to England. He said himself at Malta, where he called on his way, that the purpose of his visit was 'to obtain the benefit of medical advice and to pay a debt of gratitude he considers he owes to the English people'.[1]

The Italian Government, however, felt sure that there must be some other reason. He had long been publicly complaining that the Government had denied freedom of speech to some of his friends and had imprisoned others. Indeed, ever since his march on Rome had been checked at Aspromonte he had been complaining that the Ministers in Turin were, to use his own words published later in his *Memorie*, 'preparing a nauseous reaction, and spending the riches of Italy in hiring spies, police agents, priests and similar rabble'.[2]

The thought that he might express such opinions in London, that he might collect money for some new adventure, that he would be received with an enthusiasm which would encourage his revolutionary supporters, filled the Italian Government with foreboding.

The British Government were nervous enough themselves. Lord Palmerston had made it clear to Garibaldi's sponsors that the visit must be a private one, that the General should be discouraged from accepting invitations to public entertainments at which he might be induced to make embarrassing speeches. He had already appealed to England to help the American north against the southern slave-owners, and was known to have received Polish emissaries at Caprera and to have said that he wished his health were strong enough for him to join in their fight against Russia. Guerzoni, who was one of his companions on the voyage, said that he did, in fact, talk of securing English help for Poland and Greece as well as for Denmark.[3] And afterwards he told both Mme Schwartz and Jessie Mario that it was Denmark's plight which had taken him to England.[4] But when at the time Lord Shaftesbury and Lord Tennyson both asked him whether or not his visit had a political motive, he said it had not and repeated the reasons he had given at Malta.[5]

Certainly when he arrived at Southampton on 4 April wearing plain dark clothes, leaning heavily on a walking stick, yet bowing politely to the crowds who stood to cheer him in the pouring rain, it seemed that the fears of both the British and Italian Governments were unjustified. He made a short speech in scarcely intelligible English, confirmed his acceptance of an offer from the Duke of Sutherland to go and stay at his house in London, and was then driven away to the Mayor's house, acknowledging the shouts of the crowds with quiet dignity.

The next morning he surprised his hosts by getting up at dawn and leaving the house to go and call on his friends who were lodged elsewhere. But he returned before nine o'clock in good spirits; and later on that morning the people of Southampton renewed their welcome with 'a perfect tumult of enthusiasm' as he drove to the Town Hall, wearing his red shirt and poncho now, to attend an official reception. He made another speech, expressing once again his gratitude to the English people 'with evident deep feeling, but with so strong a foreign accent and symptoms of effort to overcome the difficulties of pronunciation that his delivery was remarkably slow'. Nevertheless, *The Times* correspondent found it 'almost impossible to describe the enthusiasm with which these few remarks were greeted'; and later on that day, when he went aboard a vessel at the pier to spend a few days in the Isle of Wight at Brook House, the home of Charles Seely, Member of Parliament for Lincoln, he was sent on his way with 'such demonstrations of affection and respect as are seldom seen ever in England'.[6] 'It was,' another correspondent thought, 'more boisterous than a battle.'[7]

Life was quieter in the Isle of Wight. He was visited there by Shaftesbury and by Mazzini whom he greeted with gratifying friendliness, speaking to him 'in the old patois of the lagoons of Genoa'; and he went to visit Tennyson, who was enchanted with this 'noble human being' who had the 'divine stupidity of a hero'. 'I had expected to see a hero,' Tennyson wrote 'and I was not disappointed. . . . He is more majestic than meek, and his manners have a certain divine simplicity in them such as I have never witnessed in a native of these islands, among men at least.'

'He came here and smoked his cigar in my little room,' Tennyson told the Duke of Argyll, 'and we had half an hour's talk in English, tho' I doubt whether he understood me perfectly, and his meaning was often obscure to me. I ventured to give him a little advice. He denied that he came with any political purpose in view, merely to thank the English for their kindness to him, and the interest they had taken in himself and all Italian matters, and also to consult Ferguson about his leg. Stretching this out he said, "There's a campaign in me yet." '8

On 9 April he was taken across the Solent in the paddle-steamer *Fire Queen* to visit Portsmouth and here again men were struck by his air of 'quiet dignity' as he walked up the dock where the 'half quavering exclamations from some of the ladies were caught up by the gentlemen, and communicated like an electric shock to the crowds of mechanics'.9

The greatest acclamations, however, were yet to come. On 11 April he was taken in a special train to London where about half a million people had turned out to welcome him. They lined the streets; they filled the windows and the roofs and the overhead railway bridges; they clapped and shouted and cheered; they sang Garibaldi's Hymn above the noise of the bands, they called out encouragement and good-natured insults to the representatives or the working men's committees, the friendly societies and the trade unions who marched so proudly in the procession; they waved their red scarves and their red handkerchiefs, and some of them laughed and some of them cried, and some pushed forward to touch him. And once a little girl ran up to him with a bunch of flowers and the 'calm, melancholy look' disappeared from his face as he picked her up and kissed her, and the cheers were more frantic than ever.10 'He came, the prisoner of Aspromonte,' the Countess Martinengo Cesaresco wisely commented, 'not the conqueror of Sicily, a distinction that might have made a difference elsewhere, but the English sometimes worship misfortune as other peoples worship success. No sovereign from overseas was ever received by them as they received the Italian hero.'11

It was quite true. There had never, in fact, been scenes quite like these in London before; nor have there ever been since. The good-will had 'seldom been equalled and probably never excelled'. It was 'most emphatically a people's welcome,' *The Times* correspondent insisted, 'a working-men's reception from first to last'. And this was one of the most remarkable things about it. There had been no official interference. The 1,500 police on duty had orders only to supervise the traffic. They were not to interfere in the organisation, not even to keep the route of the procession open. Yet although the excitement was close to hysteria, not a single serious accident was reported. There were none of the usual scenes of drunkenness, no pocket-picking, no tempers lost. It was as though the whole working-class had turned out to congratulate itself, in the most delightfully good-natured and wonderfully invigorating way, on having produced a hero who was the admiration of the world.

The excitement continued for days. Everywhere that Garibaldi went, or was expected, crowds gathered to cheer him; the courtyard of Stafford House was thronged with people hoping to catch a glimpse of him; and the Duke's servants found a ready market for bottles of soapsuds from his washbasin. Special performances of a Garibaldi musical show were given; Garibaldi biscuits became more popular than ever; ' "Garibaldies" in the science of millinery the feminine for the Garibaldi shirt', became once more the height of fashion.

He had become the height of fashion himself, as well as 'the darling of the lower classes'. He had always been a source of fascination for the aristocracy, and he already numbered many noblemen amongst his host of admirers. But now he was lionised in an almost universal way. There seemed scarcely a person in London who did not want to be introduced to him. From bishops in the House of Lords, to Florence Nightingale (a regular contributor to his funds) in Park Street, there came scores of approaches for the honour of his conversation and company. Even the Prince of Wales came to see him and was 'very much pleased with him'.

He is not tall, but such a dignified and noble appearance [the Prince told his mother], and such a quiet and gentle way of speaking – especially never of himself – that nobody could fail to be attracted to him. . . . He asked a great deal about you, and . . . referred to Denmark and said how much he felt for all the brave soldiers who had perished in the war.

Though, of course, it would have been very different for you to see him, still I think you would have been pleased with him, as he is so *uncharlatanlike*, if I may use such an expression . . . and though his undertakings have been certainly revolutionary, still, he is a patriot and did not seek for his own aggrandisement.[12]

He dined with Palmerston and Lord Russell and the Gladstones; he exchanged walking sticks with the Foreign Secretary at Pembroke Lodge, and at Cliveden he planted a tree – which still stands in uncomfortable proximity to a bronze statue of Prince Albert – for the Duchess of Sutherland; he was given banquets in Fishmongers Hall and in the Reform Club; he was made an honorary freeman of the City of London; he was taken to Woolwich Arsenal, to the Britannia Works at Bedford to see the new steam plough, to Barclay and Perkins's brewery in Southwark, to the Crystal Palace, to the royal farms at Windsor – the Queen had been careful to leave for Balmoral a few days before – and to Eton College where masters and boys alike shouted 'after him as if he had just won them the match against Harrow'.

And everywhere he went he combined modesty and dignity, a quiet friendliness with a warm sympathy that was as captivating as it was memorable. As Gladstone later said, those who saw him then for the first time could 'never forget the marvellous effect produced upon all minds by the simple nobility of his demeanour, by his manner and by his acts'. When he entered the room to meet the leaders of the Government, Gladstone told John Morley, 'he advanced with perfect simplicity and naturalness yet with perfect consciousness of his position – very striking and very fine'.[13] Even when he smoked a cigar in the Duchess of Sutherland's boudoir, 'such a sacred spot', so the Earl of Malmesbury thought, 'that few favoured mortals have ever been admitted in its precincts' let alone allowed to smoke in it, he carried it off with grace and quiet confidence. His complete and instinctive self-possession were 'truly quite remarkable'.[14]

There were those, of course, who were left unimpressed and unmoved by his performance, who believed it to be a contrived veneer – one of Garibaldi's own officers, Colonel Giacinto Bruzzesi, once said of his leader that 'if he were not Garibaldi he would be the greatest tragic actor known'.[15] And there were those, of course, who were envious, and those who were exasperated by the people's extravagant homage.

Karl Marx thought the whole thing 'a miserable spectacle of imbecility';[16] Disraeli, though few Tories followed his example, refused all invitations to meet the fellow;[17] while Queen Victoria, though she confided to her journal that she thought Garibaldi was 'honest, disinterested and brave',[18] was still 'half-ashamed of being the head of a nation capable of such follies'.[19] The visit of the Prince of Wales to Stafford House she thought unpardonable. She was 'very much shocked' and wrote to the Princess Royal of 'the incredible folly and imprudence of your thoughtless eldest brother going to see him without my knowledge'.[20]

She expressed herself in similar terms to Lord Russell:

'The Queen much regrets the extravagant excitement respecting Garibaldi which shows little dignity and discrimination in the nation, and is not very flattering to others who are similarly received. The Queen fears that the Government may find Garibaldi's views and connections no little cause of inconvenience with foreign governments hereafter, and trusts they will be cautious in what they do for him in their official capacity. Brave and honest though he is, he has ever been a revolutionist leader.'[21]

The Queen was assured by Lord Palmerston that good advice had been given and would continue to be given to Garibaldi to avoid his 'getting into the hands of men who would only make him a stepping-stone to get themselves into momentary notoriety. His simplicity of character,' Palmerston added, rendered him 'somewhat open to such attempts'.[22]

It was very useful, therefore, that Garibaldi had been 'taken up by the aristocracy and not left in the hands of agitators who would have endeavoured to use him for their own purposes'.

'There is something very attractive in the unassuming simplicity of Garibaldi's character, in the total absence of affectation or conceit or vanity,' Palmerston emphasised, 'and though he is evidently not a man of superior talent he speaks very sensibly on general subjects, and has good and generous feelings.'[23]

But the Queen was not satisfied. It was all very well for Lord Palmerston to assure her of the charm of Garibaldi's character; it was all very well of Lord Russell to tell her that he was 'very frank and open in countenance and manners', and it was all very well for Earl Granville, the Lord President of the Council, to tell her in a long and airy letter:

> Garibaldi has all the qualifications for making him a popular idol in this country. He is of low extraction, he is physically and morally brave, he is a good guerrilla leader, he has achieved great things by 'dash', he has a simple manner with a sort of nautical (natural) dignity, and a pleasing smile. He has no religion, but he hates the Pope. He is a goose, but that is considered to be an absence of diplomatic guile. His mountebank dress, which betrays a desire for effect, has a certain dramatic effect. His reception at Southampton and in London shows that no amount of cold water would have damped the enthusiasm of the middle and lower classes.
>
> His political principles, which are nearly as dangerous to the progress and maintenance of real liberty as the most despotic systems, are thought admirably applicable to foreign countries.
>
> The joining of the aristocracy, including some Conservative leaders, in demonstrations in his favour, although making the affair more offensive and more ridiculous to foreign nations, has been of great use in the country. It has taken the democratic sting (as to the country) out of the affair.[24]

But the Queen still deeply regretted that 'Government should have lavished honours usually reserved for Royalty upon one who openly declares his objects to lead the attack upon Venice, Rome and Russia, with the sovereigns of which countries the Government in her name professes sentiments of complete friendship and alliance'.*[25]

The Queen's attitude was understandable enough. At the Crystal Palace (which could not otherwise have been filled by so many enthusiastic people – as *The Times* correspondent provocatively commented – 'by anything other than the prospect of again beholding their Queen among them,') Garibaldi spoke of 'poor little

---

* Massimo d'Azeglio agreed with her; and in a letter to Sir Anthony Panizzi he said that he deplored the fact that a man who set himself above the laws of the State should be received by the heir to the British throne and by the leaders of the British Government – *Lettere ad Antonio Panizzi di uomini illustri e di amici italiani 1823-1870* (Florence, 1880).

Denmark', a country which, following Prince Albert's example, Victoria was determined should not be supported by Britain in her quarrel with Germany. And on another occasion, amidst loud cheers, the General called upon the 'generous English nation' not to abandon Poland, a country in arms against Alexander II, a fellow sovereign with whom the Queen had once been a little in love. Worse than this it was reported in the Press that Garibaldi (who had repeatedly spoken of the workers being his 'brothers all over the world') had had talks with all the most notorious European revolutionaries in London – Karl Blind, Ledru-Rollin, Louis Blanc and Alexander Herzen – and that he had declared himself to be a pupil of Mazzini.

He had made this declaration about Mazzini after a meal at Herzen's house.

> I want to say something which I ought to have said long ago [he had announced]. There is a man here amongst us who has rendered the greatest service to our country and to the cause of freedom. When I was young I sought for one able to act as the guide and counsellor of my youthful years. I sought for a guide as one who is thirsty seeks the water-spring. I found one. He alone watched while all around him slept, he alone kept and tended the secret flame; he has ever since remained my friend. His love of country, his devotion to the cause of liberty, has ever remained constant, fervent and strong. This man is Giuseppe Mazzini – my friend and teacher.[26]

On hearing these generous words Mazzini was overcome with emotion and could only murmur in reply, 'È troppo' as he grasped the General's hand. The Queen, however, when she read the report in the *Globe* was horrified, and immediately wrote to Lord Granville to complain sardonically that the Government's object of keeping Garibaldi out of dangerous hands had 'hardly been obtained'.[27]

Nor, she believed, could it be said that his behaviour with her Ministers had been discreet. He had told Lord Russell that he thought the Emperor Napoleon 'would finally be at war with England', and that since he 'admired England beyond all countries in the world', his sword-arm and those of his friends would accordingly be at her service. And he had, with a sudden and alarming display of passion, told Palmerston, when warned that revolution in Venice should be delayed, that it was 'never too soon to break the chains of slaves anywhere'.[28]

The Queen was, therefore, profoundly relieved when she was told that on 18 April Garibaldi was not, after all, to visit the numerous provincial towns whose invitations had been accepted, but that he was instead being taken home to Caprera in the Duke of Sutherland's yacht. She was informed by Palmerston that those who had 'taken an interest about him, and especially Lord Shaftesbury, thought that politically, and with regard to his health, it was very desirable that these visits should not be made. Mr. Ferguson, the surgeon, upon being consulted, gave a written opinion that the exertions of mind and body, which such visits would involve, would be more than the General in his weak state of health could bear'.[29]

The news that Garibaldi was to return to Italy almost at once raised a storm of protest in the country. It was widely accepted that his health was being used merely as an excuse to get rid of him, that the Government had put pressure to bear on him to go, that the Emperor Napoleon and other foreign rulers had protested against his reception and conduct. The Working Men's Reception Committee, in a widely quoted announcement, protested that 'General Garibaldi is in good health, and that the cause of his intended departure is not illness but pressure exercised upon him by members and adherents of the Government, and especially by Mr. Gladstone'.*[30]

There were good grounds for these beliefs: in the first place it was

---

* Lord Clarendon was horrified by these allegations and in a letter to *The Times* declared 'in the most solemn manner, and on the word of a gentleman' his 'firm belief' that all the members of the Government were animated by the same 'ardent desire (without reference to anything or anybody but the General himself) to urge that and that only which was indispensable to his personal welfare'. It was the 'General's own and unsuggested decision to give up the provincial journey altogether' – *The Times*, 23 April 1864. Lord Clarendon added privately to Gladstone: 'Do not you think that he ought in a letter to some personal friends to state frankly the reasons which have induced him to go? He alone can put a stop to all these mischievous reports. He ought to say that no government, English or foreign, has to do with his departure and that he goes solely because the state of his health does not permit him to fulfil his engagements.' – John Morley, *The Life of William Ewart Gladstone* (London 1903), ii, 113.

quite true that there was far from general agreement amongst the doctors who examined Garibaldi that he was unfit to carry on with his tour, his own Italian doctor insisting that he was perfectly capable of it. It was also true that there had been diplomatic protests about the visit from all over Europe – from France where Louis Napoleon was aghast at Garibaldi's publicised visit to Louis Blanc, from Prussia where, as Crown Princess Victoria told her mother, the shock of his reception in London was very great and where 'the very mention of his name' was greeted with horror and indignation',[31] and from Italy, itself, where as Henry Elliot said the 'extreme irritation and annoyance was hopeless to try to appease'. In Italy, indeed, all the ills of the moment – from the Opposition victories in the by-election to the closure of several universities due to the rioting of students against new examination regulations – were attributed to the English demonstrations. And the Italian Ambassador in London was instructed to show his categoric disapproval of the reception – a reception which was, in fact, boycotted by every other ambassador with the exceptions of those of the United States and Turkey; and which, Odo Russell said,[32] offended everybody in Rome.

Then there were protests from the English Roman Catholics. Archbishop Manning in an open letter to Edward Cardwell, M.P., expressed his dismay that the Archbishop of Canterbury should have attended a reception in honour of a 'representative of the Socialist revolution in Italy', of an advocate of 'theories which I need not describe'.[33] Protestant organisations, too, found cause for complaint about Garibaldi's 'attenuated belief', a fault that Gladstone himself could not but lament.

When Gladstone was asked to suggest to the General that his provincial tour of nearly fifty towns might well be curtailed to about six of the largest, it was understandable that people supposed he had suggested much more than this.

And Garibaldi himself believed that Gladstone had at least meant much more, and intimated to a friend that the implication was that he was no longer welcome. Gladstone had not intended to make this implication so plain, but he had been somewhat embarrassed by his delicate task; he had endeavoured to express himself in a round-about way so as to spare the General's feelings; and his Italian was, in any case, not up to putting the matter as subtly as he would have wished. Garibaldi said that it would be impossible to decide which provincial visits to make and which to cancel, and that he would, therefore, make none at all. He would go home.

He was, in any case, quite ready now to do so. He had, it seems, already discussed the possibility of an early return to Caprera before his conversation with Gladstone. For on the morning of 16 April he had gone to Ugo Foscolo's tomb at Chiswick with Sir Anthony Panizzi; and, according to Louis Fagan, who accompanied them, it was then that the possibility of Garibaldi's return home was first mentioned.[34] James Stansfeld, Mazzini's friend and defender, who had seen a good deal of Garibaldi in London, was quite sure that the cancellation of the remainder of the tour was Garibaldi's own decision.[35]

He had become bored by long dinners which he did not enjoy, and by long speeches which he did not fully understand; he had come to realise, too, that the political support he had hoped for would not be given him. On his way back from an evening party at the Swan Brewery, Fulham, he had asked George Jacob Holyoake, the secularist radical, how it was that the English people had accorded such enthusiastic receptions to Kossuth and yet appeared to have done nothing on behalf of Hungary.[36] The parallel with his own case seemed striking: a French journalist in the *Courier du Dimanche* had prophesied that Garibaldi would get from the English plenty of '*plum puddings, turtle's soup et sandwiches*' but no money for muskets.[37]

There were other reasons, too, apart from his disillusionment: neither Menotti nor any other members of his suite were happy in England. They had not been invited to many of the receptions and, while the General himself had been generously entertained in London, first of all at Stafford House and then at the Seelys' town house in Prince's Gate, they had been given rooms in a cheap hotel. It was as though everyone in London agreed with the Duke of Sutherland who, according to Lord Granville, liked Garibaldi but thought that the doctor, the secretary and the eldest son were all 'ruffians'.[38]

Perhaps, too, Garibaldi was finding the attentions of his hostesses a little suffocating. The ladies of the Duke of Sutherland's household were, Lord Granville thought, 'temporarily a little out of their minds'.[39] Certainly both Harriet, the Dowager Duchess, and her daughter-in-law Anne, wife of the third Duke, were utterly infatuated with him.

The day before he sailed home in her son-in-law's yacht, the *Ondine*, the dowager Duchess wrote the first of many letters which she addressed to him from Cliveden in her ungrammatical French:*

Dear General and Friend,

Allow me to express all the pain I feel at your departure and the emptiness you have left in my heart! Come back, dear General, and give me the joy of seeing you again. Although I cannot expect that the company of a woman who is no longer young [she was 58] can satisfy you, nevertheless I shall try to divert your attention from other women who still possess the blessings of youth and good health. Thus, I too shall, at least, be able to enjoy your presence. Write to me. With most affectionate greetings.

Your
Harriet Sutherland[40]

Three days before, her daughter-in-law had written the first of her many letters from Stafford House:

My General,

Sadly I see the hour pass when I had hoped to read with you, to speak with you. But you are not coming. I must, therefore, try to express myself in writing. Yesterday evening, when I told you that you would be always in my thoughts, together with those who for me represent all that is most dear and most sacred, your reply hurt me. Did you not understand me, General? Did you not understand, then, that I give you all that I have? – true worship of your glorious life, of your noble deeds, a true and profound affection, rendered holy by the admiration for your very noble character. I could never deceive you, not with a single word. Then give me a little of your affection. The words which you spoke to me this morning are very dear to me.

Anne Sutherland and Cromarty[41]

At the same time Mrs. Seely at Prince's Gate was beginning her correspondence with him on an even more intimate note:

---

* Garibaldi's rather formal replies to some of these letters are preserved at Dunrobin Castle.

Beloved General,

When, alas, you left me yesterday, my heart was full of anguish. I went to take another look at your small bed and, full of emotion at the place where your noble head would not rest again for a long time, I stood contemplating it with a heavy heart when I noticed near the bolster the kerchief which you used. Oh, my dearest General, what a comfort it was to me! I cannot let it out of my sight. It is the grey one which you wore round your neck at Brook House and with which I covered your dear head when it was windy. I had already wanted to have it as a souvenir, but had not dared to ask you for it. Now it is here. Well, tell me that you present it to me.

Your faithful and devoted friend
Mary Seely[42]

The next day she wrote again:

Just one word of affectionate goodbye, dearest and most noble General Garibaldi. Your visit was truly the greatest glory of my life! The hope of seeing your beloved face again in our old England and in my house is my most fervent wish. Beloved General! God bless you and protect you from all danger! May He make you ever victorious and happy.

Your always devoted and affectionate,
Mary Seely[43]

A few days after this letter was written, Garibaldi sailed from Fowey harbour in the *Ondine*. He had gone to Cornwall to spend the last few days of his visit with Colonel Peard who lived at Penquite. But now it was time to return: Mazzini had already pressed him to act against Venice and since then two officers, first a colonel and then a general, had been sent by Victor Emmanuel with confidential messages also urging him once more to arms.

3

'THE SCOURGE OF ITALY'

No sooner had Garibaldi arrived back at Caprera than Victor Emmanuel again involved him in intrigue. One of the two confidential agents who had pressed him to return from London to discuss a new attack on Austria now sailed to Caprera once more to press on him the King's ideas.

Garibaldi himself was prepared to consider them; but he was strongly advised by those of his lieutenants whom he had summoned to a council of war on Ischia – where he had gone ostensibly to take the mud baths for his rheumatism – that the King was merely trying to use him to get one of his sons on a Balkan throne. Victor Emmanuel, disturbed and soured by the General's triumph in England, was, they urged, trying to get him out of the way on an expedition outside Italy without the knowledge of the Government. And, in order to prevent this expedition sailing, one of his friends gave a newspaper enough information to force the King to back quickly away.[1]

In the summer of 1866, however, the King renewed the suggestion that Garibaldi should land in Dalmatia. An opportunity had at last been presented – by Bismarck's determination to assert Prussian domination over Austria – to take Venice into the Italian Kingdom. In expectation of this opportunity, which would at last provide the royal army with the chance to gain something for itself rather than as a gift from Garibaldi or Louis Napoleon, immense amounts of money had been spent on armaments and equipment, so that when Austria offered Venice to Italy as a price for staying out of the war, the Government refused. In the hope that they might not only win Venice, but Trieste and the Tyrol as well, the King and General La Marmora, his new Prime Minister, were determined to fight.

Longing to be allowed an independent command in Dalmatia, to 'throw the firebrand of insurrection' in the Venetian provinces of the Austro-Hungarian Empire, Garibaldi anxiously awaited his summons. But La Marmora delayed approaching him as long as possible.

He did not want an insurrectionary war, any more than he wanted Italy to fight a war whose strategy was dictated by Prussia. Nor did he want – and nor did Cialdini and the rest of the Italian military command want – Garibaldi to be let loose with his volunteers on a separate and uncontrollable expedition. So when Garibaldi was finally called upon to play his part, he was despatched to Salò with orders to advance northwards in the general direction of Trento and the Tyrol, while the regular forces moved against Venetia.

The volunteers were as ill equipped and ill supplied as they had been in 1859, and their numbers included a far higher proportion of adventurers and ruffians who had enlisted for excitement and loot. Though much was achieved in spite of these limitations, their campaign was marked by none of those startling successes with which their leader had made his name. Garibaldi himself was wounded in the thigh early on, and was obliged to conduct the operations for the rest of the month from a carriage. At Bezzecca, helped by his sons Menotti and Ricciotti and his son-in-law Canzio, he scored an important, though minor victory; but soon afterwards, when in sight of Trento, he was ordered to withdraw. For on other fronts the campaign had been disastrous: the regular army had been decisively checked by the Austrians at Custozza, and the navy had been defeated off the island of Lissa. Their allies, the Prussians, however, overwhelmed the Austrians at Königgrätz (Sadowa), and retired from the war leaving Venice to fall into the hands of Victor Emmanuel and to become, at last, a part of united Italy.

But Rome, the 'symbol of United Italy', still remained outside the union. And Garibaldi could not get it off his mind. During the rest of that year, 1866, he was ill and often in bed, for the wound in his foot had opened up again, compelling him once more to use crutches to get about the house. He was, as he told Mme Schwartz, 'nailed here by my dreadful rheumatism'. Obsessed by the thought that Italy had been disgraced at Custozza and Lissa and by the terms of the peace – Austria had refused to cede Venice directly to the country she had defeated and had handed it to Louis Napoleon who presented it 'like second-hand goods' to Italy – Garibaldi was also disheartened once again by the Italian peasants who had shown no inclination to help the volunteers against the Austrians in the recent campaign. He was determined that the seizure of Rome must be done in so gallant a way, and by such gallant Italians, that the stain of dishonour would be washed away.

Early in 1867 he returned to the mainland, renewing his demands for national action, storming against the priests, the 'scourge of Italy', and against the Papacy, 'the negation of God', rousing the enthusiasm of the people and persuading himself once again that they would follow him to death. He believed that the equivocal hints of the Government betokened their support, and that their denials of responsibility were intended only for the ears of foreign diplomats and Frenchmen.[2]

Once again the Government felt obliged to arrest him; for the French troops, under the terms of the '*Convenzione di settembre*', had now withdrawn from Rome on the understanding that Italy would recognise and protect the Pope's sovereignty. The General was escorted back to Caprera.

★   ★   ★

The Government, however, continued to give the volunteers their secret support, and Garibaldi deputed his son, Menotti, their leader. At the beginning of October several parties of volunteers crossed over the Papal frontier, but met with such little enthusiasm on the part of the Romans that Garibaldi decided he must leave Caprera to lead the invasion himself.* And so on 14 October, with his beard dyed black, he managed to evade the warships which lay at anchor off Caprera, and in a punt he slipped away first of all to Mrs. Collins's house on La Maddalena and then, with Giovanni Basso, to Sardinia where his son-in-law Canzio was waiting for him with a fishing smack.

By 20 October he was in Florence, since the 'September Convention' the new capital of Italy, and for two days he remained there, making speeches and arousing the enthusiasm of the people for a march across the Roman frontier.[3] The King, alarmed by the reaction of the French and concerned that the Government were entirely losing control of the situation, demanded that Garibaldi should be openly denounced, and gave orders for his arrest. Rattazzi, now Prime Minister again, resigned. Cialdini was asked to take his place, but said

---

* 'Rome', Ferdinand Gregorovius wrote in his journal on 13 October, 'remains entirely quiet' – *The Roman Journals of Ferdinand Gregorovius, 1852–1874* (ed. Friedrich Althaus. Trans. Mrs. Gustavus W. Hamilton, London, 1907), 293.

that no government which failed to come to terms with Garibaldi could hope to last. Eventually another General, Menebrea, was persuaded to take office.[4]

Leaving the military men and the politicians arguing behind him, Garibaldi marched. Nearly all his old officers and his friends tried to dissuade him;[5] but, encouraged to believe that all he had to do was to 'fire a few musket shots even in the air' and the Italian army would be with him,[6] he launched his attack, pushing past the papal forces at Monterotondo. His march, though, had been made too late. Louis Napoleon, given due warning of his intentions, had sent a strong French force back to Civitavecchia. Mazzini warned Garibaldi of his danger, and advised him to retire towards Naples and await a more favourable opportunity. But Garibaldi 'obstinately marching to defeat was in no temper to listen to anybody, Mazzini least of all'.[7] And on 3 November he came upon the French army, armed with the new Chassepot-rifle and supported by papal troops, at Mentana.

'Garibaldi commanded his men in person,' the American consul in Rome reported, 'and endeavoured many times to check the retreat of his forces. They could not, however, stand against the greater coolness and steadiness of the advance of the regular troops. . . . It is generally reported in the Italian papers that the pontifical force was defeated and only saved by the presence of the French. This is utterly untrue.'[8]

There could be no doubt, though, that Garibaldi's ultimate defeat was overwhelming. His army suffered heavy casualties, lost 1,600 men as prisoners, and was driven back in confusion across the frontier.

Garibaldi was himself arrested for the last time, protesting in vain as the police pulled him out of the special train he had ordered to take him back to the coast, that the King and the politicians had encouraged him to attack Rome and then abandoned him.* He

---

* He had certainly been misled not only as to the real attitude of the King and the Government, but as to the willingness of the Romans to support him. 'In fact,' the American consul in Rome reported, 'their unwillingness cannot be questioned.' The action had been 'deprecated by all persons in Rome of whatever political opinion they might be'. And in the countryside the people 'without exception expressed themselves in favour of the existing government, generally giving as a

was taken first to Varignano and then escorted back to Caprera.⁹*

reason, however, that should the Italian Government take possession their taxes would be more than doubled. I can bear witness to the cordial welcome the papal troops received in every town that they entered. Though from my observation of the Italian people, I should say it was quite possible that Garibaldians were received with equal enthusiasm'. – Howard H. Marraro, 'Unpublished Documents on Garibaldi's March on Rome in 1867' in *The Journal of Modern History* (June 1944), xvi, 2 – Document 2.

* 'I have heard both from French and Pontifical officers,' Odo Russell told Lord Stanley, 'that the Garibaldians at Mentana stood the *chassepôts*, field pieces and grapeshot so well and fought so bravely that many of the 615 killed were found to be also covered with bayonet wounds. General Kanzler told me that he had offered the prisoners their freedom if they would sign an engagement never to take up arms against the Pope, but one and all had refused to accept their liberty on that condition'. – Noel Blakiston (ed.) *The Roman Question: Extracts from the despatches of Odo Russell from Rome, 1858–1870* (Chapman and Hall, 1962), 347.

4

CAPRERA

Garibaldi looked an old man now. He was pale and thin, his face lined with pain and disappointment, and his hair and beard were almost white. He felt bitter and betrayed, resentful towards the politicians and the Court, the French, the Church, the Italian Army and Mazzini, whom he blamed unjustly for the desertion from his force before the battle of Mentana, denying now that the man had ever been his master.[1]

'In great need of money,' as he put it, he settled down to write a novel, holding the pen with difficulty in his stiff fingers and on some days unable to grasp it at all.

It was a distressingly bad book. Even though the name of its author would have ensured it some sort of success, nineteen publishers declined it.[2] Flattered, however, by some of his hangers-on into believing that the book had great merits and persuaded that the publishers were unresponsive fools, he persevered until the book was published – in Italian as *Clelia*, and in English and German as the *Rule of the Monk*. Recording the adventures of eight noble-minded lovers who end their lives at Mentana, it was described by one much quoted reviewer as 'almost more pitiable than absurd'.[3] Followed by two others, *Cantoni il volontario* and *I Mille* – both of them to some extent autobiographical and neither of them translated into English – it presented its ecclesiastical characters as villains of the most horrendous evil; and it was, indeed, by putting such characters in this and his other novels, that he hoped his attacks on the Church (now the declared enemy of nationalism and liberalism) would reach a wider public.

Some of his more honest friends had begged him not to publish *Clelia*, and Mme Schwartz had decided when she read the manuscript that she must go to Caprera to dissuade him.

She arrived in July 1868, and found a curious menage – Battistina with her daughter Anita, now an unruly girl of nine, another young peasant woman, Francesca Armosino, and a pale, rather plain baby, who was called Clelia.

Francesca Armosino had come to the island two years before with Garibaldi's daughter Teresa. She had had an illegitimate child by a soldier and was then employed as a wet-nurse for Teresa's baby. Mme Schwartz described her as a 'rough-looking woman',[4] and certainly in her photograph she appears to have been peculiarly ill-favoured, with strong, coarse features, broad and flat. But Garibaldi had always been attracted by women of this sort. Clelia was their child.

Clelia's half-sister, Anita, had only recently arrived with her mother from Nice where they had been living on an allowance provided by her father. The allowance, the mother protested, was not enough and she had come to Caprera to ask Garibaldi to increase it. For some time Garibaldi had been hoping that Mme Schwartz would adopt Anita, take her away from her mother whom he described as a 'wicked woman', and give her a good education. The idea had originally come from Mme Schwartz, but Garibaldi had agreed to it and had asked Mme Schwartz to go to Nice to talk to Battistina. The mother had, on that occasion, refused to part with her child; and so Garibaldi now brought up the subject again.

He told Battistina that he could not increase her allowance, that indeed the time had come for Anita to be properly educated under Mme Schwartz's care, and that he would therefore be obliged to halve it. The poor mother burst into tears, 'rushed headlong from the room in which, with closed doors and windows, and candles lit, sentence had been passed upon her. Going straight away to bed, she refused all food, said she was ill and rejected all attempts to console her.'[5]

Eventually, she was persuaded to leave the island on Mme Schwartz's promising that she would make up the allowance to its original amount, would treat Anita as if she were her own daughter and would bring her to visit her in Nice. But when Anita saw her mother go, she threw herself to the ground 'like a mad girl', and a few days later when Mme Schwartz left (having failed to persuade Garibaldi not to try to get his novel published), the distraught Anita became hysterical again, throwing herself on the deck of the steamer and later hitting her new guardian who was by now more than ever convinced that the girl needed the discipline of a strict school.

This discipline, she felt sure, Garibaldi was incapable of giving her. He was – and 'many instances of this' were known to her – extremely weak with his children. And soon after she had placed the difficult Anita in a school at Winterthur in Switzerland, she was given fresh evidence of this 'weakness'. She received a letter from the General enclosing one for his daughter, a far too indulgent one, Mme Schwartz decided, for so unruly a child. He wrote to say that he was satisfied with the conduct of his 'Anita amatissima', knew that she was obedient and doing all she could to spare Mme Schwartz the least anxiety. 'I hope to have good news and reports from the school in which you are placed,' he concluded, 'and I will send you a present if I learn that your behaviour is worthy of your name. Your affectionate father, G. Garibaldi.'[6]

It was a short letter, for his personal letters were nearly always short and, in any case, he was busy with his novels. He spent weeks on end at his desk writing slowly when his hand was stiff, and hobbling about in the garden when he could not write at all. He had come to realise as well as anyone, he said, that his romantic works were 'worthless'.[7] But they were written only for the money. He had tried to support his family by selling the blocks of granite with which the island abounded, but the cost of cutting and transporting them exceeded the price paid for them. He had sold the yacht that the English had given him, but the agent's enormous profit had accounted for most of the proceeds. He had accepted another gift from his English admirers – the purchase price of Mrs. Collins's land and of the remaining small strips which made up the other half of Caprera.*

* Mrs. Collins, whose cantankerous husband had now died, had written to Julie Salis Schwabe, a German-born woman who had married a Manchester banker and become a naturalised Englishwoman. She asked Mrs. Schwabe if she knew of anyone willing to buy her land on Caprera which she had decided to sell for £1,400. She was thinking presumably of Garibaldi of whom Julie Schwabe was a devoted admirer. Mrs. Schwabe got in touch with Mrs. Roberts and between them they collected the money from others of the General's friends in twenty donations. The Duke of Sutherland offered to put up the whole sum, but the General, as Mrs. Schwabe said, 'dare not offend some of the vulgar minds around him who would charge him with leaning towards aristocracy and all sorts of things if he accepted such a gift from a Duke'. So the Duke put up £300, in contributions of £100 each from himself, his wife and his mother. The whole transaction, as Mrs. Roberts said, was '*kept perfectly quiet*'. – *Italia, e Inghilterra nella prima fase del Risorgimento* (ed. Emilia Morelli, *Pubblicazioni dell Istituto Italiano di Cultura di Londra*, 1952), 429–35.

But he had found his new property no more profitable than the old. The quiet months spent in hard, dispiriting work, passed slowly. And then in 1870, France declared war on Prussia, and the old General was soon to feel once more the call to arms.

★   ★   ★

By the time the battle of Sedan had deprived Louis Napoleon of his empire, nearly all the French troops had been withdrawn from Rome in a vain attempt to avert the catastrophic defeat. And on 3 November 1870 Victor Emmanuel's troops entered the Holy City, and Italy was unified at last.*

Both Bixio and Cosenz were there as generals in the regular army; but care had been taken to keep Garibaldi out of the way. He was held back, as he complained to his son-in-law, a 'prisoner on Caprera'. And the long-awaited event did not, in any case, greatly excite him when he was told of it: he had not taken part in it, he had not fought.

His fighting days, however, were not over yet. At the beginning of the Franco-Prussian War he had spoken of his enthusiasm for the 'noble Germanic nation at last rewarding Napoleon for all his villainies'. But now that the detested Emperor, that 'execrable tyrant', had been overthrown, and the new French Republic had bravely rejected the Prussian terms for a humiliating peace, his sympathies changed. He offered his services to the Republic, believing that 'individual liberty, the liberty of the nation, the France of 1789 are in peril'; and he urged that it was 'Italy's duty to fly to the assistance of France now that Napoleon no longer dishonours her'.[8] The gesture was highly characteristic. It was not only that France, so decisively beaten at Sedan, had aroused his compassion for the downcast; it was not only that he believed all that he read of Prussian atrocities; that he felt forgotten and cut off from Italian life and from the world at Caprera; that he felt a need to indulge his

---

* Italy transferred her capital to Rome in July 1871. The King established his court at the Quirinal Palace, formerly Pio Nono's summer residence; and in November that year the first complete Italian Parliament was opened in the new capital. The Pope was assured the status of a reigning monarch in the Vatican by the law of Guarantees; and it was not until 1929 that a more satisfactory relationship between the Vatican and the Quirinal was created by the Lateran Pacts.

taste for the dramatic. It was also that he had a clear and uncomplicated vision of the war as a struggle between Republic and Reaction, between Freedom and Oppression.*

The 'Garibaldian chiefs' as Jessie Mario described them, 'were beside themselves with annoyance'. And the French Government, nervous of the reaction of the conservatives and the Catholics, did not show itself as anxious to receive his assistance as he was to fly to it. On 7 November, however, he landed at Marseilles and, although he was at first offered by the embarrassed Gambetta a purely token force, by the end of the month he was in command of an international corps in the Côte d'Or, where a French journalist found him with his 'white beard and pale face looking like a soldier with one foot in the grave'.[9] He could not walk because of his old wound and had to be carried about on a stretcher.

Jessie Mario faithfully joined him at Dijon to offer her help once more in the hospitals, and she 'could not but shudder at the thought of Garibaldi, of both his sons, of Canzio, the father of Teresa's nine children, and the very finest flower of Italian youth trying their strength against that gigantic mass of solid fighting forces silently approaching. Garibaldi's face was stern and grave.'[10]

There were Poles under his command as well as Italians, Englishmen and Americans, Spaniards and Irishmen, and many Frenchmen who wanted to fight for their country but felt disinclined to submit to the more rigorous discipline of army life. The rough-and-ready manners of the entire force, in fact, particularly in regard to the Church, earned them a reputation which their occasional military successes did not ameliorate.

He himself considered the part he took in the Franco-Prussian War as the crowning military achievement of his career. And the Prussian General, Edwin von Manteuffel, praised 'the great speed of

---

* He had never, in fact, been so decidedly Prussophile as the actionist party in general, maintaining reservations, even at the beginning of the war, about the 'masked despotism of the Berlin government'. Both the poet Carducci and Agostino Bertani (who in August 1870 called Germany 'the standard-bearer of progress and civilisation') changed their minds, as he did, once Louis Napoleon had fallen and France once more became the 'France of 1789, the saviour of the human race, the sister nation' – Federico Chabod, *Storia della politica estera italiana dal 1870–1896* (Laterza, Bari, 1951), i, 28–31.

his movements', the wisdom of the dispositions he made when under fire and his 'energy and intensity in attack'. His successes were, admittedly, only partial successes and were not followed up, but 'if General Bourbaki had acted on his advice the campaign of the Vosges would have been one of the most fortunate of the war of 1870–1'.[11]

It was an opinion which another Prussian commander partially endorsed. The Garibaldians, according to the official historian of the operations of General Carl Wilhelm von Werder, successfully restricted the Prussian movements. 'Nothing decisive could be done to destroy this nuisance, the enemy force consisted mostly of flying columns, which, marching only at night, appeared each day at some different point in the line of outposts to surprise patrols and attack small parties.'[12]

The Garibaldians were not so successful when they appeared in the open to offer pitched battle, and once, when encouraged to do so by Ricciotti Garibaldi's spectacular success in surprising a column of 500 reinforcements on their way to the Second Army, they were driven off the field.

But although the operations of Garibaldi, when considered as a whole, furnish a tragic list of efforts wasted and opportunities missed, yet it cannot be denied, as Michael Howard has observed, 'that during the last fortnight of November and the first fortnight of December, he operated against Werder to considerable effect'.[13]

And although it was both tactless and inaccurate of Victor Hugo to suggest that he was the only general on the French side not to be defeated in the war, Garibaldi could at least go home safe in the knowledge that, despite his age and his infirmities, he had not disgraced himself.

*   *   *

He returned to Caprera from this his last campaign at the end of 1871. The homecoming was a sad one. His daughter Rosa, born to Francesca Armosino the year before the war, had died while he was away, and her 'angel remains' lay buried under a juniper tree. He missed her very much. She was like the first Rosa who had died so many years ago in Montevideo. 'Of the *piccine*,' as he called them, there remained only Clelia now. She had a 'good heart' but otherwise she was 'like Anita'. 'These two children,' he told Mme Schwartz, 'are very far from rivalling the two Rosas.'[14]

To forget his sorrow he turned with renewed energy to his work. There were his memoirs to re-write; and he was anxious to finish them before his hand failed him altogether, and before his memory, which was never good, grew even less reliable. There was also an ever-increasing correspondence, for now that his days of action were finally over, he was interesting himself in a score of different subjects from the Socialist International and the International Court of Justice, to trade unions, female education and the abolition of capital punishment, from the extension of the franchise (still limited to less than 3 per cent. of the population) to a scheme to divert the course of the Tiber and drain the swamps of the Campagna.

He rarely left Caprera; and although he had been elected to seven out of the eight Parliaments since 1860 he hardly ever took his seat, preferring to send messages to be read out by some other Deputy. The messages were often didactic and sometimes majestically arrogant, for, living so much cut off from any outside influences other than those of his admiring companions, he had long since grown to believe not only in his own legend but in the significance of his own opinions. And sometimes, it had to be admitted, these opinions were not insignificant, for all the ridicule that his less honest and generous critics heaped upon them.

His idealistic, romantic socialism, his belief that people must be loved before they could be ruled, his supposition that the fulfilment of nationalist ambitions in Europe would be followed by a federal union, his persistent advocacy of a benevolent dictatorship to replace for a time the corruption of self-seeking politicians and ineffectual parliaments, were all seen as typical Garibaldian fantasies. But there was also seen to be much sound sense in what he wrote about the neglect of Sardinia and the South, the problems of social reform and education, the causes and cures of brigandage and the plight of the starving poor, the vast sums squandered on colonisation and armaments instead of on the internal needs of Italy.

His views were often muddled and contradictory, of course, often clouded by regrets that the unification of Italy had cured so few of the evils he had expected it to cure. They were often conditioned, too, by the personal and deeply resented rebuffs and disappointments of his later career, by fierce prejudices, by recurrent pain and illness, so that he frequently expressed himself in the form of invective, both virulent and unjust. Elections, newspapers, the army, the rich, the freemasons (of whom he had once been Grand-Master), the Papacy (of which his detestation increased with the years), Mazzini (of whom he now wrote as 'a hindrance to the cause of Italy'), even the monarchy, were all attacked and vilified.

Yet he remained in private life, as he had always been, gentle, courteous and lovable. There was sometimes a hint perhaps that his vision of himself as a man of destiny, the conscience of Italy, the prophet of a new religion, had impaired the simplicity and modesty of his character. He could never see how tasteless, how incongruous and how absurd were those lurid prints of him that depicted his Messianic features on the walls of so many poor homes – blessing the faithful, suffering on the cross, ascending to heaven, his ver-milion shirt bulging against the azure sky. He never tired of reading about himself, of receiving idolatrous letters and enclosing in his reply a whisp of hair, a button, a piece of red thread. But then he could never see a joke, and that after all was part of his strength.

He was not, and he admitted with pride that he was not, a clever man. He was more inclined to be ruled by instinct than by reasoning. He saw problems starkly without gradations of emphasis. But this very lack of *chiaroscuro* in his vision, this certainty unclouded by doubt, had always been the main source of his power and of his influence. And he was never in any sense arrogant at home.

Washing his children under the pump to make sure they were as clean as he always was, cutting his big strong Tuscan cigars in two and smoking them half at a time, putting honey in his coffee to save the price of sugar, eating raw shrimps at a table where a newspaper served as a cloth, tidily patching and mending his clothes, he remained quite artlessly unaffected.

The Press had always made much of his poverty, and offers of loans and gifts had reached him in such numbers that he had felt compelled to refuse them in a public letter: 'I have never been poor because I have always known how to cut my coat according to my cloth. During my sojourn in the South American republics I possessed only one shirt on and one shirt off which I kept under my saddle, just like when I was Dictator of the Two Sicilies. . . . I have now enough and to spare, so I decline any further offerings, especially from working men's societies. Their sympathy makes me proud, but they are more in want than I am.'[15]

Similarly he had refused to accept a pension and a capital sum voted him by the Assembly, telling Menotti that he would not be able to sleep if he accepted it, that he would have to cover his face with shame every time he heard of 'government depredations and public misery'.[16] And once when Nicola Fabrizi persuaded General Cialdini to offer Garibaldi the pay he would have received had he not thrown away his General's commission in Naples in 1860, he indignantly refused the offer, maintaining vehemently that he was not like Cialdini 'a general of the army and one who lives on the blood of the people'.[17]

But now when a new leftist Government offered to help him again he felt bound to accept, for he was heavily in debt to the Bank of Naples to which he had guaranteed a loan for Menotti. Protesting to the end, he finally gave in, and Jessie Mario found him looking 'pale and agitated' after the decision had at last been taken.

'I never thought,' he said to her as though he had been utterly disgraced, 'that I should be reduced to the state of a pensioner.'[18]

As soon as the money arrived he seemed anxious to be rid of it, immediately paying off the Bank loan and his debts, settling sums on Francesca and the children, and then lending most of the rest to his friend Luigi Orlando whose Leghorn shipbuilding firm was facing bankruptcy.

*   *   *

The Government had saved itself and the old General the disgrace of his own bankruptcy. But there were other worries, other tragedies.

One day he had a pathetic letter from Anita, the envelope simply addressed 'Garibaldi'. She begged him to take her home. She was sixteen now, and was living with Mme Schwartz in Crete where she was desperately unhappy. Her father sent Menotti to bring her back to Caprera where she arrived 'well and already a woman but with a bigger load of lice' than her father had 'ever seen on any human creature'. Francesca 'has begun combing her,' Garibaldi added in a letter to Mme Schwartz which she did not choose to reproduce in her published collection, 'and hopes that a month of daily cleaning will free the girl from her unwelcome guests.'[19]

Anita was not to enjoy her newly-found liberty for long. Two months after her return to Caprera she was playing with Clelia by the sea one morning when she suddeny felt ill; that afternoon she was lying feverish on her bed. She had contracted meningitis; and she did not recover.

For her father it seemed a time of death. Mazzini had already died; and Garibaldi had sent a telegram to Genoa, 'Let the flag of The Thousand be unfurled above the bier of the *grande Italiano'*.[20] As Jessie Mario said, it was the highest honour that he could pay – to no one else did he pay it.[21] Massimo d'Azeglio also was dead, and La Farina and Manin and Sterbini, Brofferio, Farini and Rattazzi, Cardinal Antonelli, Manzoni and Dumas, Oudinot and Louis Napoleon. In 1878 King Victor Emmanuel died, and Pio Nono, La Marmora and Pallavicino

Garibaldi himself lived on, stiff and tired and pale, intermittently in pain from his rheumatism and his wounds, eating little, pushing himself slowly about in an iron wheelchair; worrying about Italy, about the problems of the South, *la questione meridionale*, that the events of 1860 had bequeathed to United Italy. He could move his arms and legs now only with the greatest difficulty, but he had a bath often, as he had always done – more often than his doctor thought he should – and he was still as proud as ever of his long hair, now quite white, which Francesca Armosino carefully and dutifully brushed for him.

He had married Francesca at last. After twenty years he had managed to obtain a divorce from Giuseppina Raimondi on the grounds that the contract had been made under Austrian law which permitted divorce in cases of non-consummation. And so, before he died, Garibaldi could legitimise Clelia, and an adored little boy, Manlio, born in 1873.*

The marriage took place on 26 January 1880. It seemed to make him very happy. He sat in his chair smiling cheerfully, dressed as

---

* Manlio, a handsome young man of great promise, died at the age of twenty-seven. He was a lieutenant in the Navy. Clelia, who did not marry, died in her father's house at Caprera (now a museum) in 1959, a fortnight before her ninety-second birthday. Both Menotti (1840–1903) and Ricciotti (1847–1924) became generals, as did Teresa's husband, Stefano Canzio, and between them they provided Garibaldi with twenty-three grandchildren.

always in his white poncho with a red handkerchief round his neck, and on his head one of those round hand-embroidered caps that Mme Schwartz used to send him every year.

Francesca, proud and swarthy, was dressed in white. She had made him a good companion. It had not mattered that she was a simple peasant woman without grace or beauty or conversation, for he had never liked to think of himself as other than a simple man. His marriage certificate described him simply as '*Giuseppe Garibaldi, agricoltore*'. It was the description he had long preferred. And that was all he was now.

The smouldering passion was spent. It was as though the writing of his memoirs, the recollections of past insults, the resurrection of old resentments, had damped the fires within him.

* * *

Francesca moved his bed nearer the window so that he could look out towards the sea. It was a high bed with long black iron legs, and for hours on end he would lie on it, with the mosquito net drawn back, leaning on a pile of pillows, watching the rolling of the waves.

At the end of May 1882 he lay there, and felt the life draining out of him at last. He was seventy-four. He was suffering from bronchial catarrh and found it difficult to breathe, and an effort to talk. But when on the afternoon of 2 June two finches came fluttering on to the balcony, and the people in the room went towards the open window as though to drive them away for fear they would disturb him, he said, 'Let them stay there, perhaps they are the spirits of my two baby daughters come to take me away'.[22]

Beyond the balcony he caught sight of a steamboat and he asked if it was bound for Sicily. They told him that it was and he smiled. It was a hot afternoon, they remembered, with a gentle wind fluttering the muslin curtains. He passed his hand across his forehead and murmured, 'I am sweating'.

He asked for Manlio. But before the little boy came into the room, his father had died.[23]

* * *

Garibaldi had expressed a wish to be burned, not cremated. He hated the idea of being 'put into one of those ovens'. He wanted to be burned in the open air as Shelley had been.

'Tell me the exact story of your poet's fire-burial,' he had once asked Jessie Mario. And when she had finished, he said, 'That is the right way. It is a beautiful and healthy thing, too.' And then he had added as a last bitter comment on those whom he had attacked for so long, 'Only the priests oppose it. It hurts their trade.'[24]

He gave careful instructions to a friend: 'Make a fire of acacia – it burns like oil – and put me in my red shirt, my face upturned to the sun. When my body is burned put the ashes into an urn – any pot will do – and place it on the wall behind the tombs of Anita and Rosa. I mean to finish so.'[25] He had confirmed these instructions in his will, telling his wife not to let anyone on the mainland know that he was dead until she had carried out his wishes. And he had added a characteristic afterthought: 'You will need a lot of wood.'

But he did not finish so. There were protests from those who 'revolted at the thought that the body of their Duce should be burned and his ashes mixed with firewood' – he ought, they said, to be embalmed and buried on the Janiculum, or at least in the Pantheon. There were protests, too, from those who were nervous of offending the Government or the local officials, or the Church. Only the obedient and loyal Francesca urged that the wishes of her husband should be carried out just as he had ordered; but she was disregarded.[26]

So Garibaldi was buried, solemnly and ritually, near his house, in the presence of representatives of the Royal Family, of the Government and the Army, of numerous deputies and officials, and members of the diplomatic corps. And as though in protest at this violation of his wishes, the sky darkened when his body was lowered into the earth, and a strong wind came up, lifting the white dust from the leaves of the olive trees. Then, suddenly and blindingly, the rain poured down; and a vast block of granite, which was later laid over his grave, cracked and broke.[27]

REFERENCES

For full titles see Sources

References are given to the page numbers of English translations of Italian books where these translations are available. I have not, however, always followed exactly the version of the translator. And for their assistance in providing the new translations or in helping me to translate books not available in English I am grateful to Miss Jane Carroll, Miss Geraldine Ranson, and Signorina Maria Bianchi.

PART I

1 *'Apostles of a New Religion'*
Pages 3–16

1. *Memorie nella redazione definitiva*, 30–229; *Memoirs* (Werner), i, 92, 30–38.
2. John Morley, *Life of Gladstone* (London, 1903), ii, 110.
3. *Memoirs* (Werner), i, 297, 3, 16; ii, 304.
4. Sacerdote, i, 47; *Memorie in una delle redazioni anteriori alla definitiva*, 6–7; Parris, 14; Guerzoni, i, 13–15.
5. *Memoirs* (Werner), i, 10.
6. Sacerdote, i, 51; Mack Smith, *Garibaldi*, 5, 7; Guerzoni, i, 19; Fratta, 11–12.
7. *Memorie nella redazione definitiva*, 23–24.
8. *Memoirs* (Dumas), 39.
9. *Memorie nella redazione definitiva*, 27.
10. Harold Nicolson, *Congress of Vienna* (Constable, 1946), 37.
11. Collins, 279.
12. Galvani, *Francesco IV* (Modena, 1847), iii, 194, q. King, *Italian Unity*, i, 18.
13. Hales, *Mazzini*, 218–20.
14. Salvemini, *Mazzini*, 158.
15. King, *Mazzini*, 156.

16. Salvemini, *Mazzini*, 159.
17. Letter to Sismondi, 5 Nov. 1832, q. Salvemini, 126; Salvemini, *Scritti*, 214.
18. Hobsbawm, 120, 132.
19. Collins, 283.
20. Hobsbawm, 132.
21. Salvemini, 13.
22. Mazzini, *Life and Writings*, v, 259, 319, 343.
23. Guerzoni, i, 40–41; Sacerdote, i, 77.

2   *'An eagle hovering in the upper heights'*
Pages 17–23

1. *Memoirs* (Dumas), 39.
2. *Epistolario* (Ximenes), i, 3.
3. Mario, *Supplement*, 42.
4. *Memoirs* (Dumas), 51.
5. *Memoirs* (Werner), ii, 23.
6. *Ibid.*, i, 87.
7. *Ibid.*, i, 92.
8. *Ibid.*, i, 78.
9. Mario, *Supplement*, 449.
10. *Memorie in una delle redazione anteriori alla definitiva*, 45–46; *Memoirs* (Werner), 79.
11. *Memoirs* (Dumas), 89.
12. Annita Italia Garibaldi, *Garibaldi en America, Anita Garibaldi;* Giacomo Emilio Curàtulo, *Anita Garibaldi;* Giuseppe Bandi, *Anita Garibaldi, passim.*
13. *Memoirs* (Werner), 129.
14. Mario, *Supplement*, 52.
15. Winnington-Ingram, 93; Sacerdote, i, 226–227; Guerzoni, i, 179–81.
16. *Memoirs* (Werner), i, 239.
17. For Garibaldi's campaigns in America see Sacerdote, i, 98–265; *Garibaldi condottiero*, 11–59; Guerzoni, i, 50–213; and Candido, *Garibaldi: Corsaro riograndense*, 3–153.

3   *'A Man of Destiny'*
Pages 24–44

1. Nielsen, ii, 99.

2. Farini, i, 143 *et seq.*; King, *Italian Unity*, i, 72–85; Collins, 283–8; Nielsen, ii, 90–104.

3. Nielsen, ii, 106; King, *op. cit.*, i, 170.

4. Nielsen, ii, 107–108, 110; Hales, *Pio Nono*, 18–19.

5. Hales, *Pio Nono*, 21.

6. Nielsen, ii, 110.

7. *Ibid.*, i, 136; Constantin de Grunwald, *La vie de Metternich* (Paris, 1938), 304–6.

8. Mazzini, *Scritti edite ed inedite* (E.N., xxxvi), 35.

9. Garibaldi, i, *Scritti e discorsi*, 82–85.

10. Hales, *Pio Nono*, 63.

11. *Memoirs* (Werner), i, 261; Sacerdote, i, 308; Guerzoni, i, 215–17.

12. *Memoirs* (Dumas), 202; Sacerdote, i, 313–15.

13. *Memoirs* (Werner), i, 267.

14. Guerzoni, i, 169.

15. Cavaciocchi, 87; Trevelyan (1), 50.

16. *Memoirs* (Dumas), 203.

17. *Scritti e discorsi*, i, 90–92.

18. *Geschichte Frankreichs von der Thronbesteigung Louis Philipps bis zum Fall Napoleon III*, (1879), iii, q. Berkeley, 392.

19. Sforza, 13.

20. *Ibid.*, 15.

21. *Scritti e discorsi*, i, 99–101.

22. *Memoirs* (Werner), i, 274, 293.

23. Farini, ii, 105–12.

24. Berkeley, 395, 396.

25. Spellanzon, *Storia del Risorgimento*, v, 942–4; Nielsen, 157–60; Berkeley, 430–3; Hales, *Pio Nono*, 89–91; De Liedekerke, 117.

26. Nielsen, 165.

27. *Memorie in una delle redazioni anteriori alla definitiva*, 177.

28. Ossoli, iii, 186.

29. Hoffstetter, 333.

30. Conti, 53; Farini, iii, 53.

31. Mazzini, *Life and Writings*, v, 33–34.

32. *Ibid.*, 143–4.

33. Martinengo Cesaresco, *Liberation of Italy*, 132.

34. Mazzini, *Life and Writings*, v, 194.
35. Salvemini, *Mazzini*, 78–79, 83.
36. Farini, iii, 305–6.
37. Ossoli, iii, 209.
38. Vaillant, 34.
39. Farini, iv, 3.

4   *The Siege of Rome*
    Pages 45–70

1. Trevelyan (1), 119.
2. Mazzini, *Life and Writings*, v, 201.
3. *Ibid.*, v, 200–2.
4. *The Times*, 11 May 1849.
5. Trevelyan (1), 109.
6. King, *Mazzini*, 128–33.
7. 'Brani del diario 1849 di S. H. Anthony', in *Italia e Inghilterra nella prima fase del Risorgimento*, entries for 28 April and 3 May 1849.
8. Conti, 125–6.
9. Hales, *Pio Nono*, 115–33; King, *op. cit.*, i, 326–33. For Mazzini's Republic also see Ghisalberti, 'Mazzini e la repubblica dei Romani'; *Roma da Mazzini a Pio IX*, 19–45; and *Rapporti delle cose di Roma* (de Liedekerke); Bonomi; Ovidi; Rodelli, Spada; Gabussi; Griffiths.
10. *The Times*, 12 May, 17 May 1849.
11. Ghisalberti, 'Mazzini e la repubblica di Romani'; Trevelyan (1) 103–4, King, *Italian Unity*, i, 331–2.
12. Farini, iv, 35, 36.
13. Clough, i, 255.
14. Spada, iii, 555–8; Trevelyan (1), 149.
15. Mario, *Supplement*, 95.
16. Pieri, 420; Koelman, i, 248–9.
17. Koelman, ii, 281–4, 345.
18. Loevinson, ii, 192.
19. Koelman, ii, 286.
20. Fuller, 214; Farini, iv, 8–9.
21. Farini, iv, 8–9.
22. Story, 134.
23. *Ibid.*, 152.

24. Dandolo, 195–6.
25. *Ibid.*, 189, 191.
26. *Ibid.*, 196–7.
27. Pieri, 420; *Garibaldi condottiero*, 91–97.
28. Vaillant, 8; Vecchi, *Storia di due anni*, ii, 179; Trevelyan (1), 127.
29. Farini, iv, 17–18.
30. *Ibid.*, iv, 19.
31. Loevinson, i, 163.
32. Pieri, 422; Trevelyan (1), 105–34; *Garibaldi condottiero*, 97–104; Loevinson, i, 163–5; Gaillard, 178; Vecchi, *Storia di due anni*, ii, 193–4; Koelman, ii, 277–92.
33. *Epistolario* (Ximenes), i, 349; ii, 41.
34. James, 154; Clough, i, 255.
35. Ossoli, iii, 211.
36. Mazzini, *Life and Writings*, v, 204.
37. Mario, *Supplement*, 98.
38. *Memoirs* (Werner), ii, 12, 19.
39. Guerzoni, ii, 272.
40. Bourgeois and Clermont, 71.
41. Loevinson, i, 207–8.
42. Pieri, 423.
43. *Ibid.*, 424.
44. Dandolo, 204.
45. *Ibid.*, 205, 207.
46. Farini, iv, 85.
47. Guerzoni, i, 251; Loevinson, ii, 188.
48. Trevelyan (1), 141.
49. Dandolo, 214.
50. *Garibaldi condottiero*, 102.
51. Farini, iv, 51.
52. Morelli, *Tre Profili*, 116, 114–15, 98.
53. Trevelyan (1), 153.
54. Pieri, 424.
55. Dandolo, 205.
56. *Garibaldi condottiero*, 103–4; Trevelyan (1) 154–8; Pieri, 423–5; Loevinson, i, 166–200; Vecchi, ii, 235–7.

57. Pieri, 423; Trevelyan (1), 158.
58. Farini, iv, 52.
59. *Ibid.*, iv, 85.
60. Dandolo, 222.
61. Mario, *Supplement*, 102.
62. *Scritti e discorsi*, i, 128.
63. *Memoirs* (Werner), i, 293.
64. Bourgeois and Clermont, 171; Pisacane, 254-5.
65. *Epistolario* (Ximenes), i, 37.
66. Morelli, *Tre Profili*, 120.
67. Gamberini, 6-10; Trevelyan (1), 164.

5   *The French Attack*
Pages 71-80

1. Hoffstetter, 120-1; Trevelyan (1), 179-80.
2. Dandolo, 243-50.
3. Pieri, 427-30; *Garibaldi condottiero*, 104-11; Trevelyan (1), 167-87; Sacerdote, i, 361-5; Loevinson, i, 224-30; Vecchi, ii, 260-3; Guerzoni, i, 305-13; Koelman, ii, 328-59; Gaillard, 241-2.
4. Dandolo, 235.
5. Pisacane, 258.
6. Loevinson, i, 230.
7. Clough, i, 256.
8. Fuller, iii, 207.
9. Story, 167.
10. Trevelyan (1), 191-2.
11. Mazzini, *Life and Writings*, v, 403-4.

6   *The Fall of Rome*
Pages 81-99

1. Guerrazzi, 155.
2. Trevelyan (1), 203.
3. Hoffstetter, 163.
4. Memoirs (Dumas), 261-4; Curàtulo, *Garibaldi e le donne*, 69-70.
5. *Epistolario* (Ximenes), i, 37.
6. Hoffstetter, 241; Trevelyan (1), 208.

7. King, *Mazzini*, 200.
8. *Memoirs* (Werner), ii, 244.
9. *Ibid.*, ii, 284.
10. King, *Mazzini*, 200.
11. John, Viscount Morley, *Recollections* (1918), i, 80.
12. Farini, iv, 209–10.
13. *Ibid.*, iv, 188.
14. Dandolo, 257.
15. *Ibid.*, 257.
16. Fuller, iii, 211–12.
17. *Ibid.*, 216, 218.
18. Clough, i, 256, 262.
19. *Ibid.*, i, 262–3.
20. Trevelyan (1), 196.
21. Hoffstetter, 192.
22. Morelli, *Tre Profili*, 125.
23. Hoffstetter, 200–1.
24. Dandolo, 269.
25. *Ibid.*, 276–7.
26. Vecchi, ii, 295; Dandolo, 267.
27. Sacerdote, i, 379; Loevinson, i, 263–7; Vecchi, ii, 296.
28. Koelman, ii, 451–3.
29. Sacerdote, i, 381; Loevinson, i, 268; *Scritti e discorsi*, i, 147.
30. Gabussi, iii, 468.
31. Mazzini, *Life and Writings*, v, 207.
32. King, *Mazzini*, 137; Mazzini, *Life and Writings*, 214.
33. Ossoli, iii, 216–17.
34. Clough, i, 265.
35. *The Times*, 17 July 1849.
36. Clough, i, 266.
37. Farini, iv, 242.
38. Clough, i, 267.
39. Bittard des Portes, 423.
40. Hoffstetter, 307; Koelman, ii, 455–7.
41. *The Times*, 17 May, 10 July 1849; Trevelyan (1), 237.

7 *The Retreat to San Marino*
Pages 100–109

1. Mario, *Supplement*, 114.
2. *Memoirs* (Werner), ii, 23.
3. Hoffstetter, 333, 365.
4. Sacerdote, i, 394; Trevelyan (1), 275; Belluzzi, 177; Franciosi, 54–55.
5. *Scritti e discorsi*, i, 150.
6. Franciosi, 55.
7. Sacerdote, i, 397; Trevelyan (1), 280.
8. *Memorie nella redazione definitiva*, 305–6; Sacerdote, i, 399; Guerzoni, i, 357–9; Belluzzi, 193–205.

8 *The Flight to Portiglione*
Pages 110–120

1. Bonnet, 6–22; Sacerdote, ii, 405–10; Trevelyan (1), 288–97.
2. Sacerdote, ii, 413; Spellanzon, *Garibaldi*, 41–52.
3. Bonnet, 24–36; Trevelyan (1) 300–1; *Memoirs* (Werner) 38.
4. *Memorie nella redazione definitiva*, 313–14.
5. Sacerdote, ii, 418–21.
6. Stocchi, 673–8.
7. Sacerdote, ii, 424; Trevelyan (1), 314–15.
8. *Memorie nella redazione definitive*, 316–18.
9. Trevelyan (1) 323.
10. De Biase, 79.
11. *Ibid.*, 79; Sacerdote, ii, 427.
12. Mario, *Supplement*, 117–18; Trevelyan (2), 10–11.
13. *Lettere ad Antonio Panizzi*, 479.
14. Mario, *Supplement*, 119.
15. *Memoirs* (Werner), ii, 38.

9 *'A Place to Settle'*
Pages 121–132

1. Gay, 'Il secondo esilio di Garibaldi' in *Nuovo Antologia* (1910); *New York Post*, 28 June 1859; *Century Magazine* (1907), 175–82; *North American Review* (Jan. 1861); Larg, 175–81; Marraro, *American Opinion*, 164–8.

2. *Memorie nella redazione definitiva*, 327–8.
3. La Bolina, *La vita e la gesta*, 96.
4. Trevelyan (2), 25; Mario, *Supplement*, 123.
5. Mario, *Supplement*, 124.
6. Ciàmpoli, 72.
7. Trevelyan (2), 21–22.
8. King, *Mazzini*, 162.
9. Curàtulo, *Garibaldi e le donne*, 29, 265–7.
10. *Ibid.*, 29.
11. Trevelyan, (2), 30.
12. Vecchi, *Garibaldi at Caprera*, 34–35.
13. Melena, 43.
14. *Ibid.*, 26.
15. Curàtulo, *Garibaldi e le donne*, 139–40.
16. Melena, 25.
17. Curàtulo, *op. cit.*, 6.
18. *Ibid.*, 136–7.
19. *Ibid.*, 147.

10 *'Viva La Francia!'*
Pages 133–145

1. Whyte, *Cavour*, 60.
2. Mundy, 316.
3. Paléologue, 76; Cowley, 85.
4. Paléologue, 76.
5. Greville, vii, 175.
6. *Ibid.*, vii, 175; Elizabeth Longford, *Victoria R.I.* (Weidenfeld and Nicolson, 1964), 256, 276.
7. Salvatorelli, *Pensiero e azione*, 143.
8. *Ibid.*, 144.
9. Pallavicino, ii, 138; iii, 98–102.
10. *Ibid.*, ii, 438; Grew, 9, 25, 29.
11. Maineri, 333.
12. Pallavicino, iii, 511.
13. La Farina, q. Maineri, 502.
14. Maineri, 312.

15. Grew, 119, 118.
16. *Ibid.*, 120.
17. Omodeo, *Cavour*, ii, 168–9; Grew, 112.
18. *Carteggi di Cavour: Cavour e l'Inghilterra*, i, 463.
19. Maineri, 338; Chiala, ii, 144; Grew, 45, 112.
20. Harold Kurtz, *The Empress Eugénie* (Hamish Hamilton, 1964), 104.
21. *Ibid.*, 105.
22. Matter, iii, 61.
23. Thompson, 178; Massari, 173; King, *Italian Unity*, ii, 46–47; Trevelyan (2), 72; de la Gorce, ii, 348; Matter, iii, 57–61.
24. Della Rocca, 132.
25. Cowley, 160; Kurtz, Eugénie, 111.
26. Michael St. John Packe, *The Bombs of Orsini* (London, 1959), 281; de la Gorce, ii, 349–53.
27. Cowley, 176.
28. *Ibid.*, 175.
29. *Letters of Queen Victoria*, 1st series, iii, 391–2.
30. *Quarterly Review*, July 1879, q. Trevelyan (2), 78.
31. Castelli, 83.
32. *Ibid.*, 85; de la Rive, 260; Paléologue, 212; Matter, iii, 187–8.

11   *War in the Alps*
Pages 146–162

1. Mario, *Supplement*, 148.
2. Sacerdote, ii, 451–9; de la Rive, 257; Trevelyan (2), 83–84; Guerzoni, i, 411–22.
3. Chiala, iii, xcv; Grew, 175.
4. *Scritti* (Bologna, 1892), ii, 43, q. Salvemini, 149.
5. Salvatorelli, *Pensiero e azione*, 152.
6. *Memorie di Garibaldi nella redazione definitiva*, 343.
7. *Lettere ad Antonio Panizzi*, 412.
8. Melena, 36–41.
9. Carrano, 194–5.
10. Sacerdote, ii, 459–60.
11. Guerzoni, i, 432.
12. *Garibaldi condottiero*, 141–7; Guerzoni, i, 433–52; Sacerdote, ii,

References 379

460–3; Trevelyan (2), 90–96; Carrano, 258–81; *Memorie nella redazione definitiva*, 346–60.

13. Bixio, *Epistolario*, i, 263.

14. *Cornhill Magazine* (Jan. 1908): 'War Journals of John Peard', (Ed. Trevelyan).

15. *Ibid.*

16. Mario, *Supplement*, 179–81.

17. Giovanni Visconti Venosta, *Ricordi di gioventù* (Milan, 1908), q. Trevelyan (2), 107.

18. *Memorie nella redazione definitiva*, 361–88; Guerzoni, i, 452–85; *Garibaldi condottiero*, 147–70; Trevelyan (2), 101–9; Sacerdote, ii, 464–70; Carrano, 325–495. Nievo, 310–14.

19. *Memorie nella redazione definitiva*, 385; Pieri, 598–623; Cowley, 185–91; Thompson, 190–2; de la Gorce, iii, 102–13; Matter, iii, 226–46.

12 *'Love and Duty'*
Pages 163–172

1. Chiala, *Politica Segreta*, q. Thayer, ii, 114.

2. Thayer, ii, 108; Mario, *Posthumous Papers*, 282.

3. Whyte, *Cavour*, 387; Omodeo, *Difesa del Risorgimento*, 311; Salvemini, *Scritti*, 20.

4. *Scritti e discorsi*, i, 184.

5. Melena, 63; Guerzoni, i, 487–96; Sacerdote, ii, 471–4.

6. *Scritti e discorsi*, i, 194–6; Melena 68–69.

7. Melena, 66–79.

8. Curàtulo, *Garibaldi e le donne*, 6–7.

9. Melena, 84.

10. *Ibid.*, 125.

11. Mario, *Supplement*, 141.

12. Sacerdote, ii, 497.

13. Curàtulo, *Garibaldi e le donne*, 303–4.

14. Russell, *Later Correspondence*, ii, 231–2; Walpole, ii, 313.

15. Guerzoni, i, 497–508; Hancock, 249–53; Whyte, *Cavour*, 335; Thayer, ii, 155–60; King, *Italian Unity*, ii, 104–7; Grew, 226–8; Ricasoli, *Lettere*, iii, 467–74; *Memorie nella redazione definitiva*, 389–401; La Farina, *Epistolario*, ii, 235–7, 256; Chiala, iii, cclv; Carandini, 286–94.

16. q. Trevelyan (2), 121.

17. Grew, 229; Mario, *Supplement*, 203.

18. Mack Smith, *Garibaldi*, 84.

19. Sacerdote, ii, 499.

20. *Ibid.*, ii, 500.

21. Curàtulo, *Garibaldi e le donne*, 307.

22. Sacerdote, ii, 501; Guerzoni, i, 509; Curàtulo, 297–307; Fratta, · 144–52.

23. Ciàmpoli, 127.

PART II

1 *'The Negation of God'*
Pages 175–199

1. Philip Magnus, *Gladstone* (London, 1954), 98–99; Lacaita, 25–41.

2. Elliot, 6.

3. Settembrini, i, 192.

4. *Ibid.*, ii, 263; Forbes, 253; Galton, 35; Arrivabene, ii, 222–8.

5. Settembrini, ii, 264.

6. Martinengo Cesaresco, *Italian Characters*, 1.

7. Magnus, *op. cit.*, 100.

8. Gladstone, 8, 9.

9. q. Magnus, *op. cit.*, 100.

10. Acton, 246.

11. Lampedusa, 17–19; *Gattopardo*, 25–28.

12. q. Whitaker (Scalia), 263.

13. Elliot, 7.

14. *Ibid.*, 8–9.

15. *Ibid.*, 9–10.

16. Mario, *Supplement*, 135.

17. Ciàmpoli, 73.

18. Pieri, 556–62.

19. Romeo, *Risorgimento in Sicilia*, 326.

20. Crispi, *I Mille*, 72.

21. Mazzini's letter 2 March 1860.

22. Ciàmpoli, 127; Mario, *Garibaldi*, 255; Crispi, *Memoirs*, i, 113.

23. Crispi, *Memoirs*, i, 106.
24. *Lettere ad Antonio Panizzi*, 408.
25. Grew, 232.
26. Chiala, iii, 208.
27. Crispi, *Memoirs*, i, 113.
28. *Ibid.*, i, 115.
29. Ciàmpoli, 127.
30. Crispi, *Memoirs*, i, 116.
31. *Ibid.*, i, 132.
32. Mario, *Garibaldi*, 255.
33. D'Ideville, i, 116–17.
34. *Memoirs* (Werner), i, 259, 262; ii, 119, 218; *Scitti e discorsi*, i, 227–32,
35. Whyte, *Cavour*, 363.
36. *Memoirs* (Werner), i, 259; ii, 133, 218, 119.
37. Oliphant, 174–7.
38. Dumas, *Emma*, 117–18.
39. *Ibid.*, 124.
40. *Ibid.*, 122.
41. MS Carte Farini, Biblioteca classense, Ravenna, q. Parris, 207–8.
42. Trevelyan (2), 198.
43. Russell Papers: Hudson to Russell. R.P.G.D. 22-66, q. Mack Smith, *Garibaldi and Cavour*, 30.
44. *Carteggi di Cavour : La Liberazione del Mezzogiorno*, i, 36.
45. *Ibid.*
46. Curàtulo, *Garibaldi, Vittorio Emanuele e Cavour*, 177.
47. Abba, *Storia dei Mille*, 84.
48. Mack Smith, 'Cavour's Attitude to Garibaldi's expedition to Sicily', *Cambridge Hist. Journal*, 368; Crispi, *I Mille*, 98.
49. Persano, i, 81.
50. Elliot, 84, 55.
51. Chiala, iv, cxx.
52. *Carteggi di Cavour: La Liberazione del Mezzogiorno*, i, 36.
53. Mack Smith, *op. cit.* in *Cambridge Hist. Journal*, 360.
54. Arrivabene, ii, 25–26.
55. Passerin d'Entrèves, 72–83.

56. *Carteggi di Cavour: Cavour-Nigra*, iv, 294; Bianchi, viii, 691.
57. Ricasoli, *Lettere*, v, 94.
58. Chiala, iii, 809.
59. Crispi, *Memoirs*, i, 149-50.
60. Guerzoni, ii, 34.
61. Bandi, 19; Trevelyan (2), 190.
62. Stefan Türr, *Risposta all' opusculo Bertani* (1867), q. Crispi, *Memoirs*, 154; Dumas, *Emma*, 123.
63. Crispi, *Memoirs*, i, 154; Mario, *Bertani*, ii, 46.
64. Bandi, 29.
65. Sacerdote, ii, 518.
66. Colapietra, 'Intorno al pensiero politico di Garibaldi,' *Nuovo Rivista Storica* (a 43, 1959), 1.

2   *The Sailing of The Thousand*
Pages 200-210

1. Dumas, *Emma*, 132.
2. Bandi, 36-44; Abba, *Storia dei Mille*, 25-30; Pecorini - Manzoni, 15; Trevelyan (2), 200-7; Pieri, 653-7; Guerzoni, ii, 37-44; Sacerdote, ii, 521-9.
3. Bandi, 53-60.
4. Trevelyan (2), 222.
5. Bandi, 60-62.
6. Guerzoni, ii, 47-57; *Scritti e discorsi*, i, 242-5; Ciàmpoli, 145.
7. Bandi, 70-72.
8. Chiala, iii, 245.
9. *Ibid.*, iii, 246.
10. *Ibid.*, iii, 252.
11. Persano, 20.
12. Mack Smith, *Garibaldi and Cavour*, 25.
13. Crispi, *Memoirs*, i, 162.
14. *Daily News*, 22 May 1860, q. Trevelyan (2), 234.
15. Winnington-Ingram, 197-8.
16. *Ibid.*, 198; Gabriele, 6-32.
17. Crispi, *I Mille*, 126.
18. Bandi, 133.

19. Archivio Bertani, q. Mack Smith, *Garibaldi and Cavour*, 10; *Scrittt e discorsi*, i, 251.
20. De Cesare, i, 154.
21. Trevelyan (2), 248.

3 *The Battle of Calatafimi*
Pages 211-218

1. Bandi, 141-3.
2. Sacerdote, ii, 256.
3. Guerzoni, ii, 78; Trevelyan (2), 260; Bandi, 168.
4. Mario, *Bertani*, ii, 56.
5. Ciàmpoli, 150.
6. Guerzoni, ii, 71-83; Pieri, 659-64; *Garibaldi condottiero*, 232-3; Sacerdote, ii, 551-61; Trevelyan (2), 252-64; Bandi, 144-71; Menghini, 30-31, 424-5.
7. Romeo, *Il Risorgimento in Sicilia*, 377.
8. Holyoake, i, 221.
9. Forbes, 334; Arrivabene, ii, 300.
10. Abba, *Storia dei Mille*, 137-8; Alberto Mario, 264; Trevelyan (2), 268-9; Guerzoni, ii, 84-85; Sacerdote, ii, 563-4.
11. Trevelyan (2), 270-7; Pieri, 664-7; Guerzoni, ii, 85-88.
12. Guerzoni, ii, 89-91; Pieri, 667-9; Trevelyan (2), 272-82; *Garibaldi condottiero*, 233-5; Sacerdote, ii, 570-5; Pecorini-Manzoni, 384-5.

4 *The Capture of Palermo*
Pages 219-237

1. Trevelyan (2), 266.
2. Mundy, 100-2.
3. *Ibid.*, 105.
4. *Ibid.*, 107.
5. *The Times*, 8 June 1860.
6. Mundy, 108.
7. Abba, *Da Quarto al Volturno*, 108-11; Pecorini-Manzoni, 49-51; Guerzoni, ii, 91-96; Pieri, 668-9.
8. *The Times*, 8 June 1860.
9. Abba, *Da Quarto al Volturno*, 113-16; Guerzoni, *Bixio*, 198-200; Menghini, 59-61, 429-30; Pecorini-Manzoni, 49-50.

10. *The Times*, 8 June 1860.
11. *Ibid.;* Pecorini-Manzoni, 52; Abba, *Da Quarto al Volturno*, 117; Guerzoni, *Bixio*, 200.
12. *The Times*, 8 June 1860.
13. *Ibid.*
14. Mundy, 111.
15. *Morning Post*, 26 June 1860, q. Trevelyan (2), 304 n.1.
16. Cava, ii, 87.
17. Trevelyan (2), 307.
18. Pecorini-Manzoni, 59–61; Abba, *Storia dei Mille*, 189–91; Cava, ii, 85–89; *Garibaldi condottiero*, 235–6; Guerzoni, *Garibaldi*, ii, 96–108.
19. Mundy, 145–6.
20. *Ibid.*, 147–58.
21. Elliot, 39.
22. Mundy, 158–9.
23. *Ibid.*, 166.
24. Crispi, *I Mille*, 157.
25. Mundy, 179; De Cesare, ii, 231–43; Abba, *Da Quarto al Volturno*, 119–30; De Sivo, iii, 218–29; Guerzoni, ii, 111–20; Pieri, 673–4; Trevelyan (2), 313–24; Sacerdote, ii, 576–95.

5 The Dictator of the Two Sicilies
Pages 238–246

1. Arrivabene, ii, 62.
2. Alberto Mario, 3–4.
3. Dumas, *Emma*, 219.
4. *Ibid.*, 136.
5. A. Craig Bell, *Alexandre Dumas* (Cassell, 1950), 320.
6. Dumas, *Emma*, 165.
7. *Ibid.*, 214.
8. Nievo, 237.
9. Guerzoni, ii, 124–5.
10. *Scritti e discorsi*, i, 273.
11. Blakiston, 110.
12. Bianchi, *Storia documentata*, viii, 663–4; Thompson, 206; del a Gorce, iii, 390.

13. Chiala, iii, 282, 273.
14. D'Ideville, i, 129.
15. Elliot, 26.
16. *Ibid.*, 55.
17. Persano, 463.
18. Whyte, *Cavour*, 416; Crispi, *Memoirs*, i, 238–9.
19. Omodeo, *Difesa del Risorgimento*, 309.
20. Mack Smith, *Garibaldi and Cavour*, 101, 123.
21. Grew, 342–3.
22. Crispi, *Memoirs*, i, 247.
23. *Ibid.*, i, 255.
24. Crispi to Mazzini, *Ibid.*, i, 255; Mario, *Bertani*, ii, 84–112.
25. Omodeo, *Difesa del Risorgimento*, 310.
26. *Ibid.*, 312.
27. Chiala, iii, 305; Salvemini, *Scritti*, 20; Cavour, *Liberazione del Mezzogiorno*, i, 329; Mack Smith, *Garibaldi and Cavour*, 129.
28. Pianell, 12–20; De Sivo, iii, 120–4, 310–12; Trevelyan (3), 71–77; Pieri, 677–9.

6   The Battle of Milazzo
Pages 247–260

1. Forbes, 72.
2. Trevelyan (3), 80–84.
3. *Ibid.*, 85.
4. Forbes, 98.
5. Pieri, 682–3.
6. *Ibid.*, 683; Pecorini-Manzoni, 399–400; Trevelyan (3), 94–95; *Garibaldi condottiero*, 236–7.
7. Forbes, 107.
8. *Ibid.*, 107–8.
9. Pieri, 682.
10. Alberto Mario, 38–40.
11. Forbes, 120–5; Trevelyan (3), 99–100; Guerzoni, ii, 136–46.
12. Cavour, *Cavour-Nigra*, iv, 98.
13. Chiala, iii, 300.
14. Cavour, *Cavour-Nigra*, iv, 122–3.

15. Cavour, *Liberazione del Mezzogiorno*, ii, 2; Cavour, *Cavour-Nigra*, iv, 123.
16. Bianchi, viii, 333; Chiala, iii, 307, 311, 349.
17. D. Guerrini, 'La Missione del Conte Litta' (*Risorgimento Italiano*, Feb. 1909); Mack Smith, *Garibaldi and Cavour*, 125–7.
18. q. Crispi, *Memoirs*, i, 365.
19. Guerzoni, ii, 148.
20. Russell, *Later Correspondence*, ii, 265, 260.
21. Beales, *England and Italy, 1859–1870*.
22. Mack Smith, *Garibaldi and Cavour*, 137.
23. Lacaita, 138–45; Thompson, 207.
24. Alberto Mario, 43.
25. Crispi, *Memoirs*, i, 362.
26. Alberto Mario, 43.
27. Dumas, *Emma*, 259.
28. G. Manacorda, 'Vittorio Emanuele II e Garibaldi nel 1860 secondo le carte Trecchi' (*Nuova Antologia*, June 1910), q. Mack Smith, *Garibaldi and Cavour*, 158; Omodeo, *Difesa del Risorgimento*, 310–11.
29. Ciàmpoli, 168.
30. Trevelyan (3), 119–23; Guerzoni, ii, 159; Mario, *Bertani*, 165–80.

6 Calabria
Pages 261–274

1. Gabriele, 186–90; Pianell, 45–46; Trevelyan (3), 126–8; Pieri, 687; Guerzoni, ii, 157–61.
2. q. Trevelyan (3), 130; Guerzoni, *Bixio*, 229.
3. Forbes, 132.
4. Mundy, 187.
5. Trevelyan (3), 129–30.
6. Alberto Mario, 109.
7. *Ibid.*, 109.
8. Arrivabene, ii, 115–29; De Cesare, ii, 390–3; De Sivo, iii, 372–7; Forbes, 167–78; Alberto Mario, 120–47; Morisani, 120–40; Pianell, 50–82; Pieri, 687–8; Trevelyan (3), 130–8.
9. Forbes, 153, 157, 195.
10. Alberto Mario, 123.

11. Arrivabene, ii, 149-50; Du Camp, 146; Trevelyan (3), 142-3; Guerzoni, ii, 163.

12. Du Camp, 149; Trevelyan (3), 144; Pieri, 691-2; Guerzoni, ii, 164.

13. Arrivabene, ii, 151-6; Trevelyan (3), 144-9; Pieri, 692; Forbes, 196-200; Alberto Mario, 158-68.

14. Forbes, 179.

15. Rosi, *I Cairoli*, 343; Trevelyan (3), 151; Arrivabene, ii, 157-65; Adamoli, 148-52.

16. Mario, *Bertani*, ii, 456-7; Bertani, *Ire politiche*, 74-77.

17. Forbes, 225-6; Arrivabene, ii, 158-69; Trevelyan (3), 153-65; Pianell, 80-88; De Cesare, ii, 420-4; *Garibaldi condottiero*, 251-5; Sacerdote, ii, 621-3; Guerzoni, ii, 165-70.

7 Naples
Pages 275-293

1. Dumas, *Emma*, 333.

2. Acton, 474-80; De Cesare, ii, 410-24.

3. De Cesare, ii, 408; Acton, 481.

4. De Cesare, ii, 426.

5. Arrivabene, ii, 182; Acton, 487.

6. Sacerdote, ii, 626.

7. Galton, 23-26.

8. Du Camp, 27.

9. *Scritti e discorsi*, i, 296-7; Galton, 26; *The Times*, 15 September 1860; Arrivabene, ii, 192-4; Acton, 489-91; Fratta, 278-89.

10. Acton, 490.

11. Forbes, 237.

12. Galton, 27-28.

13. *Ibid.*, 29.

14. Elliot, 70.

15. Cava, 13 n.

16. Elliot, 82.

17. *Ibid.*, 82, 84-85, 90, 92, 97.

18. Maraldi, *Documenti francesi sulla caduta del regno meridionale* (Naples, 1935), q. Acton, 496.

19. Galton, 66-67.

20. *Carteggi di Cavour: Cavour-Nigra*, iv, 212–13; Whyte, 426; Thayer ii, 377; Mario, *Bertani*, ii, 208; Ciàmpoli, 181.
21. La Bolina, *Cronachette*, 62–63.
22. Elliot, 73–74.
23. Galton, 31, 51–52.
24. Arrivabene, ii, 234–5.
25. Butler, *Meuricoffre*, 60, 78.
26. Salvemini, *Scritti*, 426.
27. Nicomede Bianchi, *Storia documentata*, viii, 338.
28. Thouvenel, i, 238.
29. Pieri, 712–18.

8   The Volturno
Pages 294–314

1. Trevelyan (3), 231; Franci, ii, 212.
2. Trevelyan (3), 237.
3. Franci, ii, 220–50; *Garibaldi condottiero*, 264–7; Pieri, 701–2.
4. Trevelyan (3), 239.
5. Arrivabene, ii, 264; Bandi, 300–10; Ciàmpoli, 192–3; Menghini, 339–40.
6. Colet, iii, 13.
7. Pecorini-Manzoni, 463–4; Trevelyan (3), 242.
8. Trevelyan (3), 251.
9. *Garibaldi condottiero*, 267–76; Pieri, 702–11; Arrivabene, ii, 251–62; Menghini, 330–70; Du Camp, 310–25; Bandi, 302–12; Adamoli, 159–63; Franci, ii, 250–80; Sacerdote, ii, 634–42.
10. Butler, *Meuricoffre*, 62–73.
11. Elliot, 93; see also Colet, iii, 34–35.
12. Galton, 54.
13. Mario, *Garibaldi*, ii, 3.
14. Chiala, iii, 349.
15. Mario, *Bertani*, ii, 269.
16. MSS. of Achille Fazzari, q. Trevelyan (3), 262.
17. Salvatorelli, *Pensiero e azione*, 158.
18. Mack Smith, *Garibaldi and Cavour*, 373–4; Crispi, *I Mille*, 360–2; Pecorini-Manzoni, 277–81.

19. Mundy, 257-8.
20. Elliot, 101.
21. Alberto Mario, 283.
22. *Ibid.*, 284.
23. Della Rocca, 196.
24. Alberto Mario, 284.
25. *Ibid.*, 285.
26. Arrivabene, ii, 292.
27. Alberto Mario, 285.
28. *Ibid.*, 287.
29. *Ibid.*, 288.
30. Mack Smith, *Garibaldi and Cavour*, 235.
31. Arrivabene, ii, 291-3.
32. Alberto Mario, 288.
33. Mario, *Supplement*, 299.
34. Della Rocca, 194-5.
35. *Ibid.*, 197-8.
36. Chiala, iv, 34.
37. Guerzoni, ii, 231-2.
38. Elliot, 108.
39. Crispi, *Memoirs*, i, 487.
40. q. Acton, 505.
41. Persano, iv, 119.
42. Mario, *Supplement*, 141.
43. Mundy, 280.
44. *Scritti e discorsi*, i, 329-30.
45. Mundy, 284-7; Sacerdote, ii, 654-5; Guerzoni, ii, 230-4.

PART III

1 '*Roma o Morte!*'
Pages 317-338

1. Sacerdote, ii, 445.
2. *The Letters of Queen Victoria*, 2nd series, iii, 434.
3. Vecchi, *Garibaldi at Caprera*, 51-52.
4. *Ibid.*, 11.

5. Vecchi, *Garibaldi at Caprera*, 21-23.
6. McGrigor, 312-13.
7. *Ibid.*, 45.
8. Vecchi, 50-51. For private life on Caprera also see Curàtulo, La Bolina, Nuvolari, Sacchi.
9. Chiala, iv, 34; Whyte, 435-6, 452; Thayer, 459-62.
10. D'Ideville, i, 180.
11. *The Times*, 23 April 1861.
12. D'Ideville, i, 179.
13. Thayer, ii, 468.
14. D'Ideville, i, 182.
15. *Scritti e discorsi*, i, 363.
16. *The Times*, 23 April 1861.
17. Guerzoni, *Bixio*, 267-8.
18. *Scritti e discorsi*, i, 358-82; Sacerdote, ii, 659-61; Matter, 446-54; Whyte, 454-56; Salvemini, *Scritti*, 21-22; Guerzoni, ii, 258-66.
19. D'Ideville, i, 181.
20. Mario, *Garibaldi*, ii, 33-35.
21. Thayer, ii, 478; D'Ideville, i, 219.
22. q. Thayer, ii, 478.
23. Thayer, ii, 480-1.
24. Crispolti, 'Cavour alla vigilia della morte', *Corriere della Sera*, 6 Jan. 1911, 1; Thayer, ii, 486.
25. Paléologue, 293-4; Whyte, 460-3; de la Rive, 278-291; Thayer, ii, 478-91; Castelli, 93-101.
26. Countess Alfieri's statement in de la Rive, 282.
27. Forbes, 118.
28. Guerzoni, ii, 298-300.
29. Sacerdote, ii, 670-81.
30. Mack Smith, *Garibaldi*, 130.
31. *Ibid.*, 131.
32. De la Gorce, iv, 171; Salvemini, *Scritti*, 427.
33. Sacerdote, ii, 682.
34. *Ibid.*, ii, 682.
35. *Ibid.*, ii, 686.
36. *Ibid.*, ii, 687.

37. Lampedusa, *op. cit.*, 217; For Aspromonte campaign see Abba, Adamoli, Bruzzesi, Guarnone, Luzio, Guerzoni, ii, 301–31; Sacerdote, ii, 681–8; de la Gorce, iv, 170–9.

38. Salvemini, *Scritti*, 34.

39. Mario, *Posthumous Papers*, 329–30; McGrigor, 193–9.

2 *London, 1864*
Pages 339–351

1. *The Times*, 29 March 1864.

2. *Memoirs* (Werner), ii, 291.

3. Guerzoni, ii, 347.

4. Melena, 176; Mario, *Supplement*, 371.

5. *Alfred Lord Tennyson: A Memoir by his son* (London, 1899), 419; Mack Smith, *Garibaldi*, 139.

6. *The Times*, 5 April 1864.

7. Holyoake, *Bygones*, i, 240.

8. *Alfred Lord Tennyson, op. cit.*, 419.

9. *The Times*, 11 April 1864.

10. *The Times*, 12 April 1864.

11. Martinengo Cesaresco, *Liberation of Italy*, 353.

12. Royal Archives J.36–137, q. Philip Magnus, *King Edward the Seventh* (John Murray, 1964), 84.

13. Morley, *Gladstone*, 110, 109.

14. Mario, *Posthumous Papers*, 334–5; *The Times*, 16 April 1864.

15. Bruzzesi, *Memorie*, 197.

16. Mack Smith, *Garibaldi*, 140.

17. *Ibid.*

18. Royal Archives, Queen Victoria's Journal, q. Elizabeth Longford, *Victoria R.I.* (Weidenfeld & Nicolson, 1964), 363.

19. Mack Smith, 140.

20. Kronberg Letters, 28 April 1864, q. Longford, *op. cit.*, 363.

21. *Letters of Queen Victoria*, 2nd series, i, 169.

22. *Ibid.*, 3.

23. *Ibid.*, i, 169.

24. *Ibid.*, 175–6.

25. *Ibid.*, 174–5.

26. *Evening Standard*, 20 April 1864; Mario, *Supplement*, 372. See also Herzen.

27. *Letters of Queen Victoria*, 2nd Series, i, 174.

28. Mack Smith, *Garibaldi*, 142.

29. *Letters of Queen Victoria*, 2nd Series, i, 172.

30. *The Times*, 22 April 1864.

31. *Letters of Queen Victoria*, 2nd Series, i, 189.

32. Mack Smith, *Garibaldi*, 145; Blakiston, 285.

33. *The Visit of Garibaldi to England. A Letter to the Rt. Hon. Edward Cardwell, M.P.* (from Henry Edward Manning, London, 1864), 10.

34. Fagan, ii, 251.

35. Holyoake, i, 241.

36. *Ibid.*, 241.

37. *Courier du Dimanche*, q. Guerzoni, ii, 391.

38. *Letters of Queen Victoria*, 2nd series, i, 176.

39. *Ibid.*, 176.

40. Curàtulo, *Garibaldi e le donne*, 276.

41. *Ibid.*, 289.

42. *Ibid.*, 260.

43. *Ibid.* For Garibaldi's various speeches and less public observations while in England see *Scritti e discorsi*, ii, 218–34 and Guerzoni, ii, 347–93.

3 'The Scourge of Italy'
Pages 352–356

1. Guerzoni, ii, 393–411.

2. *Scritti e discorsi*, ii, 367–70; Sacerdote, ii, 713–22.

3. *Scritti e discorsi*, ii, 421–5; Falconi, *passim*.

4. Salvatorelli, *Concise History*, 580–1; Luzio, 118.

5. Mario, *Supplement*, 384.

6. Melena, 208, 210.

7. King, *Mazzini*, 212.

8. Marraro, 'Unpublished Documents on Garibaldi's March on Rome', *Journal of Modern History* (June, 1944), Doc. 2.

9. Sacerdote, ii, 737–8.
   For Mentana campaign see Abba, Adamoli, Barrili, Luzio, Sacerdote,

ii, 728–38; Pieri, 776–81; *Garibaldi condottiero*, 316–52; de la Gorce, v, 246–315; Delord, v, 212–25; Guerzoni, ii, 514–48;

4 *Caprera*
Pages 357–368

1. Curàtulo, *Il dissidio*, 206; Salvatorelli, *Pensiero e azione*, 152.
2. Melena, 260.
3. The Saturday Review, q. Melena, 336.
4. Melena, 256.
5. *Ibid.*, 257.
6. *Ibid.*, 259.
7. Mario, *Supplement*, 452.
8. Chabod, i, 28.
9. *Nouvelle Presse Libre*, 15 Jan. 1871; q. Melena, 293.
10. Mario, *Supplement*, 407.
11. q. Mario, *Supplement*, 421–22.
12. Ludwig Löhlein, *Feldzug 1870–1871. Die Operationen des Korps des Generals von Werder* (Berlin, 1874), q. Michael Howard, *The Franco-Prussian War* (Rupert Hart-Davis, 1961), 409.
13. Howard, *op. cit.* 409; See also G. Theyras, *Garibaldi en France* (Autunn, 1888) and J. P. T. Bordone, *Garibaldi et l'Armée des Vosges* (Paris, 1871); *Garibaldi condottiero*, 355–411.
14. Melena, 302.
15. Mario, *Supplement*, 453–4.
16. *Ibid.*, 452.
17. La Bolina, 84–86.
18. Mario, *Supplement*, 454.
19. Curàtulo, *Garibaldi e le donne*, 190.
20. Sacerdote, ii, 757.
21. Mario, *Supplement*, 437.
22. Sacerdote, ii, 773.
23. *Ibid.*, ii, 773; Fratta, 414.
24. Mario, *Supplement*, 459.
25. *Ibid.*, 459.
26. Sacerdote, ii, 773.
27. Mario, *Supplement*, 459; Guerzoni, ii, 615–17; Sacerdote, ii, 773–5.

SOURCES

ABBA, G. C., *Da Quarto al Volturno. Noterelle d'uno dei Mille* (Bologna, 1909).
— *Cose Garibaldine* (Turin, 1907).
— *Ricordi Garibaldini* (Turin, 1913).
— *Storia dei Mille* (Turin, 1904).

ACTON, HAROLD, *The Last Bourbons of Naples, 1825–1861* (Methuen, London, 1961).

ADAMOLI, GIULIO, *Da San Martino a Mentana: Ricordi di un volontario* (Milan, 1892).

AGRATI, CARLO, *Giuseppe Sirtori* (Bari, 1940).

ANSIGLIONI, GIUSEPPE, *Memorie della battaglia del Volturno* (Turin, 1861).

ARDAU, GIUSEPPE, *Carlo Pisacane* (Milan, 1948).

ARRIVABENE, COUNT CHARLES, *Italy under Victor Emmanuel: A Personal Narrative* (London, 1862).

AUBERT, R., *Le Pontificat de Pie IX, 1846–1878* (Paris, 1952).

BANDI, GIUSEPPE, *I Mille: Da Genova a Capua* (Florence, 1903).
— *Anita Garibaldi. Con documenti sulla vita di Garibaldi in America* (Florence, 1932).

BARRILI, A. G., *Con Garibaldi alle porte di Roma* (Milan, 1895).

BEALES, DEREK, *England and Italy, 1859–1860* (Nelson, London, 1962).

BELLONI, ERNESTO, *Scritti inediti* (Treviso, 1866).

BELLUZZI, RAFFAELE, *La ritirata di Garibaldi da Roma nel 1849* (Rome, 1899).

BERKELEY, G. F-H. and J., *Italy in the Making. 1 January 1848 to 16 November 1848* (London, 1940).

BERTANI, AGOSTINO, *Ire politiche d'oltre tomba* (Florence, 1869).

BERTI, G., *I democratici e l'iniziativa meridionale nel Risorgimento* (Feltrinelli, 1962).

BERTOTTI, E., *Goffredo Mameli e la repubblica Romana del 1849* (Genoa, 1927).

Sources 395

BIANCHI, LORENZO E MARIO PAZZAGLIA, *La gesta garibaldina* (Zanichelli, Bologna, 1959).

BIANCHI, NICOMEDE, *Storia documentata della diplomazia Europea in Italia dell'anno 1814 all'anno 1861* (Turin, 1865–72).

— *Il Conte Camillo Cavour. Documenti editi ed inediti* (Turin, 1863).

BITTARD DES PORTES, RENÉ, *L'Expédition française de Rome.*

BIXIO, NINO, *Epistolario* (Ed. Emilia Morelli, Rome, 1942–54).

BLAKISTON, NOEL (ed.) *The Roman Question: Extracts from the Despatches of Odo Russell* (Chapman and Hall, 1962).

BONNET, GIOACCHINO, *Lo sbarco di Garibaldi a Magnavacca* (Bologna, 1932).

BONOMI, IVANOE, *Giuseppe Mazzini triumviro della Repubblica Romana* (Milan, 1946).

BOURGEOIS, ÉMILE and CLERMONT, E., *Rome et Napoléon III 1849–1870* (Paris, 1907).

BRIZI, ORESTE, *Le bande garibaldine a San Marino* (Arezzo, 1850).

BRUZZESI, GIACINTO, *Memorie del Colonello Giacinto Bruzzesi* (Milan, 1894).

— *Dal Volturno ad Aspromonte* (Milan, n.d.).

— *Dopo 25 anni* (Arona, 1885).

— *Una parola sulle molte storie Garibaldine. Lettera a Giuseppe Bandi* (Milan, 1882).

BUTLER, JOSEPHINE, *In Memoriam Harriet Meuricoffre* (London, n.d.).

CANDELORO, GIORGIO, *Storia dell'Italia moderna* (Feltrinelli, Milan, 1956–8).

CANDIDO, SALVATORE, *Giuseppe Garibaldi. Corsaro riograndense* (Istituto per la Storia Risorgimento Italiano, Rome, 1964).

CARAGUEL, CLEMENT, *Souvenirs et aventures d'un volontaire garibaldien* (Paris, 1861).

CARANDINI, FEDERICO, *Manfredo Fanti* (Verona, 1872).

CARLETTI, CHARLES GOURAUD, *L'Italia. Sue ultime rivoluzioni* (Florence, 1852).

CARRANO, FRANCESCO, *I Cacciatori delle Alpi nella guerra del 1859* (Turin, 1860).

CASE, L. M., *Franco-Italian Relations 1860–1865: The Roman Question and the Convention of September* (Philadelphia, 1932).

CASTELLINI, GUALTERIO, *Pagine garibaldine, 1848–1866* (Rome, 1909).

CAVA, TOMMASO, *Difesa nazionale Napolitane* (Naples, 1863).

CAVACIOCCHI, ALBERTO, *Le prime gesta di Garibaldi in Italia* (1907).

CAVOUR, CAMILLO DI, *Carteggi di Cavour: Cavour-Nigra dal 1858 al 1861* (Zanichelli, Bologna, 1926–9).
— *La Liberazione del Mezzogiorno e la formzaione del Regno d'Italia* (Bologna, 1949–54).
— *Cavour e l'Inghilterra. Carteggio con V.E. d'Azeglio* (Bologna, 1933).
— *Carteggio Cavour-Salmour* (Bologna, 1936).
— *La Questione Romana negli anni 1860–1861. Carteggio del Conte di Cavour con Pantaleoni, Passaglia Vimercati* (Bologna, 1929).
— *Epistolario* (Bologna, 1962–   ).
— *Lettere edite ed inedite di Camillo Cavour* (ed. Luigi Chiala, Turin, 1883–7).

CHABOD, FEDERICO, *Storia della politica estera italiana dal 1870 al 1896* (Vol. I. Laterza, Bari, 1951).

CHAMBERS, LT.-COL., *Garibaldi and Italian Unity* (London, 1864).

CHIALA, LUIGI, See Cavour.

CIÀMPOLI, DOMENICO, See Garibaldi.

CLOUGH, ARTHUR HUGH, *The Correspondence of Arthur Hugh Clough* (Ed. Frederick L. Mulhauser, London, 1957).

COLET, LOUISE, *L'Italie des italiens* (Paris, 1864).

COLLINS, IRENE, *The Age of Progress* (Arnold, 1964).

CONTI, GIOVANNI, *La Repubblica Romana del 1849* (Rome, 1920).
— *Correspondence Respecting the Affairs of Italy 1846–1849* (London, 1849).

COWLEY, EARL, *The Paris Embassy during the 2nd Empire* (Ed. Col. The Hon. F. Wellesley, London, 1928).

CRISPI, FRANCESCO, *I Mille* (Milan, 1910).
— *The Memoirs of Francesco Crispi* (Trans. Mary Prichard-Agnetti from the documents collected and edited by Thomas Palamenghi-Crispi, London, 1912).

CROCE, BENEDETTO, *Storia del Regno di Napoli* (Bari, 1925).

CUNEO, G.B., *Biografia di Guiseppe Garibaldi* (Genoa, 1876).

CUPÀTULO, GIACOMO EMILIO, *Anita Garibaldi* (Milan, 1932).
— *Garibaldi e le donne, con documenti inediti* (Rome 1913).
— *Garibaldi, Vittorio Emmanuele, Cavour nei fasti della patria* (Bologna, 1911).
— *Il dissidio tra Mazzini e Garibaldi* (Milan, 1928).

DALLOLIO, ALBERTO, *La spedizione dei Mille nelle memorie bolognesi* (Bologna, 1910).

DANDOLO, EMILIO, *The Italian volunteers and Lombard Rifle*

Brigade. *Being an Authentic Narrative, 1848-1849* (London, 1851).

D'AUNAY, ALFRED (A. Descudier), *Mémoires Authentiques sur Garibaldi* (Paris, 1864).

DE BIASE, CORRADO, *L'arresto di Garibaldi nel settembre 1849* (Florence, 1941).

DE CESARE, RAFFAELE, *The Last Days of Papal Rome, 1850-1870.* (Trans. Helen Zimmern, London, 1909).

— *La fine di un Regno* (Città di Castello, 1900).

DE GAILLARD, LEOPOLD, *L'Expédition de Rome en 1849* (Paris, 1851).

DE LA GORCE, PIERRE, *Histore de la Seconde République Française* (Paris, 1887).

DE LA RIVE, WILLIAM, *Reminiscences of the Life and Character of Count Cavour.* (Trans. Edward Romilly, London, 1862).

DE LESSEPS, FERDINAND, *Ma Mission à Rome* (Paris, 1849).

DELLA PARUTA, FRANCO, *I democratici e la rivoluzione italiana* (Feltrinelli, Milan, 1958).

DELLA ROCCA, GENERALE, *The Autobiography of a Veteran* (Trans. Janet Ross, London, 1899).

DE LIEDEKERKE, AUGUSTO DE BEAUFORT, *Rapporti delle cose di Roma 1848-1849* (Ed. Alberto M. Ghisalberti, Istituto per la Storia del Risorgimento Italiano, Rome, 1949).

DELZELL, CHARLES F. (ed.), *The Unification of Italy* (Holt, Rinehart and Winston, 1965).

DE SIVO, GIACINTO, *Storia delle Due Sicile dal 1847 al 1861* (Trieste, 1868).

D'IDEVILLE, HENRY, *Journal d'un Diplomate en Italie* (Paris, 1872).

DI NOLFO, ENNIO, *Storia del Risorgimento e dell' unità d'Italia* (continuazione dell' opera di Cesare Spellanzon, vol. 6, Rizzoli, Milan, 1959).

DU CAMP, MAXIME, *Expédition des Deux-Siciles* (Paris, 1881).

DUMAS, ALEXANDRE, *On board the 'Emma': Adventures with Garibaldi's 'Thousand' in Sicily* (Trans. R. S. Garnett, London, 1929).

DURAND-BRAGER, Jean Baptiste Henri, *Quatre mois de l'expédition de Garibaldi en Sicile et en Italie* (Paris, 1861).

ELLIOT, HENRY, *Some Revolutions and other Diplomatic Experiences by the late Rt. Hon. Sir Henry G. Elliot: Ed. by his daughter* (London, 1922).

FAGAN, LOUIS, *The Life of Sir Anthony Panizzi* (London, 1880).

FALCONI, ANGELO, *Come e quando Garibaldi scelse per sua dimora Caprera* (Cagliari, 1962).

FARINI, LUIGI CARLO, *The Roman State, 1815–1850* (London, 1851–4).
— *Epistolario* (Ed. Luigi Rava, Bologna, 1911–14).

FONVIELLE, ULRICH, *Souvenirs d'une chemise rouge* (Paris, 1861).

FORBES, C. S., *The Campaign of Garibaldi in the Two Sicilies: A Personal Narrative* (London, 1861).

FRANCI, GIOVANNI DELLI, *Campagna d'autunno del 1860* (Naples, 1860).

FRANCIOSI, PIETRO, *Garibaldi e la Repubblica di San Marino* (Bologna, 1891).

FRATTA, ARTURO, *Garibaldi: Passione e battaglie. Collane di cultura Napoletana, 8* (Fausto Fiorentino, Naples, 1961).

GABRIELE, MARIANO, *Da Marsala allo stretto: Aspetti navali della campagna di Sicilia* (Giuffrè, Milan, 1961).

GABUSSI, GIUSEPPE, *Memorie per servire alla storia della rivoluzione degli stati Romani* (Genoa, 1852).

GALTON, FRANCIS (ed.), *Vacation Tourists in 1860* (London, 1861).

GAMBERINI, CESARE, *Schiarimenti sui fatti accaduti a Roma nel giugno 1849* (Bologna, 1884).

GARIBALDI, ANNITA ITALIA *Garibaldi en America* (Buenos Aires, 1930).
— *Anita Garibaldi* (Buenos Aires, 1931).

Garibaldi, Condottiero (Ufficio storico del Ministero della Guerra, Rome, 1932).

GARIBALDI, GIUSEPPE, *Le memorie di Garibaldi in una delle redazioni anteriori alla definitiva del 1872* (Bologna, 1932).
— *Le Memorie di Garibaldi nella redazione definitiva del 1872* (Bologna, 1932).
— *Autobiography of Giuseppe Garibaldi: Authorised Translation by A. Werner. With a Supplement by Jessie White Mario* (London, 1889).
— *The Memoirs of Garibaldi* (Ed. Alexandre Dumas: Trans. R. S. Garnett, London, 1931).
— *Garibaldi's Denkwürdigkeiten* (Ed. Elpis Melena, Hamburg, 1861).
— *Scritti politici e militari. Ricordi e pensieri inediti* (Ed. Domenico Ciàmpoli, Rome, 1907).
— *The Life of Garibaldi Written by Himself with sketches of his companions in arms. Translated by his friend and admirer Theodore Dwight* (New York, 1859).
— *Lettere e proclami* (Ed. Renato Zangheri, Milan, 1954).
— *Scritti e discorsi politici e militari* (Bologna, 1934).

— *Diario del Generale Garibaldi dal 1864 al 1876* (Istituto per la Storia del Risorgimento Italiano, MS.).

— *Epistolario di Giuseppe Garibaldi* (Ed. Enrico Emilio Ximenes).

GHISALBERTI, ALBERTO M., *Roma da Mazzini a Pio IX* (Giuffrè, Milan, 1958).

— *Massimo d'Azeglio* (Rome, 1953).

— *Uomini e case del Risorgimento* (Rome, 1936).

GIUSTA, GIUSEPPE, *Da Talamone a Palermo* (Turin, 1907).

GLADSTONE, W. E., *Two Letters to the Earl of Aberdeen on the State Prosecutions of the Neapolitan Government* (London, 1851).

GOBETTI, PIERO, *Risorgimento senza eroi* (Turin, 1926).

GRAMSCI, ANTONIO, *Il Risorgimento* (Einaudi, Turin, 1949).

— *Sul Risorgimento* (Ed. Elsa Fubini, Editori Riuniti, Rome, 1959).

GREENFIELD, K. R., *Economics and Liberalism in the Risorgimento* (Baltimore, 1934).

GREGOROVIUS, FERDINAND, *The Roman Journals of Ferdinand Gregorovius 1852–1874* (Ed. Friedrich Althaus. Trans. Mrs. Gustavus W. Hamilton, London, 1907).

GREVILLE, CHARLES, *The Greville Memoirs* (Ed. Roger Fulford and Lytton Strachey, London, 1938).

GREW, RAYMOND, *A Sterner Plan for Italian Unity: The Italian National Society in the Risorgimento*) (Princeton University Press, 1963).

GRIFFITH, G. O., *Mazzini: Prophet of Modern Europe* (London, 1932).

GUALTIERI, LUIGI, *Memorie di Ugo Bassi* (Bologna, 1861).

GUARNONE, F., *Aspromonte* (Palermo, 1923).

GUERRAZZI, FRANCESCO DOMENICO, *l'Assedio di Roma* (Leghorn, 1864).

GUERZONI, GIUSEPPE, *La vita di Nino Bixio* (Florence, 1875).

— *Garibaldi* (Florence, 1882).

HALES, E. E. Y., *Mazzini and the Secret Societies* (Eyre & Spottiswoode, 1956).

— *Pio Nono* (Eyre & Spottiswoode, 1954).

HANCOCK, W. K., *Ricasoli and the Risorgimento in Tuscany* (London, 1926).

HERZEN, ALEKSANDR, *Garibaldi a Londra* (Ed. Lavinia Bornero, Milan, 1950).

HOBSBAWM, E. J., *The Age of Revolution 1789–1848* (Weidenfeld & Nicolson, 1962).

HOFFSTETTER, GUSTAV VON, *Tagebuch aus Italien* (Zurich, 2nd edn., 1860).

HOLYOAKE, GEORGE JACOB, *Bygones Worth Remembering* (London, 1905).

Italia e Inghilterra nella prima fase di Risorgimento (Ed. Emilia Morelli, pubblicazione dell' Istituto Italiano di Cultura di Londra, 1952).

JAMES, HENRY, *William Wetmore Story and his Friends* (Thames and Hudson, London, 1957).

JEMOLO, ARTURO CARLO, *Church and State in Italy, 1850–1950* (Trans. David Moore, Blackwell, Oxford, 1960).

KING, BOLTON, *Mazzini* (London, 1902).

— *A History of Italian Unity* (London, 1898).

KOELMAN, JAN PHILIP, *Memorie Romane* (Ed. Maria Luisa Trebiliani, Istituto per la Storia del Risorgimento Italiano, Rome, 1963).

LA BOLINA, JACK (Augusto Vittorio Vecchi), *Cronachette del Risorgimento italiano* (Florence, 1920).

— *La vita e le gesta di Garibaldi* (Modena, 1882).

LACAITA, CHARLES, *An Italian Englishman, Sir James Lacaita, 1813–1895* (London, 1937).

LA FARINA, GUISEPPE, *Epistolario* (Ed. Ausonio Franchi, Milan, 1869).

LARG, DAVID, *Giuseppe Garibaldi* (London, 1934).

Lettere ad Antonio Panizzi di uomini illustri e di amici italiani, 1823–1870 (Ed. Luigi Fagan, Florence, 1880).

LEYNADIER, CAMILLE, *Mémoires Authentiques sur Garibaldi* (Paris, 1864).

LOEVINSON, ERMANNO, *Garibaldi e la sua legione nello stato romano* (Rome, 1902, 1904, 1907).

LUZIO, ALESSANDRO, *Aspromonte e Mentana: Documenti inediti* (Florence, 1935).

— *Garibaldi, Cavour, Verdi* (Turin, 1924).

LUZZATTO, GINO, *L'economia italiana dal 1861 al 1894* (Banca Commerciale italiana, 1963).

MACK SMITH, DENIS, *Cavour and Garibaldi 1860: A Study in Political Conflict* (Cambridge University Press, 1954).

— *Garibaldi: A Great Life in Brief* (Knopf, New York, 1956).

— *Italy: A Modern History* (University of Michigan Press, 1959).

MAINERI, B. E. (Ed.), *Daniele Manine Giorgio Pallavicino: Epistolario Politico, 1855–1857* (Milan, 1878).

MARIO, ALBERTO, *The Red Shirt* (London, 1865).

MARIO, JESSIE WHITE, *Agostino Bertani e i suoi tempi* (Florence, 1888).
— *The Birth of Modern Italy: Posthumous Papers.* Ed. the Duke Litta-Visconti-Arese (London, 1909). Supplement to Werner's translation of Garibaldi's autobiography (see Giuseppe Garibaldi).
— *Garibaldi e i suoi tempi* (Milan, 1905).

MARRARO, HOWARD, *American Opinion on the Unification of Italy, 1846–1861* (New York, 1932).

MARTINENGO CESARESCO, COUNTESS EVELYN, *The Liberation of Italy, 1815–1870* (London, 1895).
— *Italian Characters in the Epoch of Unification* (London, 1890).

MASSARI, GIUSEPPE, *La vita ed il regno di Vittorio Emanuele II* (Milan, 1878).
— *Il generale Alfonso La Marmora* (Florence, 1880).

MATTER, PAUL, *Cavour et l'unité Italienne, 1856–1861* (Paris, 1927).

MATURI, WALTER, *Interpretazioni del Risorgimento* (Einaudi, Turin, 1962).

MAZZINI, GIUSEPPE, *Edizione nazionale degli scritti editi ed inediti di Giuseppe Mazzini* (Imola, 1906–43).
— *The Life and Writings of Joseph Mazzini* (English trans. London, 1891).

MCGRIGOR, SIR CHARLES R., BART., *Garibaldi at home: Notes of a visit to Caprera* (London, 1866).

MELENA, ELPIS (Baroness von Schwartz), *Garibaldi: Recollections of his Public and Private Life* (London, 1887).

MENGHINI, MARIO, *La spedizione Garibaldina di Sicilia e di Napoli, nei proclami nelle corrispondenze, nei diarii* (Turin, 1907).

Military Events in Italy 1848–1849 (Translated from the German by Lord Ellesmere, London, 1851).

MINGHETTI, MARCO, *I mei ricordi* (Turin, 1888).

MONNIER, MARC, *Historie de la conquête des Deux-Siciles* (Paris, 1861).

MONTI, ANTONIO, *Pio IX nel Risorgimento italiano* (Bari, 1928).
— *Vittorio Emanuele II, 1820–1878* (Milan, 1941).

MORANDI, CARLO, *I partiti politici nella storia d'Italia* (Le Monnier, Florence, 1963).

MORELLI, EMILIA, *Tre Profili.* (Quaderni del Risorgimento, 9. Edizione dell' Ateneo, Rome, 1955). See also Bixio.

MORI, RENATO, *La questione romana 1861–1865* (Le Monnier, Florence, 1963).

MORISANI, CESARE, *Ricordi storici: I fatti delle Calabrie nel Luglio ed Agosto 1860* (Reggio, 1872).

MOSCATI, RUGGIERO, *La fine del Regno di Napoli* (Le Monnier, Florence, 1960).

MUNDY, REAR ADMIRAL SIR RODNEY, *H.M.S. Hannibal at Palermo and Naples during the Italian Revolution 1856-1861* (London, 1863).

NAZARI-MICHELE, IDA, *Cavour e Garibaldi* (Rome, 1911).

NIELSEN, FREDRIK, *The History of the Papacy in the XIX Century* (Trans. under the direction of Arthur James Mason, Vol. 2, London, 1906).

NIEVO, IPPOLITO, *Lettere Garibaldini* (Ed. A. Ciceri, Einaudi, Turin, 1961).

NISCO, NICOLA, *Storia del Reame di Napoli dal 1824 al 1860* (5th ed. Naples, 1908).

— *I generale Cialdini e i suoi tempi* (Naples, 1893).

Nuove Questioni di storia del Risorgimento e dell' unità d'Italia (Marzorati, Milan, 1961).

NUVOLARI, GIUSEPPE, *Come la penso* (Milan, 1881).

ODDO, GIACOMO, *I Mille di Marsala* (Milan, 1863).

OLIPHANT, LAURENCE, *Episodes in a Life of Adventure* (Edinburgh, 1887).

OMODEO, ADOLFO, *L'Opera politica del Conte di Cavour* (Florence, 1941).

— *Difesa del Risorgimento* (Einaudi, Turin, 1951).

— *L'eta del Risorgimento italiano* (7th edn., Naples, 1952).

— *Figure e passioni del Risorgimento italiano* (Rome, 1945).

OSSOLI, MARGARET FULLER, *The Memoirs of Margaret Fuller Ossoli* (London, 1852).

OVIDI, ERNESTO, *Roma e i Romani, 1848-1849* (1903).

PALÉOLOGUE, MAURICE, *Cavour* (Trans. Ian F. D. Morrow and Muriel Morrow, London, 1927).

PALLAVICINO, GIORGIO, *Memorie di Giorgio Pallavicino Trivulzio, pubblicato per cura della moglie* (Turin, 1882).

PAOLUCCI, D., *Da Riso a Garibaldi* (Reprinted from *Archivio Storico Siciliano*, Palermo, 1904).

PARRIS, JOHN, *The Lion of Caprera* (Arthur Barker, London, 1962).

PASSERIN D'ENTRÈVES, ETTORE, *L'ultima battaglia politica di Cavour* (Turin, 1956).

PECORINI-MANZONI, CARLO, *Storia della 15a Divisione Türr* (1876).

PERSANO, CARLO POLLION DI, *Diario privato-politico-militare sulla campagna navale degli anni 1860 e 1861* (Turin, 1880).

PIANELL, GENERAL, *Memorie* (Florence, 1902).

PIERI, PIERO, *Storia militare del Risorgimento: Guerre e insurrezioni* (Einaudi, Turin, 1962).

PISACANE, CARLO, *Guerra combattuta in Italia negli anni 1848-1849: Narrazione di Carlo Pisacane. Repubblicata per cura del Prof. Luigi Maino* (Rome-Milan, 1906).

RICASOLI, BETTINO, *Lettere e documenti* (ed. Tabarrini and Gotti, Florence, 1887–95).

— *Carteggi di Bettino Ricasoli* (Ed. Nobili and Camerani, Zanichelli, Bologna, 1939–57).

RICHARDS, B. F. (Ed.), *Mazzini's Letters to an English Family* (London, 1920).

RODELLI, LUIGI, *La Repubblica Romana del 1849* (Pisa, 1955).

ROMEO, ROSARIO, *Il Risorgimento in Piemonte* (Einaudi, Turin, 1963).

— *Il Risorgimento in Sicilia* (Laterza, Bari, 1950).

— *Risorgimento e capitalismo* (Laterza, Bari, 1959).

ROSELLI, GENERAL PIETRO, *La spedizione di Velletri* (Turin, 1853).

ROSELLI, NELLO, *Carlo Pisacane nel Risorgimento italiano* (Turin, 1932).

— *Saggi sul Risorgimento ed altri scritti* (Turin, 1946).

ROTA, ETTORE (Ed.), *Questioni di storia del Risorgimento e dell' unità d'Italia* (Marzorati, Milan, 1951).

RUGGERI, E., *Narrazione della Ritirata di Garibaldi da Roma* (Genoa, 1850).

RUSCONI, FERDINANDO, *19 anni di vita di un Garibaldino* (Florence, 1870).

RUSSELL, LORD JOHN, *The Later Correspondence of Lord John Russell, 1840-1878* (Ed. G. P. Gooch, London, 1925).

SACCHI, LUIGI, *Una visita all'isola di Caprera del pittore Luigi Sacchi* (Milan, 1860).

SACERDOTE, GUSTAVO, *Vita di Garibaldi* (Rizzoli, Milan. New edn. 1957).

SAFFI, AURELIO, *Ricordi e scritti* (Florence, 1892–3).

SALVADORI, MASSIMO, *Cavour and the Unification of Italy* (Van Nostrand, New York, 1961).

SALVATORELLI, LUIGI, *Il pensiero politico italiano dal 1700 al 1870* (Turin, 1935).

SALVATORELLI, LUIGI, *Pensiero e azione del Risorgimento* (Einaudi, Turin, new edn. 1960).

— *A Concise History of Italy* (Trans. Bernard Miall, London, 1940).

SALVEMINI, GAETANO, *Scritti sul Risorgimento* (ed. Piero Pieri and Carlo Pischedda, Feltrinelli, Milan, 2nd edn. 1963).

— *Mazzini* (Revised English edn. trans. I. M. Rawson, Cape, 1956).

SAMPIERI, DOMENICO, *Storia e storie della prima spedizione in Sicilia* (Rome, 1893).

SARDAGNA, FILIBERTO, *Garibaldi in Lombardia, 1848* (Milan, 1927).

SCHWARTZ, MARIE ESPÉRANCE VON, see Melena.

SETTEMBRINI, LUIGI, *Ricordanze della mia vita* (Turin, 1933).

SFORZA, GIOVANNI, *Garibaldi in Toscana nel 1848* (Rome, 1897).

SIMONCINI, LORENZO, *Giuseppe Garibaldi e Ugo Bassi in San Marino* (Rimini, 1894).

SPADA, GIUSEPPE, *Storia della rivoluzione di Roma dal 1 giugno 1846 al 15 luglio 1849* (Florence, 1868).

SPELLANZON, CESARE, *Garibaldi* (Saggi di cultura moderna, XXV. Parenti, Florence, 1958).

— *Storia del Risorgimento e dell' unità d'Italia*, (Vol. 5, Rizzoli, Milan, 1950).

SPINI, GIORGIO, *Risorgimento e protestanti* (Naples, 1956).

SPRIGGE, CECIL, *The Development of Modern Italy* (London, 1943).

TAYLOR, A. J. P., *The Italian Problem in European Diplomacy, 1847–1849* (Manchester, 1934).

— *The Struggle for Mastery in Europe* (Oxford, 1954).

THAYER, WILLIAM ROSCOE, *The Life and Times of Cavour* (London, 1911).

— *Throne-Makers* (London, 1899).

THOMPSON, J. M., *Louis Napoleon and the 2nd Empire* (Basil Blackwell, Oxford, 1954).

THOUVENEL, A. (Ed.), *Le Secret de l'Empereur* (Paris, 1889).

TORRE, FEDERICO, *Memorie storiche sull'intervento francese in Roma nel 1849* (Turin, 1851–2).

TRAUTH, MARY PHILIP, *Italo-American Diplomatic Relations, 1861–1882* (Washington, 1958).

TREVELYAN, GEORGE MACAULAY (1) *Garibaldi's Defence of the Roman Republic (1848–9)* (Longmans, Green, London, new edn. 1949).

— (2) *Garibaldi and the Thousand (May 1860)* (Longmans, Green, London, new edn. 1948).

— (3) *Garibaldi and the Making of Italy (June-November 1860)* (Longmans, Green, London, new edn. 1948).

TROLLOPE, THOMAS ADOLPHUS, *What I Remember* (London, 1887, 1889).

TÜRR, STEFAN, *Riposta del Generale Türr all' oposculo Bertani 'Ire d'oltre tomba'* (Milan, 1874).

VAILLANT, GENERAL, *Le Siège de Rome en 1849* (Paris, 1851).

VECCHI, CANDIDO AUGUSTO, *La Italia storia di due anni, 1848-1849* (Turin, 1856).

— *Garibaldi at Caprera* (London, 1862).

WALPOLE, SPENCER, *Life of Lord John Russell* (London, 1889).

WHITAKER, TINA (Scalia), *Sicily and England: Political and Social Reminiscences, 1848-1870* (London, 1907).

WHYTE, ARTHUR JAMES, *The Political Life and Letters of Cavour 1848-1861* (London, 1930).

— *Evolution of Modern Italy* (New edn. Oxford, 1951).

WINNINGTON-INGRAM, REAR-ADMIRAL H. F., *Hearts of Oak* (London, 1889).

ARTICLES

ASHLEY, EVELYN, 'A Garibaldi Reminiscence.' *National Review* (1899).

BOLLEA, L. C., 'Cavour e la spedizione delle Marche.' *Il Risorgimento italiano* (10, 1917).

BRAUN, MARTIN, ' "Great Expectations": Cavour and Garibaldi 1859–1951.' *History Today* (October, 1959).

CADOLINI, GIOVANNI, 'Garibaldi e l'arte della guerra.' *Nuova Antologia* (1 May and 16 May 1902).

CAMPANELLA, A. P., 'La difesa di Palermo nel 1860 nelle memorie di Heinrich Wieland.' *Il Risorgimento* (Anno 16, Milan, February 1964).

CARLO, ARNO, 'Garibaldi, Cavour e la spedizione dei Mille.' *Il Risorgimento italiano* (January, 1908).

CARRAROLI, P., 'Garibaldi nei discorsi di Felice Cavallotti.' *Bergomum* (35, 1961).

COLAPIETRA, RAFFAELE, 'Intorno al pensiero politico di Garibaldi.' *Nuova Rivistica Storica* (Anno 43, Jan. to April 1959).

DE ROSSI, EUGENIO, 'Le Marcia di Garibaldi da Roma a San Marino.' *Rivista di cavalleria* (January, February, March, 1962).

GANDOLFI, A., 'Garibaldi Generale.' *Nuova Antologia* (June 1883).

GAY, H. NELSON, 'Il secondo esilio di Garibaldi (1849–1854) da documenti inediti.' *Nuova Antologia* (June 1910).

GHISALBERTI, ALBERTO M., 'Mazzini e la repubblica di Romani.' (*Il Risorgimento*, February 1952).

GREENFIELD, KENT ROBERTS, 'The Historiography of the Risorgimento since 1920.' *The Journal of Modern History* (7, 1935).

MACK SMITH, DENIS, 'Cavour's attitude to Garibaldi's expedition to Sicily.' *Cambridge Historical Journal* (ix).

MARIO, ALBERTO, 'Personal Reminiscences of General Garibaldi.' *Macmillan's Magazine* (July, 1882).

MARRARO, HOWARD, 'Documenti italiani ed americani sulla spedizione Garibaldina in Sicilia.' *Rassegna Storica del Risorgimento* (44, 1957).

— 'Unpublished American Documents on Garibaldi's March on Rome in 1867.' *The Journal of Modern History* (June, 1944).

MONDINI, LUIGI, 'Vittorio Emanuele, Cavour e Garibaldi.' *Nuova Antologia* (479, 1960).

MORELLI, EMILIA, 'Mazzini nel 1860.' *Nuova Antologia* (85, 1960).

NICOLOSI, C., 'L'arte militare Garibaldina.' *Rivista di Fanteria* (1903).

PEMBERTON, W. BARING, 'Garibaldi's Englishman: The Story of Colonel John Peard.' *History Today* (December, 1959).

RAVA, LUIGI, 'Fanti, Garibaldi e Luigi Carlo Farini.' *Nuova Antologia* (September, 1903).

ROMEO, ROSARIO, 'Cavour e Garibaldi.' *Lo Spettatore Italiano* (1954).

SALVATORELLI, LUIGI, 'Pio IX e il Risorgimento.' *Il Lavoro* (2 October 1936).

SILVA, P., 'La Politica di Napoleone III e l'Italia.' *Nuova Rivista Storica* (11, 1927).

SPRIGGE, CECIL, 'Il 1860 visto da un inglese.' *Lo Spettatore Italiano* (1954).

STOCCHI, G., 'Un paragrafo inedito della vita di Giuseppe Garibaldi.' *La Rassegna Nazionale* (June 1892).

TREVELYAN, G. M., 'War Journals of Garibaldi's Englishman.' *Cornhill Magazine* (January and June, 1908).

VALSECCHI, FRANCO, 'Garibaldi e Cavour.' *Nuova Antologia* (479, 1960).

INDEX

Printed in Great Britain
by Amazon

22239113R00273